THE BYZANTINES

THE
BYZANTINES

EDITED BY
Guglielmo Cavallo

TRANSLATED BY
Thomas Dunlap
Teresa Lavender Fagan
Charles Lambert

The University of Chicago Press
Chicago & London

The University of Chicago Press, Chicago 60637
The University of Chicago Press, Ltd., London
©1997 by the University of Chicago
All rights reserved. Published 1997
Paperback edition 2000
Printed in the United States of America

09 08 07 06 05 04 03 02 01 00   2 3 4 5 6

ISBN: 0-226-09791-9 (cloth)
ISBN: 0-226-09792-7 (paper)

Originally published as *L'Uomo bizantino,* © 1992, Gius. Laterza & Figli.

Library of Congress Cataloging in Publication Data

Uomo bizantino, English
    The Byzantines / edited by Guglielmo Cavallo; translated by
Thomas Dunlap, Teresa Lavender Fagan and Charles Lambert.
        p.   cm.
    Includes bibliographical references and index.
    ISBN 0-226-09791-9 (cloth). — ISBN 0-226-09792-7 (pbk.)
    I. Byzantine Empire—Civilization.   I. Cavallo, Guglielmo.
    II. Title.
    DF521.U6513   1997
    949.5—dc20
                                                          96-1967I
                                                          CIP

⊗The paper used in this publication meets the minimum requirements of
the American National Standard for Information Sciences— Permanence of Paper
for Printed Library Materials, ANSI Z39.48-1992.

CONTENTS

Translators' Note

Chapters 2, 4, and 5, originally written in English, have been given in their English versions with editing. The chapters originally written in Italian, French, and German have been checked against their original-language texts.

INTRODUCTION

Guglielmo Cavallo

AFTER THE FADED IMAGES OF Byzantium as either sophisticated or sophistical had finally been abandoned, they were replaced by the equally stereotypical vision of a static, immutable society, impervious to change, in which the Roman Empire ground to a halt. Despite some resistance, this idea is also tending to disappear. Attention has now shifted to the Byzantines themselves, to the features that distinguished them from earlier civilizations, and to the cultural characteristics that were specific to Byzantium.[1] These characteristics developed during the period that began with the birth of the new capital of Constantinople around A.D. 330 and culminated with its fall into Turkish hands on May 29, 1453, although they came to a head between the seventh and the twelfth century. However, during the thousand-year life of Byzantium, with its many ethnic groups, who really were the Byzantine people?

Let us consider a ceremony: the imperial procession. This was the continuation, and culmination, of those processions that had already represented public life in its most solemn form in the largest cities of the late Roman Empire. In Constantinople, the New Rome on the Bosporos, the impressive structure and significance of the procession were maintained until the late Middle Ages. Although certain details changed with the passage of time (changes that reveal other, more profound, changes), the constant feature of the procession was its value as "ceremony," or *taxis* in Byzantine Greek. In these skillfully elaborated events, each individual and social group had a specific role to play. The procession was led by standard-bearers, followed, in ascending order, by the civil and military hierarchies, and finally by the emperor himself surrounded by handpicked members of the imperial guard and by the eunuchs of the bedchamber. The procession passed before the capital's civil authorities, public servants of varying ranks, groups of scribes and schoolteachers, doctors and law-

1

yers, the compact ranks of merchant and artisan guilds, and a crowd of soldiers, peasants, day workers, slaves, paupers, holy men, and outcasts of every kind, while choirs, named after the ancient Circus factions, sang the praises of the emperor, "God's lieutenant" on earth,[2] in rhythmical, repetitive cadences like those of the holy liturgy. When the emperor reached Hagia Sophia, he entered the church, received the welcome of the patriarch, bishop of bishops, disappeared behind a screen where his eunuchs removed his crown in honor of the heavenly lord, and participated in the service according to the complex rules of the ceremony. After having left the church, he distributed gold to the priests, the choristers, and above all to the poor, since Christ himself might be dressed in the rags of a beggar.

The identity of the Byzantines can be pieced together from the individual facets seen in these ceremonial processions: the poor, the peasant, the soldier, the teacher, the woman, the entrepreneur, the bishop, the functionary, the emperor, and the saint. Although *taxis* stood for ceremony, it also meant "order." The author of the dialogue *On Political Science,* possibly Menas Patrikios, commented: "Imperial authority will unleash from itself, so to speak, a political light and will instill it in the highest state offices that are subordinate to it, governing through these, according to a scientific system, those at the second and third levels and below; the optimates will thus take part with justice in the life of the state and will arrange everything in perfect agreement, and all the other orders of the state will be organized in the best possible way."[3] However one identifies the Byzantines, it is clear that, in society as in the ceremonial procession, each person had a particular place in the "order" of the world. An individual might move within that order—social mobility was not unknown in Byzantium—but the order itself remained unchanged. *Anōmalia,* or irregularity, was dangerously similar in meaning to disorder.

Terrestrial order was merely the imperfect reflection of celestial order. At its summit was God's lieutenant, the emperor, whose court mirrored that of heaven (or, rather, the average Byzantine regarded the court of heaven as the exalted archetype of that found in Byzantium). It is not surprising that the monk Kosmas, the chamberlain of Emperor Alexander (912–913), provided the most vivid description of the heavenly palace before withdrawing from the world.[4] The process of osmosis was constant. Taxes had to be paid to the emperor's tax collectors, and failure to fulfill this duty was regarded as a sin. A tenth-century text lists slander and envy, fornication and usury, rancor and avarice, pride and murder. These, and other sins, were recorded by demons in detailed registers or *telōnia,* kept between earth and heaven. They could be expunged only after a full confession during which the soul expiated itself of its crimes.[5] In exactly the same way, the failure to pay taxes, annotated in registers by the emperor's collectors, could be expiated only by payment or torture. The emperor, in his turn, was obliged to guarantee provisions, as long as his subjects were loyal. The only person who played no part in the relationship between the emperor and his subjects was the pauper, who paid no taxes because he had no money and whose daily bread depended on charity.

In the tenth century the victorious emperor John I Tzimiskes (969–976) passed through the Golden Gate of the capital in his ancient Roman triumphal chariot. However, the chariot bore an icon of the Virgin Mary, now regarded by Byzantine emperors as *sustratēgos,* or "assistant commander."[6] This exemplifies the synthesis between the inheritance from Rome and an Oriental sense of religion that, from the late classical period, was the basic typological factor in Byzantine civilization. The proximity of the Hippodrome to the church of Hagia Sophia in Constantinople was another, perhaps more intrinsically "popular," symbol of the fact that the dualism between Roman tradition and Christianity had been overcome.[7] The two pillars of Byzantium therefore were the Roman Empire and the Orthodox religion. Kosmas Indikopleustes wrote:

> As regards the empire of the Romans, which rose along with Christ, it will not be destroyed over the course of centuries. I dare say that, despite being a result of our sins and in order to make us mend our ways, some barbarian enemies sometimes rise against the Roman state, nonetheless, because of the strength of those in power, the empire remains undefeated, since Christian dominion does not shrink but expands. In fact, it was the first empire of all to believe in Christ, and it obeys Christian principles. That is why God, lord of all, preserves it undefeated.[8]

Byzantine citizens, therefore, had an empire whose values—ideal and, above all, religious—they defended against foreign, or "barbarian," values. One of the most specific features of the Byzantines is visible here: their awareness of belonging to an empire. This basic awareness insured the continuity of New Rome and the East when the western empire collapsed.[9]

Many centuries after Kosmas, Michael Psellos wrote a significant passage describing Emperor Romanos III (1028–34) as

> instilled with classical literature, and also an expert on that culture, which is the heritage of the Latin people . . . Wishing to model his kingdom on that of the ancient and celebrated Antonines, of the virtuous Marcus Antoninus and of Augustus, he was obsessed by these two things: the study of literature and the discipline of arms. As regards the latter, he was also perfectly incompetent, while for literature, he understood only enough to

brush the surface. . . . Dismissing literature for a short time, the emperor turned to arms. The debate turns to greaves and cuirasses, and the hypothesis under examination is the following: to conquer all barbarians, both of the East and of the West. And he wished to demonstrate this not solely by words, but with the power of his weapons. Now, if these two interests of the emperor had been, not a daydream, but an honest mastery of both disciplines, they could have been very useful to the state; but all his initiatives came to nothing.[10]

Whether the picture that emerges of Romanos' personality is true, or merely the work of a writer at the service of another dynasty of emperors, it should be noted that Psellos approves, and considers essential to the state, Romanos' aims: to model his empire on that stretching from Augustus to the Antonines, to repel barbarians, and to study classical culture, Greek and Latin literature. However, it is essential that we understand the nature of this culture. After the reign of Emperor Herakleios (610–641), little remained of the Latin culture that had penetrated the East, especially during the era of Justinian (527–565), apart from the legal system and fossilized specimens of bureaucratic and military language. It was Greek learning, late antique Hellenism, both pagan and Christian, that provided Byzantine culture with its particular character. The breach that had been opened in the seventh century could not be closed, and even the Latin peoples of the Middle Ages were regarded as barbarians. Niketas Choniates, devoting "laments, vain tears, and inexpressible moans" to a Constantinople offended by barbarians, said that the city "had lost its capacity for speech" and remarked: "Who could bear the sound of the Muses to reecho in a land that is now deprived of culture and completely barbarous?"[11] The Byzantine people were clearly proud of their inheritance from ancient Rome and of the prestige of their entirely Greek culture.

The Hippodrome, the great church of Hagia Sophia, imperial processions: Byzantium was a world of spectacle and ostentation, and the Byzantines were fascinated by games, liturgies, and pomp. Foot races and horse races, displays of wild beasts or exotic animals, tightrope walkers or bareback riders on galloping horses delighted the enthusiastic crowds packed into the Hippodrome, a meeting place for rich and poor alike. The streets were lined with musicians, singers, dancers, jugglers, charlatans, conjuring artists, and monstrous beings, both human and animal.

At the very heart of Byzantine spiritual life was the liturgy. In the largest churches, however, this was a gaudy affair, exalted by the colors of the mosaics and icons, by the sparkle of precious ornaments and gems, by the splendor of the robes, by the flames and reflections of the lamps, by the turning pages of the ceremonial books, and by the cadence of the chants. If the transient pomp of the world is so splendid, Porphyry of Gaza wondered, what splendors must await the just in heaven? The Byzantines were attracted not only by the spiritual nature of worship but also by its magnificence, by the evocative power of its trappings, which carried it into a borderland between the immanent and the transcendent, providing the soul with a foretaste of the ceremonial delights of heaven.[12]

The imperial processions were organized in an equally spectacular way, with the emperor swathed in splendid crimson and gold silk, the dignitaries weighed down with precious ceremonial robes, and the standard-bearers, with their *vexilla* of the ancient Roman rulers and "dragon" banners and standards waving in the breeze. The route taken by the procession was lined with garlands of flowers, fabrics, and silver. The solemn audiences granted by the emperor were also extraordinary spectacles, astounding both eye and ear. They took place in a room where mechanical animals, operated by complex devices, appeared noisily and without warning. The throne actually rose up to the ceiling before the startled delegations, overwhelmed by the din.

Even Byzantium's wealth and poverty were ostentatious. Pomp was visible not only in the rich imperial processions but also in the silent and majestic approach of bishops clad in brocade, and in the movements of high-ranking officials and of the rich. Toward the end of the ninth century, the widow Danielis, wishing to see the emperor, traveled from her estate in the Peloponnese to the capital. She moved in a luxurious litter, borne on the shoulders of ten of the three hundred strong young slaves who were accompanying her for this purpose. This old, and extremely rich, woman also had an immense retinue of servants and brought the emperor a gift of five hundred slaves, including a hundred eunuchs. The widow knew that these would be acceptable at the palace, where eunuchs were commoner than flies in a stable in spring.[13] Poverty was equally on show, as paupers cried in the streets: "Give us your small change of silver and bronze to buy our daily bread—everyone says that starving to death is the worst way to go." Here the scene was filled with beggars, idiots, runaway peasants, the untreated sick, and prostitutes, who wandered the streets in search of shelter in hovels, in doorways, under porticoes, and in pigsties. Even philanthropy was on display, as can be seen from the foundations and charitable institutions that existed to succor these wretches.

Sanctity itself was transformed into exhibition. This reached its most extreme form in the stylites, ascetics who lived on the tops of pillars in order to attract attention. Holy fools displayed to the public the results of their mortification: St. Andrew Salos (the Fool) "suffered intolerable cold, the ice froze him, everybody hated him, and the children of the city beat him, dragged him around, and slapped him pitilessly; they would put a rope around his neck and drag him behind them in the light of day, or they would rub his face with ink and coals." [14]

Cruelty was equally striking and extreme. Descriptions of the martyrdom of saints were full of horrific details, as blood gushed from deep cuts in the flesh, and guts spilled out from quartered bellies to mingle with the filth of the streets. Insolvent peasants were flogged or were torn to shreds by ravenous dogs. In the palace itself, abysses of ferocity awaited the unfortunate. The emperor could plant "shadows in the eyes," cut off "the extremities of the body as if they were bunches of grapes," and become "the butcher of men." [15] The emperor himself could be the victim of these spectacles of cruelty. In the eleventh century, it was Michael V who trembled with fear, waved his hands, shook his head, and bellowed dismally as his eyes were plucked "out of their sockets" by the executioner, to the delighted roar of the crowd. [16] At a later date, Andronikos I Komnenos was exposed to the mob on the back of a mangy camel, dressed in rags and with one eye poked out. Beaten about the head with sticks, plastered with dung, run through with skewers, and tortured with boiling water, he was "led into the theater," to be exhibited in unseemly triumph. [17] The Byzantines, in other words, experienced public life and religious experience, wealth and poverty, charity and cruelty, as emotion and spectacle.

The end of Byzantium heralded the end of the world. The many prophecies of this nature identified the historical and political significance of the Byzantine Empire with that of the Kingdom of Christ. The emperor was obliged to defeat his enemies, mirror images of the Antichrist, while his subjects were expected to preserve the empire not only as a political reality but also as a system of values, as they awaited the Second Coming of Christ and the final triumph of God's lieutenant on earth. [18] Political orthodoxy, based on the conformity of Byzantine society and its members, and patterns of thought depended on this identification. Conformity was expressed by obsequiousness to tradition, regardless of the fractures and discontinuities that existed, particularly in the seventh and eleventh centuries. [19] According to classical parameters, however, tradition primarily involved subjecting oneself to authority in political life. This effectively meant sanctioning the existing order at all times and in all situations. The same was true for social relations. Individuals had to be guided by their superiors, whose wishes had to be obeyed even when the superiors were inept. Independence was not considered a value. The highest positions were occupied by dignitaries and officials, who lived at court, and by ascetic monks, who lived in the desert. These two groups already submitted directly to the authority of the emperor or of God. Not to submit to authority was equivalent to placing oneself outside the natural order. Secret accusation, slander, condemnation, execution, and murder were all permitted in order to restore the disturbed order and reinstate the power of values such as devotion and resignation.

The ideal was *mimēsis,* or the imitation of models. The emperor himself practiced *mimēsis* by imitating Christ. The Byzantines turned to models, and to tradition, for answers, and their behavior, by avoiding sudden changes, initiatives, and innovations, inevitably became a part of the tradition. Let us consider certain aspects. The free market was rigidly controlled by the state, which conceded no more than was necessary, or indeed expected, to merchants and artisans. As merchants were encouraged by the nature of their trade to behave dishonestly, it was only just that limits should be imposed. Nor was there any point in artisans trying to increase their earnings by attempts to improve traditional techniques. The desire for riches was disapproved of; the best thing was to make do with what one had, however little it might be.

The poor thus occupied an essential place in the Byzantine order as objects of *philanthrōpia* ("love of mankind"). Anna Komnene described the concern demonstrated by her father, Emperor Alexios I, toward orphans, the sick, and the needy:

> At meal-times all women and men who were worn out with sickness or old age were summoned to the emperor's table; most of his rations were set before them, and he invited his retinue to follow his example in giving. . . . All children who had lost their parents and were afflicted by the grievous ills of orphanhood were committed to the care of relatives and to others who, he knew, were respectable people, as well as to the abbots of the holy monasteries, with instructions to treat them not as slaves but as free children, to see that they had a thorough education and to teach them the Sacred Scriptures. Some he introduced into the orphanage which he had personally founded.

Alexios ordered the building of a second city within the imperial city: a city of "wretches" where the blind, the lame, the paralyzed and maimed, and those disfigured by disease flocked together. Although Alexios could not order cripples to "stand up and walk," as Christ had done, he could provide them with helpers who would assist them in their movements and other activities, or even, as an act of charity ordered by God, provide these forsaken people with incomes from the land or the sea.[20] Without the suffering of the poor to be alleviated, there would have been no one to receive a portion of state finances or private riches. The emperor himself, "terrible" in his authority, could win the love of his subjects by his *philanthrōpia.* The wealthy individual could also use part of his riches in a fair and saintly way. Liberality was thus expected from everyone, although no suggestion was ever made of radical economic or social reform. "Every man should remain in the condition in which he was called," or even "Do not move the ancient boundary-stone which your forefathers set up," were the biblical verses that every Byzantine must have borne in mind.[21]

Traditionalism lay at the roots of education, in the widest sense, and of the forms it took. Education might be regarded as the basic acquisition of the alphabet, and literacy was an important feature of the Byzantine world, symbolized by the figure of St. Basil teaching children by tracing letters in the sand. In hagiographical accounts, school and the love of study formed part of the life and education of the saint, who was taught to read and write by a human teacher or by divine inspiration. In the final analysis, we see the gradual emergence of the authority of writing and of the written tradition, according to an idea that had already begun to develop during the late Roman period: whatever is written has absolute value and must be obeyed. The most authoritative texts were the Scriptures and the laws. Even illiterate Byzantines knew that these texts—with their Orthodox figures of Christ and his earthly representative, the emperor—had the authority to regulate, and dispose of, their lives.

This is the source of the bookish mentality of Byzantine life, revealed by the obsessive repetition of references, quotations from other texts, reminiscences, and the fixed repertory of notions divorced from experience, of familiar concepts, and of absolute certainties. It can be seen in the elaboration of summas and excerpts from traditional learning and of repetitive anthologies. It was a mentality that depended on books even when action was crucially required (the warrior, Nikephoros Uranos, based his battle strategy on an anonymous compilation of extracts), or when people sought answers to existential doubts in works of astrology, dream interpretation, oracles, or magic. Such texts were also used when explanations for otherwise irrational events, whether individual or social, were being sought or whenever a need for mystery was felt. They offered a glimpse into the future and provided the curious and anxious with a sense of life beyond its earthly limits.[22] Byzantine bookishness, in other words, was also a sign of insecurity and of psychological instability.

The models for the highest cultural levels remained the "classics," not only those of pagan antiquity but also Christian texts, above all the writings of the church fathers who were frequently represented on the walls of Byzantine churches. Even the methods adopted for teaching were unchanged. In the twelfth century, Nikephoros Basilakes, a teacher at the patriarchal school, continued to adhere to late classical study techniques, to the extent that "we cannot avoid the impression that time stood still."[23] Ideas of the essential and the useful dominated the books that were written and read in Byzantium, since whatever was useful was inevitably essential. It was useful to the soul to absorb, and to follow, moral teachings. Usefulness, or *ōpheleia*, can be used to justify a simple, "popular," language and style. But Byzantine literature was considered inelegant unless it exhibited rhetorical flourishes, a stubborn recourse to classical terms, and an artificial search for time-honored expressions and constructions. Thus John VI Kantakouzenos described the great plague that struck Byzantium in 1348–49 by quoting, almost to the letter, Thucydides. This is what lies behind the "atemporal" nature of Byzantine literature. Comparisons cannot, therefore, be based on "ancient" and "modern" but on the ability to use models. This ability sometimes resulted in mere virtuosity, erudite disquisition, and subtlety as an end in itself. It is obvious that this class, or perhaps "caste," of erudite men of letters formed a very small part of the population. Nonetheless, they wielded enormous influence, as a result of their surviving writings, in the conservation and representation of the Byzantine inheritance.

The monk and the saint, in their turn, were dependent on biblical tradition, but they also relied on the writings of the desert fathers and the oldest hagiographical texts. Tales of saintliness became a series of repeated tropes. In order to be recognized as such, a saint had to be "narrated" by means of consolidated and conventional phrases, verses, and terms. Anyone who aspired to holiness was obliged to base his behavior on sequences described in sacred texts, the Scriptures, the *apophthegmata* (sayings of the fathers), and edifying works and on the teachings of the *gerōn,* or ancient monk, who had already acquired traditional wisdom, the only kind that could never err.

But the most striking form of traditionalism was that of Byzantine visual art, particularly the icon, the pivot of spiritual (and political) life in Byzantium. It was a static art based on ready-made and familiar codes. For the Byzantines the reality of the sacred image, which was considered a portrait, coincided with the reality of the iconographic formulas from which it was composed. These had been established once and for all and could not be changed, since they had been universally recognized as belonging to a specific image. The monk Kosmas recognized the apostles Andrew and John in his dream because they resembled the figures he had seen in icons! To change these iconic codes would have meant falsifying portraits of Christ, the Virgin, saints, and angels, the authenticity of which was guaranteed by the fixed nature of the "iconic manner." Sacred images were eternal, and real, precisely because they had been rendered abstract through the use of formulas. Figures were presented frontally, with their gaze directed at the observer, a code that enabled the Byzantines to recognize, and become involved in, the images. The standardization of icons calmed and elevated the soul, opposing the calm and immutable nature of sanctity to the agitated and changeable world of the devil.

The only break in tradition occurred in the eleventh century. This not only involved the political system, with the arrival of the so-called "gouvernement des philosophes"[24] imposed by the emperors of the "civil-ian party" and the rise to power of new classes. It also affected literature, which opened to new experiences, art, which began to explore gesture and movement, and ideas, as certainties were upset by the search for new forms of knowledge. But these novelties were destined to be reabsorbed into traditional archetypes. Everything that seemed to bring renewal in the eleventh century disappeared during the political, social, economic, and monetary reaction that took place when the military aristocracy placed the Komnenos dynasty on the Byzantine throne.[25]

Byzantine art took the human face as the reference point and fulcrum of representation, while the body remained hidden beneath the drapery of clothes. This was no accident. The image's interior strength, in which its individuality was expressed, was concentrated in the face. Individuality was another basic characteristic of the Byzantines.[26] It could be found in all members of society and sometimes led to selfishness and excessive in-terest in oneself, in which everything was permitted without the impedi-ment of friendship, loyalty, or rectitude. But this individuality also pro-duced isolation and represented one of the most marked breaks with Byzantium's late Roman past. Society in the West had been reorganized along new lines. From the age of Herakleios on, however, the collapse of city life and the crisis of social relations in Byzantium forced individuals back into themselves and into solitude. Peasants—the mainstay, along with soldiers, of Byzantine society after the seventh century—were sin-gled out by cruel and rapacious tax collectors and were forced to bear the major burden of taxation. In a rigidly hierarchical system such as that of Byzantium, each official was directly responsible to his superior, while the highest ranks answered only to the emperor, who could deprive them of both life and limbs. The emperor himself was enclosed within the soli-tude of the palace, often surrounded by empresses and eunuchs, intrigues and plots, and was liable to be thrown to the fury of the mob. No one felt safe, and the most common emotion must have been insecurity. This was what lay behind the intimacy with saints and the obsessive depen-dence on icons, as well as the appetite for the occult, dream interpreta-tion, and astrological predictions. Neither emperors nor intellectuals were immune. In the midst of this instability, which was also a distrust of soci-ety, the only possible ethical position was that of the middle way, of mod-eration, humility, and . . . isolation. We are back where we started!

The holy man, who chose to seek a more direct and certain contact with God, was also alone. He withdrew from the world and its tempta-tions in order to seek refuge as a monk in a "separate" life. In doing so, however, he sometimes pushed his separation from human contact to extremes by living as a stylite, on the top of a pillar, as if to indicate his detachment from the world. Alternatively, he behaved as if he were mad, creating a barrier of incommunicability between himself and the rest of society. At their most socially integrated, in a monastery or in the city, or as bishops caring for the spiritual and material needs of the faithful, holy men also represented a defense of Orthodoxy, a path for the salvation of the soul that every Byzantine desired. In Byzantium, therefore, the value of holy men was never questioned. Holy men, and particularly monks, had won the trust of God by defeating the "wild beasts" of sin with prayers, vigils, fasting, discomfort, and humiliation. As a result, they could insure individual salvation and protect the well-being of the empire—so often elusive because of human weakness—in the face of a terrible celestial authority. Although the forms his mission took were both interior (spiritual victory over oneself) and exterior (the salvation of others), it was conducted by the monk in solitude. Byzantine monasticism, in fact, had no orders, and monks followed their own paths in a profoundly individualistic way. It was impossible to be a monk without leading a life of solitude and mortification, and those who sat at the table of an inept and corrupt emperor, eating "large, fresh fish" and drinking "the purest scented wine," wore the "habit dear to God" only to their shame.[27]

For those who did not devote their lives to the spirit, there was the family, the "sum of individualisms" that was the basis of Byzantine social structure.[28] The solidity of the family was both the consequence and a further cause of the isolation of the individual from other forms of social organization. It was also within the family that the dignity of the woman's role was recognized, by the laws and by tradition. Women were at the center of the ordered world of the Byzantine family, administering the family's wealth in a severe and industrious way. Sometimes living with his wife as if they were brother and sister, a Byzantine man could reconcile marriage and chastity. Outside the family, or the confines of a monastery that followed the rules of an honest life, however, women were seen as nothing but shameless temptresses of sexual desire. For Byzantine culture, women hung in the balance between the Virgin Mary, mother of Christ, and Eve, the seductress, who had led Adam and the entire human race into temptation.

It is clear, therefore, that Byzantine traditionalism and conformity also provided security and a refuge for a society of lonely, insecure individuals.

The ten chapters in this book display the mechanisms underlying the history of Byzantium: its politics, economy, agriculture, army, administration, and, indirectly, society and culture. As a result, the Byzantines begin to emerge, with all their behavioral patterns, drives, and contradictions, from a world marked by continuity and discontinuity, by conformity, but also, it must be noted, by a striking modernity. Byzantium invented the modern centralized state, experimented with "statutory" forms of poverty and public and private welfare from a very early period, accepted "capitalistic" types of economic expansion, allowed women—within the confines of a widespread antifeminism—a dignity and social role practically denied them until this century, and introduced forms of scholarship (editions of texts, ways of reading) that are part of the modern world.

As citizens of an earthly world that was the faded and inadequate projection of Heaven, and subjects of "God's lieutenant," the Byzantines lived as individuals within a hierarchy. This hierarchy was characterized by a respect for orthodoxy and the value of tradition. It sought fair measure, while being attracted to the fascination and horror of excess. The Byzantines were the proud inheritors of an empire that crushed its enemies because it was protected by Christ, "who scatters those seeking war and does not take pleasure in the spilling of blood"[29] and who gave the righteous the power "to walk without danger or offense on snakes and scorpions."[30]

NOTES

1. A. Kazhdan and G. Constable, *People and Power in Byzantium: An Introduction to Modern Byzantine Studies* (Washington, D.C., 1982), which considers *homo byzantinus* "in the sense of Byzantine people and their place in society" (p. 16). See the introduction, pp. 1–18.

2. For this concept, see A. Ducellier, *Byzance et le monde orthodoxe* (Paris, 1986).

3. *Menae Patricii cum Thoma referendario de Scientia politica dialogus*, 5.60–61, edited and translated into Italian by C. M. Mazzucchi (Milan, 1982), pp. 74ff. See also A. Pertusi, *Il pensiero politico bizantino*, ed. A. Carile (Bologna, 1990), 6–16.

4. This is examined and commented on by C. Mango, *Byzantium: The Empire of New Rome* (London, 1980), 151–53. On the equivalence of the earthly and heavenly palace, see A. Giardina, "L'impero e il tributo," *Rivista di filologia e di istruzione classica* 113 (1985): 307–27.

5. Mango, *Byzantium*, 164ff.

6. Niketas Choniates, *Historia*, ed. J. L. van Dieten (Berlin-New York, 1975), 567.49–50.

7. On the Hippodrome of Constantinople as heir to the Circus Maximus of Rome and symbol of classical Rome transposed to the East, see G. Dagron, *Naissance d'une capitale: Constantinople et ses institutions de 330 à 451* (Paris, 1974), 320–47.

8. Kosmas Indikopleustes, *Topographie chrétienne*, 2.75, ed. W. Wolska-Conus, vol. 1 (Paris, 1968), 391.

9. S. Mazzarino, *Stilicone. La crisi imperiale dopo Teodosio*, 2d ed., ed. A. Giardina (Milan, 1990), 232–44.

10. Michael Psellos, *Chronographia,* 3.2, 4, edited by S. Impellizzeri, introduction by D. Del Corno, commentary by U. Criscuolo, translation by S. Ronchey, vol. 1 (Milan, 1984), pp. 72ff and 74ff.

11. Niketas Choniates, *Historia,* 579.82–580.88.

12. B. Lazarev, *Storia della pittura bizantina* (Turin, 1967), 22–24; V. V. Byčkov, *L'estetica bizantina: Problemi teorici* (Galatina, 1983), 148–52.

13. The episode is considered by A. Guillou, *La civilisation byzantine* (Paris, 1974), 199.

14. Nikephoros, *S. Andreae Sali vita,* 9.67 (*Bibliotheca Hagiographica Graeca*³, 117 = *Patrologia Graeca* 111 [Paris, 1863], col. 708AB), translated, from an unpublished critical text of L. Rydén, by P. Cesaretti, in Leontios of Neapolis, Nikephoros, priest of Hagia Sophia, *I santi folli di Bisanzio. Vite di Simeone e Andrea* (Milan, 1990), 142.

15. Niketas Choniates, *Historia,* 548.5–7, praises Alexios III Angelos (1195–1203) for not having committed such acts typical of emperors, even though his judgment of other aspects of Alexios is more severe.

16. Michael Psellos, *Chronographia,* 5.49–50, pp. 242ff.

17. Niketas Choniates, *Historia,* 349ff.

18. These prophecies have been collected and commented on by A. Pertusi, *Fine di Bisanzio e fine del mondo: Significato e ruolo storico delle profezie sulla caduta di Costantinopoli in Oriente e in Occidente,* posthumous edition by E. Morini (Rome, 1988). See, in particular, the conclusion, pp. 151–55.

19. Kazhdan and Constable, *People and Power,* 117–39; A. Kazhdan and A. Cutler, "Continuity and Discontinuity in Byzantine History," *Byzantion* 52 (1982): 429–78; A. Kazhdan and A. Wharton Epstein, *Change in Byzantine Culture in the Eleventh and Twelfth Centuries* (Berkeley-Los Angeles, 1985), esp. 24–73.

20. Anna Comnena, *Alexiad,* 15.7.2–7, ed. B. Leib, vol. 3 (Paris, 1945), pp. 215–17; English translation by E. R. A. Sewter, *The Alexiad of Anna Comnena* (Harmondsworth, 1969), p. 492.

21. 1 Cor. 7:20; Prov. 22:28.

22. On the bookish mentality of the Byzantine people, see my "Il libro come oggetto d'uso nel mondo bizantino," *Jahrbuch der Österreichischen Byzantinistik* 31 (1981): 395–423.

23. Mango, *Byzantium,* 147.

24. P. Lemerle, "'Le gouvernement des philosophes': L'enseignement, les écoles, la culture," in *Cinq études sur le XIe siècle byzantin* (Paris, 1977), 195–258.

25. See Lemerle, ibid., and R. Browning, "Enlightenment and Repression in Byzantium in the Eleventh and Twelfth Centuries," *Past and Present* 69 (1975): 3–23.

26. Kazhdan and Constable, *People and Power,* 19–36; A. Kazhdan, *Bisanzio e la sua civiltà* (Rome-Bari, 1983), VII–XV.

27. Niketas Choniates, *Historia,* 558.31–36.

28. Guillou, *La civilisation byzantine,* 212–19, 234–36.

29. Niketas Choniates, *Historia,* 654.62–655.63.

30. Ibid., 302.35–37.

1

THE POOR

Evelyne Patlagean

T HE POOR AND POVERTY today form a category in general use, one
we know to be subject to precise but inherently relative social and
economic definitions. Anyone who studies early Byzantine society
of the fourth to sixth century immediately encounters in the literary
sources the omnipresence of this condition and of those who lived it: the
indigent huddling under porticoes, infants abandoned in the streets, cripples, invalids, country folk forced to the cities for various reasons, starving, in search of a pittance, laborers in search of day work, beggars, both
disabled and able-bodied. Is the radical and violent novelty of this portrait
due to unprecedented social conditions or to the workings of the testimonies given about them? At such a decisive turning point in the history of
the empire, the question deserves to be asked.

Certain Greek words do, however, already tell us a great deal. Since
Homer's time there have been essentially two words used to designate two
types of poverty: the *penēs* had an activity, but his efforts were not enough
to provide him with a satisfactory and secure living; the *ptōchos* was reduced to passive impoverishment and depended on others for everything.
Other words, such as *deomenos*, "the needy," were used to define poverty
as a condition reflecting a lack, a defect, a condition considered serious
enough so that, in the third century, it led to legal discrimination at the
heart of the free population: the poor person (in Latin, *pauper*) could not
testify. A person was classified as poor if he did not have 50 gold coins
(*aurei*), as specified in a text taken from the *Digest,* thus valid in 533. At
that time, 50 gold coins was a modest but in no way negligible sum. The
ancient mind also defined the rich by possessions, in their case by what
was surplus. The poor possessed less, and the rich more than was absolutely necessary. The surplus owned by the rich was to be transformed
through "magnanimity," or charity within the framework of the city and
to its benefit, as Aristotle states in the *Nicomachean Ethics.* This concept

15

thus did not place the rich in opposition to the poor, as Christian preaching would do in the fourth century. Although still entirely classical in the training of its preachers, the Christian church had its own sources, the Septuagint and the New Testament, in other words, the texts and references of a civilization foreign to the classical city. The Greek of these sources somewhat obliterated the distinction between *penēs* and *ptōchos*, which the preachers nevertheless were able to preserve. There were many texts, on the other hand, beginning with the Beatitudes, to which so many sermons were devoted, including the Psalms, such as Psalm 112 (113):7, "Raising the poor from the dust," that could be read above the doors of charitable institutions! The rich man also figured here in a position of excess that had to be resolved: there was still an ancient concept at work here, but as it became Christian it introduced two essential changes. First, the beneficiaries were no longer fellow citizens who applauded the magnificence of homage to the common values of the city, but poor people who expected charity in exchange for which they would offer their intercession. It followed that the rich were no longer defined relative to a happy medium (*to metrion*); their entire fortune had to be obliterated through charitable redistribution.

However, the social and cultural history of the fourth through the sixth century did not yet rest entirely on those Christian notions. They were only being introduced into cities that still retained the strength of their traditional forms but, at the same time, were receiving the new form of a church of bishops recruited from socially high-ranking citizens. The blossoming of the church in the Greek language is situated between A.D. 370 and 450; following that period, episcopal discourse turned toward other objectives. Moreover, Christianization was manifest in the rise of monasticism, which, in its very essence, was foreign to the city (even though monks were still occasionally found there) and which was destined to serve a key function in the era's response to the poor and to poverty itself. Monasticism did not preach but rather told exemplary stories, "tales useful to the soul," in which the presence of the poor was just as strong as it was in episcopal preaching. Then, in increasing numbers after 450, the monastic movement composed the Lives of its illustrious men, biographies intended to maintain the fervor of their commemoration as well as devotion to their monasteries and, in some cases, their tombs. The influence, impact, and lessons of monasticism were manifest in the episcopal church itself, as seen in the testimonies of the greatest men associated with it: Basil of Caesarea, Gregory of Nyssa, and John Chrysostom.

To these works by well-known authors, and to others that will not be mentioned specifically here, may be added the still numerous inscriptions as well as ecclesiastical directives and imperial legislation. From this quite extensive group of texts, which can in addition be analyzed using nonwritten documentation from archaeological sites, as well as images and currency, there emerges a truly unprecedented model of social relations of which the poor are the cornerstone, without prejudice, it goes without saying, to other models that remained in use, that of the city or the imperial state. Therefore one cannot escape the question asked at the outset regarding the historical and dialectical relationship between a certain situation and a discourse that comments on it. Through that commentary, what do we discover?

THE POOR IN THE LATE ANTIQUE SOCIAL STRUCTURE

First, we learn rather graphically what day-to-day poverty truly was. The diet of the poor was both insufficient and unbalanced compared to what was considered normal in that society as well as on an absolute scale; their lodgings were uncertain, most often rented; their burial places were unmarked or in common grave sites, at least in the cities. Their conjugal or family life, when it existed, was inseparable from their work, remained constantly linked to its ups and downs, and was therefore unstable. Jobs held by the poor were partially or completely unskilled and highly discontinuous: easy, common tasks such as basket making or simple services such as caretaking. The poor also provided the countryside with the temporary muscle power that it needed and supplied construction sites with the unskilled labor that was so often in demand intermittently between 450 and 550. Remuneration was in keeping with the services rendered: meager, completely or partially in kind, or at best paid in fractional gold coins or in the bronze coins used for the most frequent everyday transactions. However, the discrepancy in value between that coinage and gold continued to grow, despite the introduction of a heavy bronze coin by Emperor Anastasios in 498; from his reign on, gold was the coin used for paying taxes. The possibility of a poor worker accumulating such funds remained slight or nonexistent, while his instability and lack of qualifications placed him at the bottom of the scale of productive workers, in both the city and the countryside.

We also find the poor who were suffering. Accidents and illness would plunge the *penēs,* who already survived only with great difficulty, into the distressful condition of the *ptōchos.* The elderly (with old age being defined as the inability to work) and orphaned or abandoned children could not provide for their own needs. Moreover, it is likely that the health of the poor was adversely affected by malnutrition and probably by a more fragile psychological state. In any event, endemic illnesses and infirmities had more serious social and practical consequences for them. Christian preaching surely found in their condition the edifying or miraculous motifs of its gospels. But was that preaching not a function of the situation itself? Before imperial legislation of the sixth century suggested as much, all written or nonwritten sources in fact indicate a history that begins with the poor surging in great numbers into a still ancient Christian society whose traditional framework they appeared to be breaking apart, and that ends with the structure itself being changed because of them.

Above all there was an apparent rise in relative population growth in the first half of the fifth century and perhaps in the second half of the fourth. This might have occurred simply if the normal course of marriages and births was not disturbed by any decisive factor for more than one or two generations, whereas provincial epigraphy shows, in spite of probable infant mortality, families with several children, although these families were probably not very poor. This period was in fact free of any major disturbances. On the other hand, there had been an ascetic rejection of marriage since the end of the third century in the East, where it had first affected the Egyptian peasantry, but its effects could not yet be measured. In the absence of ecological or technical upheavals, and in a time of exceedingly slow evolution of social structures, only demographic growth can explain the problems that existed after 450. Cities were swelling with a population that was streaming in from the countryside and that could not find work. There was a marked change in the degree and frequency of urban violence—city dwellers against representatives of power, ethnic and denominational groups and factions of the Hippodrome against each other—in both Antioch and Constantinople. The insistence of Justinianic legislation seems to indicate a new increase in the abandonment of babies and children on public roads. Cenobitic, or community-based, monasticism underwent an unprecedented rise, as seen in both hagiographical literature and the construction of large centers such as Qal'at Sem'ān in northern Syria, where several thousand men worked in the reign of Zeno (474–475). Even imperial policies, taking into account their monetary aspects, presuppose adequate manpower, whether one looks at work done on the frontiers, as in Dara under Anastasios, or at the initial attempts of Leo I (457–474) at reconquest, an undertaking that was later pursued obstinately by Justinian (527–565). This increased population began to decline in the reign of Justinian because its margin was actually rather narrow and its ability to renew itself quite fragile. The population declined after 550 through wars (in spite of the supply of barbarian forces), from the cumulative effects of monasticism, provincial disturbances, Jewish and Samaritan uprisings in Palestine, and Persian attacks in Syria, and finally because of a decade of various calamities including the great plague of 542–544. But the population increase lasted long enough in that publicly Christian empire to encourage the development of a religious and social model destined to survive the conditions that had brought it about and that was justified by the existence of the poor.

POVERTY IN IDEOLOGY AND IN LAW

The motif of the poor surely goes back to evangelical origins, and solidarity with the needy and the outcast to the first Christian communities. Constantine, the first Christian emperor, established the foundations for this model by what he delegated to the church in exchange for tax exemptions: responsibilities for assistance or activities in the public interest, such as funeral services in Constantinople; for that purpose, eleven hundred shops in the capital, among the buildings of the Great Church, were declared exempt, if one may trust the reference in the analogous measure of Justinian. In doing this, Constantine was merely applying to that new entity, the church, a traditional principle for a newly conceived responsibility. But in the second half of the fourth century, civic discourse, perhaps in its own way, confirmed the emergence of the problem when it pointed out newcomers in the city, who were considered dangerous in the eyes of the classical city, but who, by contrast, were valued from the Christian perspective. As an example, Julian cited to a priest of his restored polytheism the effectiveness of Christian and Jewish aid: and no one had a more modern sensibility in his time than that nostalgic emperor. For his part, Libanios attributed responsibility for unwarranted demonstrations at the theater to homeless foreigners without work or families, who were, moreover, few in number. Preaching "love of the poor," Gregory of Nyssa described the poor lowered by strips of cloth onto the outskirts of cities, destroyed by a horrible new illness he had never seen before, apparently leprosy. From that point on, one could cite multiple texts that create a social definition of the poor: uprooted, alone, unstable, without resources, often physically stricken.

Also at that time, new responses to the situation began to emerge. One notes the connection between charity and sexual abstinence, discussed so well by Peter Brown, and the concomitant Christianization of the traditional values of charity. The nature of charity henceforth changed both with regard to recipients and to the content of the donations. Preaching began to develop the theme of almsgiving and its heavenly rewards. Hagiography presented as examples the unbridled charity of unmarried, wealthy, and devout women such as Macrina, the sister of Gregory of Nyssa, or the young widow Olympias, a follower of John Chrysostom. For his part, the bishop assumed a role that was as original as was his authority itself in comparison with the ancient city. John Chrysostom mentions in a homily the register of the poor, of virgins, and of widows that was kept by the church of Antioch. Two laws (in 416 and

418) mention the traveling nurses of the patriarch of Alexandria (*paraba-lani* or *parabolani*), and Basil of Caesarea himself offered a complete example. He in fact resolved a crisis that resulted from a shortage of supplies in his city, most likely in 368. At the gates of the city he established a place to welcome the homeless and the ill, specifically lepers, it seems. It was in this period that the hospital was invented, a major historical turning point, although we must be careful not to define the first hospitals in a mistaken manner using our present-day notion of the institution, for the two definitions are as far apart as the centuries that separate them. The primary function of the hospital of Christian antiquity was to collect those in need of aid and especially those that were physically incapacitated and could not provide for themselves. It remained difficult, however, to classify the able-bodied poor in a city that was in the process of being Christianized, and a law of 382 prohibited them from begging in the capital.

Monasticism went beyond the urban framework or, more precisely, abolished it. But it was connected in more than one way with the question of poverty and the poor. First, monks, who renounced all social, family, and carnal attachments as well as all possessions, were the most disposed toward the concerns of Christian charity and the uprooted souls who needed it. Second, at the end of the fourth century, monasticism exhibited three basic, already well-observed forms: a stable life in a community, the life of the hermit, and a wandering life that was willingly urban and often unorthodox. All three forms substituted a regulated type of poverty, venerated by the public and supported by donations, for the risks of common poverty. It is possible that at least some women and men, who are mentioned much more often in Greek texts, might have preferred the first type of poverty to the second. Finally, monasticism was already describing the features of its holy men, whose ascetic feats were crowned with miraculous powers that made them imitators of Christ; and miracles of providing and of healing were naturally of great importance to the poor.

All of this was clearly perceptible and, at the same time, still in flux and in a nascent state between 370 and 420. The picture is much sharper for the years 451–565. Sources from that time no longer leave any doubt about the reality and urgency of the problem of poverty and the poor. If homilies fall short in this regard, legislation, historiography, hagiography, and archaeology are equally rich in concrete and contemporary information on the two types of poverty, that of the working poor and of those unable to work.

Poverty began to be given juridical status, beginning with the worker, even one who had a specific trade that provided for him and his family. A law of 539 renewed the prohibition from testifying for those who had fewer than 50 gold coins, unless they were sponsored by a third party;

otherwise, the person could only be interrogated under torture, like a slave. In the fifth century the discrepancy in punishments for the same offense placed the poor in the same position as the *humilior* during the late empire. The poor man's different legal status was particularly evident with regard to marriage. Granted, a law of 454 condemned the confusion of the practice between *infamia* and poverty. But another law, of 538, ratified a social scale for different forms of marriage wherein the poor, soldiers, and peasants—"the lowest layer of the urban population"— were seen as recognizing marriage through cohabitation because they were, said the legislator, "uninvolved in civic life" and absorbed in their occupations, whose stability was the foundation of marriage thus conceived, as Libanios had already noted.

A degree lower one found the mobile, able-bodied poor. Their movements were generally extensive, from the countryside toward the cities, but they were also drawn toward the Holy Land or toward a region of monastic development such as northern Syria after 450. During the reign of Justinian, dependent peasants, slaves, and taxpayers fled, which was nothing new. Constantinople became filled with people who did not know how to do anything, whereas skilled labor, solidly settled into guilds, maintained its price, and even increased it, without its membership growing, it would seem. A series of laws of the 530s suggests an increase in social pressure. A law of 535 was aimed at procurers who recruited poor and often very young girls from the countryside, who were lured by offers of clothing and shoes, sometimes sold by their own families, then held by termless contracts; such evils, at one time limited, invaded the entire capital. The same year the police force in the capital, too often the accomplice of the thieves, was reorganized. In 539 a special magistracy was created to purge Constantinople of the many able-bodied unemployed men living there, who were likely to slide into a life of delinquency. Begging was once again made illegal. Those who had come from the countryside and the provinces were sent back, not without first seeing the abuses whose victims they might have become. Those who had a home in the city were employed in the public works jobs that always required additional manpower, specifically in energy, construction, baking, and truck farming. In 541, from a report by a priest from Thessalonike, a law again focused on the case of young abandoned children that were picked up to be raised as slaves. This was just before the great plague, which produced casualties perhaps on a par with a relative demographic surplus. Other texts add to the picture of criminality and violence. A law of 539 prohibited the manufacture and private sale of weapons in the capital and in all cities, with the exception of "small cutlasses that could not be used for bellicose acts." As noted earlier, this period witnessed serious urban violence and even waves of terror caused by gangs that claimed to be factions of the Greens and the Blues. There was a series of riots, but, although it appears reasonable to assume some connection between able-bodied poverty and criminal marginality, our sources are not very precise in this regard. Only one riot is explicitly attributed to the "poor" (*ptō-choi*): it occurred in 553 as the outcome of a measure that was unfavorable to the bronze coinage that was used exclusively by the poor.

Outside the cities, or from one city to another, the displacement of the able-bodied poor led them wherever they could offer their unskilled services, primarily on the many types of construction sites that cropped up in great numbers throughout this period. But they were also led toward the monasteries themselves. In the course of that century, the rise in the number of monasteries outside the cities was so great that it cannot simply be attributed either to spiritual motivations developed in the literature of monks, or to the simple effect of coincidental factors. Certainly socially complex, monasticism in any event provided a solution to the poverty experienced in that society. As mentioned, the monk in fact exactly reproduced the extreme conditions of active poverty. But the brotherhood to which the individual resigned himself guaranteed the stability of that condition, even to the point of assuming responsibility for the brothers whom illness or old age had rendered inactive.

The brotherhood itself never failed because of its enterprises, such as the production of oil in northern Syria or around Bethlehem, but especially because of the exemptions, revenues, and constant donations that recognized the spiritual and social role henceforth played by the monks. At various sites, archaeology contradicts the model of an absence of individual possessions. In Bawīṭ in Upper Egypt, founded in the sixth century, or in the monastic settlement of Kellia, developed from the fifth century on, archaeology reveals the opulence of personal dwellings. Nevertheless, for many people monasteries remained a haven of stabilized poverty. In addition, some Syrian monastic domains, even in the sixth century, were also, or perhaps primarily, places of asylum; monastic leaders were well aware that certain vocations were only evasions. Finally, monasteries were able to offer temporary employment to passing travelers. For their part, hermits survived by farming and crafts, most often rudimentary; their solitude and separation from village life were only relative. As for wandering monks, they continued to appear in the streets and the roads, despite canonical prohibitions that were vigilant against the heretical subversion for which they were in fact often responsible.

The invalid poor also traveled along the same routes: toward the cities and the large monasteries, toward Constantinople, northern Syria, or especially the Holy Land. "Tales useful to the soul" continued to portray individual models of direct lay charity, such as the beggar who saved enough to give alms to those even poorer than he was. Groups of laymen turned assistance to the poor into one of the aspects of the devout life that connected them. Egypt had its brotherhoods. Curiously, "services" (*diakoniai*) in Antioch and Constantinople seem to have been connected to Monophysite groups. "Compassionate" associations (*philoponiai*) separated the sexes: we have seen the relationship between charity and chastity that was already established in Christian thinking in the fourth century. Members donated money for the distribution of clothing, for example, and they themselves went through the streets at night looking for the sick to gather up and the dead to bury. But the primary role fell to benevolent aid establishments that, undoubtedly not by chance, began to develop a durable typology in this period. Assistance conceived in this way in fact classified the unfortunate ones it intended to help and distributed them among different institutions: there were homes for infants (*brephotropheia*), orphans (*orphanotropheia*), the aged (*gerontokomeia*), the ill (*nosokomeia*), the indigent (*ptōchotropheia*), and poor travelers (*xenodocheia*), as well as the convent founded by Theodora for girls rescued from a life of prostitution. Reality obviously could not have been so compartmentalized. As we have seen, lepers were *ptōchoi* par excellence, and *xenon* came to mean "hospital" in the sixth century. In other words, if the hospital from now on took root in the landscape, its ultimate purpose remained assistance more than healing, caring for the poor and especially those whom illness had rendered incapacitated. As we will see, this did not mean that there were no doctors to be found.

Churches and monasteries added on a "guest house," but specialization appeared, for example, in the Palestinian monastery of the abbot Theodosios, who died in 529. As a hagiographer wrote, he put the words of the apostle, "to each what he needs" into practice. He therefore provided assistance appropriate to each affliction: leprosy, hunger, isolation. The legal status for "pious homes" was then developed along the lines of the principles adopted by Constantine for church property: tax exemptions in exchange for services judged to be in the public interest, and the inalienability of property. Privileged in such a way by virtue of the tasks that fell to them, these establishments were either independent or belonged to laymen, including the emperor, bishoprics, and even other monasteries. Preaching, which had flourished in the second half of the fourth and the beginning of the fifth century, was lacking here, insofar as it had turned toward theological themes, but its teachings had established a tradition. That tradition continued to be expressed in inscriptions on buildings and in testaments, and was stimulated this time by the large volume of hagiographical works written by monks. Historical sources note gestures of charitable generosity made by emperors: the distribution of alms, the foundation or endowment of a hospital or a leprosarium. In this regard the emperor was not simply the foremost layman or a leader concerned with solutions to a pressing social problem. His legislation on the subject was justified by the traditional imperial virtue of *philanthrōpia,* which here assumed its Christianized form, specifically oriented toward the poor. Testaments in favor of the poor were guaranteed against all protests by a law of 455, renewed in 531. An heir responsible for building a hospice remained under legal surveillance until its completion. A bequest in favor of Christ or of a saint was interpreted as being intended to benefit the poor and was directed toward the nearest institution or distributed, again under legal control, by the presiding bishop. However, with regard to public assistance, bishops no longer seemed to play the primary role they had in the time of Basil of Caesarea, although their position in the provincial towns remained as important as it was in the fourth century. This was certainly not true of the patriarch of Alexandria, judging from the Life of John the Almsgiver (d. 620), written by his contemporary and intimate friend Leontios, bishop of Neapolis in Cyprus. But Alexandria was a special case. Granted, too, that Archbishop Hypatios of Ephesus wrote a letter around 531–537 to the "faithful" (*pistoi*) of the city (a group often attested), to whom he prescribed a rule concerning funeral services guaranteed by the local church; this document was written at exactly the same time as the Novel on the same subject relative to the Great Church of Constantinople. Nevertheless, after 450 the service of providing assistance appears to have passed for the most part and for a long time into the hands of the monks, even if monastic initiatives, such as they were, remained legally subordinate by canon law to episcopal authorization.

One might object that this interpretation is inspired by the predominance of hagiographical literature, in particular that which was written in the sixth century to the glory of the great convents of Palestine. But the flourishing of the genre is itself significant compared to the eclipse of episcopal preaching. Free, at least in principle, from any ties to the world, devoted to an "angelic life," monks appeared and asserted themselves as mediators of salvation through alms and intercession. Because of this, their communities received goods, revenues, donations, a continual influx of gifts both large and small. On the other hand, their discipline, which no longer had any relationship to the ancient city-state, rendered them supremely available everywhere to aid the fluid population of the poor. Their presence was therefore, conversely, a factor of attraction, toward the Holy Land, for example. Poverty and the assistance it received had henceforth to be viewed as having two levels of meaning: as a social and political urgency, undeniably; but also as an essential and indispensable element in the Christian dialectic of salvation. The poor man was a figure of Christ, but charity was the imitation of Christ, shown clearly in the exemplary and exceptional case of the saints through the typology of their miracles. To be unaware of this spiritual reading would lead to a misinterpretation.

The issue of healing and of doctors is sufficient to prove this. The hagiographer monks were certainly aware that illness, and therefore the need to be cured, involved all levels of society: their gallery of those cured by miracles proves this, and their purpose was to show the superiority of prayer for the sick and of the miraculous cure of the saint over the physiological and also venal practices of the doctor. In truth, the relationships the monks and their establishments had with the medical world were much more complicated and varied than that, and do not concern us here. But, in principle, the "pious homes" were dedicated to the meritorious work assured by those who, in supreme and perfect misfortune, combined in themselves both illness and poverty.

I have devoted a great deal of time to this early period because it was to be the matrix for a model that henceforth escaped and survived it. This model was born of the encounter of certain circumstances with the Christian transformation of classical civil society and its emperor. It was a model guaranteed to be classic in its own right by the authority retained by the Greek church fathers and Justinianic legislation throughout the centuries. In this model, one distinguishes the ambivalent definition of a poverty stricken with civil incapacity, yet invested with primordial spiritual value; the Christianization of almsgiving; the privileged status henceforth given to institutions that provided assistance; and finally, the role assigned to everyone—monks, bishops, laymen, and the emperor himself—as interlocutors of the poor in the work of salvation. The period during which this model was developed drew to a close with the Arab conquests in the seventh century, a development that cut the empire off from its very populated and active southern regions.

POVERTY IN BYZANTIUM FROM THE SEVENTH TO TENTH CENTURY

The empire then entered into a "dark" century, at the end of which social balances appeared to be modified, a century of continual wars and of the first prohibition of the cult of images, which continued from 729 to 787. All of this was reflected in a marked decrease in the number of rhetorical and hagiographic sources. Legislative work, however, continued. As we have seen, Justinianic legislation tended to give poverty a civil, legal, and penal status, thereby continuing the early attempts made in the era of the Severis. This work reached its conclusion in the law code of 726, the *Ecloga,* which prescribed, at least for certain offenses, the alternative of a financial penalty for the "rich" guilty party (*euporos*), or of corporal punishment if the offender was "needy" or "completely indigent." Existing disabilities were obviously renewed. Discrimination in types of marriage was de facto abolished, as the blessing of marriages by the church was made obligatory by a law of Empress Irene (780; 797–802). The codifications of Basil I (867–886), the *Prochiron* and the *Epanagoge,* repeat these laws, which are also found in the *Hexabiblos* of Constantine Harmenopoulos, a judge in Thessalonike, where he published his work in 1345.

Within the category thus formed, one still found the same two types of poverty: the poor incapable of providing for their own needs, and those who were able to perform some activity. At the end of the eighth century, the first type were again found in institutions that had not changed but that were part of a different society. The Second Council of Nicaea, which restored the images for the first time in 787, initiated a clarification of the status of clerics, monks, and their institutions. Based on the judicial and canonical laws of the preceding period, its canons in turn served as a point of departure for the era that opened with the ninth century, from the very beginning an era of recovery. Nevertheless, the new era had as its framework a society whose structure and balances had changed. In particular, the ancient city-state had given way to the city, whose relative importance seems undeniably to have lessened. Bishops and monks were still in place, and the ninth century marked the triumph of monastic primacy. But the issues involved in the authority claimed by the church over laymen and the emperor himself now concerned discipline and devotion. Neither eloquence nor hagiography, which were also undergoing a revival at the time, gave the passive distress of the destitute the original role it had played until the dawn of the seventh century. Granted, the Life of Theophylaktos of Nikomedeia (ca. 765–ca. 840), written around 900 by a cleric of his church, still presented the exemplary portrait of a bishop who appeared to continue the tradition of episcopal charity. Theophylaktos, writes his hagiographer, was first employed by Patriarch Tarasios (784–806), who was devoted to charity himself. Upon his arrival in the see of Nikomedeia, Theophylaktos had a group of buildings constructed that included a chapel of Sts. Cosmas and Damian, furnished with beds, blankets, everything necessary for the "destitute," and with an income; he brought in doctors and a serving staff, and the complex took on the form of a monastery. At the time he was writing, the author continues, the "medical home" (*iatreion*) thus created still existed and was functioning. Furthermore, Theophylaktos kept a register of the poor, including their names, family, origin, and description; those listed benefited from a monthly distribution of food. This is reminiscent of the list of the poor found in the West in the same period. This practice also continued in Nikomedeia, as did the personal participation of the bishop in the care of the sick. An imitator of Christ, Theophylaktos in fact visited the sick every day, and on Good Friday, after spending the night in prayer, he gave them a warm bath with his own hands, especially the lepers. This remarkable narrative is quite similar to the episcopal examples of the late fourth century, and to the double aid given to the destitute, whether healthy or sick. The aid given to the sick remained primarily a work of Christian piety, but the role of medical care was taken into account explicitly enough so that the hospital derived its name from it, no longer a "shelter," as in the time of Justinian: it was a hospital, *iatreion,* and no longer a *xenon.*

The Life of Theophylaktos remains unique in the hagiography of the ninth and tenth centuries because of its detail. Indeed, "compassion" (*sympatheia*) and "almsgiving" (*eleēmosynē*) remained relevant traits in hagiographical encomiums, but they were far from always being stressed. The founders of the Studios monastery, for example, who dominated the monastic world of that time, throughout the ninth century were occupied above all with their conflict with imperial power. The regulations of the city monastery that is described in the Life of Theodore the Studite (d. 826), and that soon became a model, includes nothing that resembles the episcopal organization we have just seen or that recalls the large monasteries of the sixth century. The Studios monastery appointed a monk to "receive guests," a *xenodochos,* who was to receive them with religious respect, wash their feet, and give them a bed and blankets. Luke the Stylite (d. 879) gave freely during his years of service in the army, but his Life gives no details. Other hagiographical works obscure the linkage of illness and poverty insofar as they stress the relationship between medicine and miracles. This is the case in the Miracles of St. Artemios of Constantinople, a collection that continues well into the eighth century, and in the Life of St. Sampson, which can be dated from the seventh or the beginning of the eighth century. This latter narrative claims to be the life of the founder of a hospital already located in Constantinople in the reign of Justinian; the author praises both the saint's medical knowledge and thaumaturgical power, which was manifest at his tomb. Monasticism also survived outside of cities. But again, there was no longer anything in common between the crowds of the needy in the fifth and sixth centuries and those who visited the monks of Olympos in Bithynia or of Latros in the ninth century. These latter convents were certainly not without hospices (*xenodocheia*), such as the "very large" foundation described in the Life of Michael Maleinos (d. 961). But if the Lives of these monks indeed repeat the ancient schema in which a flight from the world and asceticism are crowned by the power to perform miracles, those miracles lost the concrete social context in which sixth-century hagiography had placed them.

One is easily tempted to explain this change by a different demographic distribution that tended to deplete the cities and also by a general decrease in population. We have already noted the combination of factors that seem to have led to a reduced population after 550, before the Arab conquest removed from the empire its most populous regions. There was great insecurity in the provinces in the seventh and eighth centuries, and repeated plague epidemics until the middle of the eighth century, following which it did not reappear until the fourteenth. If this general hypothesis is true, we can understand why the cities were no longer poles of attraction. Moreover, noncontextual factors played against them. The empire's territory was henceforth divided into districts, "themes," for military purposes, so that the cities lost their traditional position. Athens, Corinth, and Sardis in Lycia declined; Ephesos and Magnesia on the Meander River were considerably diminished; and the sources reveal a reduction in the size of Constantinople itself.

A noticeable recovery began to occur in the ninth century, though when it began and the scope of its influence varied from place to place; it would bear fruit in the tenth and especially in the eleventh century. Scenes unfolded in the tenth-century capital that recalled similar ones in the sixth century. Thus in 927–928 the empire endured an extraordinary winter that hastened an evolution in the countryside that will be discussed below. At that time, Emperor Romanos I had shelters built under the porticoes, and ordered a monthly distribution of silver coins to the poor who ended up there; he also saw to it that each month a third of a solidus was given to the poor (*penētes*) in the churches. Perhaps these poor were listed in registers like those in Nikomedeia. St. Andrew the Fool for Christ's Sake, whose Life can be dated from the second half of the tenth century, also slept under the porticoes, suffered from cold and hunger, encountered prostitutes, gathered the alms that the other poor had stolen from him, but his Life is a narrative written by an author in an ancient style. The old Justinianic model of a pious foundation remained valid and productive. Patriarch Photios thus complained in a letter he wrote in exile (868–869) that his enemies had gone so far as to expel and rob the poor (*ptōchoi*) lepers whom he had settled "in consideration of (his) sins." The model preserved its patrimonial, fiscal, and at the same time religious advantages. A law of Nikephoros II Phokas (964) provides important documentation in this regard. The emperor states on the one hand that the poverty of monks is nothing but a memory and that their possessions were growing with never-ending donations, which were badly managed by them; on the other hand, the foundations intended for the sick or the elderly had by now exceeded the demand for their services. Consequently he implored the monks to return to the model of the ancient fathers of the desert, and he prohibited the establishment of any new monasteries, except in remote and uninhabited places. Only those donations intended to revive existing establishments would be authorized. The emperor further recalled the evangelical precept of selling one's goods and distributing the proceeds to the poor. In a word, the four-century-old model had some perverse contextual effects.

The tenth century marked a clear development in the motif of imperial charity, manifested in a change in forms of protocol. In 899 Philotheos' manual of ranks and court ceremonials, the *Kletorologion,* portrayed "twelve poor brothers" among the guests at the imperial table on Christmas day. Every day Romanos I (920–944) welcomed three poor people to his table, each of whom received one gold solidus, and three poor monks under the same conditions on Wednesday and Friday fast days; one notes in passing the indication of a departmentalized poverty. Constantine VII enlarged and endowed a leprosarium where he appears to have cared for the sick with his own hands. This was certainly true of John I Tzimiskes (969–976), and later became traditional, for it represented a supreme imitation of Christ. And the emperor maintained a privileged relationship with the Christ-model, since Christ himself was considered to be the heavenly emperor (*basileus*) at that time.

The history of the countryside in the ninth and tenth centuries introduces poverty as a status, in a social classification that remained predominantly fiscal. The "poor" (*penēs*) was once again compared to the "rich" (*plousios*), and above all to the "powerful" (*dynatos*), in a pairing that was certainly not new, but that now appeared as the exact Greek equivalent of the Carolingian pair, *potens/pauper:* and we can see that in the Byzantine world, in the same period, as well, the "poor" was defined less by a material deficiency than by a social weakness. Yet there was also some innovation that emerged from the darkness of the eighth century: all taxpayers appear to have been divided up into "soldiers" and "civilians." The first group, listed in a district fiscal register, were bound, they themselves or a member of their family, to armed service for which they had to provide their own equipment at their own expense; this obligation was secured on owned land that benefited through compensation in the form of a tax exemption. Yet two references from the beginning of the century mention "poor" (*ptōchoi*) soldiers: the first reference, in the chronicle of Theophanes, was the vexatious enrollment by Nikephoros I (802–811) of destitute recruits who had to be equipped at the expense of their villages; the other, in the Life of Philaretos, cited below, mentions a soldier who owned nothing more than a wagon and a horse. His horse died, and only the charity of St. Philaretos enabled him to replace it. Destitution here resembles a condition.

But let us return to the "poor" of the countryside, which had not changed its structure. Peasants were still owners or tenant farmers of the land they cultivated. The vast majority of them belonged to village communities, some of which were independent, while others belonged to great estates. This meant that land rents were divided between the imperial fisc and the large landowners; it was in the interest of the landowners to have the largest number of tenants possible while paying the least amount of taxes. This situation had existed for a very long time. Already at the end of the fourth century, landowning peasants were caught between the tax collectors who pressured them and the "powerful" who had the means to intervene using armed force, or political influence between public power and their tenant farmers, and thus to attract the holdings of others into their own property, indeed, to transform independent peasant farmland into de facto holdings. A law of 328, repeated in the *Code* of Justinian, paired the Latin terms *potentiores/tenuiores.* Justinian's Novels, in Greek, placed the *dynatoi* in the same position. In the ninth and tenth centuries the opposite of the "powerful" had become the "poor."

The Life of Philaretos the Almsgiver (d. 792) was written in 821–822 by his grandson and godson, the monk Niketas. Philaretos was born of a good family, like his wife, and was "extremely rich" (*plousios*), primarily from his large landholdings. The impoverishment of this new Job began with the Arab incursions, from which his neighbors witnessed him reduced to passive poverty (*ptōcheia*), for he could no longer keep or cultivate the land that belonged to him. His neighbors then divided his land among themselves, leaving Philaretos only his family home and the land it was built on. Now those neighbors turned out to be of two different sorts. Some achieved their ends through solicitations, these were the "peasants" (*geōrgoi*); the others through force, these were the "powerful," whom Niketas called not *dynatoi,* but *dynastai,* a word that had an even stronger public connotation. Thus impoverished, Philaretos nevertheless continued to perform charitable acts for the "destitute" (*ptōchoi*) of the countryside. Other hagiographic narratives document the tenth century. The Life of Paul of Latros, or Paul the Younger, (d. 955), a monk at Mount Latros in the region of Miletos, includes an episode that unfolds in an area of imperial estates entrusted to the management of a *prōtospatharios,* and on the fringes of which lived the "poor" (*penētes*). They were attacked by their neighbors, who acted as bandits and all belonged to the same family: this was also a case of social weakness, which the *prōtospatharios* attempted to defend; but the power of his enemies was such that, without the intervention of the saint, he would have paid dearly for his actions.

Michael Maleinos (d. 961) came from an important family in the Charsianon theme near the Kizil-Irmak River. He distributed his estate before he took up monastic vows. He therefore gave his personal belongings to the "destitute" (*ptōchoi*), and, says the hagiographer, one could then see herds and heaps of goods of all kinds in the hands of the "poor" (*penētes*), who were thus neighboring peasants. It is also appropriate to cite the Life of Nikon Metanoeite (Repent!), which is situated in the second half of the tenth century and was written at the earliest at the end of the eleventh century. This story begins during the reign of Nikephoros II Phokas (963–969) in a northern theme in Asia Minor. "One day his father sent him out to inspect their holdings," which were considerable. "He saw all the labor and hardship of those who lived there as dependent peasants and were endlessly forced to work the land. He took pity on the lives of the poor (*penētes*), difficult, oppressive, and he declared" his intention to take monastic vows.

Two historiographical texts of the tenth century go in the same direction. The Life of Basil I, written in the palace around the middle of the century, leaves room in its praise for the fiscal mercy of the emperor, manifest in an absence of record keeping that left the poor free to encroach upon neighboring land. Then Leo the Deacon, the historiographer of John I Tzimiskes (969–976), tells how the latter behaved after assassinating his uncle, Nikephoros II Phokas, whom he succeeded. He divided his considerable estate in two: half was used to establish and endow a leprosarium opposite the capital, the other was divided among the surrounding "peasants" (*geōrgoi*) who lived near the property in question. Thus peasant poverty was not only a status, but in this was characterized as the difficulty of acquiring land and the means for work, both of which were distributed free of charge, as seen in exemplary texts. The "poor" were also considered to be weak. This point is illustrated by the legislation of the tenth century, which was motivated by a general social evolution and by the famine of 927–928.

The laws that followed were expressed in opposing terms that were not new but were given a contemporary meaning. The objective was to preserve peasant property, and therefore the interests of the fisc, from monopolization by the "powerful," who were appropriating parcels of land using various means, and who often ended up absorbing the entire rural commune of which they had become members. The details of these imperial laws do not concern us here. These measures were repeated until the great law of 996, proof that the movement could not be checked. That legislation shows the advantages of establishing a social classification. The law of 935 detailed the categories of the "powerful": titularies of a dignity or an office, senators, governors of a theme, archbishops, metropolitans, abbots, administrators of religious foundations or imperial domains. In a word, if the wealth of these categories was implicit, the explicit criterion was always a delegation of public power or a form of authority: the "poor" were then defined by default.

Other laws oppose the "poor" to the "rich": thus a law dating from between 959 and 963 regarding the payment of judges by ordinary citizens distinguished "those who are well-off" (*euporountes*, already used in the penal classification of 726) from the "uncouth masses" and the "other poor." The law that crowned the series in 996 compared the "poor" (*penetēs*) to both the "rich" (*plousioi*) and the "powerful," the holders of "power" (*dynasteia*). It mentioned the "helpless" poor (*adynatos*). In the same period, similar laws also attempted to preserve the property of the "soldiers" mentioned above. The law of 967 distinguished them from "civilians" (*politikoi*) and in particular from the "poor." But the law of 959–963 introduced internal distinctions within each group, specifying on the one hand the "soldiers," who were "destitute," that is, did not have 4 lbs. of gold (288 solidi) declared to be inalienable, and on the other hand the "civilians," whose total worth did not exceed 50 solidi, in which we recognize, unchanged, the criteria of earlier times. Without going into detail, we may note that documents recording land sales from that period show prices for land parcels were much lower than that figure.

Poverty and Social Change in the Eleventh and Twelfth Centuries

The eleventh and twelfth centuries belonged to a new period, and were already preparing for a yet distant modernity. For that reason perhaps the dual definition of the poor that we have followed since antiquity now becomes somewhat confused. In the abundant textual sources, the main characters are not always explicitly named, and it may fall to us to do so ourselves, within a society that was continuing to evolve.

During the first half of the eleventh century, imperial power remained the recognized inheritance of the direct descendants of Basil I. It then passed into the hands of the provincial and military aristocracy whose lineages we witnessed rising to the forefront of political history beginning in the ninth century. The arrival of Alexios I in 1081 for a century consecrated the victory of the Komnenoi in that competition. Urban life, wherever it was found, and wherever the Turkish advance did not disturb it too much, again became active and outgoing, strengthening the movement that had begun in the tenth century. True, the best information we have once again refers to the Byzantine capital, and a study of Thessalonike, the second city in the empire, has not been done for that era as the sources might enable one to do. Finally, lay piety continued to found establishments at a faster pace than ever, something the law of 964 had undoubtedly hardly impeded. These foundations fit the definition with which we are familiar: the founder intended to labor for his own salvation and for that of his family, with the mediation of monks and the assistance of alms, and the labor could henceforth claim, for all intents and purposes, to be exempt from taxation, which would in fact make the establishment more profitable, to the benefit of the monastic community if the establishment were autonomous, and primarily to that of the founding family if it remained private property. Documents that have been preserved nevertheless show the preeminent importance attached at that time to the liturgical commemoration of the dead. The principle was certainly not new, but its development seems to be.

Sources clearly indicate that there was much activity in the cities in the eleventh and twelfth centuries, but they do not speak of urban poverty as such. Historical sources attest to the presence and pressure of the people in the capital when the throne was at stake. These "people" (*dēmos, politikoi*), historically connected to the public role and armed force of the *dēmoi* of the sixth century, were made up of "people of the workshops and the marketplace," grouped into their guilds, according to Psellos. Such was the case in 1042 when the people defended Zoe, the legitimate ruler by birth, from attack by Michael V; in 1047, during the usurpation attempt by Leo Tornikios; in 1057, when Isaac Komnenos seized power with the consent of Patriarch Michael Keroularios, himself supported by the people in the capital; and in 1059 when Constantine Doukas appeared before the guilds of the capital as an eschatological sovereign. That this population was not always or entirely well-off goes without saying, even if we cannot clearly discern these internal distinctions. The disturbances of 1042 seem, in spite of everything, to have been the most violent, even the most revolutionary, one might say. Michael Attaleiates thus notes the assault made on the homes of those who were related to the emperor or were in positions of power. These homes, he says, were robbed of "the wealth accumulated by so much injustice and by the wailing of the poor," and, of course, not only in the city. But the poverty of urban workers was not far behind that of the rural poor. Their condition worsened when circumstances led to increased fiscal pressures, such as in 1091. In the capital, which was being blockaded by the Pechenegs and the Turks, Patriarch John of Antioch gave a speech against the emperor. Alexios I had, in fact, dared to dip into the church treasury to finance the war, and John denounced that policy, which could not bring victory to the emperor. Useless, then, he continued, were those processions that drew the unfortunate from their workshops and that also forced them to buy lamps to take part in them, whereas they perhaps did not even have their daily bread.

In the countryside the conflict between the "powerful" and the "poor" still proved to be in effect in the middle of the eleventh century, as seen in the register of decisions made by the judge Eustathios. The condition of peasants still shifted between independence and dependence, under the aegis of a state that, in the reign of the Komnenoi, was itself on the side of the powerful whom it had fought against a century earlier. Archival documents show a fiscal classification based on the number of work animals an individual owned: two pair of oxen, one pair, a single animal, or none. Those who "owned nothing" (*aktēmōnes*), who "were not taxed" (*ateleis*), no doubt should be considered poor, and even more so those "free" men (*eleutheroi*) who came from places unknown and were hired by landowners, who then obtained authorization to include them on their own fiscal rolls. But in the current state of archaeological investigations, the contextual or regional variations in large part escape us.

Sources once again provide detailed documentation concerning works of public assistance in the eleventh and twelfth centuries, again focusing on the capital. Once again we may pose questions about the role that prevailing social and cultural factors played in this apparent revival. Furthermore, historical works and documents that have survived offer two different testimonies. A series of documents follow the model of the monastic rule (*typikon*) written for the Virgin Euergetis monastery in Constantinople around the middle of the eleventh century. Their main emphasis is on the liturgical commemoration of the dead: monks in the model *typikon* and the family of the founder (later the founder himself) in those of lay foundations. A hospice to welcome poor or sick travelers, daily distributions of food at the gates from the monks' table, or the dispensing of fixed quantities of bread and wine on feast days or days of commemoration were the various forms of relief offered the poor. In any event, such assistance was clearly subordinate to the liturgy. Thus Michael Attaleiates settled twelve elderly indigents in Rhaidestos in 1077, and John II Komnenos housed twenty-four old people in the Pantokrator monastery in Constantinople in 1136; there were thirty-six beds for the sick in the Kosmosoteira monastery founded by his brother Isaac near a village in Thrace in 1152. The numbers speak for themselves. Isaac Komnenos specified the prayers that were to follow the distribution of aid on feast days such as the Dormition, when a hundred poor people would raise their hands to heaven and cry out "Kyrie eleison" forty times for the intentions of the founder before returning home. The quantity of goods to be distributed was also specified and was thus limited. In the end, charity remained an integral part of the program but in a symbolic way, at least in these examples. Laypeople continued to benefit from the traditional exemptions, however, but these were also imperial favors, granted to the founder for one reason or another, and, as always, were favorable economic factors. Finally, in the eleventh century, monastic foundations were often conferred in a lifelong arrangement (*charistikē*) on lay managers, whom Patriarch John of Antioch, between 1085 and 1092, accused of neglecting the required alms and distributions.

Historiography is aware of the use of signs when it attempts to show the emperor as a supreme imitator of Christ, who was himself a heavenly emperor. The care the sovereign gave to lepers remained the symbolic form of that imitation, as recalled in a menologion for January intended for Michael IV, to whom Psellos in fact attributes that practice. Alexios I's welcoming of lepers to his table was a characteristic element of the encomium presented in 1089 by Theophylaktos, the imperial rhetorician and future archbishop of Ochrida. In fact, a leprosarium had an important place in the complex of the Pantokrator monastery dedicated by John II in 1136. Nevertheless, historiography reports imperial measures that suggest a more social reading. Michael IV founded a hospice and convent for repentant girls. Constantine IX Monomachos restored the Constantinopolitan complex of St. George in Mangana on new foundations. Alexios I set up a large complex for public assistance—an orphanage, a hospice for the poor, a leprosarium—and placed an *orphanotrophos* (foster-parent for orphans) at its head, whose duties, already noted in the sixth century, assumed new importance. Alexios also came to the aid of the nuns of Iberia, driven by events from their homeland and reduced to begging in the Byzantine capital. All of this goes back to the ancient concept of imperial *philanthrōpia*. One might, however, discern in it a more strained social situation, heightened no doubt by the course of war and perhaps also by a certain demographic pressure, a hypothesis that might be confirmed by research into the clearing of land, if such research was available. As one isolated and all the more enticing example, the village of Radolibos in Thrace exhibited increased activity between the beginning of the twelfth and the middle of the fourteenth century with deforestation in the thirteenth; one would indeed like to have a series of such examples. Whatever the case may have been, one would be mistaken to see in these measures direct responses to social conditions: the liturgical function of the poor, the expected mediation of the monks, "the love of monks" as an imperial virtue, were inseparable from actual needs.

For their part, the educated ecclesiastics of the twelfth century denounced the more shady characters of Christianity. In the streets of the capital, false ascetics displayed artificial wounds that impressed passersby. The monk Nicholas in his Life of Cyril Phileotes gave vent to a violent diatribe against the wandering monk, a sinner and a parasite, who frequented church festivals, liturgical commemorations, and the tables of others, an ancient, always disturbing figure. Komnenian literature sketches the theme of poverty among the educated. One finds it, for example, in the poetic work of "the poor Prodromos" (Ptochoprodromos), in which the author makes the wealth of the vernacular tongue sparkle with a completely scholarly virtuosity. In a poem addressed to the emperor "John the Black" (Mauroyannis), the author depicts the miserable life of a half-starved poet, whose implacable wife forbids him to enter the family home. Another poem is aimed at the abbots of monasteries in the capital, and contrasts their luxurious cuisine and bath facilities with the hardships that remained the fate of the ordinary monk whose bitterness is portrayed in the text of the poem.

In the framework of that society, the poor of Byzantium now existed on two distinct levels. On the one hand, there was still the traditional typology of the needy from a liturgical perspective joined to the secular discriminations of the law. On the other, an already modern type of poverty was emerging.

POVERTY DURING THE LAST CENTURIES OF BYZANTIUM

It would be difficult to present the entire situation in the fragmented empire from 1204 to 1261. The regions under Latin domination are, at least in part, the concern of other fields of research. The Empire of Nicaea at that time seems to have enjoyed a relative and temporary prosperity in Asia Minor. At the time of the restoration in 1261, Nicaea was in the process of decline because of the movement of populations following the advance of the Turks and by pressure from the Mongols. Patriarch Germanos II (1222–40) remained in contact with his flock in the occupied capital. He gave at least one homily on almsgiving and judgment. But the collection of his homilies (codex Parisinus Coislinianus 278) remains to be studied, as does the Thessalonian preaching of the same period. Thus we will not go into much detail on that period here. Still, it must be pointed out that the figure of the emperor retained his image of charitable virtue. That virtue, in fact, justified the saintliness that the populace recognized in John III Vatatzes, emperor in Nicaea (1222–54), (a development we will not comment on here) and that earned him the name "Almsgiver," recalling the holy patriarch John of Alexandria in the early seventh century.

The portrait again gains in relief following the empire's restoration by the Palaiologoi because of the relative abundance of documentary and literary sources, which in fact have not yet been fully examined. These sources enable us to distinguish two factors in the period's social history and in the renewed upsurge in poverty that seems manifest. On the one hand, there were many upheavals during the breakup of the empire at that time: Latin attempts at reconquest disguised as crusades, rivalries among Italian merchant republics, the Serbian state's will for power, devastating attacks by Catalan mercenaries in the fourteenth century, and the

Turkish advance in the provinces. Then the great plague of 1347 struck the empire, and, in addition, internal peace was compromised: society was divided by the conflict between Patriarch Arsenios and Michael VIII Palaiologos, and a war of succession broke out upon the death of Michael IX in 1320 that caused rifts in the empire for years. In this context, the Zealots took power in Thessalonike in 1342, apparently against the aristocracy, and held it until 1349. The Zealots were also among the enemies of Gregory Palamas, the mystical theologian of the Hesychast movement. The triumph of that movement carried Palamas to the see of Thessalonike (1349–58) and signified that conservative orthodoxy had triumphed over a Greek humanism whose modernity implied an opening toward the West. On the other hand, the economic expansion, or, more precisely, the expansion of Mediterranean trade, included the Byzantines of the fourteenth century, the monasteries on Mount Athos that owned wheat fields and vineyards, the nobles of Constantinople who engaged in business activities, and the guilds themselves that had remained active. Yet trade on a large scale remained beyond the reach of the Greeks, and the political situation at the beginning of the fourteenth century brought about a devaluation of the gold hyperpyron and thus a rise in prices. Through all of this, the poor in the countryside and the urban poor were again visible in the forefront of historical events.

Once more, however, rural poverty was not the subject of literary texts but may be found in documentary sources. For the fourteenth century, the archives of Mount Athos reveal not only inequality among the peasant farmlands of its domains, but also a fragility, an instability of the smallest among them in both area and inhabitants. There is undoubtedly a connection between that latter tendency and the noticeably large number of "free" peasants, those without land, mentioned above. At the same time, there seems to have been an increase in the actual working of those same domains, perhaps in response to the opening of the grain market in the Mediterranean. All of this is connected. However, one would be wrong to imagine that rural monasticism was entirely prosperous; a number of monks were displaced by events. In his second testament, Chariton, abbot of the monastery of Koutloumousion on Mount Athos (30 November 1370), recalls that when he assumed his duties the community was poor to the point of begging: it owned no property, nor any walls to protect it from attacks. Urban poverty is also documented, in the current state of the research, especially for Constantinople and Thessalonike, two highly important cases and, by that fact alone, exceptional.

We must first consider the economic factors that are explicit, for example, in the letters written by Patriarch Athanasios I of Constantinople to the emperor between 1303 and 1310. They describe a capital that, since 1302, was suffering from scarcities that culminated during the winter of 1306–7. Indeed, the more refugees there were, pushed into the city by the Turkish peril, the more active and harmful was the grain and bread speculation. In addition, the patriarch mentions the scarcity of gold and silver resulting from Latin demands. He calls for market controls and asks for wood for the soup kitchen he had opened to distribute food to the poor and unfortunate. He frequently insists on the unregulated behavior of officials: tax collectors mercilessly pressure taxpayers, and provincial bishops linger in the capital where they help themselves to banquets paid for by contributions intended for the poor (*ptōchika*). These complaints were hardly new, but they became louder with the harshness of the times, which the patriarch emphasized, moreover, on many occasions, attributing it, as was appropriate, to the sins of Byzantium: adultery, magic, and sorcery, but also to the oppression of the poor.

Social relationships, and thus forms of poverty, began to change in this period as a result of the economic changes mentioned above. Granted, the earlier model remained clearly perceptible. The treatise *On Offices* (Pseudo-Kodinos), written between 1347 and 1368 at the latest, specified that on Holy Thursday the emperor should wash the feet of twelve poor people, who should first receive gifts of clothing and 3 gold coins; the gesture was explicitly Christlike. The *typikon* of Our Lady of Sure Hope, a convent founded by a niece of Michael VIII, provided for distributions of fixed quantities at its doors on the anniversaries of deaths and on holidays, intended, declared the founder, for "my brothers in Christ, the needy." The Life of Maximos Kausokalybites, a follower of Gregory Palamas who died around 1365, was written by Theophanes, abbot of Vatopedi and then a metropolitan in Thrace. His work revives the ambiguity between true misery and asceticism that, in the early period, characterized the exemplary figures of hagiography. During the time he lived in the city, Maximos, in rags and barefooted, spent his nights like the other poor, at the doors of the church of the Blachernai. But he stood out because of his tears of penitence and, during the day, by mimicking a madman, to the great edification of all. One also encounters once again a poverty among the educated: clerics, monks, and scholars. For the latter group, poverty was of course partly a literary motif, but it must also have had some basis in reality. The testament of Patriarch Isidore in 1350 was concerned with the poor clerics and monks in the capital. Finally, the importance that preaching took on again at that time and its return to themes of social morality recall the urban conditions of waning antiquity. Patriarch Philotheos and the archbishop of Thessalonike, Gregory Palamas, once again preached on almsgiving and on "the love of profit" (*philargyria*). The evil of usury, which Basil of Caesarea had once dealt with, was the subject of a homily by Gregory Palamas. It was also the theme of a collection of writings by Nicholas Kabasilas (b. 1320), nephew of the

archbishop of Thessalonike, Neilos Kabasilas, that includes two composi-
tions and an address to Empress Anna of Savoy. Usury was also the subject of an address by Demetrios Kydones to Emperor John V. In spite of
the classical precedents, we are indeed in the fourteenth century. This is
made clear in the *Dialogue between the Rich and the Poor,* written
around the middle of the century by a Constantinopolitan teacher and
man of letters, Alexios Makrembolites.

In this work one does, of course, find classical definitions, but with a
new asperity: the poor are close to the angels and to God, morality is on
their side; the rich live in a state of excessive accumulation; equilibrium
should be restored, and the poor should again assume their role as inter-
cessors. The evocation of their daily life is also traditional but nevertheless
offers some detail: "the smallest silver and bronze coins come to us, and
just enough for our daily bread." The work also mentions brutality: "everyone says that to die of hunger is the most painful of all deaths." One
becomes rich, continues the author, through knowledge or trade, by sav-
ing or by pillaging, and for many through power or an inheritance. The
poor define themselves as those who labor on the land, in houses, on
boats, or as artisans—in short, all those who make up the urban population—and they include illegal traffickers among the rich. The rich reply
that there are two extremes in society, both equally criminal, and a happy
medium; the poor challenge this view. All of this already sounds quite
contemporary, and in fact other passages break with tradition. The poor
loudly complain of working for little or no profit and that the rich avoid
meals, relationships, and above all marriage with them. They challenge
the notion that to be poor is to become alienated from God. Did such an
idea exist at that time? That would already be quite modern. Finally, the
poor recall the old system of public assistance, which no longer functioned; the rich justify themselves by stressing that general conditions
were once much better and that there were fewer poor people. The dis-
continuance of the old system may in fact be attested in the treatise *On
Offices* mentioned above, which notes that the title of *orphanotrophos*
no longer corresponded to an actual responsibility.

The Palaiologan period also linked poverty, lack of education, religious dissidence, marginality, and sometimes delinquency. This is seen in
the conflict that arose between Michael VIII and Patriarch Arsenios, a
monk, faithful to the Laskarid dynasty that Michael had betrayed in the
form of the young John IV. The Arsenites mounted an opposition to the
Palaiologan emperor that was strengthened by hostility toward the Latins
but was socially complex. They included priests, monks, and laymen of
modest means, together with wandering messengers of what would soon
become a schism, "those wearing sackcloth" (*sakkophoroi*), a name that
recalls both ancient asceticism and heresy. The register of audiences held

at the patriarchal tribunal tells a similar story. For example, in June 1316 there was the case of the priest Garianos, who was accused of heretical activities. He claimed to be a native of Anatolia and from a good, pious family. With his wife and children, he had left his home because of enemy attacks; they then wandered in search of a home and driven by the scarcity of wheat that was common at that time. He stopped at a place that, according to the accusation, was in fact a stronghold of the Bogomils, who tended to his needs. It was here that his problems began, which were solved, in fact, by the case being dismissed. Other audiences portray priests, monks, and nuns implicated in affairs of magic and heresy or of morals.

This description of the Palaiologan period remains incomplete, not only because the Greek sources of the fourteenth and fifteenth centuries have not yet divulged all their information, but also, and perhaps above all, because the definition of that Greek world in which we have attempted to describe the poor itself becomes a question. It would, in fact, be necessary to integrate into our inquiry the Greek populations under Venetian or Frankish rule, the Greek Empire of Trebizond, which was conquered by the Turks in 1461, and also the first generations that lived under Ottoman rule, documented by Greek sources as well as by Turkish documents.

From what we have just read we may draw two conclusions. First, the old model of the working poor, the destitute poor, and public assistance, that Justinianic model with ancient roots, linked to that of imperial power, and based on the Christian economy of salvation, resisted history for centuries. It even went beyond the frontiers of the empire, spreading to countries evangelized by the Greek Orthodox Church, such as Russia. It is only fair to say that Latin Christianity, based on essentially common foundations, developed a similar model and was aware of Justinianic legislation; it would be necessary to compare them. Second, at the end of the political history of Byzantium, another type of poverty appears to have broken through that venerable model, a modern type of poverty like that of the West.

SELECTED BIBLIOGRAPHY

Canon Law and Ecclesiastic Literature
H. G. Beck, *Kirche und theologische Literatur im byzantinischen Reich* (Munich, 1959); for Hagiography, see also *Bibliotheca Hagiographica Graeca*³, ed. F. Halkin. 3 vols. (Brussels, 1957), together with the supplements published in 1969 and 1984; a complementary source for the law and jurisprudence of the Church of Constantinople is *Les Regestes des actes du patriarcat de Constantinople,*

vol. 1: *Les actes des patriarches,* fasc. 1–3, ed. V. Grumel (Paris, 1932–47), fasc. 4, ed. V. Laurent (Paris, 1971), fasc. 5–6, ed. J. Darrouzès (Paris, 1977–79).

Editions of Canons and Canonic Commentaries
G. A. Rhalles and M. Potles, *Syntagma kanonon.* 4 vols. (Athens, 1852–59).

Imperial Law
Codex Iustinianus, ed. P. Krueger (Berlin, 1877); *Novellae,* ed. R. Schoell and W. Kroll (Berlin, 1895); and for legislation after Justinian, *Jus Graecoromanum,* ed. I. Zepos and P. Zepos. 2 vols. (Athens, 1930–31).

Secular Literature
H. Hunger, *Die hochsprachliche profane Literatur der Byzantiner.* 2 vols. (Munich, 1978), esp. vol. 1, pp. 243–441, for historiography up to the beginning of Latin rule (1204).

Inventories of Sources
Patlagean 1977 (see below, General Literature) deals with the fourth through the seventh centuries, with the exclusion of Egypt, for which one can see Wipszycka 1972. Laiou-Thomadakis 1977, Lemerle 1979, and Patlagean 1987 draw upon archival sources, which for Byzantium are available from the end of the ninth century.

On the "Ptōchoprodromos"
H. G. Beck, *Geschichte der byzantinischen Volksliteratur,* pp. 101–5 (Munich, 1971); M. J. Kyriakis, "Poor Poets and Starving Literati in Twelfth Century Byzantium," *Byzantion* 4 (1974): 290–309.

General Literature
Brown, P. *The Body and Society: Men, Women, and Sexual Renunciation in Early Christianity.* New York, 1988.

The Correspondence of Athanasius I Patriarch of Constantinople: Letters to the Emperor Andronicus II, Members of the Imperial Family, and Officials, edited, translated, and with commentary by A.-M. Maffry Talbot. Washington, D.C., 1975.

Gauthier, P. "Les dossiers d'un haut fonctionnaire d'Alexis Ier Comnène, Manuel Straboromanos." *Revue des études byzantines* 23 (1964): 168–204.

———. "Diatribes de Jean l'Oxite contre Alexis Ier Comnène." *Revue des études byzantines* 28 (1970): 5–55.

Laiou-Thomadakis, A. E. *Peasant Society in the Late Byzantine Empire: A Social and Demographic Study.* Princeton, 1977.

———. "The Byzantine Economy in the Mediterranean Trade System: Thirteenth-Fifteenth Centuries." *Dumbarton Oaks Papers* 34–35 (1980–81): 177–222.

————. "The Greek Merchant of the Palaleologan Period: A Collective Portrait." *Praktika tes Akademias Athenon* 57 (1982): 96–132.

Lefort, J. "Radolibos: Population et Paysage." *Travaux et Mémoires* 9 (1985): 195–234.

Lemerle, P. *The Agrarian History of Byzantium from the Origins to the Twelfth Century: The Sources and Problems.* Galway, 1979; rev. ed. of idem, "Esquisse pour une histoire agraire de Byzance: Les sources et les problèmes." *Revue Historique* 219 (1958): 32–74, 254–84; and 220 (1958): 43–94.

Patlagean, E. "La pauvreté à Byzance au temps de Justinien: aux origines d'un modèle politique." In *Études sur l'histoire de la pauvreté (Moyen Age-XVIe siècle),* edited under the direction of M. Mollat, vol. 1, pp. 59–81. Paris, 1974.

————. *Pauvreté économique et pauvreté sociale à Byzance, 4e–7e siècles.* Paris, 1977.

————. "Les donateurs, les moines et les pauvres dans quelques documents byzantins des XIe et XIIe siècles." In *Horizon marins, itinéraires spirituels* (= *Mélanges M. Mollat*), ed. H. Dubois, J. C. Hocquet, and A. Vauchez, vol. 1, pp. 223–31. Paris, 1987.

Pseudo-Kodinos, *Traité des offices,* introduction, text, and translation by J. Verpeaux. Paris, 1966.

Ševčenko, I. "Alexios Makrembolites and his *Dialogue between the Rich and the Poor.*" *Zbornik Radova Vizantološkog Instituta* 6 (1960): 187–228; reprinted in idem, *Society and Intellectual Life in Late Byzantium.* Variorum Reprints, London, 1981.

Wipszycka, E. *Les ressources et les activités économiques des églises en Egypte du IVe au VIIIe siècle.* Brussels, 1972.

2

THE PEASANTRY

Alexander Kazhdan

W HEN WE SAY "BYZANTIUM" we usually mean Constantinople, the imperial court, and urban life. But like all medieval countries, Byzantium was predominantly rural. Even though we have no reliable figures to categorize the Byzantine population, it goes without saying that the vast majority of Byzantines lived in rural areas. Emperor Leo VI (886–912), in his military manual, the so-called *Taktika,* stated that there were two occupations necessary for the well-being of the state: that of the peasants (*geōrgikē*) who nurtured and raised the soldiers, and that of the soldiers (*stratiōtikē*) who defended and protected the peasants. In the same vein, Emperor Romanos I Lekapenos (920–944), in an edict of 934, stressed that there were two conditions required for the normal existence of a society: the payment of taxes and military service. Peasants were considered as the main taxpayers who supported the state and its military machine.

The general word for the peasant was *geōrgos,* "soil tiller." There were other terms to designate the peasant, some vaguer, some more specific: for example, *oikodespotai,* "house owners," and *chōritai,* "land dwellers." In later documents the villagers appear mostly as *paroikoi,* a word that evolved from designating a settler to meaning a dependent peasant. Among specific terms applied to specific categories of the rural population were words like *dēmosiarioi,* those obliged to pay state tax (*dēmosion*); *xenoi* (aliens); *eleutheroi* (free from taxes); *zeugaratoi* (owners of a pair of oxen); *aktēmōnes* (have-nots); *kalybiotai* (hut owners); *kapnikarioi* (hearth owners)—terms that stressed either a person's property status or relation to the fiscal system. The term *agroikos* (rustic) had mostly a derogatory connotation, "common" or "boorish."

The peasants were first and foremost dwellers in villages. The classical term for the village (*kōmē*) continued in use in narrative sources, but in documents (beginning with the third-century papyri) it was replaced by the word *chōrion,* which in the classical language meant "place." It is hard to draw a strict distinction between the village (*chōrion*) and an urban settlement. At any rate, we do not know of formal ordinances granting a site city privileges after the sixth century. The terminology was fluid, and the same settlement emerges in the available texts as city (*polis*), castle (*kastron*), or *chōrion;* in fact, a compound word, village-city (*kōmo-polis*), is characteristic for this borderless situation. Fortifications were not the landmark of urban status: the Crusaders were astonished to observe a Peloponnesian city, Andravida, that had no city ramparts; on the other hand, some monasteries and villages were strongly fortified, especially in the later centuries. Nor had agriculture become the exclusive activity of villagers: thus we possess a fiscal record of a town, Lampsakos on the eastern shore of the Hellespont, written in 1218–19, that lists 173 households in the settlement, of which 60 are characterized as urban and 113 as peasant. Nothing is known of manufacturing in Lampsakos, but there were mills, vineyards, and salt pans there, as well as fishing and harbor incomes and taxes. Athens was a famous city, more considerable than Lampsakos, but at the end of the twelfth century its archbishop, Michael Choniates, lamented that a number of fields spread out where houses once stood and that even the Stoa had been transformed into a pasture. Even within the ramparts of Constantinople, there were vineyards and fields.

How did the Byzantines themselves define the city? The same Michael Choniates mentioned fortifications, an entrance bridge, and a large population as typical features of a city, but he was inclined to suggest another, a moral definition: the peculiarity of the *polis,* he says, is "not in the strong walls or tall houses, the creations of carpenters, as the ancients imagined, but in the existence of pious and courageous, chaste and just men."

RURAL SETTLEMENTS

The *Treatise on Taxation* preserved in the Bibliotheca Marciana in Venice distinguished three types of rural settlements: the *chōrion;* the hamlet (*agridion*); and the estate (*proasteion*). The *chōrion* is a regular village; according to Angeliki Laiou's calculations, the fourteenth-century village in Macedonia contained an average of thirty-three households. We have no substantial data for other periods or regions, but a passage in the eleventh-century historian John Skylitzes allows one to draw a tentative conclusion concerning the size of the Byzantine village. Skylitzes says that circa 1039 a supplementary payment (the so-called *aerikon*) was imposed on all *chōria* in accordance with their "power"; the payment varied from

4 to 20 nomismata (gold coins) yearly. Taking into consideration the rate of this supplementary payment as it still existed in the fourteenth century, we can hypothesize that the legislator envisaged the average village as containing fifty to one hundred and fifty households.

Also quite hypothetically, we may assert that the village in Asia Minor was on average larger than that in the northern Balkans. Although even here a *chōrion* might contain 450–500 inhabitants, smaller villages were frequent, and place names such as Monospitia ("of one house") occur.

A village included a *kathedra* (literally, "seat"), a structural center of the settlement, the point from which a fiscal description of a village began. The *Treatise on Taxation* distinguishes two main types of the *chōrion*: sometimes the village had a single *kathedra,* that is, was centrally oriented; in other cases it was polyfocal, consisting of multiple *kathedrai,* that is, the peasant houses lay dispersed.

The *agridion* was in fact the third type of rural settlement, a hamlet separated from the maternal nuclear village. If the owner of such a hamlet did not dwell there and allowed the land to be worked by his slaves or hirelings, the *agridion* was classified as a *proasteion.* The word *proasteion* literally meant suburb, and the term was used time and again in this classical sense in literary texts. Documentary sources, however, ignored its etymological connection with the city (*asty*) and employed it exclusively to denote estates, usually of an insignificant size. In later texts the distinction between *agridion* and *proasteion* disappeared, with *agridion* being used to designate an estate with a dependent population.

A regular village included common lands: hills covered with forests, pastures, groves of chestnut, walnut, and other trees, sea and lake shores. Streams were also considered to be held in common. But the main territory of the village was divided among its households; the household and its terrain was called *stasis* as a physical unit and *stichos* ("line") as a fiscal unit, as an entry in fiscal surveys. Documents describe a *stasis* as including houses, vineyards, kitchen gardens, trees, fields, sometimes pastures and springs or wells. These lands were usually divided into small parcels. A fourteenth-century survey describing ten households in the village of Aphetos given to the monastery of Chilandar on Mount Athos allows a unique insight into this fractioned structure of the household: these peasants possessed from five to thirty-three parcels each. Their parcels were dispersed across different parts of the village's territory, and many were really diminutive; the average size of a field in the household of Theodore Thraskes was only 3.5 modioi (a modios was approximately 0.08 ha.). The lands of a *stasis* or of an estate formed a certain hierarchical ladder of which the most precious were called *autourgia* ("operated without assistance"). This category encompassed properties producing the most revenue: olive groves, vineyards, meadowlands, as well as salt pans, water mills, brickyards, or fish ponds. Below *autourgia* on this scale of property stood regular fields, *chōraphia* in Byzantine terminology.

Documents not only contrast *chōraphia* with vineyards and pastures but usually with *gē* (land); the latter designated primarily the larger tracts of land, whereas a *chōraphion* rarely surpassed 10 modioi. Among them one can distinguish the inner and outer fields, probably those located closer to the *kathedra* of the village and those (newly cultivated?) on the outskirts of the settlement. The *chōraphia* were closed units encircled by ditches and fences or at least boundary markers; they could have common borders with allotments of different types such as vineyards, olive groves, and gardens as well as roads and buildings. They were not considered as shares in the open fields nor were they subjected to systematic redistribution.

AGRICULTURE

Even after the loss of Syria, Egypt, and North Africa, Byzantium preserved a territory of diversified soil and climate. The most common features, however, were the predominance of rocky soil, the scarcity of water, and warm summers. This resulted in relatively small-sized fields, in the development of horticulture and viticulture, and in stock breeding characterized by transhumance.

Byzantine agriculture was polycultural, with grain production playing a substantial role, even though there are reasons to surmise that the share of bread in the human diet decreased in comparison with the late Roman Empire. Daily bread consumption in that period was three to six pounds per person, according to Evelyne Patlagean, whereas by the eleventh and twelfth centuries the average daily ration was reduced to one and a half pounds. This decrease of bread consumption can be explained by the loss of the empire's major granaries—Egypt, North Africa, and later Sicily—but it is hard to imagine that such a contraction would not be supplemented by the development of other crops. In any case, we can observe some changes in the nature of grain produced in Byzantium.

Archaeological finds from Egypt demonstrate that just before the Arab conquest of the country in the seventh century hard wheat (*triticum durum*) began to spread there; hard wheat was the major grain in the tenth-century finds from Beycesultan in Anatolia. It was easier to thresh and store than the soft wheat of Roman times.

Wheat was cultivated in Asia Minor, whereas in the Balkans barley played a greater role. The figures now available are scanty but nevertheless indicative. Michael Choniates testifies that one year from his estates on Euboia there were harvested 14 medimnoi (whatever that means) of bar-

ley and 11 medimnoi of wheat. The will of a certain Skaranos of 1270/
74 lists stored grain, with barley and wheat represented almost equally:
27 modioi of barley and 31 modioi of wheat (here modios designates the
amount of grain used to sow over the surface of a modios of land). On
the other hand, the survey of 1073 for the estate of Baris (western Asia
Minor) listed 260 modioi of wheat and 150 modioi of barley; in 1192,
the small monastery of St. Marina near Smyrna possessed 120 modioi of
wheat, whereas barley was not mentioned at all.

Besides wheat and barley, rye was known, probably a medieval innovation. The finds from Beycesultan revealed only an insignificant amount,
but in the will of Skaranos we find more reference to rye (45 modioi)
than to wheat. Though millet was cultivated as well, the eleventh-century
dietician Symeon Seth is very skeptical about millet, asserting that it is
injurious to the stomach. Oats also became known, at least in the
Frankish Peloponnese.

The Byzantines cultivated both winter and summer crops; Nikephoros Gregoras, a fourteenth-century polymath, observed young and ripe
grain in the fields at the same time. Winter crops were sown in November,
mostly between the 11th and the 30th of the month. Abundant autumn
rains were beneficial in bringing the grain to fruition.

Beans followed grain in the Byzantine diet. Again our figures are accidental: in the estate of Baris a small amount of beans was stored, only 5
modioi, whereas the monastery of St. Marina owned 39 modioi, which
amounted to one-third of the wheat preserved. Various fruits and vegetables supplemented the diet: olives and grapes are frequently mentioned.
The Byzantines also planted cabbage, onions, leeks, carrots, garlic, cu-
cumbers, squash, melons, and so on. In their orchards there were various
fruit trees. The late Byzantine vernacular satire Porikologos (the Book of
Fruits) pictures a court where all the officials are fruits and vegetables,
including quince (the king of fruit), citron, pear, apple, cherry, plum, fig,
and so forth. The peach ("Persian apple") was also known. The calculations of N. Kondov demonstrate that in the northern Balkans the pear
tree was more common than the apple and the cherry tree than the plum.
The Byzantines also planted pomegranates, mulberry, almond, walnut,
and chestnut trees. Some plants were harvested primarily for industrial
purposes, for example, flax, sesame, and cotton, the latter being produced only in the hottest regions of the empire. After the loss of Syria,
South Italy remained the major center of sericulture.

Agricultural technology continued ancient Mediterranean traditions.
The "scratch" type plow without wheels continued in use from Roman
times. It consisted of the following parts: plow beam, yoke beam, stilt,
and share beam. The plow beam is the curved portion of the plow that
unites the share beam with the yoke beam. The share beam, the essential

part of the plow, narrowed to a point and was frequently strengthened by an iron tang to reduce friction and prevent splintering. Attached horizontally by doweling to the plow beam, and through it to the yoke beam, this plow was drawn by a pair of work animals, predominantly oxen, through the top layer of soil, loosening and depositing it on both sides of the resultant furrow. The exact depth of the furrow was established by the pressure on the stilt, while the oxen were controlled by a goad. By cutting only the upper layers of soil, moisture was retained below, an important consideration in semi-arid areas such as Greece and Asia Minor with their hot, dry summers.

Many illuminated manuscripts (of Hesiod's *Works and Days* or the homilies of Gregory of Nazianzos) show us the form of this wooden implement. It was evidently very light, since a plowman, returning home from the fields, could load it on the back of his ox. The oxen were harnessed by neck collars directly, at least until the tenth century when a more complicated system of harness was introduced. As the plow had no wheels, oxen harnessed at their necks could drag only a light implement.

As the plow only "scratched" the soil, it was necessary to work the field several times, a method reflected in the terms *dibolisma* and *tribolisma* denoting the second and third tilling of the soil. In many cases the quality of the soil prevented plowing and required manual tilling. Thus, in the survey of the estate of the Patmos monastery of the late eleventh century, the entire territory was calculated as 3,860 modioi; only 627 modioi were good for cultivation, and only 160 modioi could be tilled by oxen, whereas the rest needed manual work.

Byzantine terminology had a great variety of names for the spades, mattocks, and hoes used by peasants: two-pronged *dikella, makelē, liskarion, tzapion,* and the so-called agricultural axe. Of course, tilling vineyards and gardens in particular required manual labor. Miniatures of Byzantine manuscripts as well as mosaics show the *dikella* with a bifurcated blade attached at right angles to the haft, the long-handled *makelē* with a triangular blade, and other types of hoes.

For harvesting, the sickle (*drepanon*) and not the scythe was used. The peasant held the curved iron sickle in the right hand and collected the cut-off produce with the left. High stalks were left after reaping, and livestock grazed on the fields after harvesting, thus contributing to the fertilizing of the soil.

Threshing also preserved the ancient Mediterranean method. The Byzantines did not use flails; the sheaves of grain were spread over the threshing floor, usually on a hilltop exposed to the winds, and oxen or donkeys dragged a threshing sled (*doukanē*) over it. The grain was separated from the chaff with a winnowing fork or shovel. The grain was stored either in *goubai,* bunkers (pits) dug in the earth, or in *pithoi,* large earthenware vessels, many of which have been discovered in archaeological excavations.

Various types of mills were in use. Querns or hand mills (*cheiromyla*) are known. The Life of St. Luke Steiriotes tells the story of thieves who stole a *cheiromylon* from the saint but were severely punished for their impious crime; querns were usually brought along on military expeditions. More often the sources mention mills powered by animals such as old oxen, donkeys, or even horses. This type of mill had been the predominant device for grinding grain in the Roman Empire: a law of 364 describes an average bakery as having both animals and slaves. It continued to exist in Byzantium: the tenth-century *Book of the Eparch,* a collection of the statutes of Constantinopolitan guilds, mentions the animals that turned millstones. But gradually mills powered by animals were replaced by water mills (*hydromylōnes*).

Water mills had been built in late antiquity: a fifth-century water mill has been excavated in the agora at Athens. Its axle ran between the sockets from the wheelrace to the pit in the mill-room; on the shaft, where it crossed the pit, a vertical tympanum was set, meshing with the larger horizontal tympanum whose vertical shaft moved the millstone. In Rome, mills powered by water from an aqueduct are attested in the fourth to sixth centuries; they became common in Byzantium. Two types are known: winter mills that worked only when streams were in full spate and the year-round *ergastēria* (workshops, a typical designation for mills). Windmills (*anemomylōnes*) were used in Byzantium later than in the West and are rarely mentioned in the sources, but they evidently existed in the fourteenth century.

Probably in the tenth century, a new device was invented: a machine powered by oxen for preparing dough. We first hear of it from the Life of St. Athanasios of Athos when the saint made one for his large monastic community. The implement was adopted by neighboring communities, and in the eleventh century several monasteries on Mount Athos acquired oxen especially to power the "dough mixer." Certainly, the machine was too complex to find much use in individual households.

Bread was baked in ovens in the form of loaves, which were sometimes flat. In the fourteenth century, Nikephoros Gregoras complained that he had to eat (and was barely able to) loaves produced in peasant households where they were baked in ashes. Soldiers on campaign ate *paximadion,* bread baked twice and dried in the sun so that it formed hardtack.

Olives provided a staple food and, when crushed in an olive press, yielded oil for cooking and lighting. Until the Arab conquest, Syria and North Africa were the major areas of olive production. When these regions were lost in the seventh century, olive cultivation was concentrated on the coasts of Asia Minor, Greece, and in southern Italy. There were no olive groves in Anatolia, and olive trees are only occasionally mentioned in documents concerning Macedonia. It is worth noting that the so-called Farmer's Law, a controversial collection of regulations for the countryside produced in the seventh or eighth century, knows nothing of olive cultivation. On the other hand, English observers of the twelfth century report that no other place in the world produced so many olives as the southern Peloponnese.

The production of olive oil was fairly complicated, involving pitting the olives and separating the oil from the dregs. Several oil presses of the fifth through seventh century, discovered in Syria, reveal this process. The olives were piled into a vat with two stone rollers at the end and crushed by the rollers so that the dregs could be removed and the olive paste collected in round baskets and placed in the second vat, one on top of the other, under the horizontal beam. Then the beam was lowered, crushing the olive paste, and the oil flowed into the vat below. The oil was then drawn into another nearby vat that was filled with water; there impurities fell to the bottom, while the oil came to the surface and was then drawn off into another vat. The press had to be operated carefully, as the olive pits, if crushed, would impart a distasteful flavor, and completely removing the impurities was very difficult.

Unlike olive groves, vineyards were planted across almost the entire territory of the empire. Together with the *chōraphion*, the vineyard was the most typical form of cultivated land in Byzantium, where bread and wine were main dietary products. Usually the vines were untrellised; peasants used vine props of reeds or trained the vines to wrap themselves around the trees in gardens. A Latin survey from the Frankish Peloponnese defines *ambellonia* as lands on which grapes were growing as well as other plants, including olive trees. It is not accidental that the Byzantines used not only the term *ampelōn*, vineyard, but such compounds as *ampeloperibolion* and *ampelokēpion*, or vineyard-garden.

Vineyards were ubiquitous, and were often planted in mountainous areas. In fourteenth-century Macedonia, the majority of peasants possessed vineyards: 83.7–92 percent according to Kondov, 74–96 percent according to Laiou. The size of the vineyards belonging to a single household varied (according to Kondov) between 0.5 and 22 modioi, but Laiou stresses "the relatively equal distribution of vineyards" among a population economically unequal in other respects.

The vinedressers' essential tool was the *klaudeutērion* or pruning knife. The grape clusters were put into baskets or on staves and transported from the vineyards to the wine vat (*lēnos*). Before the grapes were pressed, the vat was fumigated with incense; leaves and rotting clusters, which could make the resulting must bitter, were removed from the baskets. Then the grapes were dumped into the wine vat. After first washing their feet, men climbed into the vat and extracted the juice by treading on the grapes. Next they removed the seeds from the treading floor; the must passed through a channel into a receptacle (*hypolēnion*) below the vat; then the must was placed in casks (*barelia*) to ferment. Both stationary and portable late Roman wine vats have been discovered in various parts of the empire. Several surveys of the late Byzantine period list the vats, sometimes together with *pitharia,* large vessels to contain wine; they were owned by individual peasants and placed in their courtyards.

Liutprand of Cremona visited Constantinople in the mid-tenth century; his official embassy turned into a failure, and he returned home in bitter frustration. Everything Byzantine irritated him, including the "Greek wine" that he found undrinkable since it was flavored (he says) with pitch, resin, and gypsum. Leaving aside the difficult question of taste, what Liutprand meant were the additives, such as pine needles, that produced "retsina" wine. These ingredients helped preserve the wine but also gave it a specific aroma. Other westerners may have been more interested in Greek wine (Cretan wine was especially famous), and the twelfth-century scholar Burgundio of Pisa translated several sections on wine from the Byzantine collections of ancient agronomists titled the *Geoponika.* This work contains five books devoted to wine making, but it is difficult to judge how much they reflect tenth-century practice as opposed to an ancient bookish tradition.

We know very little about processing other agricultural products. Flax, which is hardly mentioned in the *Geoponika,* played a significant role in Byzantine agriculture: the survey of 1073 testifies that the *proasteion* of Baris had stores not only of wheat, barley, and beans but also of flax seeds (*linokokkoi*). The seeds were processed in special workshops called *linolaiotribika* and made into oil.

Flax fibers were processed in other workshops, called *linobrocheia,* usually located on the banks of a river or lake because the process required water. The fibers were used to produce textiles. The linen industry was highly developed in late Roman Egypt, but after Egypt fell to the Arabs in the seventh century, linen cloth was imported into Constantinople primarily from Bulgaria and northern Asia Minor, the regions of the Strymon River, Pontos, and Kerasous.

A hot, dry climate caused frequent droughts in Byzantium and accounted for the constant concern about water. In the late Roman Empire, a developed irrigation technique existed primarily in Egypt and in the western provinces. In Egypt, various water-lifting machines continued in use: the water screw, suction pump, compartmented wheel, bucket chain, and so on. Data concerning similar devices in Palestine, Syria, or Greece are scanty. Asia Minor and Greece relied more on collecting water (from streams, rain, or aqueducts) in cisterns than irrigating lands by canals and water-lifting gears. The monastic rule (*typikon*) of the Kosmosoteira monastery near Aenos in Thrace describes a complex construction for collecting water that flowed from the spring via a conduit into a receptacle protected from the sun and dirt. In other cases, special workers were busy carrying water in buckets.

Water was occasionally used for irrigating vineyards, gardens, and olive groves. A document from Crete dated circa 1118 presents a conflict between a mill owner and his neighbors, who were tillers of "irrigated *chōraphia*." The peasants complained that the construction of the mill deprived them of water for their fields. Improvement projects of considerable scale are described in a document of 1421 from Thessalonike; it relates the activity of the family of the Argyropouloi, who rented a garden from the Iveron monastery, improved and irrigated it, and enormously increased the yield and income.

LIVESTOCK AND RELATED TOPICS

The Byzantines raised various kinds of livestock: horses, cows, water buffaloes, camels, donkeys, mules, sheep, goats, and pigs. The history of animal breeding in Byzantium has not yet been written, and it poses a substantial problem. Cadastral records of the late Roman Empire suggest a serious understocking, even though we have to keep in mind that these records cover only an insignificant part of the empire's territory. The Farmer's Law, however, presents a rural society in which stock breeding seems to play a greater role than grain production: of its eighty-five articles, forty deal with cattle, donkeys, sheep, and pigs (horses are not mentioned), whereas only sixteen are devoted to land cultivation and related questions, nine to vineyards and gardens, two to agricultural implements, and four to houses and barns. Like western medieval *leges* (laws), the Farmer's Law protects the animal from the neighbor rather than the neighbor's crop from an animal causing damage. Later sources support the same impression: in the early twelfth century, the Russian pilgrim Daniil Igumen was astonished at the amount of stock he saw on Aegean islands (Patmos and Rhodes) and on Cyprus, and the Norman jongleur Ambroise emphasized in the same century the abundance of food and cattle there. As late as the fourteenth century, great landowners such as John Kantakouzenos possessed enormous herds in Thrace; while lamenting his losses, Kantakouzenos listed 1,500 mares, 1,000 pairs of oxen, 5,000 cows in herds, 50,000 pigs, 70,000 sheep (and goats?), hundreds of camels, mules, and donkeys. Especially rich in cattle and flocks were regions in Anatolia east of the Sangarios River (Paphlagonia, Cappadocia, Lykandos) and in Bulgaria.

While cattle breeding seems to have thrived on the large estates, at least until the mid-fourteenth century, the fate of the peasant's livestock in the fourteenth century was different. For some villages in southern Macedonia, fiscal surveys survive that demonstrate the drastic decline of flocks between 1300 and 1341. According to Laiou's calculations, the village of Gomatou circa 1300 possessed 1,131 sheep and goats; in circa 1320 the number of sheep and goats declined to 612, and the survey of 1341 records merely 10 animals in the entire village. If we take these figures at their face value and not as the result of an inaccuracy, the question arises about what caused this decrease. Are the contemporary political disturbances in Byzantium (the civil war, the razzias of mercenaries, the Serbian invasion) sufficient to explain these catastrophic changes? In any case, in the mid-fourteenth century, raising livestock was not prosperous in Macedonian villages.

Camels were typical of Egypt, Syria, and North Africa, but, as one can see from the above-mentioned list of losses established by Kantakouzenos, they are attested in fourteenth-century Thrace. The author of the so-called *Strategikon* of Maurice, a military treatise probably written in the early seventh century, considered camels as regular pack animals for the army, and the deposed emperor Andronikos I Komnenos (1183–85) was paraded through the streets of Constantinople on the back of a mangy camel.

Horses were not common in the Roman Empire, where the principal beasts of burden were oxen and mules, and the army relied primarily on foot soldiers. The role of the cavalry had already increased in the fourth to sixth century under the influence of mounted barbarians, and by the beginning of the seventh century the cavalry was the most numerous Byzantine troop formation. It is plausible to hypothesize, together with Count Lefebvre, that the invention of a new system of harnessing animals to a cart and plow increased the use of horses in everyday life. The horse, however, remained the animal of the rich and noble; people like Kantakouzenos possessed hundreds of horses, and *stratiōtai* were supposed to acquire a horse to go on military expeditions. But horses are rare in peasants' husbandry: as an exceptional case, a peasant could possess two horses, but less well-to-do villagers are described in fiscal surveys as owners of "half of a horse" meaning that they owned a horse together with a neighbor.

Sheep and goats were the main domesticated animals, especially among peasant households. A peasant household might own up to 300 sheep and goats, and Laiou calculates that in the village of Gomatou (southern Macedonia) a peasant household possessed a mean of nine sheep and goats. Pigs were owned in fewer numbers (usually two to five animals) and by fewer households.

Some animals grazed in neighboring groves and hills, and stories about peasant boys who drove their swine or sheep to a pasture for the whole day form a hagiographical topos. Cattle could be pastured in the woods without herdsmen, and the bell on their collars helped find a stranded animal. But the limited size of meadows and seasonal patterns urged peasants to send their flocks far from home. Nikephoros Gregoras describes peasants in the Strumica region of Macedonia who left their homes in spring for the mountains and stayed there to milk their animals. A similar situation existed in Asia Minor: thus the Life of St. Paul of Latros (tenth century) tells a story about a peasant who pastured his goats in the mountains and returned home only for the harvest, and the eleventh-century saint, Lazaros of Mount Galesios, while traveling through Cappadocia came across flocks of sheep herded by dogs that chased him to a rock and jumped after him trying to drag him down. Another holy man, Paphnoutios, was mistaken for a beast by a shepherd, who shot him with an arrow.

In colder weather, herds returned to special winter pastures (*cheimadeia*). An act of 1333 from the archive of the Athonite monastery of Kenophon mentions a *cheimadeion* in the area of Kassandreia, near which were located a field of 1,800 modioi and an oak grove, probably for the swine. A contract survived that regulated the use of such a winter pasture: two neighboring landowners were to feed their cattle on it during the winter, but from the beginning of spring, when the grass began to grow, they had to stay off it. Famous as herdsmen were the Vlachs who dwelled in Macedonia, Thessaly, and neighboring regions where they practiced transhumance; at the end of the eleventh century, the Vlachs lived in close contact with the monks of Mount Athos, providing them with dairy products. Emperor Alexios I Komnenos (1081–1118) expelled the Vlachs from the Holy Mountain to the great regret of the monks.

Livestock was used for pulling carts and plows and as beasts of burden. The animals provided valuable manure for enriching the soil. In certain areas of Asia Minor, dung mixed with straw was burned in place of wood. Animal hides supplied the leather industry. Though the processing of leather does not seem to have attained much importance in antiquity, in Byzantium leather processing and the manufacture of leather products became one of the most widespread craft professions. Leather was used not only for footgear but also for certain types of cloaks, harnesses, tents, and shields, as well as for parchment. The division of labor was relatively elaborate and comparable only to the complexity of silk production.

The primary product of livestock was food, both dairy products (milk and especially cheese, which could be prepared in and transported from remote pastures) and meat. Because our information about the Byzantine diet comes mainly from ecclesiastical texts, we are inclined to think that the Byzantines avoided meat, which in fact was prohibited for monks. Laymen, however, did not abstain from meat. A typical story comes from the Life of Theodore of Sykeon, written in the mid-seventh century: the saint hired carpenters to refurbish his monastery and strongly prohibited them from touching meat inside the monastery. According to his monastic rules, only three times a year, on the days dedicated to the monastery's patrons—Michael the Archangel, St. George, and St. Plato—were the guests of the monks to be regaled on meat. This prohibition, stresses the hagiographer, resulted not from miserliness but from the desire to preserve the holiness of the place. The foreman of the carpenters, however, did not want to obey the regulation and kept secretly "devouring" meat. In several other cases, the hagiographer of Theodore conveys that meat was a common food, even though he characterizes it negatively from his pious vantage point. Thus a man entered the church of St. George with a piece of pork, or the entire village of Apokome slaughtered an ox and ate it during a festival, but people were poisoned by the meat.

Hunting and fishing were regular activities of Byzantine life, but there was a substantial difference between the two. Hunting was the favorite entertainment of the Byzantine emperors (three of them died of injuries received while hunting) and nobles, whereas the peasants were primarily busy chasing beasts away from their houses and herds. On the other hand, fishing was actively pursued in both cities and rural areas, particularly in villages situated on the seacoast or near a river, marsh, or lake. Thus, according to the survey of 1317, the village of Toxompous, located on Lake Tachinos (in Macedonia), possessed 3,000 modioi of cultivated land and 80 modioi of vineyards. Besides this, the peasants there had special places for throwing fishing nets and had boats, an embankment, and sixty small fishing ponds; of their rent of 660 hyperpyra, 300 (or almost half) were levied for all kinds of fishing activities. It would seem that fishing was as important to these peasants as agriculture and that they were involved in commercial fishing.

Poultry is relatively rarely mentioned in the sources. Among others, the martyr Triphon is said to have fed geese in his boyhood. Both the *Geoponika* and the vernacular poem *Poulologos* (the *Book of the Fowl*) give lists of domestic fowls that include pigeons, hens, geese, pheasants, and peacocks; the two latter birds served primarily to adorn the parks and the tables of nobles. Chicken was popular in Byzantium: the hen in the *Poulologos* boasts that her chicks have been eaten by bishops, priests, ambassadors, emperors, senators, and so on; and the twelfth-century writer Eustathios, archbishop of Thessalonike, was fascinated by the chicken he was served after a tiring trip—thick white meat marinated in wine and stuffed with dumplings. Chickens formed part of the so-called *kaniskia* (small baskets), the gifts that the *paroikoi* were obliged to bring to their lords. Hen's eggs were common even in the houses of the poor, and Emperor John III Vatatzes (1222–54) encouraged the development of the poultry industry in western Asia Minor, so that he was able to present his wife with a beautiful crown acquired with money from the sale of eggs.

Apiculture, or beekeeping, was well developed in ancient Greece and continued in Byzantium. Beehives are mentioned in various texts, both hagiographical and documentary. St. Philaretos had beehives in Paphlagonia in the late eighth century, and surveys of monastic properties in the village of Gomatou in the fourteenth century list several peasants who owned *melissia,* beehives. Usually these were well-off peasants who owned a substantial amount of livestock as well as one or two beehives. But one peasant, Nicholas from Tenedos (unless Tenedaios was already his last name), seems to have been a beekeeper par excellence: in addition to fifteen beehives, he possessed only an ox and a small vineyard and paid a modest rent of 1 nomisma. It is difficult to estimate the place of apiculture in the Byzantine rural economy, but it obviously was highly developed by medieval standards at any rate. A Jewish writer of the twelfth century, Samuel ben Meir, affirmed that beekeeping in the "Greek kingdom" stood on a higher level than in his own land, northern France. Nevertheless, the Byzantines, at least Byzantine monks, also collected wild honey, as described, for instance, in the Life of St. Lazaros of Mount Galesios.

Honey was one of the major carbohydrate sources in the Byzantine diet. But the development of beekeeping in Byzantium was stimulated by another social need as well: from the seventh century on, the Byzantines began to replace ancient olive oil lamps with candles, and the workshops of *keroullarioi*, candlemakers, demanded a considerable amount of wax.

Rural Craftsmen

Although peasants produced a substantial part of their implements at home, craftsmen appear in rural areas, especially in larger villages. The three most common craft professions in the fourteenth-century fiscal inventories from Macedonia are the crafts of smith (*chalkeus*), tailor (*rhaptēs*), and cobbler (*tzangarios*). Less frequently we hear of ceramic workshops, as well as craftsmen making barrels or building boats; they all probably served the local population.

It remains unclear to what extent the Byzantine countryside was involved in trade. Certainly the peasants sold their products and paid their taxes and rents mostly in cash. Fishermen brought their catch to Constantinople and usually sold it right on the shore to fishmongers. Cattle, flocks, and pigs were driven to city markets, probably by the peasants themselves, who also participated in local fairs. But all these data do not allow us to specify the relative share of the market economy in the Byzantine household.

ECONOMIC DEVELOPMENT OVER TIME

The general pattern of the economic development of the countryside also remains problematic. The traditional view of the serious decline of late Roman agriculture was challenged by Paul Vinogradov at the end of the nineteenth century, but at that time no one paid any attention to his relatively general observations. We are more considerate now, and we are beginning to clear region after region from the stain of perpetual economic crisis in the last centuries of the Roman Empire. It seems, for instance, that in fourth-century Italy, at least in some of its provinces, grain production began to prosper, and G. Tchalenko postulated an economic upsurge in northern Syria in the fourth through sixth century. Subsequent investigations modify Tchalenko's views, but they affect his explanations more than his observations: there is no need now to connect this economic upsurge with the development of a monoculture in northern Syria (production of olive oil), but the fact that agriculture flourished at this time and that smaller households replaced larger estates has not been refuted by recent scholarship.

Was this process local or ubiquitous? The recent study by T. Lewit demonstrates that it is wrong to postulate the general economic downfall and demographic catastrophe of even the western provinces of the later Roman Empire, let alone the eastern half. But if the late Roman countryside was flourishing, how was this connected with the decline of urban life? And which concrete features did this agricultural development have? Our conclusions must be more hypothetical than not. We can tentatively surmise that grain was losing its predominance in the late Roman and Byzantine diet and that fruits and vegetables, dairy products and eggs, as well as meat were acquiring a larger role. So far as grain itself is concerned, hard wheat was replacing soft wheat, and new varieties of grain, such as rye, were introduced. The development of agricultural technique was slow but perceptible: the water mill was widely used, the new system of harnessing was introduced. It is plausible to hypothesize that raising livestock assumed a larger role; the evidence from the Farmer's Law finds independent confirmation in the development of the leather industry as well as in the size of herds and flocks in the later centuries of Byzantium.

But, all in all, the last centuries of Byzantium were far from prosperous. If Byzantine agriculture progressed in the thirteenth to fifteenth centuries, it was the agriculture of the great estates. On their domains, the great landowners produced grain, eggs, meat, and hides for markets in Italy or Dubrovnik (Ragusa). The scanty data concerning peasants' allotments are more depressing: some villages were deserted, the amount of livestock in Macedonian villages decreased, the rural population lessened. Certainly we can blame for all this the political situation and primarily the Turkish invasion. But there is an earlier parallel that should be taken into consideration: the Avaro-Slavic, Persian, and Arab conquests of the seventh century destroyed primarily urban life and somehow liberated the inner forces of the countryside. In Byzantium's last centuries, neither Turks nor western warriors and merchants struck a mortal blow against Byzantine cities; very few of them stopped existing. But the countryside evidently could not sustain the assault. Or at least this is what the documents from fourteenth-century Macedonia imply.

DWELLINGS AND UTENSILS

What little is known about Byzantine dwellings concerns primarily noble mansions and urban houses; the rural house is poorly documented in the preserved texts and is excavated in only a few areas. Local tradition determined the materials of which the structure was made: stone, brick, wood, or plastered reeds. Usually a house consisted of two or three rooms; one contained an open hearth and served as kitchen and family bedchamber, another was used for storing goods—grain and wine—poured into large *pithoi*. Sometimes the house had two storeys; the upper storey formed the living quarters, while the lower one could contain both *pithoi* and implements, as well as a mill powered by an animal. Peasants' houses had earthen floors and thatched roofs; rarely were they covered with ceramic tiles.

Peasant houses were simple to build, as the *typikon* for the Kosmosoteira monastery seems to indicate. The author of the *typikon*, Isaac Komnenos, the third son of Emperor Alexios I, made an inventory of various properties donated to the monastery, including those in Neokastron. He was thinking, he says, of moving Neokastron closer to the monastery, but was concerned about the distance between the location of the *chōrion* and the fields of the *paroikoi*. The physical transfer of the houses did not appear to Isaac to be a problem.

The plan of the house could be rectangular or irregular, especially if a smaller lean-to ("having three walls") was erected against a wall of the main building. The houses were poorly furnished; wills and monastic inventories that survive from the eleventh through the fifteenth century list icons, books, and vessels, but are strangely silent about beds, tables, and benches evidently made of wood. Ascetics in monastic cells had nothing but a bed and a table—even icons and lamps might be prohibited. Beds were used not only as a place for sleeping but for sitting and even dining. They were normally made of wooden planks with the frame placed on two trestles. The frame was provided with ropes or chains that supported a mattress filled with rushes, straw, or wool. Tables became more widespread in Byzantium than in the Roman Empire, especially by the tenth century when the Roman habit of reclining around a table for meals gave way to the medieval habit of sitting at the table. There are descriptions of precious tables—and a few have survived, such as a long table with an inlaid marble top from the refectory of the Nea Mone (New Monastery) on Chios—but all these data concern the furniture of the rich, not the peasants. It is also questionable whether writing desks and folding tables known from texts and miniatures formed an item of peasants' furniture.

Household utensils were made of various materials, and the Byzantines established a clear-cut hierarchy of materials in which gold and silver occupy a higher place than bronze, lead, and iron, and ivory was more highly regarded than ordinary bone. Rabbula of Edessa, a fifth-century Syriac church leader, is said to have ordered his clergy to get rid of silver dishes and replace them with ceramic ones, and, in the fourteenth century, Nikephoros Gregoras lamented that the poverty of the imperial court forced the gold and silver vessels to be replaced with ones made of tin and clay. The expensive materials usually did not enter into the peasant's everyday life: the hagiographer of St. Philaretos describes how the saint had been impoverished, lost his lands and stock, and retained only a beautiful house and an "ivory" table at which thirty-six people could be seated. Ivory and gold were atypical in the peasant milieu. An act of 1110 that fixed the division of property between three brothers in Thessalonike states that the furnishings in the house were made of "wood, iron, bronze, and other materials." Wood, iron, and bronze household utensils (to which ceramics must be added) were clearly the most common.

Furniture and agricultural implements were made of wood, sometimes supplemented with metalworking blades or ornaments. Wood was also used to make vessels and to carve icons, and baskets were woven of twigs, bark, or fronds. Iron was used for weapons and tools, to strengthen doors and gates, and to make anchors and chains as well as smaller objects (locks and keys, nails, candlesticks). Bronze was considered a semiprecious metal and was widely used for coins, icons, bells, surgical instruments, lighting devices, and so on; domestic bronzes included ewers, basins, pans, and various cooking vessels such as cauldrons. But it is again unclear to what extent bronze utensils penetrated the peasant household. Of all these materials, ceramics are the best preserved, but we are unable to draw a clear line between urban and rural ware. Potters worked in the countryside producing bricks, tiles, pipes, and vessels, but it is easier to distinguish the kitchenware (pots, jars, and so on) and tableware than to tell the city vessels from those used by villagers. Utilitarian wares were crudely manufactured, and some part of them was produced in peasant households, often by hand. Vessels for use in transport and storage and tableware (usually glazed and ornamented) were formed on potter's wheels and fired in kilns. In accordance with their functions, several major types of ceramic vessels can be distinguished: *pithoi,* usually embedded into the floor, served for storage, and amphoras for transport—both were gradually being replaced by wooden barrels; utilitarian flat-bottomed pots with globular bodies and long-necked jars, as a rule with one or two handles; chafing dishes to hold hot food—deep bowls set on a ventilated stand with a compartment containing live coals; table dishes—bowls and broad, shallow plates; small, usually two-handled cups; stemmed goblets and flasks. Some vessels were made of glass, but it is questionable whether glass flasks found their way into peasant households.

PEASANT DRESS

The history of Byzantine costume is yet to be written. We are relatively well-informed about court attire and liturgical garments. Peasant dress, however, is infrequently depicted in literary texts (even though many authors stressed that peasant dress had particular features), and we never can be sure that medieval miniatures and frescoes dressed their heroes in contemporary clothes and not obsolete costumes. One serious problem created by this discrepancy between literary and graphic sources is the use of trousers. Byzantine artists infrequently depicted trousers, whereas the words designating this item of dress were common in Byzantine texts. The Edict on Prices promulgated by Emperor Diocletian (286–305) mentions *bracarii,* those who made breeches. Trousers were a distinctive element of male dress: when Theodore of Sykeon, the saint of the early seventh century, exorcised a band of evil spirits, he did not allow them to depart nude; he ordered the men to cover themselves with *brakion,* trousers, and the women with *ependytēs,* a kind of tunic. The twelfth-century historian Niketas Choniates relates that the soldiers in his day used the expression "to wear trousers" as synonymous with manliness. But we do not know whether the trousers were an aristocratic, fanciful fashion (Eustathios of Thessalonike, Choniates' contemporary, was still critical of it) and whether the peasants also wore them.

When Byzantine authors speak of peasant costume, they rarely stress its specific features, except for its low quality. Thus the hagiographer of Patriarch Nikephoros I (806–815) praised his hero for his modesty and said that he wore a ragged and tattered dress (probably a cloak, *himation*) that the writer characterized as rustic (*agroikikon*) and rough. There are, however, some doubts that the villagers were always shabbily clad. We hear, for instance, that the mother of St. Theodore of Sykeon, a country prostitute, was able to provide her six-year-old son with a golden belt and an expensive garment, and when the boy later decided to quit the world, he doffed the golden belt, a necklace, and a bracelet.

We can obtain some idea of the clothing worn by the rank and file, strangely enough, from the description of the portrait of Emperor Andronikos I Komnenos (1183–85). Niketas Choniates narrates that Andronikos claimed to be a populist ruler and ordered his portrait to be set up in Constantinople outside the church of the Forty Martyrs. He was depicted there, says Choniates, not in imperial garb but in the costume of a toiling "laborer" (*ergatikos*): a short blue shirt that reached to his buttocks and was slit, evidently so as not to hamper movement, and thus differed from the long court cloaks ornamented with gold and purple. As footgear, Andronikos the laborer had knee-high white boots (high leather boots became fashionable in Byzantium) in preference to the ancient sandals. Choniates does not reveal what Andronikos wore between the small of his back and the knees—obviously this part of his body was covered—and trousers seem to have been used for this purpose.

THE VILLAGE COMMUNITY

Byzantine country dwellers considered themselves members of the village community, *koinon* or *koinotēs* of the *chōrion,* as it is called in Greek sources. Many prejudices are connected with the study of the Byzantine village community, as both acknowledgment of its existence and its denial are tinged with modern political conceptions. There was a theory that the Slavs brought to Byzantium their communal institutions and thus strongly contributed to the resurrection of the military and financial well-being of the empire by the eighth century. The Farmer's Law has been proclaimed a summary of Slavic customs and an embodiment of communal life. Another theory completely rejected the existence of communal order in the Byzantine countryside, while other theories connected the Byzantine village community with late Roman and even ancient Oriental institutions. Whatever its origin, the Byzantine village community had its specific and contradictory features.

On the one hand, it was permeated by individualistic attitudes that at least partially accounted for its economic forms: intensive agriculture (orchards, vineyards, olive trees, and so on), the stable borders of cultivated fields, the large role of handwork (with mattocks and similar implements), the use of the light plow and small yoke; all this made the Byzantine family practically independent of its neighbors. Common land existed primarily on the outskirts of the village and consisted of terrain that was not yet divided up and to which future generations would transfer their houses to build up new *agridia*.

On the other hand, the rights of the villagers, and especially relatives and neighbors, to privately owned land were highly developed: when buying new properties, the owners had to guarantee their neighbors the right to collect wood, gather chestnuts, and catch fish on their land and shores; a villager could enter another's vineyard and eat grapes there; at the sale of an allotment, the relatives and villagers had the right of *protimēsis* or preemption, that is, the peasant was obliged to offer his land to several groups of preferential buyers before being allowed to sell it outside his community. Various types of co-ownership evolved: siblings held their households together; a peasant could possess a tree or a building on land that was the property of another (the Roman principle that all superstructures—*superficies* in legal nomenclature—belonged to the land was abrogated); when a village possessed a common pasture, all the peasants who drove their livestock there were obliged to pay for its use to the village *per caput,* and then the collected sum was divided between all the members of the *koinotēs,* including those who had no animals at all.

Thus the Byzantine village, even though individualistic physically and in its agricultural work and frequently dispersed, with houses or hamlets far from the *kathedra,* formed an administrative and fiscal unity. It had its elders and probably other officials, and acted collectively in case of emergency; the village came together for work that required collective efforts and collectively hired carpenters and stonemasons; as an entity, the village also acted in judicial cases and defended its property rights against outsiders. The village had its feasts and litanies. The most substantial common need was collective fiscal responsibility: taxes were imposed on the *chōrion* as a whole; as a whole, the community admitted traveling imperial functionaries and ambassadors or billetted soldiers; the peasant was responsible for the arrears of his neighbor, especially if the neighbor fled, and his allotment could be forcibly assigned to the more dutiful tillers.

Woven together though they were, the *geōrgoi* were far from constituting a brotherhood of equals living in harmony and peace. There was no material equality within the village; some peasants were richer than others. The fiscal surveys distinguish between various categories from the *dizeugaratoi,* owners of two yokes of oxen, down to the needy *aktēmōnes* and *kapnikarioi.* There were peasants who earned their living from a single pear tree, their only property; peasants who had land but no animals to till it, so they had to rent it out; peasants who worked as hirelings (*misthioi*), for example, as herdsmen. Even though the church called for assistance to the poor, the Byzantine system of taxation was not beneficial to the needy: as a rule, the wealthier a landowner was, the lower was the rate of his payments, and the poor peasant bore a proportionally heavier fiscal burden than his richer neighbor. Those who were successful wanted to acquire more. In an edict of Emperor Basil II, we find a story of a former peasant Philokales who became influential and subjugated all and sundry in his village. Another sad story is told by the hagiographer of St. Lazaros of Mount Galesios: how a village forced some orphans out of their house, since the children were too feeble to resist, and seized all their belongings.

The population of the Byzantine village was also socially unequal. Beneath the mass of peasants were the slaves, and above the rank and file were the lords. The number of rural slaves seems to have been insignificant in the eighth century, and the Farmer's Law mentions slaves only as shepherds. Their number increased by the tenth century because of the military successes of Byzantine emperors who conquered new lands in Syria and the Balkans. Both small *proasteia* and large estates used slaves. As in antiquity, they could be sold, and their cohabitation had no matrimonial status, at least to the end of the eleventh century. To what extent the legal theory of slavery affected real life is another problem, as it is questionable whether this theory referred to peasant households in which slaves and *misthioi* functioned more as minor members of the family than as representatives of a different social stratum.

AUTHORITY

The lords of villages in Byzantine terminology were "the powerful" (*dynatoi*). The meaning of the term is not quite clear. It encompassed two major categories: secular and ecclesiastical administration on the one hand and landowners on the other. Theodosios, *protiktōr* in Anastasiopolis, appears in the Life of Theodore of Sykeon as a powerful man able to inflict harm and injustice on the *geōrgoi* living in the vicinity of the *polis*. They took their case to the local bishop, Theodore of Sykeon, who evidently also possessed some rights with respect to the peasants. Theodore summoned Theodosios and rebuked him for his acts of injustice toward the peasants, but the man did not change. Then the inhabitants of the *chōrion* Eukratous rioted, took to arms (swords and *petroboloi*, probably slings), and chased Theodosios away. Theodore again censured the *protiktōr* and asked him to stay away from the administration (*epitropē*) of villages, but the man accused Theodore of egging on the mutiny and demanded from him 2 lbs. of gold that Theodosios had been unable to collect in the rebellious village. The clash between the two authorities was solved by supernatural power: a fearful youth in a bright garment (probably St. George) appeared to Theodosios and made him repent.

The correlation between the two categories of Byzantine lords depended on the place and time. In the western Roman Empire, the noble landowner acquired more political influence than his eastern counterpart; in the East it was the functionary who wielded power and could own large stretches of land, but their families rarely stayed in power for several generations. The Farmer's Law does not mention "lords" at all; in this text, kyrios ("having authority") is the term applied to the peasant. The narrative texts contemporary with the Farmer's Law preserve few, if any, images of large landowners. By the tenth century, large estates emerge again, but at this time landownership and administrative power were integrated: the dynatos or archōn had administrative authority and therefore was able to acquire land. By the twelfth century, landowners constituted a particular social group. The rich in land and the nobles (relatives of the imperial house) bore the highest titles and held the most important (military) positions. Thus, during the last centuries of the empire, power became the attribute rather than the basis of landownership. Nevertheless, it was not always clear who was the lord of the village—its hereditary owner or an administrative and fiscal official (governor, tax collector, judge) wielding power for a limited time.

Hardships

The medieval peasantry faced manifold hardships of a physical, political, and social nature. Physical catastrophes included phenomena such as earthquakes, droughts, and flooding, freezing winters, and strong winds, which destroyed dwellings and harvests and in the final analysis caused starvation. Saints were effective protectors against the elements, and some miracles worked by them have a specifically rural character: locusts were often chased off and the harvest saved; even more interesting is the miracle of the "restricted rain," when the threshing floor remained dry while the area all around it suffered from the downpour. Saints' Lives also teem with miracles against starvation. Many times a monastic community appears to be on the brink of hunger, having consumed its last provisions, when, lo and behold, the vessels and crates turn out to be full again or a rich benefactor arrives with a train of heavily loaded donkeys.

Another physical disaster was sickness. Illness, both individual and epidemic, is probably the most pervasive topic of hagiographic literature, and the numberless patients belong to all walks of life. Some of them were peasants, but they are neither the exclusive nor even predominant category of ailing people. It is questionable whether hagiography furnishes us with dependable data for the "sociology of illness," in other words, for the study of which social layers suffered from which diseases. Neither the fear (or lack of it) of death was a distinctive trait of peasants;

Byzantine saints met death calmly as if they were entering a corridor leading to paradise, but this was an ideal rather than real behavior. Death—in war, in a shipwreck, from a disease, or at the hands of a robber—was a fact of life, and we can surmise (albeit we have no certain data) that the city was more dangerous than the countryside and that the poor and humble was less apprehensive about dying than the noble who had more to lose and usually more opportunity to commit sins. Unlike humble saints, Digenis Akritas, the chivalric hero of Byzantine epic, lamented his demise in a good, ancient manner; for him, death was separation from wealth and pleasure rather than unification with God.

Political catastrophe included hostile conquest, rebellion, or an assault by pirates. Like disease and death, it struck both the city and the countryside, and probably the peasants were more mobile and suffered less than urban residents. Mountains and hilly woods gave them a temporary refuge, livestock could be adapted to seminomadic habits of transhumance, and simple houses could be easily restored or built anew. Villages attracted the attention of conquerors less—there was little there to loot, except food and forage. At any rate, they survived the great invasions of the seventh century.

Social havoc, however, caused more devastation in the countryside than in the city. Peasants could be victimized by their lords, both secular and ecclesiastical; they suffered from the feuds between two lords who would attack the villages of their adversaries. But if we examine the complaints of Byzantine authors, they are focused primarily on two characters: the tax collector and the moneylender.

It is quite natural that Byzantine society and the Byzantine peasantry in particular saw the tax collector as the most noxious representative of the state bureaucracy: tax collectors of various types compiled fiscal surveys, levied payments, and sold fields of insolvent taxpayers. "Tax collectors with iron fangs," they were called by a writer of the late twelfth century. Nicholas Mouzalon, patriarch of Constantinople (1147–51), wrote a poem describing his stay on Cyprus and the plight of Cypriot peasants. Among other predicaments, there were tax collectors there, who rushed into villages, seized the peasants unable to pay their arrears, and bound them to trees together with hungry dogs. Flogging was a regular means of exacting money. Ammianus Marcellinus, who lived much earlier, relates that the Egyptian peasants of the fourth century were proud of the scars they had from refusing to pay taxes.

The moneylender went arm-in-arm with the tax collector. Most of taxes were exacted in cash, even though the peasants were also required to receive and feed soldiers and functionaries, build bridges and fortifications, send food and forage to the troops, and so on. Moreover, some revenues were collected only in gold coins. It is hard to imagine that peasants would have enough gold coins to satisfy the revenue service, and in cases of emergency (poor harvest, death of an ox), they had no money at all for taxes. The Byzantine moneylender provided money in both the city and the countryside; in the city, the noble borrowed money to squander it, the merchant to develop his trade, the official to fulfill the imperial assignment, and others to celebrate weddings. The peasant borrowed money first and foremost to pay taxes.

To borrow money, the peasant usually had to use his land as collateral. For the privilege of borrowing, he paid interest. The Greek word for interest was *tokos,* literally "child." Eustathios of Thessalonike, a writer who was very sensitive toward social inequality, was outraged by this inhumane etymology, and many other authors inveighed against moneylenders. Basil I even attempted to prohibit taking interest, but his measure was cancelled by his son Leo VI. In the tenth century, Romanos I ordered that all debts in Constantinople be paid off and all loan contracts be burned; both the rich and the poor, says the chronicler, benefited from this imperial rescript. But this was in Constantinople, where the mob could exert pressure upon lawmakers; the countryside was hardly so fortunate. Here a debt was often the first step toward a land sale, and neither the legal requirement of a just price nor the custom of *protimēsis* could stop the growing impoverishment of peasants. "What shall I do?" asks a peasant in the Life of St. Philatetos the Merciful who lost an ox. "How will I pay my taxes and my debts? I have no other way but to flee." Fortunately the man met Philaretos, who was so generous that he gave the peasant his own ox, but in real life a saint was not always at hand to assist the needy. The land changed hands.

We know only one segment of this process since it is mainly the monastic archives that have survived. They are lopsided in that they show primarily the growth of monastic estates. Unquestionably, secular landowners grasped their share of peasant lands and sometimes the lands of monasteries and convents.

Some peasants deprived of their land remained in their villages and rented land from its new owners, paying them taxes in cash and in kind. They also fulfilled corvées called *angareiai,* an old Persian word that used to denote a special type of state obligation (supplying horses and donkeys for the post service), but the term was transferred into the sphere of private services. Byzantine corvées were not too burdensome, rarely surpassing one day a week. Dependent peasants or "settlers" (*paroikoi* or *proskathēmenoi* in Byzantine terminology) were at the beginning allowed to leave their lords and move to new places, but in the thirteenth century they lost this right. Their duty with regard to the state was replaced by the duty to the landowner.

In fact, however, a substantial number of peasants were always on the move; some fled tax collectors, some cruel lords, and some the Turkish invaders. Available figures are scanty, but the general impression is that in the fourteenth century many villages were deserted or depopulated. Where did fleeing peasants go? Sometimes, in search of better conditions, they settled on the lands of new landowners and gained certain privileges. If caught, they could be flogged and returned in chains to their previous locale. In other cases, officials turned a blind eye and let them stay. Initially the fugitives were not taxed, even though they paid rents to their new lords; accordingly they were often named "free (from taxes)" (*eleutheroi*) or "the unknown to the treasury." Others escaped to cities, becoming journeymen, servants, or beggars.

Monasteries were supposed to provide runaways with a place of refuge. A man who took the monastic habit accepted a new name and a new social status in the relative protection of monastic confinement. Thus sons tired of the parental yoke, fugitive slaves, and ruined peasants streamed into monasteries. Some monastic communities liberally accommodated the fugitives, as full-fledged brethren or as dependent laborers. In others, *hēgoumenoi* were wary and refused to accept criminals and slaves. St. Nikon—who later was called Metanoeite (because he called for a general atonement, *metanoia*)—fled his family and hid in a monastery but was later urged to leave his place of refuge because his influential father was looking for him. He ran away with his family hot on his heels, and only a miracle allowed him to escape: the Virgin herself carried him over a wide river and out of his father's reach.

SPIRITUAL LIFE

What do we know about the spiritual life of the Byzantine peasantry? A. Gurevich has dubbed the worldview of the medieval peasant "the culture of the silent majority." Neither the western medieval nor Byzantine peasant left substantial traces of his intellectual creativity. Infrequently an object of literary presentation, he appears even less frequently as a creator. We might have expected that the so-called vernacular poetry that proliferated from the twelfth century on reflected the peasant's ideals, but the fact of the matter is that it originated in the milieu of urban intellectuals, hungry and scornful, who crowded at the gates of the imperial court. Vernacular poetry was more the child of aristocratic fancy than the outcry of peasants. We know very little about the peasant's worldview.

It goes without saying that the Byzantine countryside was Christian in its belief and rituals. Rural paganism was still alive here and there in the sixth century, but it was later eradicated leaving behind merely a few vestigial traces: ancient gods transformed into demons (and sometimes into saints?), festivals, fortunetelling. Canonists of the twelfth century censured these beliefs and by so doing allow us a brief acquaintance with them. One of these canonists, Balsamon, condemned the "demonic habit" prohibited by Patriarch Michael III (1170–76). He described it in some detail: on the evening of 23 June, men and women would gather on beaches or in certain houses and would dress the firstborn girl as a bride. After having eaten and danced in a Bacchic frenzy, moving in circles and shouting, they would pour seawater into a brass vessel with a narrow mouth. Each would cast some object into the vessel and then question the girl about good things and ill-omened ones. She would take one of the objects from the vessel at random and make a prediction while the owner held the object and listened to his fortune. In the morning they would go to the seashore, dancing in chorus and accompanied by the girl. After scooping up seawater, they would pour it on their dwellings. During the whole night they would burn haystacks, jump over them, and prophesy good or bad luck. They decorated the house in which they did the fortunetelling with gilded robes and silk fabrics, and they would make wreaths of leaves. Balsamon also criticized the popular January festival in which lay participants masqueraded as monks and clerics and the clergy disguised themselves as warriors and animals. He stressed the sexual undertones of such festivities when he complained that even saints' days became so lewd that pious women fled them in fear of being assaulted by the lecherous participants.

But these festivals were mere deviations from the established rituals, and their participants, whether peasants or Constantinopolitans, considered themselves orthodox Christians, attended the liturgy, and partook of the Eucharist in their churches. There were many churches in rural areas: we learn from the Life of St. Theodore of Sykeon about several small churches erected near the village of his origin—the *martyrion* of St. George, the chapel (*euktērion*) of John the Baptist, and that of St. Christopher; Theodore built there a beautiful shrine of St. Michael the Archangel with two adjacent chapels of John the Baptist and the Virgin. Some small churches and monasteries were erected by peasants, as Emperor Basil II noted in a rescript of 996: "In many villages," says the emperor, "it happens that a peasant constructs a church on his land, and then, with the consensus of other villagers, ascribes his allotment to this church and lives at this church as a monk; then another and yet another join him, and here there are two or three monks." In the eleventh century, Michael Psellos, an intellectual and civil official, mentioned a similar case: a poor nun (probably a peasant woman) and some other, unspecified people joined together to build a monastery but unexpectedly one of the partners backed out and refused to give his share. Psellos attempted to persuade or even compel the man to fulfill his vow. Hagiographers tell stories about saints who would settle on virgin soil and begin building a monastery, and then pious dwellers of neighboring villages would assist them, some with money, others with materials and food, and many cooperating in the construction work.

As a rule, none of these small chapels survives, with the exception of small churches cut in the rocks of volcanic tufa in Cappadocia. The area teems with these chapels, some able to accommodate a congregation of a dozen. Lyn Rodley calculates that a smaller church could be hewn out by a single mason with the help of an assistant and one or two laborers and could be finished within several weeks. Then the rock was covered with plaster and decorated. The Cappadocian cave churches present various riddles: only few of them can be dated by inscriptions and so their chronology remains problematic, although the church construction in the area seems to last from the seventh to the thirteenth century. Who constructed these buildings and for whom? Some patrons were noble; in one of the chapels there is an inscription mentioning Emperor Nikephoros II Phokas (963–969) and his wife Theophano, and another inscription bears the name of *prōtospatharios* Michael Skepides. Was there a monastic community here that could expect imperial and aristocratic grants? Did the local population, experienced in cave architecture, participate in both construction and service? We have no clear answers to these questions. Some of the chapels seem to have been abandoned soon after their completion; their paintings are clean, with no trace of soot from candles and lamps, and one can hardly imagine such a practice in a stable monastic community.

Thus we cannot identify the Cappadocian cave churches as peasant chapels, but it is plausible to hypothesize that their size and simple structure are reminiscent of country churches, taking of course into consideration the particularity of the material and building technique.

If not paganism, then perhaps heresies constituted a typical feature of peasant ideology? The most popular heresy on Byzantine territory was the dualist conception usually called by Byzantine authors Manichaeism, although it also appears under other names, including the Slavic-based Bogomilism. The term "Manichaeism" originated from the name of the third-century Persian preacher Manes or Mani, whether or not medieval heresies were genetically connected with Persian and late Roman Manichaeism. Medieval Bogomils taught that the visible world, including the human body, was created by the Evil principle that dared to rival God, the creator of the human soul. Therefore, both the cosmos and the human being are the battlefield of Good and Evil, and the best way to overcome the Evil principle is to abstain from the material elements of life, especially marriage and excessive food (meat and wine). The Bogomils were critical of the church, with its sacraments and cult, but they created their own hierarchy of the perfect and the rank and file, whose behavior they treated more permissively.

Bogomilism evidently spread among peasants. Anna Komnene, the daughter and encomiast of Emperor Alexios I, describes her father's reconciliation with the "Manichaeans": he gathered those of them "who worked with shovels and dealt with plows and oxen" and constructed for them a town called Alexioupolis or Neokastron, near Philippopolis (modern Plovdiv); he granted them fields, vineyards, houses, and other properties. Though these heretics were peasants, others were not, and we have no data from which to determine what percentage of the "Manichaeans" came from rural areas. Even more difficult than social characterization of the "Manichaeans" is the social interpretation of their dualist beliefs: is the opposition between Good and Evil a specifically peasant feature? Is the opposition of the perfect who has suppressed matter and cleansed his soul of material stains and the rank and file who tills the soil and lives with his wife typical of the countryside? The questions are easier to ask than to answer.

The peasants were viewed with disdain by arrogant Byzantine intellectuals. The *agroikos* was conceived of as poorly clad, dirty, and illiterate. Emperor Leo VI enacted that, in the city, wills required five witnesses, whereas in the countryside three witnesses would suffice. He is even more explicit in another edict, no. 43, which states that the witness in the city must be literate because there is "no shortage of literacy there," whereas in other places, that is, in the countryside, where "education and knowledge are not customary," literacy was not mandatory for a witness. From a very early age, country boys were involved in husbandry. Thus St. Ioannikios, born in the village of Marykatos in Bithynia in 754, at the age of seven was minding pigs; later he was drafted into the army, and obviously had no time for a regular education. Country elementary schools are rarely mentioned in hagiographic literature. When children were educated, their teachers infrequently were professionals; they are said rather to have been tutored by relatives, a local priest, or a local notary.

Nicolas Oikonomides studied the signatures on documents from the archives of Mount Athos and came to the conclusion that they indicate a relatively high level of literacy, even though some of them have crosses instead of signatures or badly mistaken signatures. But again we meet the sociological question: how many of these signatories were of country origin? Probably this question cannot be answered.

We know almost nothing about intellectual production in the Byzantine countryside. Balsamon relates that Patriarch Nicholas Mouzalon prescribed that the Life of St. Paraskeve be burned; it was written, says Balsamon, in the village of Kallikrateia by a peasant in a boorish manner and was unworthy of the angelic behavior of the saint. Thus at least we know that some peasants tried their skill in traditional genres of Byzantine literature and came into conflict with the official church. The Life of St. Paraskeve turned out to be "boorish," but we do not know the nature of the boorishness that irritated the patriarch and his milieu.

Very tentatively, however, we can discover slight traces of peasant legends in the available hagiographical texts, especially in the Miracles of St. George. St. George is one of those saints whose origin is enigmatic and whose activity is legendary. The legend of George the Great Martyr is known from the fifth century on, but his Miracles are of a later date. The collection of Miracles was formed gradually, and at least one of them, reflecting the monetary reform of Alexios I, cannot be earlier than circa 1100; of late origin seems to have been the most famous miracle of St. George, the slaughter of the dragon.

The geographical milieu of the Miracles seems to be the country bordering with the Saracens or Hagarenes, most probably Cappadocia; in some other texts, for instance, in the Life of Theodore of Sykeon, St. George is named the Cappadocian. The development of some Miracles is placed in the countryside, and it is worth noting that the saint's name itself, Georgios, is closely connected with the Greek word for peasant, geōrgos. It is quite plausible to surmise that it was especially popular in rural areas.

The rustic milieu is usually the setting of St. George's Miracles. Thus we read in one of them about the boys of the village of Phatrynon in Paphlagonia, one of whom promised St. George a cake (sphongaton) if the saint helped him win in children's games. Four merchants, however, gobbled up the sphongaton, steaming and fragrant, but they were punished: St. George confined them inside a church and did not let them out until they paid him a fine of 1 nomisma. Even more rustic in its content is the story of Theopistos, a well-off peasant from Cappadocia who went with his slaves or servants to plow a field, and, while they were asleep, a pair of oxen vanished. Theopistos sent his slave to work with another pair of oxen, and himself spent a week searching for the lost animals. Neighbors—a necessary element in many stories about the country— laughed at him, saying that he cannot be oikodespotēs if he neglected his oxen. But with the help of God and the great martyr George, Theopistos found his yoke of oxen right on a road.

Then the time came to repay St. George for his assistance, and the main part of the story is devoted to the bargaining of the smart peasant Theopistos and the even smarter St. George. Theopistos wanted to get off with nothing more than a kid, but St. George appeared to him in a dream and said: "Slaughter an ox, and I will come." The thrifty peasant decided that an ox was too much and that he could do perfectly well with a sheep and a ram. St. George became irritated, raised the stakes, and announced that he was a *komēs* ("count") and had a large retinue; he demanded that a pair of oxen be slaughtered. Theopistos grieved: he was afraid of his vision, but he did not want to become poor (*penēs*), although his pious wife (even her name, Eusebeia, was pious), remained optimistic, expecting that when all was said and done, the saint would make them rich. Theopistos was indecisive, and the next night he saw St. George again, this time sitting on a white steed and holding a cross in his hands. He was full of wrath and threatened to burn Theopistos' house. All this was not funny at all, and in the morning Theopistos gave his servants and relatives the command to cut the throats of all his animals—sheep, swine, and oxen, and prepare wine for breakfast (*ariston*); he also invited the poor of his village and priests who sang hymns from dusk to dawn. With the sunrise, thirty young riders arrived announcing the approach of their *komēs*. Then another group came, and finally the saint with his retinue, and he introduced himself as George the Cappadocian.

When the breakfast, consisting of meat, bread, and wine was over, the saint ordered them to bring him the bones. The guests were astonished and thought he was drunk and did not know what he was doing. But Theopistos, who was already acquainted with St. George, expected some help from the saint. So servants brought the bones and threw them at his feet. St. George prayed, and the earth shook so that everybody fell down, and then a miracle: the animals reappeared, tripled in number. The saint of this story is a good companion for Theopistos: savoring a tasty meal, knowing how to bargain, and edgy when resisted. He may be considered as the rustic saint, the patron of livestock who was able to find stranded animals and make them multiply.

We do not know whether the Lives of country saints (Nicholas of Sion, Theodore of Sykeon, Philaretos the Merciful, Ioannikios the Great) actually describe the rural milieu or only represent the hagiographical canon transferred to a country setting. We also have a secular parallel to the story of a saint peasant: the tenth-century Life of Emperor Basil I, who was born to a peasant family, gained his living as a wrestler, tamed wild horses, and ascended the throne as a pious and just ruler who cared about peasants. The Life of Basil is a programmatic piece of literature that originated in the circle of Constantine VII Porphyrogennetos (913–959), Basil's grandson, who made his ignoble grandfather a descendant of many royal families. But we can assume that, in addition to this political program, some elements of peasant folklore found their way into the Life.

Since we do not know Byzantine peasant culture, it would be very difficult to say what impact it had on the dominant cultural patterns of Byzantium. Was the "natural," circular concept of time, with its seasons, periods, and annually repeated feasts, a product of country life, whereas the idea of linear time originated in theological teleology? Did the respect for the human body that was retained by some orthodox Byzantine writers originate in the simple habits of the countryside or did it stem from classical traditions? We do not know. The Byzantine peasant remains much more enigmatic than the Byzantine *basileus* or the Constantinopolitan intellectual.

SELECTED BIBLIOGRAPHY

Carile, A. "La signoria rurale nell'impero latino di Costantinopoli (1204–61)." *Actes du XVe Congrès international d'études byzantines,* vol. 4, pp. 65–77. Athens, 1980.

Chvostova, X. "K voprosu o strukture pozdnevizantijskogo sel'skogo poselenija." *Vizantijskij Vremennik* 45 (1985): 1–19.

Dölger, F. *Beiträge zur Geschichte der byzantinischen Finanzverwaltung besonders des 10. und 11. Jahrhunderts.* 2d ed. Darmstadt, 1960.

Kaplan, M. "L'économie paysanne dans l'empire byzantin du Ve au Xe siècle." *Klio* 68 (1986): 198–232.

Kazhdan, A. *Derevnja i gorod v Vizantii. IX–X vv.* Moscow, 1977.

Köpstein, H. "Zur Veränderung der Agrarverhältnisse in Bysanz vom 6. zum 10. Jahrhundert." In H. Köpstein, ed., *Besonderheiten der byzantinischen Feudalentwicklung: Eine Sammlung von Beiträgen zu den frühen Jahrhunderten,* pp. 69–76. Berlin, 1983.

Laiou-Thomadakis, A. E. *Peasant Society in the Late Byzantine Empire: A Social and Demographic Study.* Princeton, 1977.

Lefort, J. "Le cadastre de Radolibos (1103), les géomètres et leurs mathématiques." *Travaux et Mémoires* 8 (1981) (= *Hommage à P. Lemerle*), pp. 269–313.

Lemerle, P. *The Agrarian History of Byzantium from the Origins to the Twelfth Century: The Sources and Problems.* Galway, 1979.

Litavrin, G. G. *Vizantijskoe obščestvo i gosudarstvo v X–XI vv.* Moscow, 1977.

Nesbitt, J. W. "The Life of St. Philaretos (702–792) and its Significance for Byzantine Agriculture." *The Greek Orthodox Theleological Review* 14 (1969): 150–58.

Ostrogorsky, G. *Quelques problèmes d'histoire de la paysannerie byzantine.* Brussels, 1956.

———. *Die ländliche Steuergemeinde des byzantinischen Reiches im X. Jahrhundert.* Amsterdam, 1969.

Svoronos, N. G. "Recherches sur le cadastre byzantin et la fiscalité aux XIe et XIIe siècles: Le cadastre de Thèbes." *Bulletin de Correspondance Hellénique* 83 (1959): 1–145; reprinted in idem, *Études sur l'organisation intérieure, la société et l'économie de l'empire byzantin.* Variorum Reprints, London, 1973.

3

SOLDIERS

Peter Schreiner

"I F YOU WISH TO ENJOY the fruits of peace, you must be prepared above all for war: only thus can you enjoy peace. For inaction cannot preserve anything, as the wise men say, no, you must take the initiative. I repeat: you can only enjoy peace if you are armed for war. He who is not ready for war will never enjoy peace." Thus wrote the scholar and rhetorician Thomas Magistros in the first half of the fourteenth century in his *Mirror of Princes,* and he was certainly not saying anything new. He merely dressed in more elegant words what the Roman Vegetius, author of a military handbook, had already said in the fifth century: *qui desiderat pacem, praeparet bellum* ("he who longs for peace, let him prepare for war").

War was always a part of the reality of life in Byzantium, and the soldier a part of the tableau of everyday life. During more than one thousand years of Byzantine history, hardly a year passed that did not see a military campaign. From this perspective, the soldier was perhaps the most important person in the state, though of course this statement holds true not only for the Byzantine Empire.

In Byzantium, as in other states, we encounter the soldier in a host of different forms, from the position he occupied in the hierarchy of the army to the unit in which he served. In some sense, even the general or admiral is only a soldier. Over the centuries the soldier's function, that of defending the state, remained the same, but military equipment, the soldier's role within the units, military titles, and, above all, the fundamental conditions of existence changed. It is difficult to paint a general picture of the "Byzantine" soldier, to draw a clear distinction to the Roman soldier. The attempt to do so is least successful (and methodologically most uncertain) when it comes to organizational aspects, and probably most successful when it comes to the social profile. Here we cannot go into the much-discussed topic of the continuity of antiquity in the Byzantine state, but the fact is that its military institutions, in particular, were connected to Roman antiquity and that Latin expressions, for example, were long common in the soldier's language. Thus it may seem arbitrary, or even unjustified, to begin this discussion with the sixth century, the age of Justinian. As early as the eleventh and twelfth centuries, but especially in later centuries, Byzantium had increasing recourse to mercenaries. And while the mercenary certainly performed the function of a soldier, he can hardly be described as "Byzantine." For that reason it is undoubtedly justified to end our characterization of the soldier largely with the twelfth century.

Following a brief overview of the sources and literature, this chapter focuses primarily on aspects of soldiering that relate to cultural history: the function of the soldier and the military environment; the material and social background; the role of the soldier within the state; the soldier and death; faith and religion; and the splendor and misery of the soldier. These aspects cannot encompass all areas. Questions concerning tactics and warfare have been excluded. Moreover, this discussion is limited entirely to the soldier of the land army. While the role of the fleet was not inconsiderable, especially during the period under consideration, the *specific* problems of the soldier as such were the same in the land army and the fleet. On the whole the reader should not expect a comprehensive treatment. Rather, this chapter is based on more or less incidental gleanings, and emphasis has been repeatedly placed on quotations or a summary of the sources.

SOURCES AND LITERATURE

Characterizing the soldier from the sources is a laborious undertaking. There are, in a sense, very few texts (primarily theological ones) that do *not* in some form or another speak about soldiers in particular and warfare in general. However, concrete information leaves much to be desired, as everything real and material did not fit well with the rhetorical descriptive style of the Byzantines, which they characterized as "speaking well" (*eu legein*). Questions relating to the social background, in particular, often remain in the dark.

The military handbooks, called *taktika* or *stratēgika*, continued a Hellenistic and Roman tradition and were, of course, devoted primarily to the conduct of warfare. But we do find in them statements about the appearance of the soldier, the composition of the force, and sometimes also about customs and habits. However, the special significance of these texts lies in the fact that they are spread over several centuries, thus providing statements from different historical periods: Maurice, probably the emperor of same name, composed a *stratēgikon* at the end of the sixth century, as did Emperor Leo VI at the beginning of the tenth, and a Nikephoros—presumably identical with Emperor Nikephoros II Phokas—in the second half of the tenth. It can be seen as characteristic of the decline of Byzantine military power that no such texts on military technique are attested for later centuries. Of course the *taktika* cannot be seen uncritically as historical sources for the time of their composition. They also contain material from antiquity or earlier centuries with no value concerning the contemporary period, and it is often very difficult to distinguish between material that is useful and material that is obsolete.

Disappointingly little information comes from the historians. Their attention was focused on tactics, campaigns, the course of battle, and at most the role of the general; what we are told about the individual soldier is only incidental. As is the case in other areas of the history of Byzantine civilization, hagiographic texts help us illuminate the social and economic conditions of soldiers. But here, too, the information is very selective, and it is always apparent that the description of material circumstances can never be the central concern of a saint's life. Various admonitory speeches to the emperor or to high-ranking individuals ("Mirror of Princes") represent a source for the warrior ethos that should not be underestimated. Still largely unexamined is the abundant astrological literature, which plays an interesting role in connection with religious faith (or better, superstition).

Archaeology is of very little help: we have virtually no pieces of a soldier's equipment and are forced to rely entirely on pictorial sources (manuscript miniatures, reliefs, small objets d'art). Considering how traditionalistic Byzantine art was, their evidentiary value is limited.

Given all this, it is perhaps not surprising that scholarship has not paid much attention to the soldier. A general survey does not exist. In recent years, specific questions relating to the equipment of the soldier have been brought closer to resolution. What has attracted the most attention are problems relating to soldiers' landed property, but they are still far from being resolved, if a resolution is possible at all.

THE SOLDIER AND HIS PROFESSION

A brief chapter in a handbook of warfare from the late sixth century illustrates the variety of functions the soldier performed within the army. Riding ahead of the army proper were the attacking forces, whose task it was to pursue the fleeing enemy. Protecting troops safeguarded the attacking forces from an assault by the enemy. Behind the line of battle, and possibly following it, were the medics. No campaign could be without technicians: field surveyors who picked the site of the camp and quartermasters who took care of the details of equipment and supplies. Of great importance, and repeatedly emphasized in the texts, was the function of the scouts. The two main branches into which soldiers were divided remained the same from antiquity down into our century: cavalry and infantry; the heavily armed forces in the true sense of the word was the cavalry.

Soldiers who exercised some kind of command also had special titles. At the head of the army stood the commander in chief (*stratēgos*), whose place could be taken by a second in command (*hypostratēgos*). The various divisions (Greek *meros*) were headed by a general (*merarchēs*). A division was composed of three regiments (*moiron*), each of which was headed by a regimental colonel (*moirarchēs*). In other functions within the subdivisions of the regiments (which cannot be discussed in detail here), we find the captain (*komēs*), the lieutenant (*ilarchēs*), and the platoon leader (*hekatontarchēs*), commanders of one hundred men who in turn had under them the leaders of groups of ten and five soldiers. The last in the line of command bears the title tetrarch or guardian (*phylax*). There were also a few other specialized functions outside the ranks, for example, the standard-bearer (*bandophoros*) and the bearer of the officer's mantle, who could also take over the standard-bearer's function.

Selecting soldiers was the responsibility of the commander. To that end he usually carried out yearly call-ups, and he had to pay particular attention that the recruits chosen were neither too young (*paides,* "boys") nor too old (*gerontes,* "old people"). The qualities looked for were physical strength (*ischyros*), good health and a robust constitution (*eurōstos*), bravery and cool courage (*eupsychos*), and dexterity (*euporos*). These criteria come from a tenth-century handbook of warfare and strike us as somewhat rhetorical and theoretical, since they are often psychological qualities that were difficult to measure. The list is rather a characterization of the "ideal soldier."

Great stock was placed in military exercises, which were to take place during the winter or periods without warfare. The handbook of Emperor Leo VI lists forty-eight different kinds, for both single as well as joint exercises. Special emphasis was placed, as early as the sixth century, on archery in combination with horseback riding and spear-throwing. The Iranian and Turkish peoples were always superior to the Byzantines in these skills, and thus it took constant effort on the part of Byzantine soldiers to be any kind of match for them. The handbook of Maurice gives a glimpse of the various aspects of this important skill: soldiers practiced rapid firing with the bow on foot, at a distance, against a lance or some other target, rapid firing with the bow to all sides while in motion on a horse, firing the bow while jumping with the horse, laying down the bow into the quiver while riding the horse, the quick switch from bow to lance, and much more. In reading such texts one is at times reminded of circus acrobats and not of Byzantine soldiers. In addition, there seem to have existed within the army rather theoretical instructions about a particular enemy, about his character traits and way of fighting, to which the soldier was supposed to adjust. Certain schematic images of the enemy were constructed. For example, we are told that the Franks are strong and terrifying in battle, bold and daring, but they are easily bribed because they are greedy for profit.

Despite the almost complete absence of pictorial and archaeological sources, we are relatively well informed about the appearance of the soldier, even if it is not always possible to construct a graphic image of all the details. Infantrymen always valued light clothing: a tunic reaching down to the knees and simple stitched shoes. There were also heavily armed soldiers on foot, who, owing to the weight of weapons and body armor, were allowed to ride on mules when the army was on the march. At times they also had helpers (who probably aided them in donning the armor), though the latter generally had to go on foot. The characteristic image of the Byzantine army, however, included the heavily armed horsemen (Greek *kataphraktēs*). In the sixth century, Prokopios briefly sketched their appearance, which did not change much until the tenth century, when we once again have descriptions: "Today the archers go into battle armored and wearing greaves up to the knee, and on the right side they carry their arrows, on the left the sword. Some also have a spear hanging down, while a short, strapless shield to protect the face and neck rests on the shoulders." A somewhat more detailed description is supplied by the handbook of Maurice: complete armor down to the ankles with a hood, files, and awls (to allow the soldier to repair the armor himself), riding lance with straps, bow, quiver, and sometimes even armored gloves. Remarkable is another comment by the author: small bushes should be attached to the breast straps of the horses and small flags at the shoulders of the armor, "for as much splendor as a soldier has in armament, with that much readiness he attacks, and that much fear he strikes in the enemy." Aesthetics to fend off the enemy!

The handbooks on tactics repeatedly point out the importance of constant exercise with weapons. Of course, such exercises had to be done during the time when there was no fighting, during the winter months. While the handling of new weapons and weapon systems demands of today's soldier constant practice and constant rethinking, that problem existed to a much lesser degree in antiquity and the Middle Ages, and in Byzantium hardly at all. Instead, there was another difficulty: adjusting to constantly new and different enemies.

Against the Turkish peoples, who, beginning with the Huns and stretching all the way to the Ottomans in the fifteenth century, assaulted the Byzantine Empire incessantly, practicing archery from horseback was particularly important. It is hard to imagine that Byzantine soldiers ever acquired the skill of the nomadic horsemen. In general, the practice of warfare on horseback was of considerable importance, also in the struggle against the Arabs; there was good reason why the handbook on warfare of Emperor Maurice devoted the very first chapter to archery.

Many pages could, of course, be devoted to the description of weapons; a few comments must suffice here. In general we can note, as was already emphasized, that the weapons did not undergo any fundamental changes over the centuries. Mercenaries often fought with their own weapons to which they were accustomed and were frequently also grouped into separate units. A special methodological problem in describing the weapons lies in the fact that we hardly have any weapons finds that can be unequivocally assigned to the Byzantines. Many of the artifacts found in museums of eastern and southeastern Europe may well be Byzantine, but there are no clear criteria for distinguishing the weapons of the peoples at the periphery of the empire from those of the Byzantines. We must therefore rely on the terminology in the written sources, which is often questionable, and on pictorial representations, which are often difficult to situate geographically and especially chronologically (with regard to possible models).

A basic distinction can be made between defensive and offensive weapons. Important for many branches of the army, particularly during the early and middle Byzantine periods, was armor. It could weigh up to 16 kilos and often rendered the soldier rather immobile, especially when he was fleeing; in such situations he had no choice but to abandon the heavy pieces. We should remember that many of the great battles occurred during the time of summer heat when the protective armor posed an additional burden. Even those soldiers who did not wear the heavy breast armor had iron protection for arms and legs. In some cases, however, cowhide or a certain combination of cloths was used instead of metal. Like the shield, the helmet (in its lighter and heavier forms) was always part of the armament. The offensive weapons were very diverse. Sword and knife hardly require special mention. The axe—aside from its use as a tool in constructing the camp—is known to us above all as a parade weapon, though certain types of axes were also used in battle. From late antiquity on, clubs and maces were also in use. Lance and spear have a long Roman tradition, and the notion that horsemen did not wield the spear before the twelfth century is based on the misreading of a source. As already mentioned, the bow, in all its variations, undoubtedly had the greatest importance; a kind of crossbow was probably also known. One of the oldest weapons of all, the sling, was also found in the gear of Byzantine soldiers.

Punishments for disobedience were manifold and severe. A source from the seventh or eighth century gives a catalogue of more than fifty punishments and prohibitions. The majority of transgressions were punishable by death. Only a few examples can be given here: violating the orders of the commander, even if (as in Heinrich von Kleist's *Prince of Homburg*) the favorable outcome justified the act, leaving camp, losing one's weapons or selling them (a case where the punishment could be reduced by an act of clemency), feigning illness out of fear of the enemy, desertion of any kind. Mutilation or exile was meted out to those who caused rebellion in the army. Soldiers who fled to the enemy and then returned to their own lines would be thrown to the wild animals or impaled. These punishments were put in place during a time of great military exertion on the part of Byzantium, in the conflict with the Bulgars and Arabs, when it was necessary to maintain strict discipline. It is questionable whether they were always imposed later, but in Byzantium, as in other medieval states, the use of the death penalty caused few, if any, qualms.

In addition to punishments, a number of prohibitions have also come down to us in the sources. For example, soldiers were not allowed to administer or rent someone else's property or take it in pawn, and the prohibition against engaging in agriculture and trade was taken over from Justinianic legislation. Later, in different circumstances, these stipulations were changed (especially with respect to landed property), but this cannot be discussed in detail here.

The Material and Social Background

This important area is among the most controversial for scholars because the relevant statements in the sources are few and inconsistent and are also difficult to pin down with regard to their chronological context. It is barely possible to make out a common thread among the many scholarly opinions. In principle we can assume that compulsory military service existed for the rural population, at least until the eleventh century. To that end, registers existed that were used for conscripting soldiers in case of war. To what extent the urban population was subject to conscription is, in my view, an open question: it is difficult to imagine that merchants and artisans performed military service, not to speak of those engaged in low service jobs. In addition, professional soldiers were always found in certain elite troops, for example, the imperial guard. Probably from the eleventh century on, professional recruiting largely or entirely replaced universal compulsory military service, and, in conjunction with the recruiting of mercenaries, it slowly led to the ruin of the treasury.

According to one law, men were not drafted for service "either in youth or old age." Two hagiographical works help to specify this vague statement a bit more precisely: entry into the military usually occurred at age eighteen or nineteen and was in general customary up to age twenty-four. The explanation for this extended period is probably that, as is the case today, not all young men of any given year were drafted if they were not needed. If war demanded it, men could probably be called up repeatedly up to whatever age the state thought fit. We can assume that conscription also occurred during peacetime in order to familiarize the young men with tactics and weapons, for it is hard to imagine that training was done only as part of the preparations for war. Still, we have no clear statements about this. In addition to acquiring the necessary skill for battle, young men also had to familiarize themselves with the repair of weapons. More than that was not demanded from the simple soldier and was not necessary. Only for the commander was a literary education desirable: primarily, of course, knowledge of the classical and Byzantine tactical writings, but also a study of dogma and theological authors since it promoted the moral conduct that was necessary for leadership.

The soldier was paid for the time of his service. The amount of pay and the dates on which it was paid differed from one region to the next and across the centuries. For the late sixth century we have a reference that it took place in the spring, when the armies were called up. In later centuries, soldiers were sometimes paid only after several years, usually three or four. It was possible to buy exemption from service with cash payments (in 949, for example, 4 nomismata), and landowners who could not provide anybody for service (because they were alone) were taxed instead of conscripted. We have no reliable information on the level of pay, with the exception of that for the commanders of large military districts.

One of the most frequently discussed questions is the connection between landownership and military service, for which legal stipulations exist from the tenth century on. Certainly the state never allotted land in return for obligatory military service. Rather, soldiers could acquire property with their pay, and this was primarily landed property. It would seem that taxes were waived or reduced if a landowner served in the military. We know this from a law of Empress Irene, who abolished the tax liability of widows of soldiers killed in battle, "so that they might not also have material damage in addition to their grief and sorrow." However, this regulation was soon rescinded, as we know from a saint's Life: we are told that one mother enrolled her son, the later St. Euthymios the Younger, in the military register as early as possible in order to reduce the heavy taxation. It would appear that the traditional link between landowning and military service was not legally fixed until the tenth century: at that time the size of the property and service were brought into some kind of proportion. But the impoverishment that was beginning in the countryside (the causes of which cannot be discussed here), in conjunction with efforts to create an army that was centrally controlled from Constantinople, based on pay, and involved the recruitment of foreigners, slowly spelled the end of the linkage between landownership and military service. This principle persisted, strictly speaking, until the end of the empire. To be sure, the thirteenth century (or possibly already the twelfth) witnessed another variation: the state allocated to soldiers tax revenues from specific landholdings (*pronoia*) allotted to them. The soldier, however, was no longer a peasant; for the most part, he did not live on the land but from its income. In addition, we find the mercenary; now recruited almost exclusively abroad, he often served in separate mercenary companies and (as in the West) no longer identified with the land he was to defend.

Apart from pay, soldiers were also given weapons and rations. We are relatively well informed from military handbooks and historical accounts about what soldiers ate and how they were supplied with food. Foodstuffs were generally taken along by the army, but in enemy territory the troops naturally helped themselves to whatever was available, in order to spare their own supplies. That is why enemy territory was ravaged only if the army was planning to return by a different route. The basic food of the soldier, the biscuit, was unchanged since antiquity, though it had a different name (*paximadion* instead of *boukelaton*). There was also a kind of bread that was baked a long time and then dried in the sun, and which must have been very similar to biscuits. As warm meals, there were a variety of freshly prepared gruels. The supply train also carried cured meat or bacon, though the sources also mention boiled or fried meat, which was fresh meat and had to be procured from the peasants during the campaign. In some sense, more important still than food was an adequate supply of water, which was sometimes kept fresh by adding vinegar and pebbles to it. Soldiers carried water in bottles, and the handbooks on tactics point out that those containers should not under any circumstances contain wine, a comment that points to the real preference of the soldiers. In general, though, wine was made available to the soldiers. In addition there were a number of mixed drinks: for example, sour wine mixed with rue and mallow, or a combination of milk, wine, and water. The main meal was eaten at noon, and if a battle was imminent, the soldiers would eat beforehand since they might have to go some time without food. The time for the meal was chosen at will by the superiors and was announced by a trumpet signal, which could also be used as a ruse to lull the enemy into a false sense of security while an attack was being planned.

The often lengthy absence of soldiers from their accustomed social environment naturally created problems. Thus the handbook of Leo the

Wise pointed out that lust, above all, should be banished from the army. We have only one epic source for a different approach to this problem—the attempt to control it instead of banishing it—but it may very well reflect real life: we read that brothels were set up in the field camp.

It has already been mentioned that we know of no fixed age cutoff for the use of soldiers in the army. Unresolved for the most part is also the question how disabled soldiers were cared for, since we have only one relevant reference from the sixth century. Following a mutiny at that time (during the reign of Emperor Maurice), it was decreed that veterans were permitted to live in the cities and would receive an allowance from the emperor. It seems that this referred to soldiers who were alone and could not be taken in by a family in the countryside. So far no system of veteran support analogous to what existed in Roman times has been shown to have existed in Byzantium.

THE ROLE OF THE SOLDIER IN THE STATE

Contrary to what was the case in other west European and Arab states of the Middle Ages, the role of the soldier in Byzantium was by no means limited to defense. Rather, in the tradition of the Roman military emperors of the third century, the army played a decisive part in the election of the emperor. To be sure, in this context the role of the individual soldier was not decisive (as it certainly could be in military combat); instead, he was merely the instrument in the hands of generals and troop commanders. Since the normal acclamation of the emperor (that is, one not based on the usurpation by certain units) took place, from the fifth century on, in the capital or its immediate environs, only the guard troops of Constantinople were involved in it. In a certain sense they represented the army as a whole, which meant that every individual soldier could feel that he was participating in the act and knew that he was a constitutive element—provided our modern-day historical analysis is not constructing too much of an ideal picture here. In keeping with constitutional conceptions, the army, the people (circus factions), and the senate were involved in the election of the emperor, and it was they who carried out the acclamation. The importance of these three parties varied in each case, and it was, strictly speaking, always a single party—by no means always the army—that decided the issue. In the late Byzantine period, when the rule of a dynasty (the Palaiologoi) had established itself, acclamation was merely a formal act, but until 1204 these various groups always carried decisive weight.

The role of the army discussed here should be seen as manifesting itself in two ways: in a peaceful choice to which the other groups consented, or in an act of usurpation that imposed its will on the other groups and led to the deposition of the old emperor. Only in the latter case did the army have an active role properly speaking, and we shall give a few examples here.

The historian Theophylaktos Simokattes described in detail such a usurpation in the early Byzantine period, which cost Maurice the throne and his life in 602. In the fall of 602, Emperor Maurice prohibited the soldiers at the Danubian frontier from returning home and ordered them instead to take up winter quarters on the other side of the Danube. The soldiers now broke with their commanders, chose one of their own (Phokas) as their leader, and informed the emperor that they no longer accepted his governance of the state. As the emperor refused to yield, the rebellious Danubian troops marched on the capital. However, by themselves they were not able to overthrow the emperor: only when the people, represented by the circus factions, joined the army was Phokas able to enter the city and assume the throne.

Well known and often discussed is the role of the army and the soldiers in the period between the end of the dynasty of Herakleios (685 or 711) and the assumption of the imperial office by Leo III (717). It almost seemed as though the conditions of the period of the third-century military emperors were repeating themselves. The backdrop to these events was, of course, different: the issue now was rivalry among the great military administrative districts (themes) and their leaders. First a general of the Hellas theme (Leontios) took the throne, next a fleet commander (Tiberios), then (after an intermezzo I shall disregard) an Armenian general (Philippikos), who was overthrown after two years by the troops from another theme. Those troops proceeded to install a civilian official at the top (Artemios), who in turn was chased from the throne after two years by the troops from yet another theme (Opsikion). Their candidate (Theodosios III) held the reins of power for even less than two years before he had to yield to the general of the Anatolian theme (Leo III), who was now able to reestablish a stable emperorship. To be sure, this political activity on the part of the army, unique in all of Byzantine history, coincided with a period in which the preservation of the empire against Arabs and Bulgars lay entirely in the hands of the military.

As interesting as these "mass usurpations" may be, since the events are only briefly recounted by two historians (Nikephoros and Theophanes), many details remain unknown. By contrast, another usurpation, that of Alexios I (1081), is fully illuminated by the light of history thanks to the account written by his daughter Anna. Alexios, having lived in the soldier's world since age fourteen, had several opportunities in the decade before his own revolt to practice the art of usurpation against Roussel de Bailleul, Nikephoros Bryennios, and Nikephoros Basilakes. It was not the soldiers who proposed to revolt against the reigning emperor (Nikephoros

Botaneiates); rather, it was Alexios—from an old family and one of the leading generals of the empire—who encouraged his soldiers to take this step. He assembled troops under the pretext of advancing against a city conquered by the Seljuks, put off another usurper (Nikephoros Melissenos) with a promise of collaboration, had himself proclaimed emperor by the army, and forced his way into Constantinople. This was a clear example of a military revolt, the success of which was entirely due (apart from diplomatic skill) to the support of the soldiers.

In addition to usurpations that were carried out by soldiers and brought about a change in imperial rule (or were intended to do so, since by no means all achieved their goal), there were revolts in the army that were not aimed at altering the leadership at the head of the state. It is once again Theophylaktos Simokattes (seventh century) who provides a very vivid example. The soldiers in the Sasanian theater of war were informed on Easter of 588 that their pay would be reduced by one-fourth. The pleasant task of announcing this was assigned to a newly appointed general (Priskos), who also made the mistake of failing to dismount from his horse when greeting the soldiers. And so a double discontent arose in the camp, because of the arrogance of the general and because of the reduction in pay. The soldiers gathered in front of the general's tent armed with swords and stones. Priskos ordered a picture of Christ to be carried around the camp. When the crowd did not calm down and even threw stones at the picture, the general hastily left the camp. The soldiers proceeded to plunder his tent, and they were not satisfied even when the reduction in pay was rescinded. The escaped general brought in a bishop as intermediary—surely not an everyday occurrence—and allowed the army to elect a new general. The ecclesiastical mediation failed as well, and the soldiers even toppled statues of the emperor and destroyed his portraits. Only the arrival of a high-ranking dignitary sent by the emperor from Constantinople put an end to the uprising.

This example reveals the power and influence of the soldiers, as well as the fact that very little separated a revolt in the army from the usurpation of the imperial power. As far as motives are concerned, it is obvious how close this revolt was to that on the Danube. All that was missing in the East, it would seem, was the possibility of setting up a rival emperor.

The role of the soldier within the state also becomes apparent in the series of emperors who were called to the highest office from the midst of military careers. Only a few names can be mentioned here. Justin, Justinian's uncle, came to the throne via a military career. Maurice initially belonged to the palace guard before he was sent to the eastern frontier as a general, from where he returned to Constantinople only a few months before beeing proclaimed emperor. Herakleios was the son of a general and commanded an army in Carthage, which placed into his hands the means to carry out a usurpation. Leo III was one of the great theme generals, and Alexios I, as we have seen, had grown up in the military. We could also mention those emperors who had a civilian background but who proved excellent soldiers and generals once on the throne. The most impressive example is surely Basil II, who has gone down in history as the soldier emperor par excellence and who had himself portrayed wearing a soldier's armor.

The constitutive element in the election of the emperor was the act of acclamation, whereby the chosen one was raised on a shield and shown to the masses. This custom was retained even when the new emperor did not come out of the military or when the army had not played a decisive role in his election. Whether or not the raising on the shield continued in use during the middle Byzantine period, we encounter it again (or still) in the fourteenth century, and it shows—as a sign of continuity, in a way—at least the theoretical connection between the emperor and the soldiers. Is this not a clue to the inherent significance of the soldier in the Byzantine period?

The Soldier and Death

The constant readiness to die is shared by soldiers in all cultures. "War is the painter of death," a Byzantine general said, and elsewhere he addressed the soldiers as those who are constantly practicing to die. An as yet little-studied genre of Byzantine literature, military rhetoric, provides some clues concerning the attitude toward death on the battlefield. It is perhaps surprising that the classical notion of the fame of the brave soldier is predominant, while the Christian idea of the heavenly reward seems seldom to appear. As late as the sixth century, a general who surely had not read Horace repeated that nothing was sweeter than death in battle. And the same thought is repeated in the twelfth-century novel of the metropolitan Constantine Manasses: it is better to die in battle than in bed. It would seem that, for these authors, the hereafter was in the Elysian Fields rather than in the Christian Paradise. Only rarely do there appear Christian notions about a life after a heroic death: for example, when death is described (also in accord with classical tradition) as sleep, short in comparison with the day that would come, or when angels gather the souls of the dead. Emperor Leo, in his *Taktika*, spoke explicitly about the heroes who distinguished themselves in battle for the Christians, and we are not far from the soldiers whom Nikephoros Phokas had declared martyrs. However, as far as I can see, only a single account of a liturgy for those killed in battle has come down to us.

To be sure, the heroic fighter was rarely depicted in a paradigmatic way. I mention only one exception, taken once again from the history of

Theophylaktos Simokattes. It is the story of a soldier who was in the throes of death, pierced by several arrows that could not be removed. He was taken to the camp, but the physicians, too, were helpless. The man, however, seemed determined to live only to hear the answer to one question: did the Byzantines win? Of course they had won! He then had the arrows pulled out and died.

The rhetorical sources speak effusively about the care and concern of the emperor and general for the families of soldiers killed in battle. They must look after them as they would after their own children and provide for the entire family and relatives. Reality was usually much bleaker. Providing for widows was left to the generosity of the emperor. For example, Michael I gave 5 talents of gold to the wives of soldiers killed in the war with the Bulgarians, but the scale of this charitable gift is unclear. Empress Irene, as already mentioned, granted tax relief if the military obligations attached to landed property could not be met, but it appears that Irene's successor, Nikephoros, already rescinded this reduction. A more careful scrutiny of the sources might bring to light a few additional details, but essentially survivors were provided for only in rhetoric.

Faith and Religion among the Soldiers

Militia Christi

"God is the supreme commander in war." With these words, a seventh-century historian begins a bishop's festive sermon to the soldiers. Christianity laid claim to being a religion of peace, missionary work was carried out with peaceful means, and the shedding of blood in battle was murder. Nearly ninety years ago, Adolf von Harnack, in a classic work, described the long road that led to the acceptance of military service on the part of Christians and to the characterization, in Old Testament fashion, of God as the supreme general. A soldier's profession was basically unacceptable to Christians during the early centuries. The true warriors were not the soldiers in the emperor's service but the martyrs who gave their lives for the Christian faith. Nevertheless, Christians did serve in the army, and cases of a conflict of conscience were rare thanks to a certain mutual tolerance. But the few Christian soldiers who were caught up in such a conflict became exemplary soldier saints who would acquire considerable importance in later centuries. Decisive for the fact that a Christian could serve in the army without any great scruples was the adoption of Christianity as the religion of the state, an event that had—and this is crucial for our purposes—begun in the army. Constantine's victory in 312 at the Milvan Bridge took place under the sign of the cross, however much the court rhetoric of Eusebios may have contributed to it. A mere two years later the synod of Arles (in canon 3) took an unmistakably positive attitude toward the soldier's calling by punishing desertion with excommunication.

The Soldier and the Practice of Religion

Christian customs were slow to make their way into the army. In addition, the sources are often silent in this regard or have not yet been scrutinized carefully enough, so that the examples presented here are hardly representative.

The military handbook of Emperor Maurice (second half of the sixth century) mentions (probably following old tradition) that the war cry was *nobiscum*. The military standards were blessed, and the labarum (following Constantinian tradition) was carried ahead of the army. The evening meal was concluded with the singing of the *trisagion*. Before battle a prayer must be said in camp, ending with the words "Lord, have mercy"; a priest was also present during this ritual. In the precepts of Nikephoros Phokas (tenth century), who also distinguished himself in the rest of his life by his military piety, this prayer was also ordered at the enemy's approach. While there is no mention of a military liturgy in the sixth century, we do find one in the *Praecepta* of Nikephoros. If the day of the battle was fixed, a liturgy should be held followed by a three-day fast, meaning that the soldiers could eat only once a day, in the evening. In general there was no lack of piety in the camp of Nikephoros: services were held in the morning and at night. During that time no soldier was permitted to engage in any other activity. Riders had to dismount and, like the foot soldiers, turn to face east. Transgressions were punished with lashes, shearing of the hair, or demotion. However, we can assume that such strict religious discipline in the army applied only during the time of Emperor Nikephoros Phokas. The first mention of the presence of a picture of Christ in the army occurred, as far as I know, in connection with the munity of the soldiers at the eastern frontier (588) that was mentioned earlier. Icons were also displayed to the troops in a similar, but less serious, situation in the eleventh century.

Still, certain remnants that pointed to the unholiness of war always existed. They included above all the fact that priests were not permitted to do military service. As we have seen, there were priests in the military who said prayers and conducted services. In the Life of a certain St. Nikephoros, we are told that he accompanied the army to Sicily (in 966). Priests, however, were barred from carrying arms. This prohibition had been clearly laid down already in canon 7 of the Council of Chalcedon (451): once a person had entered a clerical or monastic status, he was not permitted to take up civil or military service. The apocryphal apostolic canons, too, which were not sanctioned canonically until 692, speak a very clear language: "A bishop, presbyter, or deacon who is serving in the military and wants to hold to both, wordly service and spiritual function, shall be divested." To be sure, in spite of all this we have evidence that state institutions called on priests for military service or that the latter took up arms voluntarily.

Of course these prohibitions could also be interpreted—or rather exploited—the other way round: "timely" entry into the clerical or monastic status made it possible to avoid military service. As early as the fourth and fifth centuries, the authorities sought to prevent this "escape." We find references to this problem in the correspondence between Pope Gregory the Great and Emperor Maurice, and the dissolution of monasteries during the iconoclastic controversy and the persecution of monks could also be seen against this background.

We also encounter numerous cases in which the hardships of military service led to a withdrawal from wordly life as such. The destruction of the Byzantine army in the battle against the Bulgars in 811 and the death of Emperor Nikephoros prompted the soldier Nicholas to enter a monastery during the retreat. The Eastern Orthodox Church celebrates the memory of this warrior and monk on 24 December, and his Life, embellished with edifying stories, has survived in several versions. From the same decade comes the account of the "conversion" of another soldier, the later hermit Jacob. He was serving in the household troops of Emperor Leo V, and it appeared that he also shared the emperor's iconoclastic stance. His brother, by contrast, was a priest monk and very distressed about Jacob's sentiments. However, he did succeed in leading him back to the true path. The text, extant only in Latin, speaks of a *mirabilis metamorphosis* in which *hominem mundam transformavit in virum spiritualem* and that made a *miles saecularis* into a *miles christianus*.

However, what we encounter among the soldiers is not only faith, but also, and far more frequently than the scant references in the sources would suggest, superstition. A certain Theophilos, who was active as a court astrologer in Baghdad in the eighth century, wrote a work in which he described the various activities of war with the help of astrological tools. What follows are a few examples from this work; though extant only in excerpts, it covers no fewer than sixty pages in the modern edition. The alignment of Kronos and Selene (the moon) indicates treason and ambush, but the same constellation with Aphrodite and Selene rules out an ambush. Crucial during sieges is which zodiac the moon is in at the time of the siege. The setting of Selene, who harmonizes with Kronos, points to a fearful and powerless general and brings with it much danger. This information was certainly intended for the officers and not the individual soldier, but the use of astrological practices was of course also known to the soldiers. The example of Emperor Manuel I shows to what extent even emperors relied on horoscopes.

Also in the category of superstitious prophecies are dreams. The dream book of Achmet gives a whole series of clues connected with war and weapons, not only for the general but also the simple soldier. If the general dreams that he finds a cuirass, he will triumph over the enemy and become as rich as the cuirass is heavy. If a simple man dreams about iron weapons, he will attain riches. If the emperor sees himself in arms, he will win a victory over the enemy.

The Soldier and Religious Controversies

While ethnic problems in the Byzantine army barely persisted beyond the fifth century, it was in that same century that religious problems began in the wake of the decrees of the Council of Chalcedon. This area, too, can only be touched upon briefly in this context, and the transition from paganism (or Gnostic currents and the cult of Mithras) to Christianity has been left out entirely.

I begin with the obvious statement that a soldier is subject to the commands of his superiors. Personal religious attitude was of secondary importance. It is, in any case, questionable to what extent the individual soldier considered himself a Monophysite, say, and what he thought it meant. As far as I can determine, we have no indication that a military uprising in the fifth or sixth century was caused by the christological controversies. The intervention of troops on behalf of decisions of a council (for example, in 449 in Ephesos) came in response to orders and does not reveal the will of the soldiers involved. At times emperors surely realized the danger that could arise from religious enmity. Marcian prohibited the decisions of Chalcedon from being discussed within the ranks and barred certain religious groups from entering the army. Earlier, in 428, Emperor Theodosios II had barred Manichaeans from normal military service, accepting them only into the field army proper.

The attitude of the army in the iconoclastic controversy (which can be seen as a continuation of the religious controversies) has been frequently discussed. However, all we can do is determine where soldiers got involved; we cannot say anything about their inner attitude. Not a single revolt during the entire period is linked to the questions of icons. And the characterization of troop units as iconophile units (in the West) and iconoclastic units (in the East) has proved untenable.

The only conflict within the army that was genuinely motivated by questions of faith took place between the ninth and eleventh centuries and involved Paulicians and Bogomils. As early as the ninth century the Paulicians, within their statelike entity on the Euphrates, had raised armies that clashed with the imperial power in Constantinople. Similar in nature were the Bogomil revolts on Bulgarian territory, which Emperor Alexios still had to confront as late as the end of the eleventh century. These were in a certain sense religious wars—with all the caution with which this term should be used—and the soldiers involved may well have felt themselves to be religious warriors.

Military Saints

We have already seen that some Christians who had suffered martyrdom during their military service, as true *milites Christi,* were to be protectors and models for the soldiers. Dressed in their soldier's uniform, they were also represented pictorially (though probably not before the ninth century), and their number increased over the course of the centuries. It would seem that their cult grew in proportion to how strongly Byzantium, or Christian peoples in general, were engaged in the struggle with unbelievers, as happened in the ninth and tenth centuries and again in the fourteenth and fifteenth, when the Ottomans were threatening the Byzantine Empire and the Christian states in the Balkans.

The most widely venerated saints included Demetrios, Prokopios, Theodore (who later split into a general and a recruit), and the mounted knight George. For the most part their martyrdoms dated back to the time of Diocletian, and their earliest veneration probably goes back to the fourth century, though many questions still await clarification. The richest treasury of legends surrounds St. George, who, according to a source that is not entirely secure chronologically, was a "state saint" as early as the seventh century.

The military saint was not only the protector of the individual; like the Homeric gods, he also intervened in battle and thus boosted the confidence of the army. Many examples of this appear in the historical and encomiastic literature. During the campaign of John Tzimikces against the Russians (971), a storm suddenly arose, blowing dust into the enemies's faces and robbing them of their sight. At the same time a rider on a white horse is said to have appeared, none other than the "great martyr Theodore," who spurred on the Byzantines. A few centuries later it was the two Theodores who came to the aid of the emperor. During the campaign to conquer Melnik (1255), two men, overly tall in stature, are said to have appeared to Emperor Theodore VI Laskaris. As only the emperor and nobody in his entourage had seen them, it seemed evident that the men were the two soldier saints. They reappeared when the assault on the city was in full swing and brought the effort to a victorious conclusion for the Byzantines. At times, however, the saint also became the soldier's guilty conscience. When the Russians were besieging Constantinople in 907, the Byzantines offered to negotiate, and Oleg was offered poisoned food and drink. Oleg turned down the food, but the Greeks, according to the chronicle of Nestor, were afraid and said: "That is not Oleg but Saint Demetrios, sent against us by God."

THE GLORY AND MISERY OF THE SOLDIER

"Today the sky is different, today is a special day, today the young lords will ride out (to do battle)." Thus begins one of the oldest and most beautiful Byzantine heroic songs, the *Song of Armoures*. Here it is the border soldiers, the *akritai,* who are going into battle against the unbelievers. They are, at the time of the greatest glory of the Byzantine Empire, the great models of heroism. However, they are not realistic heroes but heroes of fabulous strength: singlehandedly they defeated entire armies. Faith and magical powers lie side by side. An angel shows Armoures a ford across the raging Euphrates, whereupon he falls upon the enemy and cuts them all down in a day and a night.

The epic glory of heroism was always the exception. A soldier was afraid and helped himself with prayer and superstitious practices. He was forced to carry out orders, and his own opinion did not matter. However, given the openness of Byzantine society, he could climb to the highest ranks. If there is anything that typifies the Byzantine soldier, it is precisely the direct relationship to the state and the emperor. Apart from some peculiarities relating to the material and social background, there are otherwise hardly any characteristics that set him apart from other soldiers in the medieval world in any fundamental way. To be sure, western sources, in particular, regarded the Byzantine soldier as somewhat spoiled and soft, an opinion that, in view of Norman military prowess, for example, may not have been entirely unjustified.

This brief overview has left out certain aspects altogether. One could speak of the fate of prisoners, which is known to us almost exclusively from intrastate agreements, though in one instance it also comes alive in the hagiographic story of the forty-two martyrs of Amorion. In old age, and this too has not been discussed, ailments plagued the soldier: even an emperor, John VIII, suffered such a bad case of gout by age fifty that he could barely write his name. One would also have to address criminality in the army, murder, robbery, and plundering, which we encounter not only in the catalogues of punishments but also as realistic descriptions in real life. Missing, finally, are not only the splendid soldier saints of religious art, but also the warriors on the silver plates of the eleventh and twelfth centuries, the simpler depictions on ceramic ware, and the graffiti on walls or sketches of soldiers on empty manuscript pages that remind us of children's drawings.

At a time when war and the profession of arms no longer seem the proper tools for advancing one's interests, an essay on the soldier may strike some as outdated. Be that as it may, the Byzantine Empire would have existed without Photios, Psellos, and Theodore Metochites, but not without the Byzantine soldier.

Selected Bibliography

Primary Sources

Ashburner, W. "The Byzantine Mutiny Act," *Journal of Hellenic Studies* 46 (1926): 80–109.

Das Strategikon des Maurikios, edited with an introduction and indexes by G. T. Dennis, translated by E. Gamillscheg. Vienna, 1981.

Leonis imperatoris Tactica sive de re militari liber. In J.-P. Migne, ed., *Patrologia Graeca,* CVII, cols. 669–1094. Paris, 1863.

Strategika imperatora Nikiphora, edited by I. A. Kulakovskij. Zapiski Imperatorskoi Akademij Nauk, s. VIII, 8, no. 9. St. Petersburg, 1908.

Le traité sur la guérilla de l'empereur Nicéphore Phocas, ed. G. Dagron and H. Mihaescu. Paris, 1986.

General Literature

Delehaye, H. *Les légendes grecques des saints militaires.* Paris, 1909.

Dölger, F., *Zwei byzantinische Reiterheroen erobern die Festung Melnik.* In idem, *Paraspora: 30 Aufsätze zur Geschichte, Kultur und Sprache des byzantinischen Reiches,* pp. 299–305. Ettal, 1961.

Garsoïan, N. G. *The Paulician Heresy: A Study of the Origin and Development of Paulicianism in Armenia and the Eastern Provinces of the Byzantine Empire.* The Hague–Paris, 1967.

Gregoriou-Ioannidou, M. *Stratologia kai stratiotike idioktesia sto Byzantio.* Thessaloniki, 1989.

Grosse, R. *Römische Militärgeschihte von Gallienus bis zum Beginn der byzantinischen Themenverfassung.* Berlin, 1920.

Haldon, J. F. *Recruitment and Conscription in the Byzantine Army c. 550–950: A Study on the Origins of the Stratiotika Ktemata.* Vienna, 1979.

Harnack, A. V. *Militia Christi: Die christliche Religion und der Soldatenstand in den ersten drei Jahrhunderten.* Tübingen, 1905.

Heath, I. *Byzantine Armies, 886–1118.* London, 1979.

Hunger, H. *Das Reich der Neunen Mitte: Der christliche Geist der byzantinischen Kultur,* esp. pp. 193–95. Graz, 1965.

Kaegi, W. E., "The Byzantine Armies and Iconoclasm." *Byzantinoslavica* 27 (1966): 48–70.

———. *Byzantine Military Unrest, 471–843: An Interpretation.* Amsterdam, 1981.

Kolias, T. G. "Essgewohnheiten und Verpflegung im byzantinischen Heer." In W. Hörander, J. Koder, O. Kresten, and E. Trapp, eds., *Byzantios: Festschrift für H. Hunger zum 70. Geburstag, dargebracht von Schülern und Mitarbeitern,* pp. 193–202. Vienna, 1984.

————. *Byzantinischen Waffen. Ein Beitrag zur byzantinischen Waffenkunde von den Anfängen bis zur lateinischen Eroberung.* Vienna, 1988.

Lot, F. *L'art militaire et les armées au moyen-âge en Europe et dans le Proche Orient,* vol. 1, esp. pp. 19–73. Paris, 1946.

Obolensky, D. *The Bogomils: A Study in Balkan Neo-Manichaeism.* Cambridge, 1948.

Oikonomides, N. "À propos des armées des premiers Paléologues et des compagnies de soldats." *Travaux et Mémoires* 8 (1981): 353–71.

————. "Middle-Byzantine Provincial Recruits: Salary and Armament." In *Gonimos: Neoplatonic and Byzantine Studies presented to L. G. Westerink at the 75,* pp. 121–36. Buffalo, 1988.

Pertusi, A. "Ordinamenti militari, guerre in Occidente e teorie di guerra dei bizantini (secc. VI–X)." In *Ordinamenti militari in Occidente nell'alto Medioevo,* pp. 631–700. Settimane di studio del Centro italiano di studi sull'alto medioevo, XV. Spoleto, 1968.

Treitinger, O. *Die oströmische Kaiser- und Reichsidee nach ihrer Gestaltung im höfischen Zeremoniell.* Jena, 1938.

Vieillefond, J. R. "Les pratiques religieuses dans l'armée byzantine d'après les traités militaires." *Revue des études anciennes* 37 (1935): 322–30.

4

TEACHERS

Robert Browning

B
YZANTINE TEACHERS, whether elementary schoolmasters or professors of grammar, rhetoric, or philosophy, were heirs of a very ancient tradition that went back to the fifth century B.C. A fragment
of a lost comedy of Aristophanes shows a schoolmaster asking his pupils
the meaning of difficult words in the poems of Homer; they had no doubt
been given a list of such words to learn by heart. The historian Thucydides tells how in 413 B.C., in the course of the Peloponnesian War, a band
of Thracian mercenary soldiers burst into the little town of Mykalessos
in Boeotia and massacred the inhabitants. "Among other things," he
writes, "they broke into a boys' school, the largest in the place, into which
the children had just entered, and killed every one of them." That there
were several schools in so tiny a town—the geographer Strabo in the first
century B.C. calls it a village—bears witness to the spread of education in
Greece in the fifth century.

It was in the Hellenistic period—roughly from the death of Alexander the Great in 323 B.C. to that of Cleopatra in 31 B.C.—that a system
of education took shape which was maintained, though with inevitable
changes, throughout the Roman and Byzantine periods of Greek history
until the capture of Constantinople by the Ottoman Turks in 1453. Education was a three-stage affair. The elementary schoolteacher, a humble
individual of low social status, who has left few traces in the record of
history, taught the arts of reading and writing, often together with simple
arithmetic. His pedagogical methods were simple and made little allowance for the psychological development of the child. Children learned first
the names and forms of the letters, then syllables, then short words, then
the basic morphology of nouns and verbs, usually without consideration
of the archaic and dialectal forms found in classical Greek poetry. They
then went on to copy and learn by heart short edifying maxims, such as
"Accept the counsel of a wise man" or "Do not trust all friends at ran-

dom." Finally, they might learn by heart short prose texts such as Aesop's *Fables*, together with grammatical and moral explanations by the teacher. His lessons were regularly reinforced by corporal punishment. We catch a glimpse of him at work in a mime of Herodas in the third century B.C. and in stray leaves from exercise books among the papyri found in the rubbish heaps of small towns in Egypt. His methods seem to have changed little, if at all, during a millennium and a half. There were no textbooks, and much learning by rote.

We know a great deal more about the activities of the grammarian and the rhetorician, the professors responsible for the next stages of Hellenistic and Byzantine education. They belonged to the small, educated, and articulate class who wrote books, and some of their books have survived. What the grammarian taught his pupils was how to read with understanding, and sometimes with critical appreciation, the literature of classical Greece. He began by teaching in much greater detail than the elementary schoolmaster the complex morphology of noun and verb as they appeared in this literature, taking account of the many deviant forms. This implied some study of the various dialects, real or artificial, in which the literature was written, and of rare words occurring only in literature. As time went on, the spoken Greek of everyday life diverged more and more from that of classical Greek literature. So the grammarian was obliged to "correct" and "purify" the speech of his pupils and to insist on their using, in all formal communication, words and inflections that they had not internalized in childhood.

For this purpose, the grammarian made use of textbooks that, though composed in antiquity, continued in use throughout the Middle Ages. One of these was *The Art of Grammar* (*Technē grammatikē*) of Dionysios the Thracian, written in the second century B.C. This short treatise, of no more than sixteen printed pages, dealt with parts of speech, morphology, prosody, etymology, and figures of speech and thought. Grammarians expounded and illustrated this succinct and elementary work in the course of their teaching, and some of them gave their teaching a permanent form as a written commentary. Many such commentaries, composed by teachers in late antiquity or the Middle Ages, survive. In their complexity and long-windedness, they dwarf and overwhelm the brief and lucid text they endeavor to explain. The other textbook much used by Byzantine grammarians was the *Canons* (*Kanones*) of Theodosios of Alexandria (ca. A.D. 500), a systematic list of brief rules for the inflection of nouns and verbs in classical Greek. In fact, it includes many forms that occur in no classical writer but were invented by later grammarians, often by false analogy. Around this treatise, too, there accumulated a body of commentaries far exceeding in bulk the text of Theodosios.

Side by side with this theoretical teaching went the practical reading of literary texts. Poetic texts were preferred, both because they were easier to remember and because they tended to contain more unusual forms and more mythological and other allusions. Above all, it was the poems of Homer that formed the stock-in-trade of the grammarian. These were written in an artificial literary language, reflecting that used in oral composition by minstrels in a preliterate age, a language containing many variant words and inflections belonging to different dialects in archaic Greek. And they were full of references to mythological figures and events that may have been familiar to schoolboys in pagan Athens, but had to be explained to their Christian Byzantine descendants. So much of the grammarian's time was occupied with detailed word-by-word and line-by-line explication of the *Iliad* or the *Odyssey,* or less frequently of Hesiod, an Attic tragedy, or the refined and allusive poetry of the Hellenistic world.

Pupils did not normally have copies of the treatises of Dionysios or Theodosios, to say nothing of the Homeric poems. Books were rare and expensive objects in both late antiquity and the Byzantine world. Teaching was oral. The grammarian dictated passages for his pupils to learn by heart and then explained them, often simply reading out or slightly paraphrasing a commentary by one of his predecessors, perhaps his own teacher. He would then go on to test their knowledge by asking questions on the subject matter of the lesson, much as did the teacher in Aristophanes' play. Progress must have been slow. A twelfth-century Aristotelian commentator mentions that the normal passage of Homer learned and explained each day was thirty lines, and that only the brightest pupils could manage as much as fifty lines. When one considers that the *Iliad* runs to 15,694 lines and that the *Odyssey* is not much shorter, one realizes that pupils could scarcely have acquired a vision of the architecture and the grand sweep of these great epics from the teaching of the grammarian. There were, however, epitomes of the Homeric poems available; but to judge by those that survive, they were unlikely to have kindled the enthusiasm of the young.

There survive some Byzantine commentaries on Homer, of varying comprehensiveness and depth, which provide some idea of how a grammarian might explain the difficult text, as well as a number of line-by-line prose paraphrases, which certainly owe their origin to a teaching situation. The immensely long, detailed, learned, and discursive commentaries on the *Iliad* and the *Odyssey* by Eustathios, teacher in the patriarchal school in the mid-twelfth century and later archbishop of Thessalonike, clearly owe something to his teaching activities. But he himself declares that they are addressed to a wider public of educated readers and may be read with or without the text of the poet. It would be unwise to suppose that the explication of Homer provided by the average grammarian was as rich, erudite, varied in approach, or as lengthy as Eustathios' magnificent "compilations" (*parekbolai*), as he entitles them. The rich critical scholia on the *Iliad* surviving in a tenth-century manuscript now in the Biblioteca Marciana in Venice, and containing the debris of the Homeric scholarship of the great Alexandrians from Zenodotos and Aristarchos to Didymos, are also quite unrepresentative of what the average grammarian taught his pupils. They are addressed to mature scholars, not to schoolboys.

The rhetorician who took over the grammarian's pupils at about the age of fourteen—there was no official regulation of such matters—taught them how to express their thoughts in speech or in writing with elegance and persuasiveness. We must bear in mind that, in a largely oral society, skill in speech was more important and more highly appreciated than it is today. In addition to teaching, the rhetorician was expected in late antiquity to give displays of his art in the theater or council chamber, to deliver panegyrics, funeral or marriage orations and the like for the leading citizens of his town, and on occasion to act as spokesman for his fellow citizens before provincial governors, praetorian prefects, or the emperor himself, and thus to serve as a vital link between the partly autonomous cities and the imperial government. In the fourth century, Libanios, professor of rhetoric in Antioch, fulfilled all these roles from time to time. As power became more centralized, the rhetorician became less and less a mediator between his civic community and a remote government, but he was still expected to give displays of eloquence and to celebrate important events in the life of his city and its ruling elite. In the middle of the sixth century, Chorikios, teacher of rhetoric in Gaza, delivered encomia, funeral orations, and the like for both laymen and bishops in the then predominantly Christian society, and also composed descriptive set pieces on churches and other buildings in Gaza. In the funeral speech on his old teacher of rhetoric, Prokopios, Chorikios observed that "the quality of a rhetorician is tested by two things, his ability to astound an audience by the wisdom and beauty of his words, and his initiation of the young into the mysteries of the ancients."

In the Byzantine world the teacher of rhetoric had little or no opportunity to play a political role, but he was still expected to appear before the public and deliver obituary speeches, encomia of leading men, and celebratory speeches on the occasion of military victories. Holders of publicly funded chairs of rhetoric might be required to deliver orations in praise of the emperor at Epiphany and of the patriarch on the feast of St. Lazaros on the Saturday preceding Palm Sunday. Teachers of rhetoric in late antiquity, and even more in the Byzantine world, might be called upon to compose speeches for their pupils to deliver on public occasions. Their ability as teachers might well be judged by these performances of their students. This public role of the teacher of rhetoric continued undiminished to the very last days of the Byzantine state. George Scholarios, who was later to be appointed ecumenical patriarch by Sultan Mehmed II after the capture of Constantinople, pronounced a memorial oration on the despot Theodore II Palaiologos in 1448. John Argyropoulos, teacher in Constantinople and later in Padua, Florence, and Rome, commemorated the death of Theodore's brother, Emperor John VIII, who died in the same year. And the death in 1450 of the dowager empress Helena, the widow of Manuel II, provided the occasion for no less than six orations by teachers and other men of letters.

The teacher of rhetoric, it will be evident, moved in circles of power and influence, both because of his role as a public spokesman and because he taught the sons of the rich and powerful. Many teachers seem to have suffered from a kind of status dissonance: without wealth, power, or influence themselves, they associated with the rich, the powerful, and the wielders of influence. This may explain the tendency they sometimes display to exaggerate and aggrandize the importance of their discipline, and hence of themselves. A typical example of this exaggeration is found in the introduction to the lectures on Aphthonios' *Progymnasmata* (an elementary textbook dating from the fourth century and used by teachers throughout the Byzantine period; see below), written by John Doxopatres, a teacher of rhetoric in Constantinople in the eleventh century.

> For those who have just come from the study of poetry and the marvels it recounts to the great mystery of rhetoric, and who are anxious to drink deeply of its inspiration and its grandeur of concepts, it is natural to feel no small wonder and to experience a not ignoble bewilderment as they set foot on its wondrous portals. Thanks to the greatness of its reputation and its extraordinary renown, it is reasonable for them to feel some confusion, and for the more noble souls among them to experience a longing and an eagerness that match their bewilderment. The more difficult they hear this study to be, the more eagerly do they prepare themselves, so that by attaining success in something that for the multitude is hard to grasp or comprehend, they may become distinguished and celebrated for their eloquence.

The teacher of rhetoric inherited textbooks from late antiquity that continued in use throughout the Middle Ages. The first was a collection of *progymnasmata* or preliminary exercises, short model texts illustrating the different genres of composition. That most frequently used by Byzantine teachers was compiled by Aphthonios of Antioch, a teacher of rhetoric in Athens in the late fourth century. Each model text is preceded by a short definition, setting out the characteristic features of the genre in question. Presumably the teacher read out, and if necessary explained, the definition and then dictated the model text. Aphthonios, following a pattern already established centuries earlier, begins with fable, goes on to narrative, *chreia* (an illustrative anecdote supporting some general proposition), moral maxim, refutation, confirmation, commonplace, encomium, censure, comparison, delineation of character, description, general question (for example, ought one to marry?), and proposal of a law. An example of the material to be learned by the pupil is the following:

> *Refutation* is the disproof of some matter. One can also refute what is neither completely obvious nor quite impossible, but occupies an intermediate position. Those who aim to refute must first discredit whoever makes the assertion and then attack his exposition of the matter, making use of the following heads of argument: first, that it is unclear and improbable, then that it is impossible or does not follow on its premises, or is unbecoming, and finally add that it is disadvantageous. This preliminary exercise contains within itself all the force of the art (of rhetoric).

He then goes on to exemplify under each of these heads the arguments for rejecting the story of Daphne, the nymph pursued by Apollo and turned into a laurel tree. The next preliminary exercise, on confirmation, sets out the arguments in favor of the truth of the story of Daphne.

In the middle of the fifth century A.D., a rival collection of *Progymnasmata* was published by Nicholas of Myra, a teacher of rhetoric, in Constantinople, and probably holder of an official chair, but it does not appear to have been nearly so widely used as that of Aphthonios, the popularity of which is demonstrated by the number of commentaries on it compiled by Byzantine teachers. These permit us an indirect glimpse of the actual teaching of the first stages of a course in rhetoric. They are far too long-winded and repetitive to be quoted here, and, to modern ears, are both tedious and uninspiring. But they evidently performed their function well enough. One can only hope, for the pupils' sake, that the challenge of oral delivery in the classroom induced teachers to enliven their presentation.

From time to time attempts were made to provide *progymnasmata* that would engage the pupils' interest more directly. Thus in the twelfth century Nikephoros Basilakes, a professor of rhetoric in the patriarchal school in Constantinople and author of a number of ceremonial and other orations, composed a new collection of *Progymnasmata*. These follow the traditional arrangement of themes. They offer several model texts to exemplify each genre, but provide no definitions; these would be supplied orally by the teacher. Basilakes also introduces a new selection of authors to be read by students of rhetoric, including examples of the florid style, such as Kallistratos and Prokopios of Gaza. His other main innovation is the occasional use of Christian material in his *Progymnas-mata*. Thus under the head of *prosōpopoeia* (delineation of character), we find "What would Pluto say when Lazaros was resurrected on the fourth day?" "What would Samson say when he was blinded by the Gentiles?" "What would Zacharias say when he recovered his voice after the birth of the Forerunner?" "What would the Virgin say when Christ turned the water into wine at the wedding feast?" "What would Joseph say when he was accused by the Egyptian woman and cast into prison?" "What would David say when he was pursued by Saul and captured by the Gentiles and about to be executed?" and "What would the maiden from Edessa say when she was deceived by the Goth?" (this last is an allusion to a celebrated story of a Christian girl who avenged herself against a Gothic soldier). Basilakes saw himself as an innovator and spoke of "this new rhetoric."

Another educational innovation, this time in the domain of the grammarian, was the so-called schedography, apparently introduced in the late eleventh century. It seems to have consisted in the use of short texts specially composed by the teacher and sometimes ending in a short passage in verse. These were dictated to pupils and then commented on in detail by the teacher. The point of the new method, which initially met with opposition from traditionalists, was that the text could be designed to illustrate particular points of grammar, lexicography, style, and construction upon which the teacher wished to concentrate the attention of his pupils. Thus some schedographic texts contain many examples of words and phrases that sound the same but have a different meaning according to how they are written—Greek has, since Hellenistic times, had a historical rather than a phonetic orthography. The correct copying of them from dictation would test a pupil's ability to select the right rendering on the basis of the context. Many schedographic texts, often composed by otherwise known professors, survive from the twelfth century, and a further series of such texts by Manuel Moschopoulos (early fourteenth century) remained in use until long after the end of the Byzantine Empire.

There was no regulation by higher authority of the curriculum followed by teachers of grammar or rhetoric. Tradition, modified by changing social pressures, in the last resort determined such matters, but individual teachers enjoyed great freedom of choice. Similarly, there was no fixed age for each stage of education. The usual age for beginning elementary school was six, and at nine or ten a pupil might go on to study under the grammarian, while the study of rhetoric might be pursued from fourteen to eighteen. But there were child prodigies—Hermogenes himself had been one—and many cases of late or interrupted study. The diversity of age among his pupils must sometimes have been a problem for the teacher. Finally, it must be remembered that only a tiny fraction of those with elementary education went on to study under the grammarian and the rhetorician.

After their preliminary studies of rhetoric, pupils would read select orations of Demosthenes and possibly Aeschines or Libanios, and compose declamations on themes set them by their teacher. These were mainly forensic speeches delivered before an imaginary court on an imaginary case under imaginary laws, or speeches put in the mouth of historical characters belonging to fifth- or fourth-century Athens. It is at first sight astonishing that youths who were being trained to occupy responsible posts in their city, in the state, or in the church should devote their energy to themes so unreal and so remote from the world in which they lived and might work. It is partly a matter of the dead weight of pedagogical tradition, which goes back to the Roman Empire and the Hellenistic kingdoms. At the same time it may be that this exciting imaginary world of pirates and tyrannicides aroused the interest of very young men much more than the workaday world of Byzantine administration and justice, and made them more ready to learn the difficult and delicate art of inventing, developing, presenting, and assessing arguments. Byzantine teachers were not fools who blindly followed ancient tradition because it was old, as will be seen when we look more closely at one or two of them.

Last in the armory of the teacher of rhetoric was the study of theoretical treatises on the subject. Those in almost exclusive use in Byzantium were the four treatises of Hermogenes of Tarsos (ca. 160–ca. 235): *On Positions* (that is, on the stance a speaker adopts toward the matter in dispute), *On How to Find Arguments, On Forms,* and on the *Technique of Grandeur.* These provide a subtle and at the same time practical introduction to the different procedures used in public communication and the effects each was designed to produce. These texts of Hermogenes in their turn gave rise to a dense mass of commentaries in the Middle Ages, which is evidence of their regular use in the classroom. No comparable theoretical handbook was produced by any Byzantine teacher.

In both late antiquity and the Byzantine Middle Ages, a training in grammar and rhetoric was the mark of the learned man, who normally belonged to a very limited social elite. Philosophy was always an optional subject, perhaps studied superficially by many, but in depth by only a few. In late antiquity there were flourishing schools of philosophy in Athens and Alexandria, and an officially appointed professor of philosophy was to be found in Constantinople in the fifth century, and no doubt in some other cities too. There was a fairly clear distinction between elementary courses, which seem to have dealt largely with Aristotelian logic and to have been addressed to a nonspecialist audience that had completed or were completing their studies of rhetoric, and advanced courses, attended primarily by those who wished to become teachers of philosophy. The content of these latter was predominantly Neo-Platonic, and they usually took the form of section-by-section commentaries on texts of Plato or Aristotle. Many of these late antique commentaries survive, though not all have been published, and most of them clearly betray their origin in the lecture room. The teacher read out or dictated a short passage of the text studied and then commented on its meaning, its place in the argument of which it forms a part, its relation to other works of Plato or Aristotle, and so on. Sometimes the exposition of the text seems to have been followed by questions from the students or by general discussion.

The Athenian school was, if not suppressed, certainly much restricted in its activity in 529, in the course of a witch-hunt by Justinian's government against pagans or crypto-pagans in positions of influence. The Alexandrian school, all of whose teachers were by this time Christians, maintained its existence until the capture of Alexandria by the Persians in 618, when Stephen, the head of the school, and probably some of his colleagues, withdrew to the safety of Constantinople.

For the next four centuries there is little trace of systematic teaching of philosophy in the Byzantine world. Some short epitomes of Aristotelian logic survive from the period, but it is very uncertain for whom they were written. They may well have been addressed to clergymen as an aid to the study of theology. The revival of interest in the literary heritage of ancient Greece in the late ninth and tenth centuries meant that texts of Plato and Aristotle and of the Neo-Platonists entered into circulation once again. The oldest surviving manuscripts of Plato—the Clarke Plato in the Bodleian Library in Oxford, the Vatican Plato, and the Paris Plato—were all written at the end of the ninth century or the early decades of the tenth, and one of them was copied for Arethas, archbishop of Caesarea, a noted scholar and bibliophile. There probably was some informal and unorganized teaching of philosophy at this time. But it was not until 1154 that Michael Psellos, who was a man of letters rather than a philosopher, was appointed by Constantine IX Monomachos as head of an imperially sponsored school of philosophy in Constantinople, with the title of *hypatos tōn philosophōn*. This title, often misleadingly translated "consul of the philosophers," means rather "chief of the philosophers" and implies that there were other teachers of philosophy in the capital as well. Psellos regarded himself as a Christian Platonist. His numerous works include some treatments of philosophical questions as well as a hodgepodge of short notes on philosophical and scientific questions. If these works represent his philosophical teaching, then it was not of a particularly high order.

Psellos' pupil and successor, John Italos, born in south Italy of a Norman father and a Greek mother, was a much more serious philosopher.

Anna Komnene, in her history of the reign of her father, Alexios I Komnenos, says that he had an enthusiastic following among the young in the late eleventh century. Of his writings there survive a series of short discussions of philosophical problems as well as commentaries on some of Aristotle's works. His application of the methods of philosophy to theological questions, his western origin, and probably his dependence on the patronage of Alexios' political enemies, brought about his downfall. In 1182 he was hauled before a tribunal, found guilty of heresy, deposed from his office, and disappeared from history. His alleged teachings are still solemnly anathematized by the Orthodox Church during the liturgy of the Festival of Orthodoxy on the first Sunday of Lent. The lesson that philosophers who infringe on the preserve of theology do so at their own risk was not lost on his successors. One holder of the office of chief of the philosophers, Michael of Anchialos, in his inaugural lecture, probably in 1167, declares that he will give Plato a wide berth and will base his teaching on Aristotle. Not surprisingly, he ended his days as patriarch of Constantinople (1170–78).

There were occasional holders of the title of chief of the philosophers during the two centuries between the restoration of the Byzantine Empire in 1261 and the capture of Constantinople by the Ottoman Turks in 1453. But much philosophical teaching and writing seems to have been done by men whose main field of activity lay elsewhere. George Pachymeres (1242–ca. 1319), statesman, historian, and polymath, wrote a learned treatise on the *quadrivium* and a long and detailed exposition of the philosophy of Aristotle. He was evidently a serious thinker, but it is not clear that he was engaged in systematic teaching of philosophy. Theodore Metochites (1260/61–1328), another statesman and polymath, composed commentaries on many of the works of Aristotle, which suggests that he was involved in some way in the teaching of philosophy. The deacon John Pediasimos, who held the office of chief of the philosophers in the first half of the fourteenth century, and was therefore an actual teacher, wrote commentaries on Aristotle's logical works.

At the same period the south Italian Greek clergyman Barlaam of Calabria, who played a prominent part in the Hesychast dispute, lectured on Plato and Aristotle in Constantinople, probably as a kind of visiting professor. Around 1400 John Chortasmenos, teacher of rhetoric and notary to the patriarch, wrote an introduction to the logic of Aristotle. His pupil George Scholarios, later patriarch of Constantinople after the Turkish capture of the city, lectured on philosophy to a small circle of young men and wrote up his lectures in the form of textbooks. The latest of all the late Byzantine philosophers was George Gemistos Plethon; his treatise on the differences between Aristotle and Plato, and the lectures on the subject that he delivered at the Council of Florence in 1438, caused a stir among Italian humanists and later led to the foundation by Cosimo de' Medici of the Platonic Academy in Florence. It is certain that Plethon taught philosophy in Mistra, the capital of the Byzantine province of the Peloponnese, where he spent the second half of his life, and he probably taught earlier in Constantinople. But whether he was in any sense a professional or officially appointed teacher we do not know.

Much philosophical teaching in the last two centuries of Byzantium appears to have been done by "gentlemen scholars" rather than by professional teachers. This was not due to a lack of interest in the classical philosophical tradition—far from it—but it rather reflected the breakdown of institutions as the Byzantine Empire was dismantled and reduced to a handful of scattered patches of territory in a region ruled by Turks or Latins. However, in the last decade of the existence of the empire, we find an officially appointed professor who taught philosophy as well as grammar. He was John Argyropoulos, one of the few Greeks of the time who had studied in Padua, and who later emigrated to Italy and taught in Padua, Florence, and Rome. His teaching, as well as his numerous Latin translations of works of Aristotle, made a major contribution to the intellectual world of the Renaissance. A portrait of him teaching in Constantinople, albeit with a traditional iconography that owes much to portraits of the evangelists, survives in a manuscript in the Bodleian Library in Oxford. This, and a somewhat earlier drawing of Manuel Chrysoloras lecturing in Florence around 1400, now in the Louvre, are the only surviving depictions of a Byzantine professor at work.

In the course of the Byzantine period, the distinction between the domains of the grammarian and the rhetorician, and to a lesser extent between those of the rhetorician and the philosopher, became blurred, and the same teacher is often found giving instruction in two subjects. Thus all postprimary education is sometimes entrusted to the same teacher. It was said of Eustathios that "When he presided over the mysteries of the literary arts, as soon as a pupil had set foot on the Muses' threshold he was at once granted a vision of their innermost sanctuary." In other words, he taught both grammar and rhetoric. Similarly we are told that "In a brief space of time, enough for an introduction to rhetoric or for setting foot on the first threshold of philosophy, his students seemed like pupils of Aristotle or like poets inspired by the Muses." But not all teachers had Eustathios' talents.

Some teachers in Constantinople received financial and other support from the government, the church, or both. But most teachers seem to have depended on fees paid by their pupils. The pattern of late antiquity, whereby city councils appointed and paid some teachers of grammar and rhetoric, broke up with the decline of city autonomy and civic initiative in the sixth and early seventh centuries.

Many "schools" consisted of a single teacher, often teaching in his own house. But in the Byzantine period, as in late antiquity, we not infrequently find in Constantinople assistant teachers, called *hypogrammateis* or *proximoi* (Latin *proximi*). Thus Christopher of Mitylene (first half of the eleventh century) mentions in a poem a school attached to the church of St. Theodore in the quarter of Ta Sphorakia, whose head teacher (*maistōr*) was Leo and whose *proximos* was Stylianos. Michael Psellos delivered a moving funeral oration on Niketas, *maistōr* of the school of St. Peter, a former schoolfellow of his. While Psellos devoted himself primarily to rhetoric, Niketas chose to become a teacher of grammar. At first, we are told, he was a *hypogrammateus,* not by choice but by law. He was already fit to be head of a school (*prokathēmenos*), but the law forbade this. In other schools, which had perhaps less institutional continuity, the older pupils helped teach the younger.

An anonymous teacher of grammar, and perhaps also of rhetoric, in Constantinople in the second quarter of the tenth century, in a letter to a court clergyman puts the matter thus: "I have pupils who pursue advanced studies, and I have entrusted to them the supervision of the less advanced, while maintaining the necessary control over their work." In another letter he writes that his older pupils interrogate the younger pupils in his presence and that he then fills in any omissions on their part. In another letter he claims that he personally checks the progress of all beginners in grammar twice a week. This use of pupils as assistant teachers is not merely an economic measure, since he states as a pedagogical principle that each student should confirm his own grasp of what he has learned by passing it on to others. The senior pupils who played the most important role as assistant teachers, and some of whom might go on to open schools of their own, formed a distinct group in the school, that of the "elect" or the "supervisors," and they seem to have enjoyed considerable independence and initiative.

Not all schools adopted these procedures, but it is unlikely that they were confined to the school of our anonymous teacher. He seems to have been, within the limitations of a traditional pedagogy, a conscientious and even imaginative teacher. Here is his report to another court clergyman on the progress of his nephew: "Your nephew is pursuing the appropriate course of studies. Twice a week his knowledge of what he is interrogated on is tested in my presence. He can repeat the text of the grammar by heart almost without error. In the Epimerisms (commentaries), he has completed the third Psalm. He can conjugate the third barytone conjugation, which he is learning by being questioned, and is taught to remember it by passing on his knowledge to others. May you continuously pray for him, and if I understand his character, our hopes for him will not be disappointed." The references are probably to the *Art of Grammar* of Dionysios the Thracian, the *Epimerisms* or grammatical commentary on the Psalms of George Choiroboskos (eighth/ninth century), and the classification of Greek verbs set out in the *Canons* of Theodosios of Alexandria (fourth century A.D.). Our anonymous professor was not so fortunate with all his pupils. Here is an extract from his letter to Alexander, metropolitan of Nicaea, a former professor of rhetoric himself:

> Since your children (probably his nephews) went about with their classmates and acted like them, devoting their attention mainly to quails and partridges, I had to divert them from such matters by admonition and punishment. I appealed to them repeatedly to obey their father's instructions and not to disregard his wishes, but without success. So I have decided to turn to you. I find them most inconsiderate toward their father, who in his turn is too clement with them. So I punished them, and they returned to their studies with diligence. But soon they once again found study boring, played truant, and passed their time buying pet birds. Once their father turned up by chance and found them occupied with these games. "Is this how you study? he asked, and went away. They should have come to me or to one of their classmates, or to their uncle. Instead, they stayed away from school. I asked their classmates about them and got different answers, some saying one thing, some another. Should they have taken refuge with you, please be gentle with them, since they come as suppliants. Should they have gone somewhere else, treat them like a good shepherd who brings the lost sheep back to the flock, so that they may not fall victim to the wolf.

Teachers often complained of the truancy of their pupils. When one thinks of the endless learning by heart involved in teaching literature in the age before printing, it is scarcely surprising that some decided to stay away from school. But there was also a social aspect to truancy. A teacher's pupils, especially in the capital, might include the sons or nephews of men whose wealth, social position, and influence put them far higher in the social pyramid than any teacher, however gifted or distinguished he might be. These youths tended to look on their teacher as a social inferior whose authority could be flouted with impunity. Theodore Hyrtakenos, teacher and minor man of letters in the early fourteenth century, writes to Theodore Metochites, chief minister of the emperor Andronikos II, in the following terms:

> I would have preferred to be present in person and to rebuke your son orally rather than in writing. Since I cannot because of the pressure of your affairs, which I would not wish to add to by my presence, I address you in absentia in writing. Your dear son is neglecting his studies and devoting himself to horsemanship; he gallops around and dashes through the streets at full tilt, speeding through hippodromes and theaters, arrogant and exultant. . . . I

have repeatedly rebuked him, but he neither blushed nor mended his ways. When he deserved it, he was beaten. Five days have now passed since he got his beating, during which he has not come to school nor paid the least attention to his studies. Horses and musical instruments are his delight. But if he did not have fine garments, nor wear a leather belt round his waist, nor ride horses with golden bridles, but traveled on foot, he himself would master his unreasonableness and not be ruled by it. It was my duty to deliver this message. It is for you to take thought henceforth for your son.

It is perhaps ironical that much of Hyrtakenos' correspondence is concerned with his own horse and his hopes of getting an allowance from the emperor for its fodder! But Hyrtakenos was a hardworking teacher of rhetoric, not a spoiled youth.

Here is a somewhat shortened account of how Michael Psellos' friend Niketas taught grammar in the school of St. Peter in the mid-eleventh century.

Grammar has long been treated as an elementary part of education, but he made it the art of arts and the science of sciences (the allusion is to a famous phrase of Aristotle), treating it as a rational structure. He carefully distinguished the dialects of Greek, and explained scientifically the rules of accentuation. He explained the sequence of verbs, the use of relative and other pronouns, and many other matters. His success in explaining poetry is proved by the number of his pupils who became examples to others. He knew that the Hellenes (that is, the pagan Greeks) spoke in riddles and concealed secret meanings beneath a trivial form, and he tore away the veil and revealed the hidden concepts. Thus the Golden Chain let down by Zeus from heaven to earth in a notoriously puzzling passage in Homer (*Iliad* 8.19–27) was for him the unmoving center of the revolving universe; the binding of Aregs represented the control of passion by the power of reason; the native land toward which Odysseus and his companions strove to return was a metaphor for the Heavenly Jerusalem.

This kind of allegorical interpretation of Homer goes back to the sixth century B.C. and was further developed by Stoics, Neo-Platonists, and Christians.

A memorial oration on Eustathios, master of the rhetoricians in the patriarchal school in Constantinople and later archbishop of Thessalonike in the last quarter of the twelfth century, describes in somewhat high-flown but nevertheless moving words the teaching of this remarkable man, who was recognized as a saint by the Orthodox Church; his portrait in fresco, dating from ca. 1320, can still be seen in the chapel of the Serbian royal monastery of Gračanica. Space permits only a few excerpts, sometimes in abbreviated form, from this text.

The lectures of Eustathios exuded honey like springs of nectar, so that his lessons penetrated to the inner depths of the souls of his listeners and remained indelible by the stream of oblivion. . . . In his daily classes he did not explain only the book in his hands, or elucidate obscurities in its interpretation. He added much material gathered from other books too, not because he gloried in inopportune digression from the matter in hand, but because he was inspired by it. . . . If a student, with a book of poetry under his arm, asked to be enlightened on the rules of meter and the rhythms of harmony and the etymology of words or the mythology of the ancients, he returned as a true initiate in these matters, acquainted with their profoundest secrets. How many who came to him as children were brought to manhood not by milk but by the solid food of learning. . . . How many who thought that they knew grammar well and could teach it to others, when they measured themselves against him realized how little they really knew? How many believed that they possessed the graces of rhetoric until they heard the Siren voice of Eustathios? How many appeared to excel in philosophy until they were compared with him and learned to know themselves and to recognize their own ignorance, and began to exchange opinion for knowledge?

Among other points that emerge from this passage is the blurring of the distinction between grammar, rhetoric, and philosophy in the teaching of the best professors in an age of innovation and exploration. Eustathios' immense commentaries on the *Iliad* and the *Odyssey*, though clearly not the verbatim text of his lectures, are certainly the fruit of long experience as a teacher, and give some idea of the richness and variety of his instruction.

Most teachers, however, were most of the time concerned with more mundane matters. One of their recurring problems was getting their fees paid. Even those who held official positions seem to have depended in part on fees from their pupils. The anonymous tenth-century teacher whom we have already met devotes several of his letters to reminding parents or guardians of their remissness in payment of fees. Unfortunately for modern scholars, actual sums are never mentioned. He does not seem in fact to have had a fixed scale of fees. In one letter he waives all claim to a fee because the addressee is a friend and the pupil a fellow countryman—probably from somewhere in Thrace—and at the same time thanks his correspondent for sending a small contribution. In another letter he tells his correspondent, probably a court official, that he always leaves his honorarium to the conscience of those who pay it, and never forces the issue. The Anonymous also complains to officials of the patriarchate and finally to the patriarch himself about the failure to pay him *eulogiai* (a religious term). This probably refers to some kind of retaining fee for teaching monks and clergy rather than to a regular salary. Even teachers holding imperial appointments did not always find it easy to get the salary due to them. Theodore Hyrtakenos writes to a series of high officials and finally to the emperor himself to request payment of what had been promised to him. This may well reflect not only bureaucratic delay but also the financial embarrassment of the Byzantine government during the disastrous reign of Andronikos II. However, such complaints are recorded from other periods too.

Another problem that a teacher might have to face was poaching of his pupils by another teacher. This was partly an economic matter, as loss of a pupil meant loss of fees. But it was also a question of prestige within a small professional group of hypersensitive individualists. Several letters of the anonymous tenth-century teacher complain of such poaching. In a letter to another *maistōr,* he writes: "I care nothing for this or that pupil whom you have enticed away from me either personally or through others, who knock on doors and kidnap my pupils as if they were my prisoners, like dogs who by swiftness of foot and keenness of scent flush out their prey for hunters. . . . It seems to me execrable and wholly alien to Christian behavior to persuade persons to poach pupils from one school and send them to another." In another, more vitriolic letter, he accuses a patriarchal official of conniving at such poaching. This sense of insecurity and mistrust of colleagues seems typical of a profession whose members enjoyed little institutional protection, unlike lawyers, notaries, and some other professional groups.

Relations between teachers, however, were not always so tense. Maximos Planoudes, monk, scholar, and polymath in the years after 1280, had wide literary and scientific interests, which ranged from Hellenistic poetry to the theory of numbers. He also knew Latin and translated many western texts into Greek, from Augustine's De Trinitate to the love poems of Ovid. In addition, he was head of a school in Constantinople that, though situated in a monastery, was in no sense a monastic school. There were at least two other schools enjoying imperial subvention in Constantinople toward the end of the thirteenth century. One was headed by a certain Chalkomatopoulos, the other by one Hyaleas. Planoudes' correspondence includes an interesting letter to Chalkomatopoulos in which he gently upbraids his correspondent for not giving enough attention to a pupil whom he had sent to Chalkomatopoulos' school.

> He is a talented youth and eager to learn. That is why I sent him to your school rather than to any other. For you are my friend and an excellent teacher. He is capable of absorbing more instruction. But his supervisors (probably older pupils acting as assistant teachers) are wasting his time. What he could learn in one day they do not cover in three. Please give him

your personal attention and instruct his supervisors to dictate more to him and devote more care to him. Why should he suffer like Tantalos in the midst of the water, and be given the same instruction as children coming straight from their nurse to school?

In another letter, to the archbishop of Crete, who lived in Constantinople because the Venetian rulers of Crete did not permit the Orthodox hierarchy to set foot on the island, he writes: "Your nephew is an enthusiastic student, and an even more enthusiastic teacher. His own enthusiasm elicits equal enthusiasm from me. He can count on getting this from me, since I hope and pray that my pupils' progress in their studies will be balanced by the development of their character and the acquisition and cultivation of virtue in other domains." The pupil in question was Manuel Moschopoulos, who later became a teacher himself and published many textbooks, including an edition of selections from classical Greek poetry with a commentary for school use and a grammar of classical Greek in the form of questions and answers. Some of his works survive in as many as sixty manuscripts and were evidently widely used by teachers for two centuries or more after their author's death. They may not display much evidence of original scholarship, but they were admirably adapted for school teaching.

A younger contemporary of Moschopoulos, George Thessalonike Lakapenos, taught both grammar and rhetoric in Thessaly, or perhaps in Thessalonike, in the second quarter of the fourteenth century. He, too, was the author of a number of schoolbooks. His selection of 264 of the two thousand letters of Libanios, with an elementary commentary, was intended for students of rhetoric and survives in many manuscripts. He also published a collection of his own correspondence with Andronikos Zaridas, a pupil of Planoudes. They have little concrete content—what they may have had was removed from them when they were prepared for publication as models of style—but they are good examples of the mannered Atticizing Greek that was much prized in the fourteenth century. This is no doubt why he equipped them with a long word-by-word commentary. A short work on grammar and an elementary commentary on the first two books of the *Iliad* are also attributed to him in some manuscripts.

The editorial activities of Moschopoulos and Lakapenos, and of others among their contemporaries, suggest that the early fourteenth century saw a change in methods and approach among teachers of Greek grammar and rhetoric. Less Homer was read, and more of other authors' works, in particular plays of Sophocles and Euripides and prose texts of the Second Sophistic, such as the *Descriptions of Pictures* of Philostratos. At the same time a body of rather elementary grammatical, rhetorical, and mythological commentary replaced the older scholia, which contained much of the debris of the scholarship of classical antiquity. Just what this change may have signified concerning the attitude of Byzantine teachers and their pupils toward their classical heritage is too complex a question to be treated adequately here.

Late Byzantine teachers sometimes display an unexpected interest in and familiarity with the scientific literature of antiquity, and in particular with astronomical literature. This is probably due in part to the more prominent role played by astrology in Byzantine life, but it also bears witness to a partial abandonment of the narrowly literary tone that had marked Greek education since Hellenistic times. Thus Demetrios Triklinios (ca. 1280–ca. 1340), a teacher of grammar in Thessalonike in the early fourteenth century, whose knowledge of ancient metrical treatises enabled him to correct many errors in the traditional text of the Attic dramatists, was also author of a short treatise on the phases of the moon. Barlaam of Calabria wrote a commentary on part of the *Elements* of Euclid and short treatises on the solar eclipses of 1333 and 1337. In this respect, teachers followed the general intellectual current of the age. Statesmen and private scholars like Theodore Metochites and his pupil Nikephoros Gregoras, clergymen like John Chortasmenos (ca. 1370–1435/7), doctors such as George Chrysokokkes and Gregory Chioniades—who later became bishop of Tabriz in Persia—the moralist and poet Theodore Meliteniotes, all wrote serious studies in the field of mathematical astronomy, sometimes drawing on Arabic or Persian astronomical literature.

It has already been noted that holders of high state offices sometimes devoted their spare time to some form of teaching. Photios, before becoming patriarch in 858, held a kind of seminar in his house, which he describes nostalgically in a famous letter to Pope Nicholas I, written immediately after his elevation to the patriarchate.

> I lived at home in enjoyment of pleasing delights, watching the labor of my students, their eager questioning, and their conversation, through which ideas are most easily brought to light, while some sharpened their minds by mathematical studies, others tracked down the truth by logical procedures, still others trained their minds to piety by studying the Holy Scriptures, which is the fruit of all other labor. Such was the company that surrounded me at home. When I left for the imperial palace, I was sent on my way by their prayers for my speedy return. . . . When I returned, that same wise company met me before my door; some of them, to whom great familiarity had been granted because of their exceeding virtue, upbraided me for my delay; for some it was enough to greet me; for others it sufficed to show that they had awaited me.

Photios' pupils, if we may so call them, were probably adolescents, if not older. The same appears to be true of the pupils of other men in exalted positions. Michael Psellos had such a circle of pupils or admirers whom he taught at home while holding a post in the imperial court. In the period after the Byzantine restoration in 1261, several high civil servants had a circle of pupils who met in their house. Theodore Metochites, chief minister of Andronikos II until his downfall in 1328, taught mathematics and astronomy to such a group, apparently with encouragement from the emperor. Metochites' pupil and protégé Nikephoros Gregoras gathered around himself a circle of like-minded young men, which met regularly to study rhetoric, philosophy, and mathematics. These gatherings probably resembled graduate seminars or meetings of learned societies rather than ordinary school classes. In one such gathering, we find Gregoras expounding his proposals for reform of the calendar. Such groups were not confined to the capital. The philologist Thomas Magistros invited Joseph the Philosopher, teacher and friend of Theodore Metochites and Nikephoros Gregoras, to visit the "seminars" (*syllogoi*) in Thessalonike and address them.

In the last decades of the Byzantine Empire, George Scholarios, the future patriarch Gennadios, taught Aristotelian philosophy to a private circle. This development of private teaching by men of learning whose principal activity lay elsewhere, though it had roots in Byzantine practice going back to the ninth century and perhaps earlier, is probably a symptom of the final breakdown of state and church patronage of higher education. It may also reflect the increasing acquaintance of Byzantines with the emergent universities of Italy and the systematic instruction in philosophy and mathematics that they provided. Demetrios Kydones, chief minister of Manual II, observes that "the study of the Stoa and the Peripatos now flourishes among the Italians." And George Scholarios, in spite of his rigidly anti-Roman theological stance, was a great admirer of the teachers of philosophy in the West. Many Byzantines had begun to realize that they might have something to learn from the despised and often hated Latins.

The West in its turn was becoming more and more aware of what it had to learn from Byzantine professors. The importance of the Greek contribution to the Italian Renaissance has been the subject of dispute since the seventeenth century, and this is not the place to reexamine the arguments in detail or in depth. It is now generally agreed that the origin of Renaissance humanism lay in the interplay of internal factors in the society of the cities of Italy and did not depend on external influence. But the contribution of Byzantine scholars and teachers, both before and after 1453, to the development of the form and content of humanist culture was significant, precisely because it satisfied a preexisting demand. That contribution was made up of various components.

First of all, Byzantine scholars brought with them Greek texts that were either unknown in the West or available only in inadequate Latin translations made in the medieval manner *ad verbum,* often made not from the Greek original, but from an Arabic translation, which itself was sometimes a rendering of a Syriac translation. We cannot reconstruct the library that the professor and diplomat Manuel Chrysoloras brought with him when he came to Florence in 1397 at the invitation of the Signoria to teach Greek. We know, however, that it included Homer, Thucydides, Plato, Isocrates, Demosthenes, and Plutarch. No doubt he also brought such teaching texts as Aphthonios and Hermogenes, as well as elementary grammatical treatises. In particular, he brought with him a copy of St. Basil's *Address to Young Men on Reading Hellenic Literature,* an influential work of which more than eighty manuscripts survive. It was eagerly seized upon by Chrysoloras' Italian pupils and was translated into Latin by Leonardo Bruni. Inasmuch as it provided the justification of an unchallengeable authority for the study of the pagan literature of antiquity, this short text supported the growing emphasis on *studia humanitatis* against powerful opposition from some ecclesiastical quarters, and so helped to shape the culture of the early Renaissance. Later teachers who came to Italy from Constantinople all brought books in their baggage, and so rapidly built up the stock of Greek texts available to the Italian humanists.

Next, Byzantine teachers introduced a style of teaching and a whole educational tradition that was unfamiliar in the West. From the writings of Bruni, Guarino of Verona, and others, we can form some idea of the enthusiasm that Chrysoloras' teaching aroused. He encouraged his pupils to look beyond the general structure of the texts they read and to examine the tropes and figures, the devices and ornaments of style, the individual words and syllables. In other words, they were taught to go beyond the Ciceronian principles of rhetoric and make use of the more subtle and sophisticated analytical procedures of Hermogenes. They were also to use their sense of language and style to detect and, if possible, emend errors in the manuscripts they used. A generation later, Michael Apostoles, a much less gifted teacher than Chrysoloras, emphasized how much his method of teaching differed from that current in the West. This critical approach to literature soon spread from the domain of Greek to that of Latin, and eventually even to the sacred preserve of biblical studies.

Third, many of the Greek scholars who came to teach in Italy possessed or soon acquired a sovereign command of Latin and played an important role in the translation of Greek texts. Translations, sometimes with commentaries, made by men like Theodore Gaza (ca. 1400–1476) and John Argyropoulos (ca. 1445–ca. 1487) not only made available many hitherto unknown Greek works but set a standard of philological accuracy that served as a model for others.

Finally, Greek teachers brought to the West not merely texts of Plato and Aristotle but also those of their ancient and medieval commentators, especially those on Aristotle. These revolutionized western attitudes to *il maestro di color che sanno* ("the master of those who know"). The late Byzantine disputes on the relative merits of Plato and Aristotle, which themselves reflected a long-standing tension within Byzantine culture, were made known in the West by the lectures that Plethon gave during the Council of Florence in 1438. One of the indirect results of this was the foundation of the Platonic Academy of Florence and the Platonic translations of Marsilio Ficino. This new input helped shape the whole of Renaissance philosophical thought. Indeed, it can be said with some reason that, without the contributions of Greek teachers, Renaissance philosophy would never have broken loose from the straitjacket of medieval scholasticism.

The influence of Greek teachers in the early Renaissance spread far beyond the bounds of Italy. One example will suffice to illustrate how the knowledge, the texts, and the values they brought with them from Byzantium were eagerly welcomed beyond the Alps. Pier Paolo Vergerio was a native of Capo d'Istria, which was in Hungarian territory in the early fifteenth century. He studied in Florence, learned Greek from Manuel Chrysoloras, and became a friend of Coluccio Salutati, Leonardo Bruni, and Guarino of Verona, all fellow pupils of Chrysoloras. In 1414 he accompanied Emperor Sigismund to the Council of Constance and then returned with him to Buda, where he lived and taught for the next twenty-six years. He gathered round himself a group of Hungarian humanists, among whom was János Vitéz, bishop of Várad, a scholar and collector of manuscripts. Vitéz, encouraged by Vergerio, sent his nephew János to Ferrara to study Greek under Guarino of Verona. The nephew later became bishop of Pećs and a notable Latin poet. In Pećs he founded the first library of Greek books in Hungary. Meanwhile King János Hunyadi, the last Crusader, appointed Vitéz as teacher of his son and successor, Matthias. Matthias not only built up a magnificent library of Greek and Latin manuscripts, later known as the Bibliotheca Corviniana, but also sponsored a grandiose international program of translation of Greek texts into Latin. Among those taking part in this project were Angelo Poliziano and Marsilio Ficino, both of whom had studied Greek in Florence under John Argyropoulos of Constantinople. It was in such ways as this that Greek schoolmasters helped directly, or indirectly through their pupils, to shape the common culture of Europe.

Selected Bibliography

Primary Sources

Browning, R. "A New Source on Byzantine-Hungarian Relations in the Twelfth Century: The Inaugural Lecture of Michael ho tou Anchialou as Hypatos ton Philosophon," *Balkan Studies*, vol. 2, pp. 173–214. Thessaloniki, 1961.

―――. "The Correspondence of a Tenth-Century Byzantine Scholar." *Byzantion* 24 (1954): 397–452; reprinted in idem, *Studies on Byzantine History, Literature and Education*. Variorum Reprints, London, 1977.

Browning, R., and B. Laourdas. "To keimenon tōn epistolōn tou kodikos BM Add. 36749." *Epeteris Hetaireias Byzantinōn Spudōn* 27 (1957): 151–212.

Choricii Gazaei opera, critical edition by R. Foerster and E. Richsteig, pp. 109–28. Leipzig, 1929.

Die Gedichte des Christophoros Mitylenaios, ed. E. Kurtz. Leipzig, 1903.

Eustathii archiepiscopi Thessalonicensis Commentarii ad Homeri Iliadem pertinentes, ed. M. van der Valk. 4 vols. Leiden, 1971–87.

Hermogenis opera, ed. H. Rabe. Leipzig, 1913.

Laourdas, B. "He syllogē epistolōn tou kodikos BM Add. 36749." *Athenā* 58 (1954): 176–98.

La Port-du Theil, F. J. G. In *Notices et extraits des manuscrits de la Bibliothèque Nationale*, vol. 5, pp. 709–44, and vol. 6, pp. 1–48. Paris, 1798, 1800 (edition of the text by Teodoro Irtaceno).

Maximi monachi Planudis Epistulae, ed. M. Treu. Breslau, 1890.

Michael Akominatou tou Choniatou ta sōzomena, ed. Sp. P. Lampros, vol. 1, pp. 283–300. Athens, 1879.

Photii patriarchae Constantinopolitani Epistulae et Amphilochia, critical edition by B. Laourdas and L. G. Westerink, vol. 3, Ep. 290. Leipzig, 1985.

Prolegomenon Sylloge, ed. H. Rabe, pp. 80–81. Leipzig, 1931.

Rhetores graeci, ed. C. Walz, vol. 1, pp. 59–120 and 423–525. Stuttgart, 1832.

Saint Basil. *Aux jeunes gens sur la manière de tirer profit des lettres helléniques*, éd. and trans. F. Boulenger. Paris, 1935.

Sathas, C. *Mesaionikē Bibliothekē*, vol. 5, pp. 87–96. Venice, 1876.

General Literature

Bolgar, R. R. *The Classical Heritage and its Beneficiaries*. Cambridge, 1954.

Browning, R. "The Patriarchal School at Constantinople in the Twelfth Century." *Byzantion* 32 (1962): 167–202; 33 (1963): 11–40; reprinted in idem, *Studies on Byzantine History, Literature and Education*. Variorum Reprints, London, 1977.

Constantinides, C. N. *Higher Education in Byzantium in the Thirteenth and Early Fourteenth Centuries, 1204–ca. 1310*. Nicosia, 1982.

Fuchs, H. *Die höheren Schulen von Konstantinopel im Mittelalter*. Leipzig, 1926.

Harris, W. V. *Ancient Literacy*, pp. 285–322. Cambridge, Mass., 1989.

Lemerle, P. *Le premier humanisme byzantin*. Paris, 1971.

Marrou, H.-I. *Histoire de l'éducation dans l'antiquité*. Paris, 1948.

Wilson, N. G. *Scholars of Byzantium*. Baltimore, 1983.

5

WOMEN
Alice-Mary Talbot

ONLY DURING THE PAST two decades have Byzantine women, with the exception of empresses, begun to receive serious scholarly attention, and the picture is not yet complete. Researchers are hampered by the fact that almost all the Byzantines who preserved records of their civilization—be they historians, jurists, or hagiographers— were men and their writings tend to focus on the activities of their male colleagues. Historical sources, which emphasize political affairs and court intrigues, diplomacy, religious controversies, and military struggles, primarily the domains of men, rarely mention women except for members of the imperial family. In the Lives of male saints, women appear on the periphery as the mothers or sisters of the ascetic or perhaps as pilgrims to a shrine or beneficiaries of a miracle. The biographies of the relatively few Byzantine women who were recognized as saints are precious sources of information because of their rarity. Likewise, fewer rules survive for nunneries than for their male counterparts; in fact, it is likely that fewer were written, as male monasteries vastly outnumbered nunneries in the Byzantine Empire. Compilations of civil and canon law with the pertinent commentaries, as well as the decisions of ecclesiastical courts, are more fertile sources on the legal status of women, a subject that still awaits systematic investigation. Monastic acts, especially those recording gifts to monasteries, shed some light on the role of female property owners, as do the few extant wills written by women.

Perusal of the surviving texts suggests an ambivalence toward women in the patriarchal society of Byzantium, best symbolized by the frequently expressed antithesis between Eve, endlessly reviled as the temptress who persuaded Adam to eat of the forbidden Tree of Knowledge and thus was the cause of original sin, and the Virgin Mary, venerated as the pure and immaculate Mother of God, whose Son came to cleanse mankind of its sins and offer the possibility of salvation and eternal life. The ninth-century poet Kassia neatly summed up the dual nature of women in the exchange she is reported to have had with Emperor Theophilos. When he pointedly attacked Eve, stating that "a woman was the fount and source of all man's tribulation," Kassia immediately sprang to the defense of her sex, retorting that "and from a woman sprang the course of man's regeneration."

There was always a tension in Byzantium between the Christian ascetic ideal of virginity and celibacy, and the promotion of marriage, which provided a legitimized outlet for sexual relations and the procreation of children, indispensable for the perpetuation of the population. Marriage was, after all, a sacrament of the church, and the family was the basic unit of society. The most important role of women was to bear children, and it is as mothers that they are most often praised. There are frequent descriptions of women as tender and loving nurturers, who were concerned not only for the physical well-being of their offspring but also for their spiritual welfare, teaching them the Psalms and telling Bible stories or tales of holy men and women. In romances, women are praised for their beauty, and their loving relationships are portrayed in a positive fashion.

On the other hand, women were constantly viewed with suspicion as sexual temptresses, were considered periodically unclean during menstrual periods and for forty days after childbirth, and were characterized as weak and untrustworthy. As a result, they were the victims of many forms of discrimination, for example, in some aspects of their legal status, in their access to education, and in their freedom of movement. They were also negatively portrayed in literature, both overtly and through unconscious choice of language and metaphors, such as the description of sins as female.

With few exceptions, those rare women who were considered to have attained sanctity were consecrated virgins and thus had rejected sexuality, or were widows whose conjugal life had ended. The ideal for saintly women was to deny their femininity and emulate men; some female ascetics ate so little that their breasts shriveled up and their menstrual periods ceased. It is significant that abbesses were encouraged to marshal their troops, to heal spiritually ailing nuns, to supervise a rigorous training regimen for their charges, even though the role of general, physician, and athletic trainer was normally limited to men. Even the occasional woman writer was not always immune from presenting a negative stereotype of her sex. Thus Theodora Synadene, the foundress of the Palaiologan convent of the Virgin of Sure Hope, urged its abbess to rise above her innate feminine weakness, to "gird her loins in a manly fashion," and to assume a manly and masculine temperament. A few years earlier, the dowager empress Theodora Palaiologina, foundress of the nunnery of Lips, stated that women are weak by nature and require strong protection.

Byzantine legislation did protect some rights of women, for example, their rights to inherit and bequeath property. Sons and daughters were entitled to equal portions of the family property. A woman was assured of her ultimate ownership of the dowry that her family presented to her husband at the time of marriage. This right to inherit and transmit family property enabled many women to amass considerable wealth, which they could use for patronage of the arts, for charitable purposes, to found a monastery, to buy more land, or to invest in a business. However, much legislation, for example, the laws on divorce and adultery, discriminated against women and placed them in a disadvantageous position. Women did go to court to appear as plaintiffs, defendants, or witnesses, but in general their testimony was considered less reliable than that of men. A synodal act of 1400 declared that the evidence of a certain Anna Palaiologina was not trustworthy because she was a woman and because she contradicted herself. The provision of the *Institutes* of Justinian that women could not witness a will was repeated by later legislation. Novel 48 of Leo VI forbade women to act as witnesses for business contracts, justifying the new law on the grounds that women should not frequent law courts where a lot of men are present and should not become involved in matters belonging to the male domain. The same law did provide, however, that women should be permitted to testify in certain situations pertaining to the female sphere, for example, with regard to the birth of a child. Moreover, despite the legal prohibitions, a number of documents bear the signatures of women witnesses.

THE THREE PHASES OF WOMEN'S LIVES

The life of the average Byzantine woman can be divided into three stages: girlhood, the period of marriage and motherhood, and, finally, if she survived her husband, widowhood and old age.

GIRLHOOD

Childhood was brief and perilous in Byzantium, even more so for girls since boys received preferential treatment. Parents prayed for male children and rejoiced twice as much at the birth of a boy, as we are told in a poem of Theodore Prodromos. There is some evidence of the use of female infanticide (by suffocation or abandonment along the roadside) to control the size of families, even though the practice was forbidden by both civil and canon law. Girls seem to have been weaned somewhat earlier than their brothers and were thus more vulnerable in infancy and early childhood to infectious diseases. As a result, their mortality was evidently somewhat higher than that of boys.

There were few educational opportunities for girls. They probably did not attend regular schools, but from the age of six or seven were taught at home by their parents or tutors. The reference made by Michael Psellos to the "fellow students" of his daughter Styliane suggests that sometimes a tutor may have taught a group of girls. More formal lessons were provided at convents, but they were usually limited to young orphans being raised at the nunnery or youthful novices who planned to take vows. With few exceptions, education for girls was limited to learning to read and write, memorizing the Psalms, and studying the Scriptures. Women of the aristocracy had more opportunities to pursue learning, and a number of them developed a serious interest in literature. Nonetheless, even a woman like Irene Choumnaina, who was praised by a contemporary historian for her depth of knowledge and her devotion to the study of the Scriptures and ecclesiastical doctrine, wrote letters marred by errors in spelling and grammar. Only in unusual circumstances, such as that of the imperial princess Anna Komnene, did a young girl read a wide range of ancient authors and study a variety of disciplines; and even in her case, as George Tornikes relates, her parents did not at first encourage her study of secular literature.

Information on the activities of girls before marriage is extremely limited but suggests that unmarried maidens spent most of their time in the seclusion of their homes, protected from the gaze of strange men and from threats to their virginity. When imperial messengers arrived at the home of Philaretos the Merciful in search of a suitable bride for Emperor Constantine VI, Philaretos was distressed when they asked to see his granddaughters, "for even though we are poor, our daughters have never left their chambers." Theodore of Stoudios commended his mother for her protection of her daughter from contact with men, and Kekaumenos advised fathers to keep their daughters confined and invisible. If girls did leave their homes for such socially acceptable purposes as attending church services, they were strictly chaperoned by parents, relatives, or maidservants. The Life of St. Nikon mentions a girl who was sent to the well by her mother to fetch water, but she evidently belonged to a lower-class family.

Thus young girls devoted most of their youth to learning domestic skills in preparation for married life and running a household. They would learn to spin, weave, and embroider at an early age. One of the few surviving descriptions of girlhood is found in the encomium written by Michael Psellos for his only daughter Styliane, who died at the age of about nine or ten, probably of smallpox. He praises her piety, modesty, and skill with the needle; as a scholar he also approved of her devotion to learning. Styliane attended church services regularly, both matins and vespers, enjoyed singing the Psalms and hymns, and was very attached to certain icons. At a tender age she became engaged in charitable work, helping to care for the sick and poor. The child was openly affectionate, embracing and kissing her parents and sitting on their knees; her death was a great blow to Psellos and his wife.

One of the few forms of recreation available to young girls was excursions to a public bath, where they might linger to chat with friends and share a picnic. A well-brought-up young woman like Theophano, the future wife of Leo VI, did not venture forth to the bath until dusk so as to reduce the chances of being exposed to the glances of strangers; she was carefully chaperoned by servants while outside the house. Girls also accompanied their parents on outings to visit shrines, see a holy man, or watch a procession. They had dolls made of wax or clay, and played catch with a soft leather ball or a game similar to jacks (*pentalitha*) using five stones. They also enjoyed games of make-believe: Theodoret of Cyrrhus describes little girls who dressed up as monks and demons. The biographer of Symeon the Fool, however, looked askance at girls singing in the street, remarking that they would grow up to be prostitutes.

MARRIAGE AND MOTHERHOOD

Betrothal

For most girls in Byzantium, childhood came to an abrupt end with the onset of puberty, which was usually soon followed by betrothal and marriage. Early marriage and procreation of children was the norm in Byzantium; the only alternative for teenage girls was entrance into a convent. Byzantine legislation originally permitted betrothal of a girl after the age of seven, a figure later raised to twelve. The laws were frequently ignored, however, and children as young as five years old might become engaged. The minimum age for marriage was twelve for girls and fourteen for boys, but the more normal age at marriage may have been closer to fifteen and twenty respectively. Very rarely we read of women marrying in their twenties, as in the case of Thomais of Lesbos who did not take a husband until she was twenty-four. One reason for the promotion of teenage marriage was the emphasis on the virginity of the bride. Another, unstated reason may have been the desire to make the most of the childbearing years; because of the high rate of infant mortality, a woman had to bear many children to insure the survival of a few. Furthermore, since many women died young (if they survived infancy, they had an average life expectancy of about thirty-five years), it behooved them to marry and begin producing children as soon as physically possible.

Marriages were arranged by the parents, for whom economic considerations and family connections were paramount. The betrothal ceremony included the presentation of *arrha sponsalicia,* a prenuptial gift, by the family of the groom, and took on the nature of a formal contract guaranteeing the engagement. If the girl broke off the engagement, her family had to return the engagement gift to the groom, supplemented by a like sum. If the groom terminated the engagement, the girl was entitled to retain the *arrha*. Normally girls accepted the bridegroom selected by their families, although there was occasional resistance, both by girls who preferred to take monastic vows and live as consecrated virgins, and by girls who violently objected to the groom selected for them. A twelve-year-old girl from Epiros, for example, betrothed from the age of five, threatened suicide if she was forced to go through with the marriage; her family managed to have the betrothal annulled in the courts. The records of the ecclesiastical courts preserve evidence of the tragic results of some of the premature betrothals and marriages, such as a girl whose marriage was consummated at age eleven, causing permanent damage to her sexual organs. Around the year 1300, Simonis, the daughter of Emperor Andronikos II, married at age five to the middle-aged ruler of Serbia, was also injured by premature sexual intercourse so that she was rendered incapable of childbearing.

The presentation of a dowry to the bridegroom by the bride's parents was an essential element of marriage. The bride retained life ownership of the dowry, which represented her share of her family inheritance, but her husband was granted the usufruct of the cash or property and rights over its administration. If the husband predeceased his wife or the marriage ended in divorce, the wife was entitled to recover full control of the dowry. On the other hand, if she predeceased her husband, then the dowry reverted to her family (if she was childless) or was inherited by her children, although the husband continued to administer it as long as he lived. The marriage contract also provided for the husband to make a substantial gift to his wife. Originally called the *donatio propter nuptias* ("marriage gift") and in the Justinianic period equal in amount to the dowry, the husband's required contribution decreased over the centuries. From the ninth century on, this gift was termed *hypobolon*, and typically was one-half to one-third the size of the dowry. If the husband died first and the couple was childless, his wife received the full *hypobolon*; if there were children, she shared the *hypobolon* with them. From the tenth century on, a supplemental wedding gift by the groom, the *theōrētron*, is also attested. It amounted to one-twelfth of the dowry, was completely under the control of the wife, and remained her exclusive property if the marriage was terminated by death or divorce.

Romantic Love

Although arrangement of marriage by parents was the norm, romantic love affairs were by no means unknown in Byzantium. At the upper levels of society, one could mention Andronikos I's passionate attachment to

Philippa, daughter of Raymond of Poitiers, with whom he dallied in Antioch, and his affair with his cousin Theodora Komnene, with whom he eloped to the Caucasus. The Life of Irene of Chrysobalanton preserves the sad tale of an engaged couple from Cappadocia. The young woman decided to break off the betrothal and take monastic vows in Constantinople, but soon realized that she had made a terrible mistake: she was hopelessly consumed with love for her fiancé, tried in vain to escape from the convent, and threatened to commit suicide if she could not see him. The young man also could not forget his betrothed and resorted to a sorcerer to help him regain his lost love. In the end the abbess Irene was herself forced to burn figurines of the embracing lovers in order to rid the nun of her passionate attachment to her former betrothed. The same work tells the story of the vinedresser Nicholas who fell in love with a nun at the convent whose vineyard he tended.

A sympathy for romantic love is reflected in the continuing popularity, at least in some circles, of late antique romances and the revival of this genre beginning in the twelfth century. They were sometimes interpreted allegorically as the struggle of the soul for salvation and its yearning for God, but must also have been enjoyed as works of escapist adventure. The epic poem *Digenes Akritas* includes many romantic episodes, notably Digenes' wooing of Eudokia. The youthful hero, who catches sight of Eudokia leaning from her window, is so smitten with her beauty that he is unable to eat or drink and returns to her castle to steal her away.

Wedding Ceremonies

Weddings consisted of the marriage rite and the attendant ceremonies and celebrations. Following a ritual bath, the bride donned white garments and left for the church. There the couple was blessed by a priest, who placed marriage crowns on their heads; the bride and groom also exchanged rings and shared a cup of wine. The couple was then escorted to the groom's house by a joyful crowd of well-wishers who sang special marriage songs called *epithalamia*. A wedding feast ensued, during the course of which the newly married couple retired to their bedroom. There the groom presented his bride with a marriage belt and their union was consummated while the wedding guests continued their revelries. In *Digenes Akritas,* the festivities lasted for three months.

The Conception and Birth of Children

The primary purpose of marriage was the procreation of children, who would continue the family line, transmit family property from one generation to the next, support their parents in old age, and assure their proper burial and posthumous commemoration. Hence barrenness was a great sorrow for a woman and her husband; Digenes Akritas and his wife were saddened daily by "the unquenchable and most grievous flame of child-lessness." A common theme in hagiography is the infertility of the future saint's parents, suggesting that this may indeed have been a problem for many couples in the medieval period. The parents of the future saintly empress Theophano (the first wife of Leo VI), for example, lamented their inability to have a child, viewing it as a fate "more bitter than death." They finally managed to conceive a child after daily visits to a church in Constantinople, where they entreated the Virgin with lengthy prayers to bless them with a baby. Some women resorted to concoctions made from rabbit blood, goose fat, or turpentine, which were rumored to promote fertility. Other sterile couples had recourse to physicians. In the Life of Antony the Younger, a landowner promised a doctor one-third of his estate if he could help them have a child. The physician (who was really the saint in disguise) demanded instead a payment of ten warhorses, to which the husband readily agreed. Magical fertility amulets were also a popular means of warding off barrenness. Some women became so desperate that they feigned pregnancy and delivery, presenting their husbands with a supposititious heir acquired from a poor woman who could not afford to raise another child. Other couples adopted a baby, as did Michael Psellos after the death of Styliane. At the time of intercourse, the husband and wife might use various folk remedies or superstitious practices in an effort to influence the sex of the child they hoped to conceive.

Most women were anxious to produce a large number of children in order to insure the survival of a few, and did not attempt to practice any form of birth control. Breast-feeding, which normally lasted two to three years, served as a natural (although unreliable) form of contraception, and thus helped to space out the arrival of children. Even so, in some cases where precise figures on the birth dates of children in a given family are available, they were born only a year or so apart, but we do not know whether these babies were breastfed. The mother of Gregory Palamas, for example, gave birth to five children in eight years, as did Helena Sphrantzes, the wife of the fifteenth-century historian. The fate of Helena's children vividly illustrates the high infant mortality of the era, as only two of the five children survived; of the others, one died at eight days, one at thirty days, and the third just before his sixth birthday.

Women normally delivered their children at home with the assistance of a midwife and female relatives or neighbors. Manuscript illustrations show women giving birth in seated and standing positions, and lying on a bed, and a birthing chair is included in a list of surgical instruments. In special circumstances, women might go to lying-in hospitals, as in the case of destitute refugee women in seventh-century Alexandria. Patriarch John the Almsgiver established seven maternity wards in various parts of the city, each ward containing forty beds. The women were permitted to remain at these hospitals for a week after they had given birth, and were then given one-third of a gold coin on their departure.

In cases of difficult labor or complications in childbirth, women resorted to medical, magical, and spiritual assistance. Thus Anna, the mother of St. Theophano, was miraculously aided during a painful labor by the girdle that her husband brought her from a church of the Virgin. A woman in labor for twenty days was finally able to give birth after St. Luke the Stylite offered her some holy bread and water. The Life of St. Ignatios relates the tale of a woman who was unable to deliver because the baby was incorrectly positioned. The surgeons were prepared to perform an embryotomy, that is, to cut up and remove the fetus in order to save the mother. The baby's life was spared, however, for a piece of the saint's cloak placed on the abdomen of the mother enabled the delivery to proceed normally. It was in fact sometimes necessary for physicians, as a final resort, to proceed with the embryotomy, and lists of surgical instruments include tools for dismembering a fetus. There is no evidence that Byzantine surgeons performed Caesarean sections. Higher female mortality resulted in part from the perils of childbearing, as women died prematurely from miscarriages, complications of delivery, and from infection or hemorrhage during the postpartum period. The process of childbirth was regarded as unclean, and the new mother was excluded from communion for forty days after delivery, unless she was in danger of dying.

The newly delivered infant was bathed and tightly swaddled. Most women breastfed their babies, but wet nurses were used if the mother's milk failed or if she died in childbirth. There is also evidence that women of the upper classes were more likely to use wet nurses as a matter of convenience. A party was held to celebrate the birth of the child, and relatives, friends, and neighbors came to visit the parents and wish the baby health and long life.

Contraception and Abortion

If a couple did decide to limit the number of children after two or three of their offspring had survived the dangerous childhood years, one method of birth control was total abstinence from sexual intercourse; henceforth husband and wife lived together as brother and sister. Little information survives on the subject of contraceptive devices and potions, but it seems that they were used primarily by prostitutes, adulterous married women, or unmarried women engaged in an illicit love affair. These women might make use of herbal ointments or suppositories that served as spermicides or barriers preventing fertilization of the egg; the vaginal pessaries were usually made of wool soaked in honey, alum, white lead, or olive oil. Women might also resort to magical means of contraception, such as the amulets recommended by Aetios of Amida consisting of a portion of a cat's liver or (even more impractical) of the womb of a lioness worn in an ivory tube attached to the left foot.

Abortion was strongly condemned by both civil and canon law, and was punished with such penalties as exile, flogging, or excommunication. Yet inevitably many women resorted to it to terminate unwanted pregnancies, especially prostitutes and other single women, such as slave girls who feared the wrath of their masters, or even nuns. Thus, before she married Emperor Justinian, the actress/prostitute Theodora reportedly underwent many abortions. On one occasion, however, her pregnancy was sufficiently advanced that she was unsuccessful in aborting it and bore a son. Prokopios comments that she probably would have killed the unwanted infant, but he was rescued by his father. A fourteenth-century synodal document records the case of a nun from the Constantinopolitan convent of St. Andrew in Krisei who had intercourse with Joasaph, a monk from the Hodegon monastery. When she became pregnant, Joasaph sought out a physician-sorcerer from whom he purchased an abortifacient potion for the substantial sum of 5 gold hyperpyra plus a cloak and a glass vessel from Alexandria. The drug did produce the desired effect, but the monk's transgression came to light and he was punished by the synod. Another method of inducing abortions was to place a heavy weight on the abdomen.

Running the Household

In Byzantium the running of a domestic household was labor-intensive: food was prepared from scratch, cosmetics and ointments were concocted, and all stages of garment making from carding wool to sewing the cloth into garments were carried out in the home. In lower-class households, women performed these necessary duties themselves, for example, child care and food preparation (sometimes including the grinding of grain). The wife of Philaretos the Merciful baked bread, gathered wild greens, and roasted meats. Women were responsible for cleaning and laundering as well as for domestic cloth making. Women of the upper classes instructed and supervised maidservants in these tasks but seem to have remained involved in spinning and weaving despite their social status. As George Tornikes commented in his funeral oration for Anna Komnene, "women are born for spinning and weaving." Even though there were professional male weavers, the distaff and loom were inextricably linked with women in the popular consciousness, and cloth making was considered to be the most appropriate occupation for them. Michael Psellos criticized the eleventh-century empress Zoe because she did not engage in the activities normally performed by women, namely, spinning and weaving. Wives of artisans may have assisted their husbands in the workshop, which was normally located in the same building as the living quarters. In the countryside the concept of household was even broader, and peasant women's domain extended to the garden and vineyard outside the house.

Dress and Jewelry

Because of the prevalent ideal of modesty for Byzantine women, they wore garments that concealed virtually all of their body except for their hands. Typical garb was a full-length, long-sleeved tunic, with additional layers added as necessary for warmth. Lower-class women might wear sleeveless tunics. Proper women were always expected to have their heads covered when they were out in public, wearing the *maphorion,* a shoulder-length veil, over a tight headdress that concealed their hair.

Despite these restrictions, however, women of means devoted much attention to their personal appearance, spending large sums of money on finely woven fabrics, sometimes embroidered and encrusted with precious stones. They further adorned their garments with brooches and jeweled sashes or belts, and wore elegant headdresses. They adorned their hair with hairpins and ornamented mesh nets and bands. The numerous preserved examples of jewelry, including earrings, bracelets, and necklaces, demonstrate the fine workmanship of Byzantine goldsmiths and the wealth of the upper classes, as well as the popularity of costume jewelry among poorer women. Much to the dismay of the church fathers, women also tried to enhance their natural beauty with cosmetics: they used bean flour to wash their faces, powdered their faces to make their complexion fairer, reddened their lips and cheeks, dyed their eyebrows black, and used eye shadow and hair dye.

Marital Relations, Divorce, and Adultery

As in other societies in which betrothals are arranged by the parents, couples in Byzantium had no expectation of romantic love in marriage but viewed their union as a sacrament ordained by God for the perpetuation of the family and, secondarily, as the merger of the economic assets of two families. The woman was expected to be obedient and subservient to her husband, to produce heirs, and to run the household. For the most part the arranged marriage seems to have worked well, and often true affection and even love developed between husband and wife. There were instances, however, in which the couple was incompatible, and sometimes marital discord led to adultery, divorce, or flight to a monastery. A synodal document records the sad outcome of premature marriage: a girl married at the age of eight came to detest her husband to such a degree after a period of five years that the synod agreed to annul the original betrothal on the grounds that it was made in contravention of canon law.

Husbands often beat their wives, sometimes as the result of excessive drinking, other times in anger at their wives' behavior or excessive spending of the family fortunes. Some of these battered wives endured their plight stoically, and some took refuge in a convent. The reverse situation was not unknown, as in Prodromos' description of a henpecked husband. Some men supported concubines, either because they failed to find satisfaction in their marriage or because their wives could not have children. Concubines usually, but not always, came from the lower classes and might be maidservants. Both men and women might be driven by unhappy marital relationships to engage in adultery, although it was severely condemned by both civil and canon law. In the early centuries of the empire, civil law specified death as the punishment for adultery; later legislation provided for the more lenient penalty of mutilation, cutting off the nose of both guilty parties. A woman convicted of adultery was sometimes sent to a convent in punishment; her husband was then entitled to her dowry. Civil law applied a double standard for adultery: husbands were punished only for engaging in sexual relations with a married woman. Canon law punished adultery with excommunication and penance.

Although both civil and canon law emphasized the indissolubility of marriage, some unhappy couples decided to go through with a formal divorce procedure. Legislation restricted justifiable causes for divorce: under Justinian a husband could seek a divorce if his wife was guilty of adultery or inappropriate behavior, such as dining or bathing with strange men, or attending circus games or the theater without his consent. Other grounds for divorce were insanity or the impotence of the husband. An alternative to divorce was the separation of the couple to enter monastic life, often on the basis of an amicable agreement, but sometimes as a solution to an intolerable marital situation.

WIDOWHOOD AND OLD AGE

Although female life expectancy in Byzantium was lower than that of men, widowhood was still a common phenomenon: husbands tended to be older than their wives and thus were likely to predecease them; also many men died in battle. Second marriages were permitted by law but condemned by some moral rigorists. The traditional image of the widow was that of an unfortunate and helpless woman, linked in the popular perception with orphans and the poor. Christians were urged to be solicitous of widows, who were singled out for special charitable distributions. Some philanthropic institutions called *chērotropheia* were established especially to house indigent widows. Some women who lost their husbands entered convents where they found physical sustenance and emotional support.

In Byzantium, however, as in other societies, widowhood was a stage of life in which many women achieved the greatest esteem and power. Since widows were normally middle-aged or elderly, they were no longer viewed as sexual temptresses but as mature, reliable, and respectable. In the early church there was a special ecclesiastical order of widows who performed charitable services. Numerous widows attained greater financial security by recovering total control over their dowries; many of the most generous Byzantine patronesses were in fact widows at the time when they founded churches or monasteries or commissioned works of art. Danelis, who owned vast estates in the Peloponnese in the ninth century, is an example of an extremely wealthy widow. Many widows became the heads of households, even when they lived with adult sons. The data for certain villages in early fourteenth-century Macedonia indicates that 20 percent of households were headed by widows.

BEYOND THE HOUSEHOLD: WOMEN OUTSIDE THE HOME

There has been considerable discussion of the question of the seclusion of Byzantine women and the degree to which they were confined to their homes. As mentioned earlier, young girls, especially those of good family, were carefully chaperoned to protect their virginity and reputations. With regard to married women, there were wide variations in practice, depending on the woman's social class, whether she resided in the city or the countryside, and perhaps on the era in which she lived. Peasant women obviously had to spend a great deal of time outside the house, tending the garden and feeding the chickens. Poorer urban women, who had no servants, had to do their own shopping and sometimes held jobs outside the home. Since they lived in small houses, there were no separate women's quarters to which they could retire. Middle- and upper-class women, on the other hand, tended to be more confined to their homes and may have spent most of their time in certain rooms reserved for their use. The historian Agathias commented that after the earthquake of 557 the social order in Constantinople was disrupted, as women of the nobility mingled freely with men in the streets. Likewise in 1042 during the popular rebellion that overthrew Emperor Michael V and brought Zoe to the throne, Psellos remarked with amazement that some women, "whom nobody till then had seen outside the women's quarters, [were] appearing in public and shouting and beating their breasts and lamenting terribly at the empress's misfortune." He also noted that young girls joined the mob that attacked and destroyed mansions belonging to the family of Michael V. The historian Attaleiates, when describing the earthquake that struck Constantinople in 1068, commented that women forgot their innate modesty and ran into the streets. In the mid-fourteenth century, the noble women of Constantinople rushed to Hagia Sophia to help clear the rubble when the church's great dome partially collapsed during another earthquake.

In wartime, especially during sieges, women left their homes to help defend their city, carrying stones to repair the walls or for use in catapults and slingshots, bringing wine and water to the thirsty troops, and nursing the wounded. Sometimes women even assumed military command, as when Irene, wife of Emperor John VI Kantakouzenos, was placed in charge of the garrison at Didymoteichon during the civil war of 1341–47, or in 1348 when she took responsibility for the defense of Constantinople during her husband's absence. Even in ordinary circumstances, however, women were frequently to be found outside the home, for work and for worship, for recreation and for burial of the dead.

WORKING WOMEN

As we have seen, women's primary duties within the home were raising children, preparing food, and making cloth. Many of the jobs that women held outside their own homes were an extension of these basic household occupations. Women employed as cooks, bakers, and washerwomen were performing traditional female labor but were paid to perform this work for other households or for institutions. There is evidence that some women made cloth not just for their own families but on a larger scale in urban workshops. A short eleventh-century treatise by Michael Psellos describes a Constantinopolitan festival of Agathe, held on 11 May, which was celebrated by women engaged in the carding and spinning of wool and the weaving of cloth. The festival included church services as well as dancing; at one point in the ceremonies the participants evidently gathered around a representation (in fresco?) of women carding and weaving, some less skillfully than others; the incompetent workers were whipped in punishment. These women may have been members of a cloth makers' guild. There is even firmer evidence that women were associated with the silk makers' guild.

There is very little data about women working as other kinds of artisans, although they probably assisted their husbands or sons, as suggested by the panel on an ivory casket in Darmstadt which depicts Eve working the bellows in a smithy while Adam is at the forge.

Women were also active in retail trade, especially as the sellers of groceries; female purveyors of bread, vegetables, fish, and milk are attested. This was no doubt seen as a suitable occupation for women because many of their dealings were with other women (or their maidservants) doing the grocery shopping. Retail vendors sometimes peddled their goods from house to house, thus obviating the need for their customers to leave their homes. Neither cloth production nor retail trade was exclusively limited to women, however, since the sources describe male weavers, grocers, butchers, and fishmongers.

Women not only worked as salaried employees in retail operations, but sometimes owned the stores or workshops themselves. The sources mention women owners or part owners of an ointment/perfume shop and of a dairy shop; they also ran exchange offices, engaged in trade, invested in mining operations, and owned mills.

Another category of professions is those involving intimate contact with women and/or children which were necessarily practiced by women: examples are matchmakers, gynecologists, attendants in the female ward of a hospital, midwives, wet nurses, children's nurses, maidservants, deaconesses, hairdressers, and attendants at public baths for women. The sources mention with some frequency female physicians, who not only served as obstetricians and gynecologists but may also have cared for women suffering from a variety of ailments. One of the physicians at the female ward of the hospital at the Pantokrator monastery in Constantinople was female, as were all the nurses and nursing assistants. These nurses received the same pay as male attendants at the hospital, but, for reasons that remain unclear, the sole woman doctor received half the salary of her male colleagues (3 instead of 6 nomismata) and a smaller ration of grain (26 modioi instead of 36). It is curious that at the hospital of the Lips convent, which had twelve beds reserved for women, the staff was exclusively male with the exception of the washerwoman. Female doctors and midwives were sometimes called as expert witnesses in lawsuits, for example, to pronounce on the virginity of a bride, to determine whether a woman was pregnant, or to attest to the birth of a child.

One should also group together disreputable occupations such as prostitutes, innkeepers and tavern keepers (who frequently functioned as prostitutes on the side), and public entertainers (dancers, actresses).

There is little information on the work of peasant women. In addition to cultivating gardens near their homes and tending domestic fowl, they occasionally worked in the vineyards, as vinedressers and harvesters, and might help with reaping grain, as is suggested by a panel on a tenth-century ivory pyxis in New York depicting Adam cutting wheat with a sickle while Eve carries the harvested sheaves on her shoulders. A thirteenth-century text states, however, that women assisted with the grain harvest only under abnormal circumstances, such as wartime. The biographer of Cyril Phileotes relates that the saint's wife worked the land with the help of her children, while he retired into seclusion within their home. Some girls and women worked as shepherdesses; an unusual case is that of the Vlach women who pastured sheep on Mount Athos. This was viewed as a great scandal, especially when it was learned that they were delivering cheese and milk to the monasteries.

ACTIVITIES OUTSIDE THE HOME

Entertainment and Diversions

Like their young daughters, married women spent most of their day at home, primarily in the company of relatives and servants. They sometimes kept birds or small dogs as pets. Evidently the family dined together on everyday occasions; but if there were male guests, well-bred women stayed in their chambers. Still there were numerous reasons for excursions outside the home: to the public baths, to churches for services, to shrines to visit relics, to see a holy man, and to attend religious processions and funerals as well as family celebrations such as the birth of a child or a wedding. It was considered unseemly for a woman to attend chariot races or other spectacles at the Hippodrome; Justinianic legislation established that a husband could sue for divorce if his wife engaged in such inappropriate behavior. Only rarely did women of the aristocracy or empresses go hunting on horseback.

Religious Activity

Worship and Pilgrimage. As in other societies in which women lead a relatively secluded existence, religious worship played a vital part in the lives of the women of Byzantium. For laywomen, attendance at church services and processions and visits to shrines provided socially approved opportunities for them to leave their homes, in addition to satisfying emotional and spiritual needs.

Women of the upper classes were able to attend services in private chapels attached to their houses, but the majority frequented churches in their own neighborhoods or even at some distance from their homes. Thus the pious St. Mary the Younger walked to church twice a day, in all sorts of weather, even though she had to cross a stream to reach the church. Her biographer tells us, however, that she remained in the darkest part of the church to worship and that when she moved to a larger city, she said her prayers at home so as to avoid the crowds in public places of worship. Within the church building, women were separated from men, being relegated either to an upper gallery or to a side aisle, depending on the size and plan of the structure. The early fourteenth-century patriarch Athanasios I suggested one rationale for such segregation of the sexes when he criticized noblewomen who came to Hagia Sophia not out of piety but to show off their jewels and finery and painted faces. Later in the century a Russian pilgrim described how at the same church the women stood behind translucent silken draperies in the galleries so that they could observe the services without being seen by the men in the congregation.

A favorite activity for women was visiting shrines, where they prayed for the health and salvation of themselves and their families, or might seek a miraculous cure from illness or injury. We are told that Thomais of Lesbos, who became a saint even though she was married and had children, used to pray at churches in various parts of Constantinople, even remaining for nocturnal vigils at the sanctuary of the Virgin at Blachernai. During the early centuries of the empire, some women, especially those from the imperial family or members of the aristocracy, made the long pilgrimage to the Holy Land. After the Arab conquests of the seventh century, however, women rarely ventured to make this perilous journey and restricted their travels to local shrines.

Involvement in Religious Controversy. Excluded for the most part from participation in political life, many women became ardently involved in the religious controversies of the day. In the eighth and ninth centuries, for example, when the emperors adopted a policy of Iconoclasm, forbidding the veneration of images, women were in the forefront of the opposition. They were passionately devoted to icons, which they venerated in churches and kept at home as their most treasured possessions. Michael Psellos vividly describes Empress Zoe's attachment to her icon of Christ, embellished with precious metal. She believed it could foretell the future and in moments of anxiety clutched the sacred image in her hands and talked to it as if it were alive. It is reported that at the very beginning of the iconoclastic period, when a soldier was dispatched to destroy the image of Christ above the Chalke Gate at the Great Palace, a group of nuns led by St. Theodosia pulled down the ladder on which he was standing. These women became the first iconodule martyrs, as they were all executed by order of Leo III. Another iconodule nun, St. Anthousa of Mantineon, was tortured by having the hot embers of burned icons poured over her body. Many women of the imperial family opposed the policies of their husbands and fathers and continued to venerate icons in the privacy of their chambers. Furthermore, it was two empresses who restored image veneration after the death of their husbands: in 787 Irene convoked the Second Council of Nicaea which reinstated icons for a short time, and in 843 Theodora, the widow of the iconoclast emperor Theophilos, presided over the permanent restoration of image veneration as official doctrine of the Orthodox Church. In the late thirteenth century, women played a prominent role in the opposition to Michael VIII's policy of reuniting the churches of Constantinople and Rome; some of his female relatives were even sent into exile for their condemnation of the Union of Lyons in 1274.

Women as Deaconesses and Religious Teachers. Women were excluded from the clergy, except for the order of deaconesses which survived until the twelfth century. Deaconesses originally assisted with the baptism of women at the time when adult baptism by immersion was customary, and then evolved into a group of women who performed charitable services, functioning as social workers and visiting nurses. Laywomen did engage in private religious teaching, instructing their children in the Christian faith, teaching them the Psalms, and telling them stories of the saints of old. Others organized private reading and study groups, as we learn from the Life of Athanasia of Aegina, who assembled neighborhood women on Sundays and feast days and read to them from the Scriptures, "inculcating in them fear and love for the Lord." Much more rare were nuns such as St. Anthousa of Mantineon, who taught the monks of the double monastery over which she presided, or Irene, abbess of the Chrysobalanton convent in Constantinople, who preached to crowds of men and women, including women and girls from senatorial and other prominent families.

Charitable Activities

An important and socially acceptable activity for women outside the home was the performance of charitable services. Wealthy women might help the needy indirectly, by donation of funds to institutions that provided social services, such as orphanages, poorhouses, old age homes, hospitals, and monasteries. Others preferred a more personal involvement in ministering to their unfortunate brethren and came into direct contact with the sick and poor. Some volunteered in hospitals, helping to feed and bathe patients; some visited prisons, consoling those in confinement; others roamed the streets, seeking out beggars and homeless people in order to give them clothing, food, and money. This spirit of philanthropy was motivated by Christian piety and was viewed as an honorable way of serving Christ. In the ninth and tenth centuries, a few women, like Mary the Younger and Thomais of Lesbos, even attained sanctity on account of their devotion to helping the poor.

Role as Mourners at Funerals

Just as women were the principal figures at the time of the birth of children, as mothers, midwives, and nurses, so women also assumed a prominent role at the time of the death of a family member. First of all, they helped to prepare the corpse for burial, washing the body, sprinkling it with fragrant oils and spices, and clothing it. Then, during the wake, they were the chief mourners, demonstrating their grief by wailing, tearing their hair, lacerating their cheeks with their fingernails, beating their breasts, and ripping apart their garments. Not only female relatives of the deceased, but also hired professional female mourners sang dirges, praising the virtues and lamenting the death of the departed one. Women mourners continued their wailing and lamentations as they accompanied the corpse to the cemetery. This practice elicited criticism by church fathers who complained that the mourning women in their paroxysms of grief resembled Maenads in a Bacchic frenzy and were indulging in shameful behavior by uncovering their heads and tearing their garments so as to reveal portions of their bodies. The church urged that funeral processions be conducted in a solemn, dignified manner and provided trained choirs of men and women to sing psalms and funeral hymns. Both male and female relatives of the deceased came to the cemetery on the third, ninth, and fortieth day after the death to make offerings at the tomb. In addition, women were assiduous in their commemoration of their deceased relatives, preparing *kollyba* (a mixture of boiled wheat grains and dried fruits) and attending commemorative services on the anniversary of their death.

Cultural and Intellectual Life

There is very little evidence that women engaged in artistic activity besides the production of fine textiles and embroideries; one case is attested of a woman in seventh-century Syria who gave drawing lessons. Likewise only a few female scribes are known, at least one of whom, Irene, was the daughter of a calligrapher, the late thirteenth-century Theodore Hagiopetrites. Theodora Raoulaina, a niece of Michael VIII Palaiologos, copied a manuscript of Ailios Aristeides that is now preserved in the Vatican.

Women of imperial and aristocratic families did, however, play an important role in the cultural life of Byzantium, especially through their patronage of the arts. Not only did they commission deluxe manuscripts and liturgical vessels, but they also founded churches and monasteries, some of which still stand. In the early sixth century, a prominent patroness was Anicia Juliana, the daughter of Olybrius, who was briefly emperor in the West in 472. As his only child, she inherited great wealth and built or embellished a number of churches in Constantinople, including St. Euphemia en tois Olybriou and the huge basilica of St. Polyeuktos, recently excavated at Saraçhane in Istanbul. Anicia Juliana was also responsible for the production of the lavishly illustrated manuscript of the herbal of Dioskorides, which is presently one of the treasures of the Austrian National Library in Vienna.

Many of the monastic complexes in Constantinople that are known to us today, either because of the chance preservation of their monastic rules (*typika*) or because of the survival of the church buildings, were founded by noblewomen or empresses. Although women occasionally founded male monasteries, it was more common for them to establish nunneries, usually intended as a future home for their daughters or themselves. Empress Irene Doukaina, wife of Alexios I Komnenos, founded the Kecharitomene convent in the twelfth century and drafted a lengthy set of regulations for its nuns. From the Palaiologan period, the Lips convent, restored by Theodora Palaiologina, widow of Michael VIII, is known both from its *typikon* and from the church she added on the south side of the existing church as a mausoleum for the Palaiologan family (Fenari Isa Camii). Theodora Raoulaina restored the convent of St. Andrew in Krisei and built the small monastery of Aristine to house Patriarch Gregory II of Cyprus after his abdication from the patriarchate in 1289. Irene Choumnaina, the young widow of Despot John Palaiologos, used much of her inherited wealth to establish the double monastery of Christ Philanthropos and became its abbess. Another of the magnificent churches that still adorns Istanbul, the *parekklēsion* of the church of the Virgin Pammakaristos (Fethiye Camii), was built by Maria-Martha, widow of Michael Tarchaneiotes Glabas, as a mausoleum for her husband. Somewhat atypical was the convent called Repentance, which was established by Justinian's wife Theodora to house former prostitutes.

In addition to the Vienna Dioskorides, as examples of deluxe manuscripts commissioned by women one could mention the *typikon* for the Palaiologan convent of the Virgin of Sure Hope, with its introductory series of portrait pages (Lincoln College Typikon), and the group of sixteen codices attributed to workshops patronized by a certain Palaiologina, perhaps to be identified as Theodora Raoulaina or Theodora Palaiologina, respectively the niece and wife of Michael VIII.

In the realm of literary production, we find a few highly educated women who were themselves writers and a number of others who encouraged literati with correspondence and outright financial support, by lending them books, and by holding literary salons. Without question the most important work written by a Byzantine woman was the *Alexiad* of Anna Komnene, daughter of Alexios I Komnenos. This lengthy and subjective history is not only the basic source for her father's reign and the First Crusade, but also provides detailed information about three generations of strong-willed imperial women: Alexios' mother, Anna Dalassene, his wife, Irene Doukaina, and Anna herself. A few women tried their hand at poetry and hymnography, the most successful of them being the ninth-century Kassia, who entered a convent after she failed to win the hand of the crown prince Theophilos. Likewise only two or three women hagiographers are attested, such as the abbess Sergia, who in the seventh century wrote a brief account of the translation of the relics of St. Olympias, the founding mother of her convent. Many centuries later, the versatile Theodora Raoulaina composed a lengthy Life of the iconodule brothers Theodore and Theophanes, the Graptoi. Abounding in classical allusions that attest to the literary tastes of its author, the work has been interpreted as a veiled allusion to the suffering endured by her own brothers who opposed the unionist policies of Michael VIII.

A number of women with literary interests became the patrons of writers and scholars. The *sebastokratorissa* Irene, wife of Andronikos Komnenos and sister-in-law of Manuel I, seems to have been particularly partial to poetry. She encouraged the work of the poets Theodore Prodromos and Manganeios Prodromos, as well as that of John Tzetzes who wrote Homeric commentaries and versified commentaries on his own collection of letters. Constantine Manasses, another of Irene's protégés, dedicated his universal history (written in fifteen-syllable verses) to his patroness, calling her "a foster child of learning." Theodora Raoulaina was an erudite bibliophile who at one point owned an important manuscript of Thucydides, was praised for her learning by her contemporaries, and corresponded with Nikephoros Choumnos and Patriarch Gregory II of Cyprus. Irene Choumnaina possessed a substantial library of secular and religious works, exchanged books with her spiritual director, commissioned the copying of manuscripts, and seems to have held a sort of salon for literati at her convent.

Monastic Life

Convents offered a variety of opportunities and services to Byzantine women. Frequently described in the sources as a safe and tranquil harbor, the nunnery was a place in which women could enjoy a calm and ordered existence in a community of sisters whose lives revolved around the daily offices and prayers for the salvation of mankind. For young women, convents were the principal alternative to marriage; for women afflicted by family troubles, illness, or old age, they offered a refuge; for poor laypeople, they provided charity in the form of food and clothing and occasionally health care. Convents also provided an institutional environment in which women were expected to have reached a certain level of education and could hold positions of responsibility.

As in the medieval West, young girls entered Byzantine convents for many reasons. Some maidens, drawn to the life of piety from childhood, preferred marriage to Christ, the heavenly bridegroom, to earthly marriage. Although most parents supported their daughters in their decision to renounce the world, there were instances in which the parents arranged a marriage against the girl's wishes and resisted her desire to take the monastic habit. Occasionally a girl entered monastic life more out of necessity than vocation; for example, she might be considered unmarriageable because she had been scarred by smallpox or was mentally ill. Although most surviving monastic rules declare that no financial contribution was required in order to enter a convent, the norm was for the girl's family to make a substantial donation to the nunnery, often the money or property that would have been her dowry. After a novitiate of three years, the girl took monastic vows.

The placement of girls in convents before the age of ten was discouraged since they were viewed as a potential disruptive influence on the monastic community; nevertheless, very young girls were sometimes admitted. There were instances of parents bringing their children to convents at a very tender age as an offering of thanks to Christ or the Virgin, especially if they had conceived the child after years of infertility or if the child had miraculously survived while her brothers and sisters had died (as in the case of the daughter of Theodora of Thessalonike). Orphan girls might also be raised in convents. These girls were taught to read and write, to chant the office, and to do handiwork. Once they had reached the age of informed consent, they could decide if they wished to remain permanently at the nunnery and take formal vows. The rule of the Lips convent stated that girls raised by the nuns from infancy or childhood had to wait until their sixteenth birthday before taking the habit.

Many women took the habit at a later stage in life, in middle or even old age. It was extremely common for a woman to enter a convent after she had been widowed; in a monastic environment, she could find spiritual solace, companionship, and support for her old age. A number of documents survive that describe the financial arrangements made on such an occasion: the widow would make a substantial contribution to the nunnery of cash or property, and in exchange would receive the tonsure, be supported for the rest of her life, and after her death would be properly buried and commemorated in annual services. In some cases the widow did not take monastic vows, but lived in the convent as a lay pensioner or remained outside the cloister and received regular allotments of food. It was not only widows who adopted the monastic habit in middle age; not uncommonly a husband and wife would agree to end their married life once their children were grown and would retire to separate monasteries.

A variety of other motives led women to the gate of the convent: for some, such as battered or unhappy wives, refugees from enemy invasions, or the mentally ill, the convent was indeed a refuge. For others, it was more like a prison or place of confinement, as in the case of empresses whose husbands had been deposed, women found guilty of adultery, or sorceresses and heretics condemned by the synod to take monastic vows to atone for their sinful behavior.

Nuns were normally of aristocratic or middle-class background, but women of the lower classes also lived and worked in convents both as private maidservants and as menial help. Despite the stated ideal of equality in a monastic community, many noblewomen who entered convents later in life found it difficult to renounce their comfortable lifestyle and were permitted to live in separate apartments with their former retainers and to take their meals privately.

The choir sisters and officials of the nunnery had to be able to read and write, and were often women of considerable education who found an outlet for their talents in the monastic environment. The mother superior, who was not only the spiritual leader of the community but also responsible for supervising the maintenance of the physical complex and the management of its financial resources, had to be a shrewd businesswoman who combined a stern will and strict discipline with a spirit of loving-kindness toward the nuns in her charge and psychological understanding of the problems that could arise in such a close-knit group of women.

Convents required the services of several officials for their administration, the size of the staff depending upon the number of nuns in a given institution, which might range from a handful to a hundred or so. In a small convent one nun might combine functions that were held by two or more individuals in a larger establishment. One of the most important officials, who had to be musically inclined and steeped in the intricacies of the liturgy, served as the *ekklēsiarchissa*. Her duties were the supervision of the church sanctuary and services, including the proper chanting of the office by the choir sisters. The sacristan (*skeuophylakissa*) was responsible for the safekeeping of liturgical vessels, while the treasurer (*docheiaria*) was in charge of finances and purchasing supplies such as food for the refectory and clothes for the nuns. The archivist (*chartophylakissa*) had the duty of safeguarding the monastic archives, principally documents pertaining to grants of imperial privileges, gifts and purchases of land, and tax exemptions. This group of officials had to have excellent skills of organization, record keeping, and financial accounting. Other positions held by nuns included those of gatekeeper and infirmarian. The steward (*oikonomos*), in charge of the management of the monastic estates, might be a layman who lived outside the nunnery, but in some convents the post was held by a mature nun with much practical experience. She was expected to go out of the cloister as necessary to visit the far-flung properties of the convent, check on the progress of the harvest, and attend to revenues from the sale of crops.

Although the convent provided an environment where women could assume major responsibility for the management of a complex establishment, there were still limitations on their independence from male authority. Because women could not serve as priests, of necessity male clergy came from outside the cloister to officiate at the liturgy. Likewise the confessor had to be a man, as was the physician who visited the convent on a regular basis. Furthermore, the convent was often placed under the authority of a male *ephoros,* or supervisor, who could overrule the mother superior if he judged it necessary.

The nuns' daily routine varied according to their specific assignment but revolved around the chanting of the office, private prayer and study of the Scriptures, handiwork such as spinning, weaving, and embroidery, and performance of household duties. Some nuns also worked in the convent's vineyard and garden. In contrast to male monasteries where monks sometimes engaged in artistic or intellectual endeavors, such as calligraphy, hymnography, musical composition, or the writing of chronicles and saints' lives, nunneries offered little opportunity for artistic expression. There were nuns who worked as scribes, hymnographers, or hagiographers, but they were rare indeed.

Convents differed in other ways from male monasteries. They tended to be smaller, less well endowed, and located in cities rather than the countryside. Nuns took seriously the requirement of monastic stability, that is, remaining for life in the monastery in which one takes vows. Unlike monks, who tended to move restlessly from one monastery to another, or to alternate between a cenobitic lifestyle and the arduous existence of the hermit, nuns almost always remained in the same convent until their death. They also lived almost exclusively in cenobitic establishments; after the ninth or tenth century, female hermits are hardly ever mentioned in the sources.

Furthermore, nuns for the most part strictly observed rules of monastic enclosure and rarely left the cloister. However, some *typika,* especially in the later centuries, as a concession to human frailty, relaxed monastic discipline and permitted nuns to visit their families upon occasion. Younger nuns had to be accompanied by mature, experienced nuns if they went out of the convent; likewise if nuns received male visitors at the gate of the convent, an older nun was supposed to supervise the visit. Occasionally nuns who held official positions at the convent had to leave the cloister to conduct various kinds of business: petitions to the synod, appearance at a law court, rent collection, visits to monastic estates, or escorting the abbess at the time of her installation by the patriarch. Ordinary nuns might go out to attend a relative's funeral, to visit a spiritual confessor or a shrine, or to perform charitable services.

Women of the Imperial Family

Empresses and other women of the imperial family have appeared occasionally in the previous pages, primarily in connection with their role as patrons of the arts or their involvement in religious controversies. In a number of ways, the lives of the wives, mothers, sisters, and daughters of emperors resembled those of other women: they spent much of their time in their private quarters; they were generally pious and assiduous in their church attendance; for many, a principal concern was philanthropy to the less fortunate members of society; others made generous contributions for the construction, restoration, or maintenance of churches, monasteries, and charitable institutions or the production of manuscripts and other works of art. Still their wealth, high birth, and constitutional position set them apart from the norm.

The most distinguishing feature of Byzantine empresses (and occasionally princesses) is that they were the only women who had any involvement in the political arena. Sometimes they played a key role in the perpetuation of a dynasty; on occasion they actually exercised imperial authority, either as regent or as sole ruler; not infrequently they exerted influence on husbands, sons, or brothers. In cases where there was no male heir to the throne, empresses or princesses could transmit the imperial power through marriage. Thus Ariadne, daughter of Leo I, took as her first husband the Isaurian chieftain Zeno, who reigned from 474 to 491. When Zeno died without leaving a son, Ariadne married Anastasios (I), who was emperor from 491 to 518. Likewise the princess Zoe, daughter of Constantine VIII, prolonged the Macedonian dynasty by her successive marriages to three men who became emperor—Romanos III Argyros (1028–34), Michael IV Paphlagon (1034–41), and Constantine IX Monomachos (1042–55)—and by her adoption of Michael V Kalaphates (1041–42). Widowed empresses like Irene in the eighth century and Theodora in the ninth served as regents for minor sons, while Anna Dalassene was entrusted with the regency by her adult son Alexios I Komnenos when he left the capital for an extended military campaign.

In a few instances an empress refused to step aside when her son attained his majority, or was unwilling to take a consort, and for brief periods held sole power. Thus Irene, after a ten-year regency, was reluctant to hand over the reins of authority to her son Constantine VI; after a power struggle, she eventually ordered his arrest and blinding in 797 and ruled in her own right for the next five years until she was overthrown. In 1042 Empress Zoe, discouraged by the manner in which her consort, Michael IV, and her adopted son Michael V had relegated her first to the women's quarters and then to a convent, ruled for a few months with her sister Theodora after a popular rebellion had removed Michael V from the throne. She was persuaded to give her hand in marriage once more, however, this time to Constantine (IX) Monomachos. Following the deaths of first Zoe and then Constantine, Theodora, the third daughter of Constantine VIII, ascended the throne in 1055 and ruled in her own name for nineteen months. Before her death she transmitted the imperial power by marriage to Michael (VI) Stratiotikos, who survived her by only a year. The Macedonian dynasty had at last totally died out, but through the sisters Zoe and Theodora it had been prolonged for almost thirty additional years, from 1028 to 1056.

Legally women could sit on the throne, but sole female rule was viewed as irregular and improper. The position of a ruling empress was ambiguous. Irene signed documents as "emperor of the Romans" and was praised for her masculine spirit, whereas on her coinage she was titled "empress." Michael Psellos sharply criticized Zoe and Theodora for their incompetence, stating that "neither of them was fitted by temperament to govern" and that the empire "needed a man's supervision." He commented that, during Theodora's sole rule, "everyone was agreed that for the Roman Empire to be governed by a woman, instead of a man, was improper." The historian Doukas attacked the regency of Anna of Savoy, likening the empire in female hands to "a weaver's shuttle spinning awry and twisting the thread of the purple robe." He deliberately used the simile of a loom, reminding his readers that handiwork, not imperial affairs, was the proper domain of women.

Only three women sat alone on the imperial throne of Byzantium; women regents were more numerous, tended to stay in power for a longer time, and sometimes played a decisive role in determining the future course of events. We should not forget that both Irene and Theodora were regents for minor sons when they reversed the iconoclastic policy of their deceased husbands and restored the traditional veneration of images.

Yet other empresses had an indirect but significant influence on events through persuasion or manipulation of their husbands. Prokopios vividly described the dramatic episode in the palace at the time of the Nika revolt (532) when Theodora persuaded Justinian I not to flee and abdicate his throne but to stand firm and crush the popular rebellion. Indeed, he was able to retain his throne and ruled for thirty-three more years. Empresses became involved in negotiations about the marriage of their children, took a strong interest in religious affairs, recommended promotions and demotions of courtiers who had pleased or displeased them, and sometimes even accompanied their husbands on military campaigns.

CONCLUSION

The Byzantine attitude toward women was ambivalent. Under the influence of two stereotyped female images, the Virgin Mary, who miraculously combined virginity with motherhood, and Eve, the sexual temptress, they vacillated between revering women as mothers and criticizing them as weak and untrustworthy. This may be a partial explanation for the wide variety of female saints, who ranged from consecrated virgins to reformed prostitutes to charitable matrons. Although the Byzantines idealized virginity and considered it superior to marriage, the family was still the key unit of their society. Women played an indispensable role in the perpetuation of the family line and in the transmission of property from one generation to the next. They assumed particular prominence at the critical passages of life: at birth, as mother, midwife, wet nurse; at marriage, as bride; at death, as mourner.

Because of the emphasis on chastity for maidens and fidelity for wives, women tended to lead secluded lives within the confines of the family home. Within this domestic sphere, however, their position was assured as they carried out the tasks of raising the children and running the household. If women did leave their families to become nuns, in effect they joined another family, the spiritual sisterhood of the convent under the leadership of the mother superior. In taking monastic vows, a woman became the bride of Christ, embarking upon a spiritual marriage while retaining her virginity. Thus a woman was always linked with a family, whether at home or in the convent.

SELECTED BIBLIOGRAPHY

Beaucamp, J. "La situation juridique de la femme à Byzance." *Cahiers de civilisation médiévale* 20 (1977): 145–76.

Grosdidier de Matons, J. "La femme dans l'empire byzantin." In P. Grimal, ed., *Histoire mondiale de la femme,* 3:11–43. Paris, 1974.

Herrin, J. "In Search of Byzantine Women: Three Avenues of Approach." In A. Cameron and A. Kuhrt, eds., *Images of Women in Antiquity,* 167–89. London, 1983.

Koukoules, Ph. *Byzantínon bios kai politismos,* 6 vols. in 7 parts; esp. vol. 2:117–218 and vol. 4. Athens, 1948–57.

Laiou, A. "The Role of Women in Byzantine Society." *Jahrbuch der Österreichischen Byzantinistik* 31.1 (1981): 233–60.

Talbot, A.-M. "A Comparison of the Monastic Experience of Byzantine Men and Women." *Greek Orthodox Theological Review* 30 (1985): 1–20.

6

ENTREPRENEURS

Nicolas Oikonomides

THE MERCHANT WAS PRIMARILY a city dweller, a townsman; he was also a traveler. In pursuit of his own financial gain, he transported goods, sometimes even ideas. He took economic and physical risks to achieve his goals. He produced nothing, rather he offered his services; thus his very existence depended on the existence of a society that did in fact have need of those services.

The artisan, too, was primarily a city dweller, but he was for the most part sedentary. He, too, needed a large number of people interested in his wares, and such a large number could only consistently be found in cities. In the Middle Ages the artisan and the merchant were often one and the same, a single person who produced and sold his wares.

In the absence of any formal business organization, artisans and merchants in the Middle Ages formed what we might call "the business world" of that time. In Byzantine Constantinople, the functions of the merchant and the artisan were frequently and commonly blended together. Following Roman tradition, they were both members of the *collegia,* those state-run organizations whose goal was to bring together practitioners of a trade, and ultimately to control them better. In the Byzantine world, the *collegia* were transformed and called first *sōmateia* or *systēmata.* Their members were designated by the collective name "those who manage stores" (*ergasteriakoi*), regardless of the type of trade that was exercised in them. Shopkeepers formed a distinct social category.

Then in the eleventh century, when the Byzantine business world experienced its only true period of success, there was an attempt to clarify the basic distinction between those who performed a manual task, "such as the tanners," whose professional organizations were called *sōmateia,* and those "who did not labor, such as the importers of fabric from Syria," who belonged to the *systēmata.* The examples chosen to define the two categories are revealing: tanners engaged in the most taxing and un-

144

healthiest of trades, so much so that they were required, insofar as possible, to set up shop outside the confines of the city. Niketas Choniates, the twelfth-century statesman and historian, also placed pork butchers, shoemakers, and small tailors in the same category as tanners, as they were considered to form the lowest level of the population of the marketplace. By contrast, fabric importers practiced the "cleanest" and least tiring trade imaginable, without participating in any way in the manufacture of their merchandise. Their profession was based on pure profit, earned from goods bought from one party and sold to another: the merchant was a true intermediary. It is clear that, in the eleventh century, professions that did not involve manual labor enjoyed a higher social prestige that was recognized even by the state. Furthermore, those professions presupposed a definite economic advantage.

Obviously, profit earned from the resale of goods was a complete contradiction of the Roman tradition that looked askance at money earned by means other than the production of goods: such profit was basically considered immoral. Such immorality was even more acute when interest loans, which were also looked down upon by the Christian religion, were at issue. Thus persons in such professions found themselves barred from joining the senate, just as freed slaves, heretics, or actors (members of *the* most disreputable profession) also were. But in spite of the immoral profit earned, a clean trade did present obvious advantages from a social point of view. The merchant "who did not work," when compared to artisans, appeared as a great lord alongside small peasants: the latter had to work the land and had rough hands that smelled like the earth; similar images might serve to compare tanners and fabric importers.

The distinction is also important from the point of view of mentalities. A capitalist conception of the world was forming, a conception that would never truly ripen, but one that gave to eleventh-century Byzantium the illusion of having a developed economy and society. The eleventh century represents an important turning point in the history of Byzantium in general and, more specifically, in the history of its business world.

THE SURVIVAL OF A MARKET ECONOMY DURING THE DARK AGES

The Byzantine entrepreneur was a product of his Hellenistic and Roman past, of the great urban centers of the Orient, the large cities of Asia Minor and the Balkans, cities that until the seventh century had known virtually no invasions and had for centuries followed a well-established urban tradition. This was the continuation of an ancient tradition, of merchants traveling throughout the Mediterranean basin, of "Syrian" merchants going to Lyon to transport fabrics as well as correspondence between hermits. This period of late antiquity will not concern us in what follows, for it is not a part of what we call Byzantium. It was the remains of a past that was destroyed in the West with the barbarian invasions.

In the East there were no barbarians (not as early, in any event) nor any formal collapse. Nevertheless, that world also became decadent and fell even before the great invasions at the end of the sixth and seventh centuries. It was an ailing world with large cities overflowing with magnificent buildings that were in disrepair. Members of the elite were fleeing the heavy municipal taxes that had, however, been created with them in mind. The archways of the monumental porticoes were walled up and transformed into hovels for the migrant populations from the countryside. True repairs were no longer undertaken, except those financed by the emperor. Thus in the sixth and seventh centuries, at the time when external events shook the cities and destroyed their buildings—attacks by Persians or Slavs, or earthquakes—an extraordinary phenomenon occurred, one characteristic of what has been called the fall of the ancient world: following the departure of the enemy, no one was interested in repairing buildings in the city. In certain cases, colonnades and their arches remained where they had fallen and have been discovered intact by archaeologists. The large cities were abandoned by their inhabitants, who most often went to settle on a neighboring hill and created new, small, fortified centers that were really more like villages; the grandeur of the past had disappeared for good. For merchants, this could only be the beginning of a great crisis.

This was the beginning of the Middle Ages, which, for Byzantium, we might situate in the seventh century, although it must actually have begun much earlier: it was in the seventh century that the change became obvious, that the urban civilization of the past definitively disappeared everywhere, except perhaps in Constantinople and in a few large cities in the East, although they had then fallen into the hands of the Arabs. A closed economy based on autarchy, characteristic of the Middle Ages, was also forming in Byzantium. Constantinople, which had never ceased to be a great city, comprised the only important consumer market in the empire—in fact, the only consumer market worthy of that name. This is why the Byzantine capital and its immediate surroundings formed an economic zone unto itself: to have access to it, merchants, both Byzantine and foreign, had to submit to strict controls and pay special duties at two stations that Justinian had established for this purpose in the sixth century: in Abydos, at the entrance to the Dardanelles, and in Hieron, at the entrance to the Bosporos. Thus, at the beginning of the sixth century, the empire was divided into two economic zones of different calibre and serving different functions: the economic zone of consumer activity in the capital and the closed economic zone in all the provinces.

Moreover, in fact, with the arrival of the Arabs on the shores of the Mediterranean, that body of water that had once united the Roman provinces became a boundary line that was bitterly disputed by two totalitarian religions, both of which placed a high value on privateering with the aim of dismantling the economic structures of their adversary. Naturally, this did not mean that commercial exchanges ceased, not even those between warring factions: Syrian merchants continued to travel to Constantinople, and the Byzantines went to Syria. But the circulation of goods diminished, and commercial activity was taken over by agents of the state rather than remaining in the hands of individuals.

Indeed, in Byzantium one then began to encounter particularly rich men who in the name of the state often formed partnerships in order to monopolize certain economic activities. These were men with close ties at court, with glorious honorific titles and obvious backing from within the emperor's entourage; imperial favor enabled them to dominate certain economic activities during a given reign, but they often disappeared as soon as their protector was overthrown, which shows the degree to which their rise was linked to a certain favoritism. They had the right to use the official seals bearing the portrait of the emperor who had conferred their authority upon them. They were most often involved in organizing the production, dying, and sale of silk, the foremost luxury commodity, which at that time, and even more so later on, was one of the most important national products in the Byzantine economy; in an economy with an ample money supply, imperial silk was also used as a supplemental currency, enabling the sovereign to pay a portion of salaries in silk fabric. This fabric, especially purple silk (and leather of the same color), was a very sought-after commodity both within the empire and abroad. By allowing it to be exported in well-controlled quantities, Byzantium kept its value, and therefore the demand for it, at very high levels.

These foreign exchanges (which were, in fact, primarily a form of bartering, especially when economically undeveloped neighbors such as the Bulgarians were concerned) provided government agents with other merchandise to sell in their own markets. Exchanges occurred at fixed border locations.

Silk was not the only item traded. The same businessmen dealt in large-scale exchanges of other goods: there was a concentration—and, one may assume, the marketing—of agricultural surpluses obtained through the collection of taxes, some of which were paid in kind; and there was slave trading, which at that time still played an important role in the economy of cities as well as in that of the countryside. We know of a case that occurred at the end of the seventh century in which a sale of slaves (these were an entire tribe of rebellious Slavs) was undertaken by a single entrepreneur for the entire empire, and lasted three years. This was certainly a huge, completely atypical operation, and clearly a very profitable one as well.

It is important to stress that in all these cases those "big" businessmen were more like government functionaries. They carried out all the activities described in the name of the state and had jurisdiction over certain regions for limited periods of time (generally the collection of taxes occurred in one or two well-defined provinces and lasted one or two years). Because of these special circumstances, they might have belonged to the upper aristocracy and might even have been members of the senate. Since they were working for the state, they were not affected by the dishonorable character of their profession, which involved the handling of money.

There were also merchants and artisans in the Constantinople marketplace, the *ergasteriakoi*, strictly speaking, restless city dwellers who ran all sorts of shops: fishmongers, butchers, grocers, bakers, wine merchants, blacksmiths, builders, weavers, dyers, tanners, perfumers. These were the small businessmen who set up shops in the porticoes of the city, in specific places reserved for each trade. Their clientele was the population of the city; their merchandise, which came from the provinces or from abroad, was burdened with various duties or taxes, in particular for being transported into the economic region of the capital. Special surtaxes on this merchandise were imposed from time to time to keep the empire's finances afloat, whereas the populist rulers, such as Empress Irene (around the year 800), temporarily abolished them, giving rise to celebrations in Constantinople.

There were also market fairs in the provinces, such as that of St. John the Theologian in Ephesos, whose annual revenues in 795 were more than 1,000 lbs. of gold (72,000 solidi); this sum—which is, moreover, quite approximate—might appear small when one considers that the St. John's fair was undoubtedly the major economic event in the region. But it appears large when one recalls that the ancient city of Ephesos was abandoned at that time and was replaced by a township called Theologos, and that the neighboring rural region had an economy that appeared to be based above all on autarchy at the local level. Figures such as those for the St. John's fair enable us to assume that the merchants of the eighth century were evolving in a much less autarchic environment—one based much more on exchange—than might previously have been believed.

Merchants thus functioned in an economy of limited exchanges but also of movement. Carrying cargo over land, a process burdened with a variety of tolls, was relatively costly and inefficient. Transporting goods by sea was more efficient but very dangerous; added to the risks of the sea there were the Arab pirates who took over the entire coastline and forced the Byzantine population to abandon it and seek refuge in fortified locations in the mountains. Small boats and ferries, which enabled exchanges between provincial ports, were destined sooner or later to fall victim to the pirates. The government thus favored the dissolution of that overly vulnerable provincial merchant marine and set out to use its human resources to reinforce the navy. By contrast, this same government, at the beginning of the ninth century, chose to invest in the merchant marine of the capital by providing the "large shipowners of Constantinople" with the financial means necessary to arm their ships better and to use them in profitable, large-scale enterprises.

The important shipowners of Constantinople—they were, in fact, merely sailors who owned their ships—had no special social prestige. When Emperor Theophilos learned his wife owned a ship that imported wheat into Constantinople, he ordered the ship burned with its cargo, for that trade brought dishonor to him. The prejudice against all commercial undertakings thus remained very much alive.

In order to raise the capital needed for his business activities, the Byzantine merchant had recourse to two alternatives, business loans or partnerships. In the case of loans, the businessman assumed all risks associated with the enterprise; in partnerships, he shared the risks with his associates.

In spite of the religious condemnation of moneylending, the emperors, who were realists, did not seriously attempt to prevent it. Rather, they chose to permit loans in order to control them better. In Justinianic legislation, we find the first "ceilings" in this regard: senators could ask for no more than 4 percent, the majority of the population no more than 6 percent, businessmen no more than 8 percent, whereas for high-risk loans, such as maritime loans, they could demand as much as 12 percent. It is clear that with these arrangements the authorities were trying to straddle the fence: on the one hand, society wished to discourage the aristocracy's participation in the capital market; on the other, the system allowed everyone to earn interest rates higher than 6 percent, in order to encourage the financing of risky enterprises.

Moreover, this situation was in fact accepted even by the church, which never attempted to prohibit laypeople from lending money at interest. It prohibited this practice by ecclesiastics with such insistence that one is forced to raise questions. The arguments put forth were the immoral character of charging interest and, above all, the ecclesiastics' prohibition from having secular employment. When all was said and done, in Byzantium moneylending was practiced with the blessing of all the authorities, who wished only to limit any excess related to it. We do not know the degree to which they were successful.

Regarding business partnerships, one can assume they occurred within a very liberal and flexible framework. To form a business partnership there had to be two or more participants: the resources pooled together for an enterprise could be capital, personal labor, or both; money came from professional businessmen, but also from individuals, people of humble origin, or even monks who wished to make a profit. The partnership was usually established for a limited time (or for a specific voyage), during which collective responsibility was in effect. At the outset, each party's contribution was assessed, and each partner's share of the profit (or loss) was immediately calculated. These were partnerships that appear to have involved small sums received from several financial backers (who thus avoided high risks) and that must have ended quickly. They were undoubtedly renewable, often with the same partners. This temporary nature of partnerships was even discernible in the case of wealthy capitalists who monopolized state concerns, notably the silk industry. Among them one encounters equal partners who often collaborated on a series of undertakings; but such relatively stable partnerships did not preclude the forming of other partnerships with other individuals. The unstable and constantly changing partnership was a basic characteristic of the oriental world of business.

Byzantium was the only ancient or medieval society to enjoy the uninterrupted use of currency, following the system of coining in three metals established by Constantine the Great. One notes that currency was issued in considerable quantities in all the reigns of this period. Currency was used above all to pay salaries, in particular those of soldiers. It returned to the public till in the form of taxes: indeed, taxes levied in kind became increasingly rare, while basic taxation took on a completely monetary form already at the beginning of the ninth century. The increase in the circulation of currency opened up new avenues for businessmen. More subtle forms of business activity were then made possible; and the monopolistic attitudes of the state and its entrepreneurs were no longer necessary to promote business in the new "capitalist" spirit that appeared to be emerging.

Capitalism Held in Check by the State

Thus there was clearly an expansion of the forms of city life within the empire, and merchants were making their presence increasingly known. Market fairs were increasing in number; they were being held in the same locations every year, and the same merchants returned bringing trunks full of money in amounts that far exceeded those found in the time of the Ephesos fair. Merchants from the provinces came to the fairs to sell their goods, but also to buy other merchandise that they would then transport elsewhere. They were true peddlers who went from market to market and who, we might assume, brought supplies to the villages on their routes.

The provincial cities were growing in importance: merchants began to establish themselves permanently in the marketplaces. This is known to have occurred in Thessalonike in the ninth to twelfth century. The city was renowned for the abundance of goods one could find there, consumer goods as well as goods for investment; it served as an outlet for its Balkan hinterlands, notably for the Bulgarians with whom it maintained constant contact by using the river routes of the Axios/Vardar and the Strymon, primarily following the conquest of Bulgaria by Basil II in 1018. Thessalonike was thus an important junction on the empire's main Balkan route, the Via Egnatia, and owing to that fact it always attracted many visitors who came there to buy supplies. Thessalonike was located on the crossroads of the north-south river routes and the east-west land route. It formed a large market where a great deal of merchandise was exchanged; in the tenth century one already heard about gold, silver, precious stones, silk and wool fabrics, all sorts of metalwork, and the manufacture of glass. Within the city there were at least two permanent markets, one called the inferior market or the so-called Slav market. In addition, in the twelfth century, during the festival of St. Demetrios, the patron saint of the city, a particularly important market fair was held, one attended by merchants from Italy, Western Europe, Bulgaria, and by peoples living even farther north than the Bulgarians. Thessalonike was truly the second city of the empire.

We find mention made of fairs held in several other cities, such as Corinth, Halmyros, Negrepont, Chios, Andros, Chrystopolis, Raidestos, Adramyttion, and Attaleia. One may safely say that the phenomenon of market fairs was a common occurrence and that the number of peddlers must have increased dramatically.

It is also true that there was an increasing number of permanent markets in the provincial cities. In Corinth, for example, the Life of Hosios Loukas as well as archaeological excavations indicate that there was a particularly active economic life there as early as the ninth and tenth centuries. In Lakedaimon there was a market where Venetian merchants came to sell their wares. In the Peloponnese there were paper and purple dye manufacturers, some of whom at least worked for the palace. Thebes, the primary agricultural city, nevertheless became an important center for the production and treatment of silk. In every city in Asia Minor it was common for there to have been at least one money changer: economic life there was thus sufficiently active to require his services on a permanent basis.

The provincial merchant was now quite active on the local level but also went to Constantinople personally to sell his merchandise. To do this he joined a cartel: all merchants who sold the same product—silk, for example, or livestock, or linen—joined together and negotiated with their colleagues in the capital, who also met with them as an organized cartel. The basic principle that underlay these relationships was a division of the empire into two economic regions: the developed region of the capital and the less developed region of the provinces. Hard competition within each of these regions was thereby avoided.

This economic development coincided with the geographical expansion Byzantium underwent beginning in the middle of the ninth century and that was well under way from the middle of the tenth to the middle of the eleventh century. The conquests of John Kourkouas, Nikephoros II Phokas, John I Tzimiskes, and Basil II added new populations and cities to the empire; there were new sources of raw materials and of manufactured products and new markets in which to sell this merchandise. In addition, the reconquest of Crete by the Byzantines (961) and their supremacy at sea brought renewed security to the seas and coastal areas. There was an increase in maritime exchanges; cities reappeared on the coasts, and ports underwent a renaissance. It was the perfect time for the bourgeoisie to thrive. As might be expected, this expansion was first seen in large urban centers, notably Constantinople, which had assumed the role of a metropolis looking outward to the entire world. The businessmen active at that time may be considered to have been truly fortunate.

The rise in business activities could only increase the demand for capital. This tendency toward an increase was already vaguely apparent at the end of the ninth century: the ceiling on interest rates increased officially by about 4.1 percent. In the eleventh century, rates changed to a different, much higher scale: 5.55 percent for senators, 8.33 percent for the average citizen, 11.71 percent for businessmen, and 16.66 percent for maritime loans. These same rates continued to apply in the twelfth century. The returns on loans became tempting, but the system was devised so that for moral reasons the richest men in the empire, the aristocrats, remained outside the realm of loan activities; moneylending was still seen as a deeply dishonorable activity.

Dishonorable perhaps, but a business that paid well and could be tempting. In his *Strategikon,* the eleventh-century author Kekaumenos, himself a soldier and aristocrat, seemed to envision that one of his ilk might be interested in moneylending. He approved of loans made to ransom prisoners (this was not controversial, as that motive was the only one for which it was acceptable even to sell ecclesiastical property), and he disapproved of all other types: one should not lend money in order to earn interest; one must not lend money to earn illicit profit, thus one must not participate in business partnerships; one must not lend money in order to obtain favors from a woman (literally, "for a diabolical love"); one must not lend money to anyone who hoped to secure an administrative post; one must not lend money to anyone who wanted to buy slaves or land, thus to those who wanted to invest in land; one must, above all, not lend money to anyone who planned to invest in a business activity. These were the types of people who, using all sorts of ruses, would attempt to obtain loans from an aristocrat: they would invite him to fancy dinners, cajole him, offer him rare perfume, give him the false impression that they were rich and worthy of trust (to do this they would often borrow from someone else so they would have cash on hand), hold out the extraordinary profits such merchandise would promise and what a shame it would be to miss such an opportunity. It is obvious that, in Kekaumenos' opinion, the typical borrower was a businessman; he might live in the provinces or in Constantinople. He even speaks of those who, with the goal of borrowing from an aristocrat, went so far as to create either real or fictitious family ties with him, have a child named after him, or serve as an intermediary in arranging a marriage. They would do anything to obtain the capital they needed, especially since they would probably receive it at a lower rate than that found on the market.

This need for capital was also evident in Constantinople. We note that businessmen, merchants or artisans, were very rarely owners of the shops in which they carried out their activities. They usually rented or subletted, as the buildings belonged either to ecclesiastical institutions in the capital or to members of the aristocracy or administration. This also occurred in Thessalonike. Since businesses were for the most part small, their owners could not tie up a substantial portion of their capital in owning a building, especially as the rent they paid to set up shop in such a building would certainly have been less than the profits earned from their business.

Most of the shops in Constantinople were located along the main street, the famous Mese, which led from the Golden Gate to the Great Palace, primarily between the Forum of Theodosios and the Forum of Constantine, in the very heart of the city. There one found bakers, jewelers, moneylenders, slave merchants, professions associated with silk, furriers, money changers and their employees who shook sacks of coins in the streets to attract customers. Near St. Sophia there were the candle makers and the bronzeworkers. Elsewhere, still in the same area, there were nail and shoe factories. Scattered throughout the city one found notaries (two per quarter), tavern keepers, and grocers; fishmongers had their wares sold in the various sections of the city by peddlers. From the eleventh century on, neighborhoods were established in which foreigners lived, notably Venetians, merchants who opened their own shops and sold retail just like their Byzantine counterparts. In addition, many western artisans settled in Constantinople and adopted local customs.

The activities of these merchants and artisans were closely monitored by the department of the city prefect, the eparch of Constantinople, an official typical of the Roman capital, head of the imperial tribunal but also governor of the city and responsible not only for maintaining public order but also for insuring that business ran smoothly. In this area of his responsibilities, the prefect was assisted by an assessor, the *symponos*, who had jurisdiction over the trades.

As the Byzantine capital was a city far larger than all others and its marketplace far more important, trades were organized there in a particular way, in the form of professional guilds with internal organizations overseen by the state. From this point of view, the strongly regulated economic life of the capital was clearly different from that of the provinces, which was left much more to the personal initiative of individual businessmen.

The way in which tradesmen carried out their business in tenth-century Constantinople seems to have been a curious mixture of free enterprise and state intervention. We are fortunate to know a great deal about this thanks to the *Book of the Prefect,* an ordinance issued in 911/12 in order to regulate the professional guilds in Constantinople. Even though it was a document conceived at the most basic level, dealing with the day-to-day functioning of specific trades, and contained no general declarations of principle, it enables us to have a glimpse inside Constantinople's business world. On the one hand, everyone was free to make use of his money as he saw fit, to spend it as he wished within the limits imposed upon him by his trade. But the state supervised and controlled all activity with five clear objectives in mind.

(1) The businessman could not compete, especially not illicitly, with other members of his trade. At the time he acquired merchandise or raw materials, he was obliged to work with his colleagues in a cartel: each person contributed the amount of money he wanted to the common till, and after the general purchase he received a proportionate share of the merchandise; in other words, everyone bought at the same price. Individual initiative and competition were thus limited to a choice of the time to buy, the level of investment, the time to sell, and the price to charge. But there were also restrictions regarding this last item.

(2) The merchant was free to set his own prices, but his profit could not exceed a certain level, which varied between around 4 percent and 16 percent of the value of the merchandise, while taking into account the expenses he incurred to obtain the goods and whether or not they were perishable. Since merchants obtained all their goods openly with the full knowledge of the municipal authorities, it was very difficult, if not impossible, to exceed the prescribed level.

(3) The merchant was subject to regulations and controls that were intended to protect the consumer: government offices verified the quality of goods brought to market. This applied to all merchandise, the most

expensive as well as the least costly. Those who sold work animals had to take them back if they were sold with undisclosed defects; and construction professionals (which included painters and sculptors) had to guarantee their work and were required to perform any repairs needed without receiving compensation.

(4) There were separate regulations for so-called prohibited goods (*kekōlymena*), those items whose sale and exportation were subject to specific controls and prohibitions. For the most part, these were precious metals and high-quality or purple-colored silk fabric. It was forbidden to work on these materials outside the workshops, especially in one's home—consequently, one was open to inspection at any time; there was no way to hide any aspect of one's work. Any purchase of goods or raw materials, even that made at an individual's home, had to be reported to the prefect, as did all sales. Thus when Liutprand, bishop of Cremona, visited Constantinople as the ambassador of Otto II, and later attempted to export prohibited merchandise, the Constantinopolitan authorities had already been informed of the purchases he had made.

(5) The government controlled all professional activities very closely, activities that were, by the way, not hereditary. In order to enter a trade, one had to have references and obtain recommendations. One then had to take a sort of entrance examination given by the leaders of the guild. The nomination was confirmed by the department of the prefect. In addition, each new participant had to distribute sums of money to his colleagues at the time he entered his professional guild. The economic importance of the custom was insignificant, but it had a considerable importance from an ethical standpoint: through such gifts, a tradesman was acknowledging his gratitude for having been accepted into the fold.

Thus the tradesman was a skilled professional; this was required by the state, which was also involved and intervened exclusively when it came time to name the heads of each trade: these were distinguished members of their group who enjoyed the confidence of their colleagues, but who also had to enjoy the confidence of the state, in whose interest they directed the activities of their guild. In other words, control over a trade was exercised internally but by someone who had the trust of the government and who seems to have been named for life. This, too, was a stabilizing factor.

From the time he entered a trade, the Byzantine worker had to be able to earn a good living while providing the city's population with the goods and services it required. And members of a trade were required to participate personally in various professional activities, even if they were of a purely ceremonial nature: fines were imposed on those who did not accept an invitation (to a procession, to the Hippodrome, or to a reception given by the prefect) without having a valid reason. The concept of order (*taxis*), which formed a primary element of the Byzantine worldview, was also evident within the professions. One might say that their very existence was inscribed in the same worldview that saw the emperor, believed to be Christ's delegate on earth, as the head of the Christian world, the object of a true cult during palace ceremonies and during official processions through the city. In the common belief that saw the empire as an enormous machine with global importance, the trades held a place that was as well-defined and, one might even say, as essential as that of soldiers or administrators.

Furthermore, businessmen, although they were socially scorned because they could not belong to the senate, were numerous; they settled in the vicinity of the palace and could often be unruly. If they had not had internal problems, they would not have been discontented and would not have had a tendency to turn against the authorities. In an autocratic state, the will of the people could be expressed only in a direct way when the popular masses gathered together in the same place, as the crowd could guarantee a certain anonymity and the security that resulted from it. The explosions of popular sentiment exhibited during races at the Hippodrome are well known. The other place where many residents of Constantinople naturally gathered together in mass and could potentially explode was the marketplace.

The social peace that was guaranteed by stifling competition among members of the same profession, and this within the context of a free economy, limited in particular the possibility of amassing large amounts of capital and developing large enterprises. The economic power and aggressiveness so necessary for making progress in business seem to have been absent, and one receives the impression that they remained absent insofar and just as long as business was good for the tradesmen of Constantinople. It remains true, however, that in sources of the ninth to the eleventh century, when there is mention of extraordinarily rich men, they were usually members of the administration, tax collectors hungry for profit, especially those who farmed out positions in finance, or even artists, like the cantor Ktenas, whose wealth tempted even the emperor. Interestingly, there were no businessmen among the few exceptionally rich men we know of.

Moreover, the state saw to it that there were no millionaires in the world of business by using several expedients. For example, a person was prohibited from belonging to more than one professional guild. It was thus impossible for an individual to take on several trades and accumulate them so as to reach an economic level greater than that of his colleagues. Naturally, many people tried to circumvent this difficulty by being accepted into other guilds by an intermediary, by a slave, for example, or in the case of a monastery, by a monk. But those were unusual situations that did not really change the general fixed image provided by the unified nature of a trade, in which each person could participate. Obviously managing several shops that sold the same goods in the same marketplace would have made no sense, as the shops would have been competing against each other.

The trades connected to the production and distribution of silk provide a particularly telling example of this. Since silk was a commodity of great value, but also in high demand, the trades involved with it were divided into several different guilds: sellers of raw silk who bought the raw material from the producers; those who made silk thread; silk dyers; silk cloth manufacturers; silk clothing sellers; and sellers of silk clothing imported from Syria. Each stage of the process was run by a separate trade, so each individual could concentrate on a single link in the chain. Thus no one person could in any way dominate that industry.

The rigidity with which each trade was distinct from others becomes clearer in a particular case described in the *Book of the Prefect*. Let us assume, the text goes, that the neighboring barbarians, the Bulgarians, for example, wanted to trade linen or honey with us; the qualified merchants of Constantinople, that is, the cloth and food merchants, would bring along other merchants, those who sold objects needed by the barbarians, usually sellers of poorer quality silk cloth. Having obtained the prefect's authorization, they all went together to the barbarians' territory to carry out the exchange, those merchants exporting their goods having the right to obtain a commission for any merchandise that was bought with the help of their goods. The distinction and protection of individual trades could hardly have been more advanced.

One can then better understand the importance the state's moderating role in the economic life of the cities had for the merchant. By guaranteeing a certain security for all members of the trades, it held their activities and ambitions in check. In a free economy, through its various controls it managed to transform merchants into individuals calmly settled into the security of their shops, somewhat as if they were lifelong functionaries. The system guaranteed everyone a good, though not very ambitious, life. But with the expansion of the economy in the tenth and especially the eleventh century, it was natural for the business world to be shaken up, for its participants to begin to aspire to more.

THE ARRIVAL OF FOREIGN SUPPLIERS

Everything discussed so far has concerned the business affairs of those who resided in Constantinople. But there were also individuals who came from outside the city to do business there; whether they were from the Byzantine provinces or beyond did not make a great difference. From the moment they arrived in the capital, they were immediately placed under the jurisdiction of the prefect: they became the responsibility of a delegate of the prefect (*legatarios*) whose duties included overseeing the activity of foreigners; they had to inform the authorities of what they were importing, receive instructions concerning the procedures to be followed in selling it, and also receive a time frame (no more than three months) during which they were to complete their transactions and leave the capital, and in the end obtain approval of the list of purchases they made in Constantinople and wished to export. From every point of view, the behavior of Constantinople's residents toward provincial visitors and foreigners was essentially the same. This is very clear insofar as prohibited merchandise was concerned, such as precious metals or high-quality silk, the exportation of which into the provinces was controlled and limited, just as if those goods were being exported abroad.

The development of business activity in Constantinople fell within the framework of the economic development of Europe, which is believed to have begun in the tenth century. We have seen how Constantinople maintained the level of economic exchanges with its neighbors, the caliphate, which was an already developed economic power, and with the Bulgarians, who had a much more primitive economy. Furthermore, Constantinople obtained goods steadily from the Far East either by using Arabs as intermediaries or directly by using the route from Trebizond, which led into central Asia. These were very active commercial exchanges, but which for the most part stopped at the Byzantine capital, for there were no more important customers farther west. This was still the situation in the ninth century.

In addition, Constantinople, which, as a large city, continually experienced problems in obtaining enough supplies for its population, had contact with the north from the Black Sea, which comprised another gate to the Far East, but which above all assured the city its supplies of raw materials. To insure the availability of such supplies, the government naturally came to the aid of businessmen with the installation of a military government (theme) in Cherson in the Crimea, which then became the center for trade with peoples from the north, primarily the Khazars, and also the Russians.

Indeed, Constantinople's opening up to the world became much more evident in the tenth century, about which we finally have significant amounts of information. Commercial contacts with the Russians, which were then established for the first time, and which are made known to us thanks to two treaties, one from 911 and another from 944, show the fundamental element that governed these economic relationships: the Russians' desire to enter into the economic zone of the Byzantine capital and to be able to obtain prohibited merchandise there. In other words, the agreement between the two states essentially concerned the arrival of Russian merchants in Constantinople and the treatment they could expect to receive there. The Russians arrived in the Byzantine capital in a convoy of boats that came down the Dnieper from Kiev, according to the well-known description by Constantine VII Porphyrogennetos: it was a dangerous voyage, and the merchants, who were still true Vikings, were of course armed—in fact, many of them were hoping to enter the Byzantine emperor's guard as mercenaries. They settled outside the city in the St. Mamas district and went to the market during the day in unarmed groups accompanied by an imperial functionary. They sold or traded their goods, and were allowed to bring back their purchases, which could include a limited quantity of prohibited goods, silk cloth in particular: each Russian merchant could export goods valued at no more than 50 gold coins, in other words, the quantity of prohibited merchandise he could export diminished if its quality (and value) was great. And at the time goods were exported, all the merchandise had to obtain the seal of the appropriate functionaries. It appears there were no limitations placed on the exportation of other merchandise.

In addition to what is said in the treaties concerning Constantinople, mention is also made of the visits that the citizens of the two lands might have made elsewhere, of the protection that the rulers had to grant them mutually. But their economic contacts were suppressed, undoubtedly because all commercial contacts made outside the zone of the capital were governed by the idea of a free market and were regulated only insofar as the two states guaranteed the safety of the participants and the goods involved in exchanges.

Furthermore, commercial contacts were being established between Byzantium and the West, beginning with Italy and in particular the small states that had, at one time or another, recognized Byzantine sovereignty. Byzantine goods appeared first in Rome, but it was primarily the merchants of Amalfi who created the first large colony of westerners in Constantinople. Their undertakings succeeded thanks to the commerce between their country and the Byzantine capital. Amalfi quickly became a noteworthy market town in Italy. And the merchants of Amalfi also participated in the spiritual life of the empire by creating, before the schism of the churches, a monastery of their own on Mount Athos.

The Venetians also began to be regular visitors to the empire. They already enjoyed a privileged status in the tenth century, and they obtained additional privileges in 997, ones that put them in a better position than other non-Byzantines who came to Constantinople. Still, at that time all agreements concerned foreigners who visited the economic zone of the capital. But we note that at that same time, around the end of the tenth century, Venetians began to settle in the Byzantine provinces to do business. They were most certainly profitable markets despite the absence of prohibited goods.

The Culminating Point

In this discussion concerning foreigners, what was the role of Byzantine merchants and artisans? It was one that, at first glance, appears to have been privileged: they stayed in their shops in the comfort and safety of the Byzantine capital, and they waited for their suppliers as well as their customers to come to them. For a vast region surrounding the city, a region that went far beyond the frontiers of the empire, Constantinople was the only truly large market because of the number of local consumers and because of its international contacts. Everyone, including the residents of the empire, hoped to sell their merchandise there; everyone also hoped to obtain supplies there. Owing to the organization described above, they all had to go through the organized trades of the Byzantine capital, whose members alone were authorized to import goods into the capital, had the right to work the raw materials that arrived there, and, finally, had the right to run a shop in the city. In addition, the system prevented them from competing against each other. It is thus not surprising that they adopted the attitude of "passive brokers"; they avoided business voyages and the associated risks, and were content with the profit insured by the status of their shops and the limited interventionism of the Byzantine state, which was concerned with restraining rather than controlling its market economy, which in principle was a free one.

There was economic somnolence, therefore, but also comfort, the accumulation of the wealth that came quite naturally with the opening of new markets and with the economic awakening of Western Europe. This awakening also occurred in Byzantium, with three fundamental differences: Byzantium had never completely fallen asleep; the acceleration of its economy had begun earlier; and it occurred in calm and serenity. The business figures rose, the opportunities for becoming rich did as well, but this all occurred within the framework of the old system, without necessitating the adoption of new forms of management or trade. The need for capital increased, and interest rates were then raised. But since the risk taken by Byzantine merchants was always minimal, and the returns they earned from business were more or less regulated, the need for higher interest loans does not seem to have arisen.

But with the increase in the number of business transactions, the economic power of the Constantinopolitan businessmen also increased. In the eleventh century when all Byzantium, victorious on all fronts, was settling into an "illusion of a lasting peace," and tended to ignore the rigors of military life in order to adopt a new lifestyle, businessmen could finally become aware of their economic power and could also cultivate their ambitions. The men of the marketplace participated directly in the political life of the empire. In December 1041, one of their own, Michael V Kalaphates ("the caulker," named after the trade practiced by his family), became emperor by being adopted by the widowed empress Zoe. This was the occasion for unprecedented joyful celebrations in Constantinople. During his procession on Easter of 1042, his colleagues from the marketplace exhibited symbols of adoration toward him. They spread bolts of richly woven silk on the ground, from the palace to the doors of the church of St. Sophia, upon which the emperor proceeded in great pomp followed by the stately retinue who guarded him. "To the right and left of the procession, rich and precious fabric was displayed, gilded and silver decorations were hung in endless succession, and the entire marketplace, decorated with garlands, indeed appeared to be celebrating." And everyone sang the praises of the new ruler.

This was a mob mentality that could quickly shift. When the next day it was learned that Michael V had carried out a coup d'état and had banished his adoptive mother, the legitimate empress Zoe, that same mob rose up against him. Under the active and fairly well organized leadership of the "people of the workshops," of the "marketplace mob," including women, the population of Constantinople rose up, fought the palace guard, and overthrew their idol of the day before. An attachment to the dynasty and to the legality of the crown won out over any impulsive class or group action.

This was the first time in a very long while that the people of Constantinople had brought about such radical political change on their own. Granted, during the revolts of the preceding centuries, the residents of Constantinople had played a role, but it was never completely determining. Most often it involved uprisings that occurred just as a rebellious and partially victorious army appeared before the capital; and these uprisings were usually led by local aristocrats who assumed leadership over the mob with the assistance of their private militias. But in 1042 there had been nothing like that. It was the market people who took the initiative and carried the revolt to its conclusion.

They demanded a role in the political life of the empire. In this specific case, as in later ones, merchants and artisans allied themselves with the legitimate dynasty. This was normal; everywhere in the world all citizens, and in particular the bourgeoisie, have allied themselves with the strong central power against the landholding or military aristocracy. By participating in the political life of their land, they were also aspiring to a better social status both for themselves and their children. This was an attitude that in many ways resembled what was to occur in Western Europe a few centuries later with the emancipation of the bourgeoisie and the centralization of power. In Byzantium that strong central authority had always existed; it was now being supported by its new bourgeoisie.

There can be no doubt that this political change—the active participation of businessmen in political life—was also the result of the economic power they had in the meantime begun to wield. From that time on, and for years to come, the emperors attempted to curry the favor of businessmen. Soon the supreme moment came, the moment when businessmen were admitted into the ranks of senators. This reform, which is attributed to Constantine IX (1042–55) or Constantine X (1057–67), provided another considerable advantage for the central authority (as would also be the case in Western Europe), the possibility of putting their hands on some of the capital accumulated by businessmen.

In eleventh-century Byzantium, to become a member of the senate one had to have obtained an imperial dignity, that of *prōtospatharios* or an even loftier title. To become *prōtospatharios,* one needed the consent of the emperor, but one also had to pay a considerable sum to the state, 12–18 lbs. of gold (864–1296 gold coins), for which one received the dignity as well as an annuity of 1 lb. of gold, which represented a return of 8.33–5.55 percent. This was a life annuity without the possibility of recuperating the invested capital. Consequently one's returns, which might have appeared attractive considering the interest rates of the marketplace (and which might have appeared even more attractive because they were guaranteed by the state), were nevertheless not necessarily profitable.

Until the eleventh century, businessmen did not have the right to participate in the system because of the traditional prejudice against their dishonorable activities. But in the eleventh century, things had changed quite a bit. The number of businessmen and their economic, social, and political roles had changed dramatically. The revolt of 1042 offers tangible proof of this. Businessmen had become real factors in political life and were recognized as such. By opening the doors of the senate to them after so many centuries of rejection, the emperors not only earned their gratitude but also enriched the public till, at that time undergoing a crisis of expansion, with their money, which was needed to fortify the state's finances. As for the Byzantine bourgeoisie, they joined the aristocracy eagerly, without being the least concerned that a portion of their capital was now destined for state revenues and might possibly be missed. Were they not assured that competition in Constantinople was controlled and limited? Were they not assured that other merchants, Byzantine or foreign, would be forced to bring their markets to Constantinople, inevitably to them? In any case, it was obvious that their newfound status was connected to their wealth, a wealth that could be predicted to become an important factor in the definition of human relations. To the Byzantine businessmen, a capitalist—or almost capitalist—future was opening before their very eyes.

In obtaining these new honorific titles, they did more than break a taboo; they also received a distinguished social position, precedence over others, and some social privileges that, though they primarily reflected formalities, were no less real and provided concrete advantages: they obtained the right to give sworn statements in their homes, where a functionary came for the purpose, and thus did not have to go to court. And if they were involved in a trial, senators were allowed to ask for a chair and sit down, like the judge, whereas everyone else in the audience remained standing. These were small advantages, but they could greatly influence the morale of everyone implicated in the trial.

The beginning of the second half of the eleventh century was the culminating point of the economic and social ascent of Byzantine businessmen. They had just established themselves economically, politically, and even socially, and saw promising prospects before them. Their situation brings to mind that of the bourgeoisie in Western Europe at the end of the fourteenth and during the fifteenth century, with one difference: in Byzantium there were no economic empires such as those of the Bardi or of Jacques Coeur. The Byzantines had their limited, safe, and ultimately indolent capitalism with wealth distributed to a large number of the members of each trade. It was a large capitalist base, but without high points. This was perhaps a weakness.

Whatever the case may have been, the Byzantine dream of the eleventh century was shattered in 1071, one might say, when the Normans definitively expelled the Byzantines from southern Italy and the Turks, having won the battle of Mantzikert, flooded into Asia Minor. These two events demonstrated the weaknesses inherent in the empire, and the ten years of civil war that followed completed its dismemberment. In 1081 a sort of restoration was undertaken in Constantinople, led this time by the great families of the landed and military provincial aristocracy, by the Komnenian dynasty that allied itself with the Doukas family. Byzantium ceased to be a vast and impersonal empire and assumed the aspect of a feudal state in which family relationships were often more important than the titles of an individual. This was the upper aristocracy that now reigned and that favored noble blood.

One of the first measures taken by the new regime was to abolish all the privileges the businessmen had just acquired. Alexios I Komnenos quickly set about cleaning up the senate. He created a completely new hierarchy of titles, reserved for aristocrats, so that the old titles that the businessmen had been given became obsolete. In addition, the revenues for the titles had already been abolished, as were all social privileges, through a new law enacted by the emperor. Already at the end of the eleventh century, the merchants' participation in the senate was a thing of the past.

Suppliers Become Competitors

The same emperor took other measures that might have been against the interests of his own merchants and artisans. Pressured as he was to confront the Norman threat in the Balkans, he turned to Venice and received the assistance of its fleet, for which he gave the Venetians unprecedented privileges: the right to trade freely throughout the empire, including the economic region of Constantinople, with its warehouses and loading docks, as well as the right to set up shops. In addition, they were exempt from the 10 percent duty that the Byzantine merchants had to pay the state for transporting and selling their merchandise. Thus the Venetians automatically found themselves in a privileged position compared to their Byzantine colleagues.

They had already obtained privileges before the tenth century. At that time they came to Constantinople and sold to and bought from Byzantine merchants. Now, in 1082, for the first time they received the right to compete directly with the Byzantine shopkeepers of the capital, and even to do so in privileged conditions. This was the principal innovation of the treaty of 1082; the security of the businessmen of Constantinople was destroyed, and open competition sprang up in the capital at the same time the Venetians did.

The treaty of 1082 was ratified at a time of necessity, when the empire was pressured from all sides. Later, emperors attempted to revoke the Venetians' privileges, but they were no longer in a position to confront their fleet. They therefore had to come to terms with the situation and extend the same privileges (without complete exemptions) to other westerners, such as the Pisans or the Genoese. But what was always the most important element in these agreements was the freedom to trade in Constantinople, which continued to be a much larger marketplace than any other.

It was precisely due to this "intrinsic" importance of the Constantinopolitan market that the effect of concessions made to foreigners was not immediately felt. First, there was the time it took for the westerners to establish themselves firmly in the eastern markets (all markets were not accessible to them; they still had to obtain oriental goods from Byzantine merchants); then there was the twelfth-century phenomenon of the great movement of groups and individuals, and Constantinople took on a completely cosmopolitan appearance. Sources mention at length all the foreigners who visited the city, some of whom were so exotic that no interpreter could be found to speak to them. It happened that small trade was carried out by the Venetians—for example, the cheese merchant mentioned by Theodore Prodromos—but business also grew very quickly, and everyone did extremely well economically. According to the same Theodore Prodromos, Byzantine shopkeepers and artisans continued to earn a very good living in Constantinople and in the provinces.

However, it was only a matter of time before the effects of competition were felt. Even the emperor sought to curry the favor of the Italians who habitually entered the port of Constantinople with their sails hoisted. Resentment grew, and the Byzantine merchants exerted pressure on the authorities. Thus a vast government action was undertaken on 12 March 1171: in a single day the Byzantine administration arrested all Venetian citizens residing in the empire and confiscated all their belongings, merchandise, and boats. It took the true pogrom of the Latins in 1182 and the clearly anti-Latin—albeit inefficacious—policy of Andronikos I Komnenos for the Italian merchants to decide to leave Constantinople. But this was just a temporary situation.

It is clear that toward the end of the twelfth century the condition of the Byzantine merchants of Constantinople had become critical because of competition from the Italians. There had been repeated attempts to get rid of them, either by using state-supported violence or with direct action. Nothing yielded the anticipated results. The economic region of Constantinople continued to be the most coveted market, but the control Byzantine businessmen managed to exercise over it continued to diminish. In fact, they exercised political control over that market and carried much weight because of their sheer numbers; but economic control escaped them, hence the violence of their reactions and their attempts to use political strength to reestablish their economic superiority. It did not work. On the other hand, soon afterwards political control also fell into the hands of the Latins following the Fourth Crusade, the capture of the city, and the creation of the Latin Empire in Constantinople. From that moment the very notion of a "protected" economic region in the Byzantine capital disappeared; and all the advantages the Byzantine businessmen had been able to retain also disappeared, in particular those connected with obtaining raw materials from the Black Sea region. The purest and most competitive capitalism was finally and definitively established on the shores of the Bosporos.

THE BYZANTINE BUSINESS WORLD
SUBJUGATED AND DEPENDENT

The Fourth Crusade opened the door to the creation of two great colonial empires in Romania: the Venetian and the Genoese. There were also the Latin states that were the direct issue of the conquest over the territory of present-day Greece. The eastern basin of the Mediterranean became an integral part of the European market, which swelled with several economic centers. Constantinople remained an important city and, what is more, an important market center owing to its geographical location; it continued to impress visitors, such as the Arab traveler Ibn Battuta, but it was no longer unique. Cities just as large and economically more powerful had in the meantime developed in the West: in the south, Florence, Venice, and Genoa had large populations and served as bases for economic operations that were larger and more aggressive than any the world had previously known. Constantinople, already under Latin domination, but also after it was reconquered by the Byzantines in 1261, was behind. It soon became the place where the developed and relatively industrialized economies of the West came into contact with the still primitive economies of the East; it thus served as a locale for the transit and redistribution of merchandise that traveled through from all directions. Indeed, it appears that, from the thirteenth to the fifteenth century, there was a closed trade route in the Black Sea, whose goal was in fact to collect the raw materials produced along the coast and bring them to Constantinople and Pera, where they would connect with the large international trade routes. Greek shipowners and businessmen were very active in this local commerce.

Moreover, already in 1261 the empire was forced once again to recognize the privileges of western merchants and allow the Venetians to settle in Constantinople, for example, and the Genoese to settle in Galata, again with complete exemptions and benefits of all kinds. Competition existed, and Greek merchants had trouble dealing with it; they were thus forced to adapt and submit to the de facto domination imposed by their Latin colleagues.

These were acts of resignation, imposed by economic realism. For a long time, but especially after 1204, the Greeks had considerable reservations about the Latins, who imposed themselves economically and who also wanted to impose themselves spiritually and subject the Greeks to the Church of Rome. These two different Christian parties were separated by violent animosities. But when one entered into the world of business, agreement was obligatory, especially since the Italian powers were always able to obtain adequate protection and opened the doors to the most lucrative enterprises of the time. Thus several Byzantines were eager to obtain Venetian or Genoese citizenship to take advantage of the privileges that went with it, without for all that forgetting their implacable hatred for those boorish, violent, and greedy Latins whose piety was debatable and whose dogma was "certainly erroneous."

The fiercely anti-Latin mind-set that characterized the average Byzantine citizen of the final centuries was also motivated by the resentment he felt against the economic imperialism of western merchants, who had settled in the East and were getting rich at his expense; it was an imperialism against which the Byzantines did not have the means to react in any effective way. A single attempt in this direction should be pointed out. In 1348, when almost all the land of the empire had passed into the hands of its enemies, Emperor John VI Kantakouzenos took some radical measures. He lowered the duties the Byzantine tradesmen had to pay to 2 percent and attempted to impose tariffs on the trade of westerners, who reacted with violence and forced him to reverse that measure. He was also forced to abandon his plans to build a war fleet worthy of the name and had to recognize officially that the Greek merchants could no longer compete with the Genoese in the trade of products coming from central Asia via the Tana route below the Sea of Azov. This was, in fact, the largest area of trade, controlled by the Venetians and the Genoese, into which Greek merchants were not at all welcome.

Whether they liked it or not, the Greek businessmen had to adopt new methods and techniques that were in use in the international markets. Loaning money with interest was regularly practiced, setting rates that often exceeded the norms established by law, from 10 percent to 25 percent or even higher; for maritime loans, the usual rate was 16.66 percent per voyage and no longer per year. Above all, there was hidden interest levied at the source, such as commissions, which were not mentioned in contracts. Usury was violently denounced by intellectuals, thus it wreaked havoc. In the cosmopolitan atmosphere of the time, it was normal to make loans at a distance using the currency of other countries; these were exchange contracts in which the interest was in fact hidden in the exchange rate established. Checks or promissory notes (which were nevertheless negotiable, making them very close to checks) even began to be used. These were common practices employed by the capitalists of Western Europe but that were also introduced and largely adopted in the Byzantine East. When the Byzantine government attempted to intervene the better to control abuses in the lending practices of its own subjects, the Byzantine capital turned toward the Latins.

Indeed, it was neither capital nor bankers that the Byzantines were lacking. First, there were many bankers in Constantinople itself, and they were powerful enough to continue to play a political role right up to the middle of the fourteenth century. They were in very close contact with their Italian colleagues, with whom they often formed partnerships. They appeared to act very cautiously, as did the Italians in the East, as well: they invested relatively small sums in several enterprises and sought the highest interest wherever they could find it, even at a distance.

The big bankers with contacts and clients in the international sphere had undeniable economic power, but they were never able to create real public banks in Byzantium, like those found in Italy at the same time; nor did they succeed in becoming affiliated with those large Italian banks. Otherwise they carried out business in the same way their Italian colleagues did: they opened up individual or business accounts, they received deposits, granted loans, carried out financial transactions through simple inscriptions in their books, exchanged foreign currency, and especially letters of exchange. They sometimes had to defend their clients' interests before the law. They also sometimes participated personally in trade activity and in commercial voyages. Although specializing in the money trade, they did not scorn the trading of goods and the profit that could be earned from it.

In forming business partnerships, the Byzantines of the last period used the same procedures as the Latins and undoubtedly maintained their accounts in a similar manner. In Constantinople one found the *commenda* and the *colleganza,* which were arrangements between the merchant (who either did or did not have any capital, but who offered his own personal work) and the financial backer who provided all or part of the capital. Other partnerships combining work and capital included the running of a shop or a workshop, or even the shipping business.

The main characteristic of these business partnerships was that most often they involved relatively small sums and lasted only a short amount of time. Like the Italians in the East, each financial investor attempted to reduce his risk and consequently simultaneously invested in several partnerships, and every merchant who went abroad was the partner of several investors; each one of them provided him with only a portion of the capital he needed for the voyage ahead. The same reserve characterized partnerships that did not involve a risky voyage, such as, for example, partnerships in the running of a workshop or a shop; one has the impression that the partners waited impatiently for the dissolution of the enterprise, at which time they could tally up the earnings and divide the profits among them. The same partners entered into several consecutive partnerships or participated simultaneously in several arrangements with different partners. These were limited and temporary; there do not seem to have been any true enterprises with interdependent and unlimited responsibility, with permanent and known correspondents in other cities, like those in Western Europe that developed and lasted for a long time. One has the impression that the most absolute individualism—a sign of insecurity, lack of confidence, and a certain economic underdevelopment—took precedence over and dictated the supple forms of partnerships that the Byzantines and the Italians of the Levant, especially the Venetians, applied.

Moreover, nationalism and strong feelings gave way when business was at issue. Partnerships between Byzantines and Italians were common, despite the few prohibitions imposed by the emperors. The Greek businessman may have been resentful of the Italians, but when the time came to make a profit, all his reticence disappeared and gave way to realism and the lure of financial gain. Thus, before declaring war against the Genoese of Galata, the Byzantine emperor gave his subjects a few days so they could settle their business affairs with their partners who were soon to become their enemies on the battlefield. Also, as seen in the account book of Giacomo Badoer, the Venetian businessman who settled in Constantinople in the fifteenth century, Greco-Latin business partnerships were very common.

Byzantine merchants went on business voyages only in the eastern basin of the Mediterranean and the Black Sea, but the large west European markets were closed to them by their Italian competitors. They carried out trade in large part using the boats of the sailors from Monemvasia, who traveled everywhere and came to settle in Constantinople and in its immediate surroundings, near Kyzikos. They transported primarily raw materials, especially objects of limited value that served as supplies for Constantinople as well as for the Italian fleets, which themselves engaged in the trade of luxury items. Long-distance Byzantine trade was thus limited and played a subsidiary role as compared to that of the Italians.

By contrast, the retail trade and artisanry of Constantinople were dominated by the Greeks. Their shops and workshops were scattered throughout a city that was now made up of thirteen distinct villages within the city walls; in the fifteenth century the large food market, the "central marketplace," was located along the Golden Horn, outside the city walls, surely in order to be near the place where the goods would be unloaded from ships. Obtaining supplies by land routes became increasingly difficult, given the gradual occupation of the countryside by the Turks. Other shops were located in the center of the city, near the Mese, and we also read of peddlers and fairs that were held in the city, such as the one held each week on the occasion of the procession of the icon of the Virgin Hodegetria.

All trades were practiced there, but we note that there was practically no production of fabrics or glass, probably because those types of crafts were abandoned by the Greeks, who were unable to withstand the competition of the developed industries in Western Europe. Otherwise, each trade seems to have been organized into a western-style guild, with a leader who was empowered to represent all the members before the authorities. This was another characteristic element that connected Greek businessmen to their Latin colleagues, who were organized in the same way.

From the end of the eleventh century, the Byzantine businessmen were once again excluded from the senate and from receiving imperial dignities, and from a social point of view they were counted among the people. However, in the twelfth and especially the first half of the fourteenth century, having reached a certain critical mass, they were once again admitted into the political and social life of the empire; they began to be called by the collective form, "the middle ones," *mesoi*, those who occupied an intermediate social position between the low-ranking masses and the aristocracy. During the civil wars and the social conflicts of the fourteenth century, these "middle" men took a position only when they were forced into it, and in those cases they stood up against the aristocrats who were rich in land and who in turn despised them.

So with the political setbacks Byzantium experienced around the middle of the fourteenth century, which resulted in the empire's loss of most of its cultivable lands, many aristocrats forgot the traditional restrictions and placed their capital in the only sector that could bring them significant returns—commercial affairs. The big names, including that of the ruling dynasty of the Palaiologoi, became increasingly frequent in the world of business. Thus in the fourteenth century the exact opposite of what had taken place in the eleventh century occurred: by adopting the trades of the "middle" men in a massive way, the aristocrats brought about the disappearance of the basic characteristic that distinguished them from those men. In a society that was becoming increasingly mercantile, good birth was of little importance; only one social distinction maintained its value, the distinction between the rich and the poor.

SELECTED BIBLIOGRAPHY

Primary Sources

Acta et diplomata graeca medii aevi sacra et profana collecta, ed. F. Miklosich and I. Müller. Vienna, 1860–90.

Jus Graecoromanum, ed. I. Zepos and P. Zepos. 8 vols. Athens, 1930–31.

Il libro dei conti di Giacomo Badoer (Costantinopoli 1436–1440), ed. U. Dorini and T. Bertelè. Rome, 1956.

Le Livre du Préfet, ed. J. Nicole. Geneva, 1893.

Constantine Porphyrogenitus. *De administrando imperio,* edited, translated, and with commentary by G. Moravcsik and R. J. H. Jenkins. Vol. 1, Budapest, 1949; vol. 2, London, 1962.

Francesco Balducci Pegolotti. *La pratica della mercatura,* ed. A. Evans. Cambridge, Mass., 1936.

General Literature

Ahrweiler, H. *Byzance et la mer.* Paris, 1967.

Antoniadis-Bibicou, H. *Recherches sur les douanes à Byzance.* Paris, 1963.

Balard, M. *La Romanie génoise (XIIe–début du XVe siècle).* 2 vols. Rome, 1978.

Bréhier, L. *Le monde byzantin,* vol. 3: *La civilisation byzantine.* Paris, 1950.

Chrysostomides, J. "Venetian Commercial Privileges under the Palaeologi." *Studi Veneziani* 12 (1970): 267–356.

Janin, R. *Constantinople byzantine: Développement urbain et répertoire topographique.* 2d ed. Paris, 1964.

Koukoules, P. *Byzantinōn bios kai politismos.* 4 vols. Athens, 1948–57.

Laiou-Thomadakis, A. E. "The Byzantine Economy in the Mediterranean Trade System: Thirteenth–Fifteenth Centuries." *Dumbarton Oaks Papers* 34–35 (1980–81): 177–222.

———. "The Greek Merchant of the Palaelogan Period: A Collective Portrait." *Praktika tēs Akademias Athēnōn* 57 (1982): 96–132.

———. *Händler und Kaufleute auf dem Jahrmarkt.* In G. Prinzing and D. Simon, eds., *Fest und Alltag in Byzanz,* pp. 53–70. Munich, 1990.

Matschke, K.-P. *Fortschritt und Reaktion in Byzanz im 14. Jahrhundert: Konstantinopel in der Bürgerkriegsperiode von 1341 bis 1354.* Berlin, 1971.

Mickwitz, G. *Die Kartellfunktionen der Zünfte und ihre Bedeutung bei der Entstehung des Zunftwesens: Eine Studie in spätantiker und mittelalterlicher Wirtschaftsgeschichte.* Helsigfors, 1936.

Oikonomides, N. *Hommes d'affaires grecs et latins à Constantinople (XIIIe–XVe siècles).* Montreal–Paris, 1979.

———. "Silk Trade and Production in Byzantium from the Sixth to the Ninth Century: The Seals of Kommerkiarioi." *Dumbarton Oaks Papers* 40 (1986): 33–53.

———. "Le Kommerkion d'Abydos, Thessalonique et le commerce bulgare au IXe siècle." In *Hommes et richesses dans l'empire byzantin,* vol. 2, pp. 241–48. Paris, 1991.

Schreiner, P. "Die Organisation byzantinischer Kaufleute und Handwerker." *Abhandlungen der Akademie der Wissenschaften in Göttingen, philologisch-historische Klasse,* s. 3, 183 (1989): 44–61.

Thiriet, F. *La Romanie vénitienne au Moyen-Âge: Le développement et l'exploitation du domaine colonial vénitien (XIIe–XVe siècles).* Paris, 1959.

Zacos, G., and A. Veglery. *Byzantine Lead Seals* Vol. 1. Basel, 1972.

Zakythinos, D. *Crise monétaire et crise économique à Byzance du XVIIIe au XVe siècles.* Athens, 1948.

7

BISHOPS

Vera von Falkenhausen

A FUNERARY EPIGRAM FOR Metrophanes, the metropolitan of Smyrna (second half of the ninth century), lauds the episcopal virtues of the deceased prelate in the following words:

> Do you seek the saintly life of a monk?
> Then let the life of Metrophanes be an example to you.
> Do you seek the proper word of the spiritual shepherd?
> Then seek it in his writings.
> Do you have the ambition to admonish and advise others,
> to care for all like a father?
> Then imitate his wise and open speech.
> For wealth consists in caring for the poor.
> That is how he reached Paradise,
> leaving behind on earth only the shadow of his body.[1]

We are not concerned with Metrophanes himself, who in his youth was involved in a vicious slander campaign against Patriarch Methodios, and whom we know as the author of biblical commentaries and spiritual poetry. He was also an uncompromising supporter of Patriarch Ignatios during the conflicts over ecclesiastical policy in the second half of the ninth century, a partisanship that earned him imprisonment, exile, and eventually even papal excommunication. The point is that the author of these somewhat awkward verses, a high-ranking imperial official, expressed here the very essence of what the Byzantines expected in their bishop: he should have spent part of his life in a monastery and at the same time be the teacher, protector, sustainer, and father of the believers entrusted to his care. Despite all the political, ideological, and social changes the Byzantine Empire experienced during its more than thousand-year history, the image of the episcopal profession hardly changed: prior life as a monk, education, leadership qualities, and social

172

activism were consistently regarded as desirable characteristics of the ideal bishop, from Basil the Great, bishop of Caesarea in Cappadocia in the fourth century, to Bessarion, metropolitan of Nicaea in the fifteenth century.

The Greek word *episkopos* (bishop), already used in the Epistles of St. Paul, means something like "overseer" or "guardian." Thus the Christian bishop was, in a sense, the overseer of the community entrusted to his care. As such he had to see to the spread of the faith and the purity of doctrine, promote social peace within his flock—*shepherd* is one of the most popular terms for the bishop—and cultivate contacts with other communities. As spokesmen for and representatives of their communities, many bishops suffered a martyr's death during the Christian persecutions. Well over fifty martyr-bishops are commemorated in the liturgical calendar of Constantinople.

The seat of the bishop was usually a city, the local center of civilian life and imperial administration; the bishop's jurisdiction included the territory of the city. The sixth canon of the Council of Sardica (342/343) clearly stipulated that bishops were not to be used in villages or small towns whose spiritual care could be provided by a simple priest, lest the episcopal name and its authority be degraded. Just as Christianity spread along the lines laid down by the geographic and administrative structures of the Roman Empire, the organization of the ecclesiastical geography and hierarchy became, almost inevitably, a mirror of the secular organization, even if the boundaries of ecclesiastical dioceses did not always overlap with those of the secular provinces: bishops resided in cities, metropolitans in provincial capitals, and archbishops (without suffragans) in cities that had special importance for some reason or another. The bishops of the great metropolises of the empire—Rome, Alexandria, and Antioch—soon adopted the title of patriarch. For, according to Byzantine notions, the primacy of the bishop of Rome rested not on the apostolic succession to Peter but on the political rank of the old capital of the empire. For much the same reason the holder of the episcopal title in Constantinople was catapulted into the rank of patriarch already during the fourth century. Only the patriarchal title of the bishop of Jerusalem, which he held from the fifth century on, was based on the specific importance of the city as the site of Christ's redemptive acts.

If the political significance of a city or province changed, ecclesiastical organization generally followed suit. The most blatant case was the already mentioned rapid rise of the capital of the Byzantine Empire, to which the First Council of Constantinople (381) assigned the second rank of honor behind Rome because it was New Rome; the fathers at the Council of Chalcedon (451) went a step further by decreeing that Old Rome and New Rome were equal in rank, for the latter was distinguished as the seat of the emperor and the senate. But many other such examples could be listed from all parts of the empire, for, according to canon seventeen of Chalcedon, the organization of the church was to follow that of the state. For example, when Emperor Justinian I, in an effort to elevate the status of his puny birthplace in Dacia, made it the administrative center of the prefecture of Illyria with the new name Justiniana Prima (today Caricin Grad in Yugoslavia), he also elevated the local bishop to the rank of metropolitan (535) and even granted him the honorary title of papal vicar. In the course of the seventh century, the bishop of the city of Ravenna, since the end of the Gothic Wars seat of the Byzantine governors of Italy, also reached metropolitan status with special privileges, at least for a short time, through an imperial edict. In general, it was probably ambitious local bishops who pestered the emperor and the patriarchs until the ecclesiastical rank of their city was finally adjusted to its secular rank. However, there were also practical reasons for such an adjustment: capital cities usually had a larger population that placed greater demands on their ecclesiastical lords. Moreover, the fact that the residences of the secular and religious authorities were in the same city could make it easier for both to carry out the duties of their offices. In any case, when it came to the organization and reorganization of the ecclesiastical map, the emperor always had the last word.

The church canons and secular laws of late antiquity defined the episcopal office something like this: the bishop should be elected by the clergy and notables of his bishopric, confirmed by the appropriate metropolitan, and consecrated by two or three bishops from the metropolitan's diocese. Simony and nepotism in the election and consecration of a bishop were strictly prohibited and in theory invalidated the ordination. The metropolitans were chosen by the patriarch on the recommendations of the synod. The patriarchs, in turn, were originally elected by their clergy, the people, and the metropolitans; eventually, however, they were chosen— and this was especially the case for Constantinople and Antioch—by the emperor on the recommendation of the metropolitans, though the emperor was at liberty to select a candidate of his own choosing. Once ordained, a bishop was, if possible, not to be transferred to another bishopric or elevated to the seat of a metropolitan or the throne of a patriarch. If he violated religious, moral, or legal norms, he could be deposed, with the secular power, if necessary, acting as the church's executive organ. The bishop should be unmarried and, if possible, without children or grandchildren, for, quite apart from the Pauline postulate of chastity, there was good reason to fear that direct heirs would use the church's wealth and offices to enrich themselves. Within his bishopric the bishop had ecclesiastical, and up to a certain point also secular, jurisdiction over the local clergy and monks; interference in the affairs of another diocese was strictly prohibited. The bishop was obligated to reside in his diocese, visit all parishes on a regular basis, and manage the church's wealth honestly, with priority given to money spent for the poor, the sick, orphans, widows, prisoners, and of course the building of churches. He was to perform his office without pay, that is to say, he should support himself and the diocesan clergy from the income of his church. As successor to the apostles, he was the spiritual teacher of his community, and for the sake of this function it was appropriate that the bishop should have a certain minimum of general education and basic knowledge of doctrine.

The clergy was not permitted to take on state posts that were civilian or military in nature or any other secular affairs, in particular financial affairs, since these things were incompatible with their clerical status (no one can serve two masters). However, Justinianic legislation gave the bishop certain supervisory functions also with respect to the state bureaucracy: together with the respectable citizens (*primates* or *possessores*), to which he belonged ex officio, and thanks to the wealth of the church (which was often considerable), the bishop not only had the right to make recommendations for the choice of the city's *defensor* and the supervisor of the food supply (*sitōnēs*), he also supervised the administration of their office. In addition, jointly with the respectable citizens, he was in charge of the city's finances, that is, of the distribution of the incoming revenues for construction projects, the food supply, aqueducts, baths, harbors, bridges, and fortifications. In fact, the names of bishops often appear with those of emperors and governors in inscriptions on public buildings that are not ecclesiastical in nature. In cases where provincial governors severely abused their authority, the bishop was to report this directly to the emperor.

From these normative sources we get a picture of the church as a parallel organization to the state administration, an organization that in turn reflected the geographic and hierarchical order of the empire almost exactly without being tied into it, and that was at the same time able to still function if the governmental administration failed or ceased to function altogether. Leaving aside the trend toward an increasing centralization of the church in Constantinople—after the loss of Egypt, Syria, Palestine, and Italy, the patriarchate of New Rome stood for the church of the empire—and with it an increase in the power of the emperor in church affairs, the norms outlined here remained essentially unchanged during the subsequent thousand-year history of Byzantium.

The prerequisites for the ideal Byzantine bishop who was to fulfill his functions in keeping with these norms could thus be summarized as follows: he should be unmarried, educated, have a social conscience to make him see when people were in need and recognize situations that needed to be remedied, and above all possess large measures of courage and personal authority to enable him to take effective action, if needed, against the abuse of power by officials and members of the ruling class. However, there was a large number of Byzantine bishoprics and a correspondingly great demand for qualified prelates: 338 bishops, archbishops, and metropolitans took part in the iconoclastic synod of 754, and 365 in the Second Council of Nicaea (787); according to an official catalogue of bishoprics from the beginning of the tenth century, the patriarch of Constantinople had under him 51 metropolitan sees, 51 archbishoprics, and 531 bishoprics, though some were no longer within the boundaries of the empire. It thus becomes clear that not every diocese could always be staffed with ideal candidates.

THE BISHOP AS TEACHER AND SCHOLAR

The chief task of the Byzantine bishop was to spread and preserve orthodox Christian doctrine inside and outside the borders of the empire. The unity of the orthodox faith was seen as an effective spiritual bulwark against the political fragmentation of the empire. In addition, it was hoped that the spread of Christianity would exert a welcome civilizing effect on the rough habits and customs of the barbarian provincials and neighboring peoples. Visible expression of the ecclesiastical teaching function, which thus had not only a purely spiritual but also an eminently political aspect, were the frontal depictions of bishops—dressed in the *omophorion* and holding the Bible in their hands—on church walls. In the patristic manuscripts, which, following classical tradition, have a picture of the author on the title page, we usually see the bishop seated at a desk writing, following the model of the pictures of the evangelists. A popular variation of this figurative type is the depiction of the great preacher John Chrysostom (fourth/fifth century) as the fount of wisdom: those around him drink the water that pours from the scroll onto his desk. Biographical scenes from the lives of sainted bishops show them for the most part in situations where they are teaching, preaching, writing, defending the faith, and condemning idolatry or heresies. Depictions of the ecumenical councils (which are often found in the narthex of churches), with the bishops around a table, are considered the image of the Orthodox Church itself.

It is very striking that as Christianity spread in the eastern Mediterranean, the most talented and intellectually most active and lettered young men were drawn into the service of the church. One cannot conceive of late antique Greek literature without the contributions of bishops such as Basil of Caesarea in Cappadocia, Gregory of Nazianzos, and John Chrysostom—the so-called three hierarchs who, as the most popular church fathers, had to be on every painted church wall—or Eusebios of Caesarea in Palestine, Athanasios of Alexandria, and Synesios of Cyrene. Education was necessary for the episcopal office, for in order to keep watch over the purity of Orthodoxy, as teachers of the communities entrusted to them, and be able to defend it against heathens and heretics, bishops had to be at least equal, if not superior, to the enemies of the faith in terms of intellectual acuity and argumentative technique. It was this same high level of education and love of philosophy and dialectic that led the East Roman clergy, in particular the bishops, to get themselves worked up into ever more subtle speculations and definitions of theological and Christological questions, which were then discussed—usually without Christian charity—at the synods and councils and either accepted as true or condemned as heretical. Until the end of the Byzantine Empire, the obligatory persecution of the defeated party—that is, the heterodox party—and its impenitent supporters that followed in the wake of these decisions repeatedly led to situations that had all the makings of a civil war.

The church fathers and bishops of the fourth and fifth centuries, most of whom came from the upper class or the upper middle class, had enjoyed a classical, that is to say, pagan, education, the same sort of education as their peers who were active in the civil service; and as a rule they did not abandon their love for classical literature in their ecclesiastical office, genuine or feigned scruples notwithstanding. In later centuries, as well, bishops and metropolitans such as Arethas of Caesarea or Alexander of Nicaea (both ninth/tenth century) commented with equal enthusiasm on classical authors and Holy Scripture, and when Leo, the metropolitan of Synada (second half of the tenth century), confessed in his last will with playful remorse that he had all too often neglected spiritual literature in favor of its secular counterpart, his contrition was surely not meant to be taken too seriously. Many Byzantine sermons are structured according to the rules of ancient rhetoric and contain allusions to classical texts. When the patriarchal school in Constantinople became the cultural center of the empire during the Komnenian period (eleventh to twelfth centuries), the spiritual professors devoted a good part of their literary work to imperial propaganda and to sophisticated entertainment for members of the imperial family and the court. If they were later sent off to a metropolitan see, the crowning achievement of their career, they placed their rhetorical skills at the service of homiletics for the spiritual edification and moral fortification of the faithful. The learned commentator of Homer and metropolitan of Thessalonike, Eustathios (end of the twelfth century) preached against the vices of the Thessalonians with such fiery and unyielding vehemence that he was driven out of the city for a time.

Despite a progressive Christianization of Byzantine intellectual life, education never became a privilege of the clergy. The education and up-bringing of the learned remained uniform, a hybrid culture of classicism and theology, and this gave rise to a situation where—apart from conse-cration, which one could undergo later, if needed—educated laymen and clergymen were practically interchangeable. The fact that Emperor Man-uel II (1391–1425) is counted among the most gifted Byzantine theolo-gians is not a unique and isolated case; Justinian had already enjoyed engaging in theological speculations. Conversely, it was quite normal when clerics like the later metropolitan of Naupaktos, Constantine Man-asses (b. 1187), wrote not only a chronicle in verse but also a love novel. And Byzantine tradition has it that the popular late antique novelists Heli-odoros and Achilles Tatios became bishops in their old age.

This common cultural background of the spiritual and secular upper class explains how laymen who, for political reasons, were called from public service directly to a bishop's see or even the throne of a patriarch—as was the case with the former *comes Orientis* Ephraim (patriarch of Antioch 527–545), or the patriarchs of Constantinople Nektarios (381–397), Tarasios (784–806), Photios (858–867; 877–886), and Constantine Leichoudes (1059–63)—were able to fulfill the duties of their office with unquestioned competence without any further theological preparation. Nektarios and Tarasios are even venerated as saints in the Byzantine Church. Nobody took offense when Emperor Theophilos (829–842) ap-pointed the famous mathematician Leo the Philosopher—who was even said to have been called to the court of the caliph because of his knowl-edge of natural science—as metropolitan of Thessalonike, on the one hand to give the great scholar, in appreciation of his scientific accomplish-ments, a proper place in society with a corresponding income, on the other to give this important city a worthy head of the church. Much the same was also true for the patriarchs Nikephoros I (806–815) and Nicho-las I Mystikos (901–907): after terminating their wordly careers more or less voluntarily and withdrawing for a brief period into a monastery, they went on to attain high honors in their ecclesiastical careers. In the long run the emperor probably could not afford to lose many well-trained people to monasticism, which was unproductive for the state.

Highly revealing in this context is a measure taken by Emperor Con-stantine VII Porphyrogennetos (913–959). Concerned over the decay of learning and science in his realm, he installed four teachers in Constanti-nople (three higher officials from the central administration and one met-ropolitan) who were to instruct young Byzantine men in philosophy, rhet-oric, geometry, and astronomy. The emperor looked after the students in person, he invited them to his table and to long discussions, and chose from among them judges, public servants, and metropolitans. This story is important, for it shows that metropolitans enjoyed the same education as judges and other servants of the state, and that they, too, were placed in dioceses chosen by the emperor. Collections of Byzantine letters, especially from the tenth to the twelfth century, demonstrate impressively the strong social and cultural cohesion of this elite group, whose members studied together in Constantinople and then went off to different parts of the empire to serve the state in a variety of careers. In a somewhat playfully rhetorical correspondence, they kept each other informed about their yearnings and complaints and about the positive and negative twists and turns in their respective careers. If one of them needed political help, he knew who was in a position to intervene on his behalf with the best prospects of success.

As a rule the education of the high clergy thus corresponded to the average education of the Byzantine upper class, and it was in individual cases and over time subject to the same kinds of fluctuations. There were uneducated bishops, such as the eunuch Antonios Paches, metropolitan of Nikomedeia and favorite of Emperor Michael IV Paphlagon (1034–41). However, the emperor's relatives who had been pushed into state offices were also considered crude and utterly uncultured; the emperor himself had risen from modest circumstances. The chroniclers tell the following story about the involuntary abdication of the pious patriarch of Constantinople Tryphon, whom Emperor Romanos wanted to replace with his own son in 931: the unsuspecting patriarch was confidentially told that many metropolitans believed he was illiterate. On the pretext that they wanted to refute this perfidious rumor, his scheming enemies had him write his name and title on a piece of parchment, to which the imperial chancery then appended the text of a letter of resignation. Even if this story is a fabrication, it does reveal what sort of reputation the intellectual abilities of the patriarch enjoyed in the capital. And Tryphon's successor, too, the imperial prince Theophylaktos, a horse lover who once interrupted the solemn liturgy of Maundy Thursday in Hagia Sophia to go off and help his favorite mare to foal, was not exactly one of the great intellects on the patriarchal throne.

Still, as a rule the demand that bishops be educated seems to have been respected. On the acts of the councils, signatures of participating prelates are almost always in their own hand. The fact that some bishops at the early synods signed their names in Syriac or Latin is a reflection of the cultural diversity of the empire, which was always multilingual. It has been calculated for the fourteenth century, for example, that one-fourth of those Byzantines who were involved in literary production were prelates: three bishops, fourteen metropolitans, and seven patriarchs. There are no comparable studies for other centuries, but it is likely that they would yield fairly similar results.

However, the more educated the freshly ordained metropolitans were, the more reluctant they were to fulfill their duty of residing in the distant provinces. After the glitter and intellectual stimulation of the imperial city, life in the provinces seemed unbearably barbaric. In his verse autobiography *De vita sua*, Gregory of Nazianzos (fourth century) described Sasima in Cappodocia as a dirty relay station at a crossroads: "A carters' village lies there in the middle of the road from Cappadocia, where the paths diverge into three directions, with no water, no greenery, altogether unworthy of a free man, a thoroughly accursed and narrow nest. Everything there is dust, noise and carts, complaints and groans, bailiffs, torture, shackles. The only residents are foreigners and vagrants."[2] The metropolitan Leo of Synada, whom we met earlier, called the emperor's attention to the harsh conditions of life in his diocese in Pisidia in a letter that was probably never dispatched in this form: "You see, we do not produce olive oil; this is something we have in common with all the residents of the Anatolikon theme. Our land does not yield wine because of the high altitude and the short growing season. Instead of wood, we use "zarzakon," which is really dung that has been processed, a thoroughly disgusting and smelly business. All the other requisites for the healthy or infirm we solicit from the Thracesion theme, from Attaleia, and from the capital itself."[3] Leo pleads with the emperor not to let him live on barley, hay, and straw, like an animal, for the land around Synada was unsuitable even for growing wheat. John Mauropos (eleventh century), a renowned teacher and literary figure from the capital, probably had good reason to feel that his promotion to metropolitan of Euchaita on the Black Sea was tantamount to banishment: apparently he had not sufficiently flattered the reigning emperor in his historical work. What depressed him was the great desolation (*erēmia*) of his province, which he described, in words borrowed from his favorite poet Gregory of Nazianzos, as "uninhabited, with no charm, no trees, no green, no forest, no shade, utterly barbarous and devoid of culture, unknown and without fame."[4] For Michael Choniates, metropolitan of Athens from 1184 to 1204, his city was simply a misery. In letters to friends in Constantinople, he lamented the great poverty of the population and the lack not only of books and educated people with whom to converse, but also of skilled artisans. He wrote that he felt like the prophet Jeremiah in Jerusalem after its destruction by the Babylonians; his episcopal residence on the Acropolis—in the Middle Ages the Parthenon had been turned into a church dedicated to the Virgin—made him feel all the more painfully that "yonder age in love with science and overflowing with wisdom has vanished, its place taken by one hostile to the Muses."[5]

However, there are no indications that bishops tried to raise the intellectual level in their cities, for example, in the area of schooling, in order to reduce the education gap between the center and the periphery. Education was in fact not an area that fell within the bishop's purview. To be sure, most bishops saw to the education of one or more of their nephews—indeed, we cannot imagine the intellectual life of Byzantium without the figure of the bishop's nephew—but these young men were usually raised and educated in the capital. As for most bishops and metropolitans themselves, any pretext was good enough to take a trip to Constantinople: participating in synods, settling diocesan affairs with the central administration or in the offices of the patriarchate, interceding with the emperor on behalf of the diocese, and so on. And once they had made it to the capital, they tried to postpone their return for as long as possible, often for years. Justinian had already taken measures against bishops who journeyed to Byzantium all too frequently. Later there was a regulation that a bishop was not to absent himself from his diocese for more than six months at a time. Leo of Synada protested against this rule, for, given the medieval conditions of travel, it allowed the titularies of distant bishoprics only enough time for the shortest of visits to the imperial city. In any case, all legal and ecclesiastical regulations concerning a bishop's duty to reside in his diocese seem to have been fairly useless. This was especially true from the twelfth century on, when the provinces of Asia Minor were progressively conquered by the Turks, and more and more bishops took up permanent residence in Constantinople with the frequent, though not always justified, excuse that they were unable to reach their bishoprics because of ongoing warfare or because their dioceses had already been conquered. In the comfort and safety of the capital, they then proceeded to participate in sessions of the permanent or standing synod (*endē-mousa*) and to discuss, in speech and in writing, the theological and political problems of the day. The episcopal teaching office was thus increasingly concentrated in and reduced to Constantinople and its immediate environs.

THE BISHOP AS DISPENSER OF PUBLIC WELFARE

One of the most engaging texts of Byzantine literature is the so-called *Strategikon* of Kekaumenos, written during the second half of the eleventh century. The author, a retired general, gathered the lessons of his life's experiences into a brief manual of advice and admonition for his son. There we read:

> If you are received into the hierarchy, as a metropolitan or bishop, for example, do not accept the election until you have obtained a revelation from up high through fasting and night vigils and have received complete certainty from God. Even if God is slow in revealing himself, be of good cheer, persist and humble yourself before God, and you will see him. Just make

sure that your life is free from impeding desires. But why do I speak of a metropolitan seat? If the choice for patriarch falls on you, you should all the more not dare to take the helm of the holy church into your hands unless God has revealed himself to you. And when you become patriarch, do not become haughty, do not let spear-bearers escort you, and do not amass money; do not concern yourself with gold and silver and costly banquets, rather you should be concerned about food for orphans and widows, about hospitals, the redemption of prisoners of war, peace, and help for the weak, but not about accumulating houses and properties and robbing your fellow man, in the process telling yourself: I am not doing this for myself and my family but for God and the church. I knew bishops who talked like that, and I had to marvel at Satan's wiliness, his knowing how to deceive us with false piety. But I say to you: St. Nicholas and St. Basil and their kind distributed their possessions among the needy already during their life in this world and preached poverty. And now that they live in heaven, should it be necessary that one rob the poor for them? . . . Day and night your zeal should be focused on the divine and the edification of the rich and the poor.[6]

To this wise old military man—who had served all over the empire, who evidently had no love for the imperial city, and who completely excluded theological and dogmatic problems from his treatise—a bishop, metropolitan, or patriarch was above all a pastor who, convinced of his divine calling, should devote himself completely to the spiritual edification and social welfare of his flock. The text implies that most prelates he knew were more concerned with advancing their own careers and enriching themselves than protecting and caring for the needy. This verdict agrees with the last will of the metropolitan Leo of Synada from the early eleventh century. With a certain self-irony, he accused himself of singing the Psalms without inner participation, neglecting his prayers and idling all day instead, riding arrogantly through the market on his horse past poor and sick petitioners without taking pity on them, and living in high style while others went hungry—by Kekaumenos' standards an anti-bishop!

Already in late antiquity, following the gradual dissolution of municipal administration and the progressive ruin of the state's finances, poor relief had fallen increasingly within the sphere of the church, and many bishops devoted themselves with great seriousness and zeal to this task. The patriarch of Constantinople John Chrysostom (397–404) not only spent less on luxuries in order to build hospitals in the imperial city with the savings, among them a hospital for lepers; but, more important, he also placed his great rhetorical talent at the service of Christian charity. In his sermons he sought to awaken the social conscience of his listeners so they might forgo ostentation and luxury in order to help the poor. Many centuries later, Patriarch Athanasios I of Constantinople (1289–93; 1303–9) was labeled by his contemporaries a new, if decidedly less eloquent, Chrysostom. He, too, preached against the miserliness, greed, luxury, and corruption of the Constantinopolitans, and set up soup kitchens for the poor and the refugees pouring into the capital from those parts of the empire conquered by the Turks. He personally took a hand in distributing the food, and something similar is also reported about his contemporary, the esteemed bishop Theoleptos of Philadelphia (1284–1324/25). Reports about the feeding of the poor, the building of hospitals, and deeds of practical charity toward widows, orphans, and prisoners are among the most popular and almost obligatory literary conventions in the Lives of sainted bishops. For example, Patriarch John of Alexandria (610–619), called "the Almsgiver," is said to have registered the poor of his city immediately after his consecration and to have fed about 7,500 every day. The sainted bishop Theophylaktos of Nikomedeia (first half of the ninth century), we are told, personally washed the sick every Saturday in the hospitals he had founded.

But over and above this, the bishop, the "good pastor," was expected to protect the weak against violence and, in case of war, protect his flock against the outside enemy. As the bishop was not permitted to fight or kill—there never was a Byzantine equivalent to the knightly prelates of medieval Western Europe—his main weapon was *parrhēsia,* frank and open speech before the powerful. The "powerful" could be the emperor or the leader of attacking enemies, but usually they were local tax officials and judges, military officers and local aristocrats. Byzantine history and hagiography is in fact full of accounts of bishops who took risks in their pastoral office: bishops who interceded with judges and governors on behalf of those unjustly condemned, who traveled to Constantinople to obtain tax relief for their diocese, who in time of war remained in their threatened city, even after the military commanders had fled, in order to suffer the horrors of conquest together with their flock (as the great philologist Eustathios of Thessalonike did), or offered themselves to the enemy as a hostage for their city (as Theoleptos of Philadelphia did).

When it came to dealing with state authorities, it usually proved advantageous if the bishop himself came from the upper class and had influential contacts in Constantinople—relatives, friends, or colleagues from student days. This not only allowed him to circumvent the slow path through the official channels and to take his complaint directly to the relevant office or even to the emperor himself; it also provided effective backing against possible threats and pressures from the local powers that be. That is why the rich, educated, and well-connected aristocrat Synesios of Cyrene, bishop of Ptolemais in the North African Pentapolis between

411 and 414, could afford to get into a fight with the corrupt governor Andronikos and excommunicate him. Against external enemies, in this case predatory desert nomads, he could, if necessary, organize a kind of local militia from the church's vassals, but even more important, through his high-ranking contacts in Constantinople he could effect the dispatch of regular troops. Synesios thus exercised his episcopal office in the manner of enlightened Roman patronage.

The metropolitan of Athens, Michael Choniates also had influential connections in the imperial city, which he could use for the benefit of his see; in fact, he even had access to the emperor. Again and again he asked for a more equitable tax levy and for help against the pirates who were ravaging the coast of his bishopric and kidnapping the locals; and, quite in keeping with the spirit of Justinianic legislation, he denounced the overbearing conduct of the large local landowners, imperial officials, and military men. But he did so with little success, as the government in Constantinople was hardly in a position to enforce its will in the provinces. Michael's colleague Nicholas, metropolitan of Corinth, even paid with his life for his courageous conduct toward a local magnate.

Parrhēsia was dangerous and rarely paid off, especially when it was directed against the emperor himself. One who had to learn this firsthand was Patriarch Arsenios (1255–59, 1261–65), who was deposed and banished because he had excommunicated Emperor Michael VIII for blinding and eliminating his youthful co-emperor. It was also something that bishops who were called upon to mediate in cases of rebellion, a not infrequent occurrence, found out for themselves. When the metropolitan of Syracuse, Theodore Krithinos, reminded Emperor Theophilos (829–842)—who was, incidentally, a fanatic for justice—that he had broken the sacred oaths with which he had assured one alleged usurper that he would go unpunished, he was banished. Less courageous than the Sicilian bishop, the metropolitans of Chalcedon, Herakleia, and Coloneia stood by, silent and impotent, as the captive emperor Romanos IV, whose inviolability they had guaranteed, was blinded.

If we consider the fates of the pastoral bishops we have mentioned, we find a sad picture: the patriarchs John Chrysostom, Arsenios, and Athanasios I were deposed; Theophylaktos of Nikomedeia, Theodore Krithinos, and Michael Choniates died in exile; Nicholas of Corinth was blinded and hurled from the acropolis of Nauplia; Eustathios of Thessalonike fell into Norman captivity and had to buy his freedom with a steep ransom; even the successful Synesios seems to have run into difficulties at the end of his tenure in office. Evidently it was dangerous and frustrating to be a "good shepherd."

Only dead bishops could be truly successful, provided they were saints. Perhaps it is in this sense that one can understand the cult of one of the most popular Byzantine saints, St. Nicholas of Myra, whom Kecaumenos mentioned as a model bishop. For our purposes it is not important that the figure behind the cult is historically a bit elusive. We are evidently dealing with a blend of two persons of the same name, a bishop of Myra (fourth century) and an abbot of Sion in the hinterland of Myra (sixth century). By the ninth century the fusion of the two into one—or better, *the*—Nicholas of Myra had already taken place. In his Lives, miracle stories, and pictorial representations, St. Nicholas is the prototype of the sainted bishop: he is a brilliant student in school, he receives the necessary consecrations as deacon, priest, and bishop, he fights against the pagan cults. Particularly revealing, however, are his interventions on behalf of those in need of help: he gives rich dowries to three girls whom their impoverished father had destined to be prostitutes; during a famine in Myra he diverts several ships that were sailing from Alexandria to Constantinople with Egyptian grain into the harbor of his suffering city; he saves three falsely condemned citizens of Myra from being executed; he intervenes successfully with the emperor and the city prefect of Constantinople against the sentencing of three generals wrongly accused of treason. St. Nicholas of Myra thus did exactly what was expected of a bishop: he gave help to the needy, food to the hungry, protection to the persecuted. And since there are no obstacles of any kind for a true saint, he also displayed his miraculous powers in a stormy sea and against attacks of Arab fleets. His cult enjoyed unbroken popularity in the Byzantine Church, even after sailors from Bari stole his relics in 1097 and brought them to Italy and Myra was captured by the Turks shortly thereafter.

BISHOPS AND POLITICS

Byzantine bishops usually respected the canon that barred clerics from serving in the military or holding government posts. When the sources speak of bishops who fought the Saracens weapon in hand and even killed enemies in battle and were suspended for doing so, it means that this prohibition remained in force in spite of all transgressions. Much the same holds true for the assumption of offices in the civil administration. While we occasionally find bishops in the function of *paradynasteuon* (chief imperial counselor) from the end of the eleventh century—for example John of Side under Emperor Michael VII or Phokas of Philadelphia under John III Vatatzes—these were probably exceptions. In principle, the strict separation of civil and ecclesiastical careers was observed.

But this does not mean that bishops were thereby forced into complete political abstinence. On the contrary, the pastoral office was inextricably intertwined with politics. Thanks to the authority of their office and the extended supervisory function over provincial administration that

Justinianic legislation had accorded them, bishops were almost invariably drawn into local political events, especially in times of crisis. Moreover, owing to the often considerable wealth of their churches, they were automatically among the "powerful" of the provinces. As bishops could, in principle, not be transferred, they were usually better informed about local conditions and had a clearer overview of the situation in their bishopric than high imperial administrative officials and governors, who generally served only a few years in the provinces assigned to them. Bishops also repeatedly assumed—voluntarily or not—the function of mediator between the imperial administration and the local population, and in so doing they could easily get caught in the middle. For example, how should a bishop act if a rebellion broke out in his province? If he called for resistance, there was a good chance the rebels would kill him and his supporters. If he joined the rebels, he had to fear the worst from a victorious emperor. Caught in such situations, many bishops were banished, blinded, mutilated, or killed, for it was not always possible to opt for the third way, that of staying out of the conflict.

It is thus understandable that the emperors had an interest in controlling the election of bishops so that not only government posts but also ecclesiastical ones were held by persons who had their confidence. Nikephoros II Phokas (963–969) even enacted a law, over the opposition of the patriarch, that gave the emperor a free hand in appointing bishops. Even if his successor had to revoke the law, imperial control continued. However, the appointment of suffragan bishops seems to have remained largely within the power of the metropolitans and local notables. In these cases, local interests were paramount, and at the periphery of the empire, in particular, in provinces where the majority of the population did not understand any Greek, it was advisable, for linguistic reasons alone, to consider candidates who were natives of the diocese or had already lived there a long time. In the fifth century, for example, the patriarch of Jerusalem ordained a sheikh as the bishop of the newly converted nomadic Saracens in the desert of Palestine.

When it came to the choice of metropolitans, however, the decision rested above all with the emperor. The regional roots of candidates apparently played no role in these appointments. As was the case with provincial governors and high administrative officials, metropolitans were placed into the dioceses assigned to them by the emperor without any regard for local ties or interests: a cleric from Argos could become metropolitan of Nicaea, and a cleric from Lampe in Anatolia could be placed in the see of Ochrid. If we take a brief look at the place of origin (where known) of the metropolitans we have met so far, we find quite a motley picture all across the empire: Arethas of Caesarea in Cappodocia came from Patras in the Peloponnese; the metropolitans of Thessalonike Leo and Eustathios hailed from Constantinople, with the latter originally intended for the seat in Myra; Michael Choniates, metropolitan of Athens, had been born and raised in Chonai in Anatolia, Theoleptos of Philadelphia in Nicaea. As was the case among government officials, among metropolitans, too, we can detect clans whose members headed metropolitan sees more or less at the same time in various parts of the empire: Alexander of Nicaea and Jacob of Larissa (tenth century) were brothers, as were the metropolitans of Side and Ankara under Michael IV (1034–41). Very often the nephews of metropolitans chose the career of the uncle who had raised them: the metropolitan of Euchaita, John Mauropos, was the nephew of the bishop of Klaudiopolis and of the archbishop Leo of Bulgaria; the uncle of the metropolitan of Chonai was himself metropolitan of Patras (tenth century); Theodore of Side and his nephew of the same name, titular of Sebasteia in Anatolia, are both known as the authors of historical works that have not survived. It could also happen, however, that a nephew was ordained as his uncle's successor, almost like an heir, for example, Nikephoros Chrysoberges as metropolitan of Sardis. This roulette with ecclesiastical offices, in which considerable economic interests were at stake owing to the enormous wealth of many sees, was centered on Constantinople. Here the candidates had studied or risen in service in the city's clergy, here they had created, in the surroundings of the court or Hagia Sophia, a lobby that supported their candidacy before the emperor. And simony, in spite of strict canonical prohibitions, seems to have been the order of the day all the way to the highest ranks of the church.

If new metropolitans subsequently did not live up to the emperor's expectations, for whatever reason, they could not be simply transferred like government officials, but it was always possible to depose them. If they proved trustworthy, however, they were at times also given tasks that lay outside their immediate episcopal duties; I have already mentioned the metropolitans who, as *paradynasteuontes,* ran the affairs of state for some of the emperors. Metropolitans were also frequently entrusted with international missions because they held an esteemed office that was also respected in distant countries, especially in Christian Western Europe, they were educated, and they could be more readily spared than provincial governors, below whom they ranked in the Byzantine hierarchy. Missions to non-Christian peoples always involved a missionary element, the readiness—at least theoretically—to engage in religious dialogue, which was always an appropriate activity for a metropolitan. The metropolitan Leo of Synada took part in an embassy to the court of Otto III (998) that concerned the marriage of the young western emperor to a Byzantine princess. Along the way Leo became involved in a coup d'état in Rome on his own initiative: he supported the expulsion of the Saxon pope Gregory V and successfully launched the candidacy of the Greek anti-pope Philagathos of Rossano, but the latter was soon deposed and cruelly punished. In his correspondence with his friends in Constantinople, Leo reported with cynical relish on his experiences as a puller of political strings in Old Rome.

The emperor made the most determined use of his right of appointment, however, when it came to the choice of the patriarch of Constantinople, who resided virtually next door to him in the capital city. In the other patriarchates, especially in Rome, because of the great geographic distance alone, the locally selected candidate was often confirmed by the emperor, provided he was orthodox in his faith and gave every indication that he would be reliable. In Constantinople, by contrast, nobody could become patriarch against the emperor's will or remain so for long. A self-confident and independent policy like that of the medieval popes, who usually had to deal with a faraway emperor and often with no emperor at all, was inconceivable for their Byzantine counterparts. A good third of the patriarchs of Constantinople were either deposed, some even twice, or stepped down more or less voluntarily. These depositions or resignations are distributed fairly evenly across all periods, and we cannot find a dynasty that dealt with its patriarchs more considerately than any of the others: Justinian I (527–565) and Alexios I (1081–1118) each deposed two patriarchs, Andronikos II (1282–1329) no fewer than four.

The ideal patriarch of Constantinople had to be of orthodox faith as defined by the emperor. He also had to be loyal and obedient for two reasons: first, as the head of the church in the imperial city, he had the possibility of influencing the mood of the population, which could be decisive especially in cases of rebellion; second, as court bishop he was in charge of imperial coronations and of weddings and baptisms in the imperial family. The first condition for being selected was thus that the candidate was known to the emperor and enjoyed his confidence. Such candidates could come from among the clerics of Hagia Sophia or the palace clergy, they could be confessors of the emperors or pious monks whose charisma had impressed them, teachers or educators of the emperor, but also imperial princes if they lacked ambition and could be manipulated. Only two imperial princes, younger sons or brothers of reigning emperors, attained the patriarchal throne: Stephen II (925–928), a brother of Leo VI, and Theopylaktos (933–956), the youngest son of Romanos I. In both instances the point was not to find an honorable position in society for the imperial relative and offspring, but to put the most pliable candidate possible on the patriarchal throne of Constantinople. Both patriarchs lived up to the emperors' expectations. The prototype of the compliant patriarch was Basil II Kamateros (1183–86), who, after the forced resignation of his predecessor, is said to have promised Emperor Andronikos in writing to do whatever he demanded, no matter how unlawful, and to refrain from doing anything that displeased him. Understandably enough, Patriarch Basil got caught up in the downfall of his emperor.

In particularly delicate or intractable situations concerning ecclesiastical policy, when the unity of the empire was truly at stake, the emperor's choice did occasionally fall on a candidate with political experience and good diplomatic instinct. When the issue was getting rid of Iconoclasm, the emperor plucked the layman Tarasios straight from the imperial chancery; despite the handicap of his uncanonical consecration, he proved a splendid tactician and patient politician. His successors Nikephoros and Methodios, who both strove, with some success, not to cause too much upheaval during the reorganization of the church following the iconoclastic controversy, were in all likelihood also patriarchs chosen for their political qualifications. Much the same holds true for Constantine Leichoudes, who, following a brilliant career in government service, was chosen patriarch of Constantinople (1059–63) to reestablish the customary relationship between the emperor and the subordinated church after the political excesses of his predecessor Michael Keroularios. And John XI Bekkos (1275–82) had proved his worth on diplomatic missions on several occasions while a high cleric of Hagia Sophia before Michael VIII appointed him patriarch with the task of ending the schism with Rome.

The reasons behind the deposition or resignation of patriarchs corresponded to the reasons for their appointment. Most frequently differences between the emperor and the patriarch on doctrinal issues were involved. This applies, for example, to the patriarchs Anthimos and Eutychios under Justinian, to Germanos I and Nikephoros I, who were forced to abdicate by iconoclastic emperors, and to the above-mentioned John XI Bekkos, who was toppled immediately after the death of Michael VIII in 1282 by his anti-unionist successors. In some cases, doctrinal issues were used as a pretext to mask political differences. Another reason for the deposition or resignation of a patriarch could be provided by a new emperor on the imperial throne or the appearance of a new dynasty. The death of an emperor frequently also ended the relationship of trust on which the interplay of palace and church was based, and for that reason the son and successor often chose a new ecclesiastical partner. On the other hand, if a new dynasty assumed the reins of power, especially if the previous one had been eliminated by force, the new ruler, still insecure in his office, often liked to draw support from the recognized authority of the incumbent patriarch; however, if he did not trust him, he chose a new one from among his clerical supporters.

An example of someone who chose the first path is John I Tzimiskes after the murder of his predecessor Nikephoros II Phokas (969). In order to have his imperial coronation carried out by the respected patriarch

Polyeuktos, he accepted all the acts of penance the latter demanded from him. A prime example of the second path is the checkered career of the famous patriarch Photios (858–867, 877–886). He had ascended to the patriarchal throne as a layman—highly uncanonical—after Emperor Michael III had deposed Patriarch Ignatios because of a difference of opinion on ecclesiastical policy. But Photios' consecration merely heightened tensions within the Byzantine episcopacy, on the one hand, and between Rome and Constantinople on the other. That is why Basil I, upon ascending the imperial throne after the murder of Michael III (867), immediately deposed Photios and reinstated Ignatios, trying in this way to win over to his side the ecclesiastical party that had been hostile to his predecessor. Following the death of Ignatios, however, he brought Photios back, either because he wished for a general reconciliation or because he did not want to do without the services of this highly talented and educated man. But no sooner had Basil I died (886) than his son, Leo VI, sent the overbearing patriarch, who had been his teacher, into exile, presumably because he had become in his view too powerful or independent.

From all that has been said, it is clear that the patriarchs of Constantinople participated in Byzantine politics more as victims than as actors. Many of them lost their freedom and their office in the struggle for orthodoxy. Even if the doctrine for which they stood in the end proved to be the correct one, that vindication rarely came during the lifetime of the emperor who held different views; the reigning emperor usually decided what was considered orthodoxy in Constantinople. But within the given framework, patriarchs with political flair and skill could certainly make something of their role, either by actively supporting the policy of their emperor or by exploiting the weaknesses of an underage or insecure emperor. Patriarch Sergios I was evidently the most important advisor of Emperor Herakleios in questions of politics as well as ecclesiastical policy, and during the latter's long absence as a result of the Persian War he was his deputy in Constantinople. During Constantine VII's minority, Patriarch Nicholas Mystikos for years determined the course of Byzantine domestic as well as foreign policy.

But if a patriarch set about trying to change the rules of the politics of power in Byzantium, he was invariably brought down. During his second term, Patriarch Photios felt so strong and so superior to his fellow men that he began theorizing about a drastic increase in the status of the patriarchal office. His formulation to the effect that the patriarch, through his works and words, symbolized the truth, and was the living image of Christ, went against traditional Byzantine ideas about the hierarchical relationship Christ—emperor—patriarch. Such a man as the head of the church of Constantinople was not acceptable to Leo VI; Photios had to go.

Deposition was also the fate of Michael Keroularios (1043–58), who, with less subtlety, had arrogated to himself visible imperial prerogatives such as wearing purple shoes. In his youth, Keroularios had taken part in a coup against Emperor Michael IV, and, after its failure, he was forced to enter a monastery. When a fellow conspirator assumed the throne in the person of Constantine IX Monomachos, he bestowed upon the monk, as consolation for his failed worldly career, the patriarchate of Constantinople, an office the latter sought to politicize as much as possible. During the negotiations over union with Rome (1053–54), the patriarch, against the emperor's will, provoked a break with the Roman legates with remarkable demogogic skill. During a revolt of the generals against Emperor Michael VI, he even rose to become emperor-maker, and he was subsequently annoyed and disappointed when the man of his choice, Isaac I Komnenos, did not give him the political maneuvering room he expected. Although the emperor was able to depose the inconvenient patriarch, Keroularios' influence on the populace of Constantinople was strong enough, even in exile, that Emperor Isaac himself soon abdicated the throne in favor of a man related by marriage to the deposed patriarch.

But with the exception of Michael Keroularios, who, with his hunger for worldly power and his remarkable ability to assert himself politically, was more like a would-be emperor than a typical patriarch, Byzantine bishops usually had as much power and freedom of action as the emperor and the state administration accorded them. As a group, however, they were able to make their influence felt in Byzantine politics, at least during the last centuries. In this context, "group" refers to the standing synod that was in session several times a week in Constantinople under the chairmanship of the patriarch. Participants with voting rights were all metropolitans and archbishops who happened to be in Constantinople at the time and the high officials of the patriarchal administration. The synod discussed and decided theological and canonical questions, problems concerning the relationship between the emperor and the church, and above all the appointment and deposition of patriarchs, metropolitans, and archbishops. The desire to take part in the synod and thus have a chance to get involved in the distribution of lucrative positions and not be shortchanged, evidently added to the desire of the metropolitans to be in Constantinople as often as possible and to stay as long as possible.

In the late eleventh century, when many metropolitans from Anatolia and Turkey fled to the capital before the advancing Turks and were unable, often for years, to return to their dioceses, the political influence of the synod appears to have grown. Impoverished by the loss of their bishoprics and condemned to inactivity in Constantinople, the frustrated metropolitans consoled themselves with synodal activities. It is surely no coincidence that the dissatisfied metropolitans played a decisive role in the

revolt against Emperor Michael VII Doukas (1078), and that at the acclamation of his successor, Nikephoros III Botaneiates, the synod appeared
for the first time in Byzantine history alongside the senate and even ahead
of the people of Constantinople as a constitutive group. As the standing
synod, the metropolitans were able to put pressure not only on the patriarch but occasionally also on the emperor.

Around the same time, a new iconographic type of the sainted bishop
emerged in Byzantine painting. This type later develop into a standard
element of apse decoration. The lower register of the apse wall often depicts two episcopal processions moving from the right and the left toward
the center of the apse where the altar stood. The individual bishops walk
to the altar slightly stooped forward, in silent prayer; their scrolls are usually inscribed with quotations from the liturgies of Basil or Chrysostom.
The number and identity of the participating bishops vary depending on
the church, the period, and the region, though the three hierarchs and
Athanasios of Alexandria are almost always present. Perhaps this new
iconographic type of the sainted bishops as a unified group can be linked
to the newly won self-confidence of the metropolitans in the standing
synod.

BISHOPS AND MONASTICISM

In the funerary epigram at the beginning of this chapter, we read that the
metropolitan Metrophanes had been an exemplary monk. This praise is
typical insofar as most Byzantine bishops began their ecclesiastical careers as monks or spent at least part of their lives in a monastery. This
monastic aspect had an old tradition in the Byzantine Church. The fact
that so many bishops came from the monastic realm was the result, not
of a canonical requirement, but of the Byzantine notion that the most
direct path to God was via monastic asceticism. When the official recognition of the Christian religion in the Roman Empire left few opportunities for martyrdom, the self-chosen ordeal of the ascetic—who led a contemplative life devoted to God with complete renunciation of all worldly
pleasures and comforts and with self-inflicted torments—was regarded as
the surest way to perfection. Having undergone such an experience, the
bishop could work in the world in accord with God's will. This was the
sense in which the early fathers of the church (Basil and Gregory of
Nyssa) interpreted the life of Moses, for example, who after many years
in the desert saw God in the burning bush and afterwards completed his
mission among his people. The monastic background thus gave the
bishop spiritual authority. In addition, there was also a very practical reason: the lower clergy in Byzantium was usually married, and as bishops

were required to be single, episcopal candidates that met this requirement were most readily found among monks and eunuchs.

Many committed monks, however, rejected the episcopal office when it was offered to them: some, like Gregory of Nazianzos, because they did not want to give up the contemplative life, some because they did not wish to be integrated into the strict institutional order of the church, and others because they feared they would inevitably compromise themselves or get their hands dirty with worldly affairs. Flight from the episcopal office became virtually a stock element in Byzantine hagiographic literature, in the Lives of sainted monks who managed to remain in the monastery, as well as those who were not able to escape episcopal consecration in the long run. Individuals such as Bishop George from the Pontic city of Amastris (b. ca. 825), who voluntarily gave up the monastic life because he did not wish selfishly to concentrate only on his own spiritual perfection but wanted to serve his fellow man, were a rare breed. Thus monasticism as a way of life was at the same time the preliminary stage of the episcopal office and its antithesis, a kind of perennial conflict in the history of the Byzantine Church.

From the very outset, Byzantine monasticism had a strongly anarchic streak: seeking to escape the city and civilization, refined cooking and classical education, and any government or ecclesiastical authority, monks headed into the desert, into trackless mountains, or even high up onto freestanding columns, to a life marked by strict, self-imposed fasting, sleep deprivation, and prayer. This heroic existence, which aroused the general admiration of contemporaries, led many monks to a certain spiritual arrogance toward the bishops who lived comfortably in the cities with bathing facilities and classical literature. This antagonism between monasticism and the bishop remained intact even when magnificent monasteries were established in cities and suburbs and when many wealthy Byzantines set up private, villa-like monasteries on their estates to which they withdrew for a contemplative life. The conflict was fought on two levels, spiritual and material. On the one hand, the conflict was about moral superiority; on the other, about control over the often enormous monastic landholdings. The legal situation was clear: the canons as well as secular law gave the bishops jurisdiction over monasteries and monks in everything relating to monastic discipline and the proper administration of monastic wealth; in practice, however, there were many ways in which both sides could subvert laws and canons. Alongside many bishops who shamelessly enriched themselves from the wealth of the monasteries under their supervision, there were many monks who escaped the disciplinary control of a bishop whose spiritual authority they did not recognize. That is why it often created a practical or spiritual dilemma when a pious monk was consecrated bishop.

John Chrysostom, himself a monk in his youth, had already said that ascetics who had lived a long time without contact with the world were unsuitable for the office of bishop. This statement proved true in the life of St. Theodore of Sykeon (sixth/seventh century). A highly venerated archimandrite when he was elected bishop of Anastasioupolis in central Asia, he failed miserably because he could not handle the practical side of his office. Theodore was unable to intervene effectively in the quarrel between oppressed farmworkers on the church's estates and the powerful leaseholders, and the conflict led to bloodshed. He was later accused of squandering church property, and there was even an attempt to poison him. At the same time, because of his absence, discipline among the monks in the monastery he had founded and headed became more lax. Saying that he could not serve two masters, the monastery and the diocese, Theodore stepped down and returned to his monks. Other monks who became bishops or patriarchs tried to use their legal rights to discipline monks and monasteries and in particular to prune back the wild growth of pseudo-asceticism, though generally with little success. Eustathios of Thessalonike wrote a tract against the excesses of monasticism in which he criticized, with irony and wit, the stylites and other holy men who showed off their stinking, self-inflicted wounds. When, upon becoming patriarch, Athanasios I of Constantinople, who himself had led the life of a wandering monk, vigorously advocated traditional monastic virtues such as obedience and stability (*stabilitas loci*), he drove the monks into the already large camp of his enemies and was eventually forced to step down.

And so it remained that, on the Byzantine scale of popularity, of all social classes the eccentrically ascetic monk, who won heaven and often the fanatical devotion of his contemporaries with all kinds of torments and hardships, ranked far ahead of the bishop, who, in service to his fellow man, had to grapple with the problems of practical life. This is revealed, for example, by the large number of monastic saints compared to the relatively few sainted bishops from Byzantine times. Evidently the latter excited the imagination of contemporaries less than the extreme ascetics and stylites, who brought a supernatural aspect into life. On the other hand—and this, too, is characteristic—there were Byzantine satires about monks who had betrayed their high ideals, but there were no such satires about bishops.

Finally, there was one more aspect of the episcopal office, one that came to the fore only when the power of the Byzantine state disintegrated. When the military fled and the civil administration collapsed during the Arab and later Turkish conquests, it was often the bishop who, as the sole and last Byzantine authority, confronted the enemy, negotiated the surrender of the city, defended the "rights" of the native inhabitants, and sought to make their lives easier. In many cases he remained in his uncomfortable position as the representative of the Christian population and tried to stay in touch with Constantinople to whatever extent possible. This is what happened during the Arab conquest of Egypt, Palestine, and Syria, and later during the Turkish conquest of the empire. There are moving reports from the metropolitan Matthew of Ephesos, who, between 1340 and 1351 under the Turkish conquerors, performed his pastoral office in the diocese entrusted to him despite harassment and hostility from the Muslim government and population: the famous Joannes church had been turned into a mosque, the episcopal residence had been seized, and the landholdings confiscated. The Christian community was made up of slaves and prisoners. His movements restricted, his correspondence impeded, pelted with stones by the Turkish inhabitants, Matthew stayed on until the patriarchal synod deposed him for heretical tendencies, one hundred years before the fall of Constantinople.

NOTES

1. S. G. Mercati, "Inno anacreontico alla SS. Trinità di Metrofane, arcivescovo di Smirne," *Byzantinische Zeitschrift* 30 (1930): 60.

2. Gregory of Nazianzos, *De vita sua,* introduction, text, translation, and commentary by C. Jungck (Heidelberg, 1974), verses 439–46.

3. *The Correspondence of Leo, Metropolitan of Synada and Syncellus,* Greek text, translation, and commentary by M. P. Vinson. Corpus Fontium Historiae Byzantinae 23 (Washington, D.C., 1985), 69.

4. A. Karpozilos, *The Letters of Joannes Mauropus, Metropolitan of Euchaita* (Thessaloniki, 1990).

5. Sp. P. Lampros, *Michael Akominatou tou Choniatou ta sozomena,* vol. 2 (Athens, 1880), 12; G. Stadtmüller, *Michael Choniates, Metropolit von Athen (ca. 1138–1222),* Orientalia Christiana 33.3 (Rome, 1934), 155.

6. G. G. Litvarin, *Sovety i rasskazy Kekavmena* (Moscow, 1972).

SELECTED BIBLIOGRAPHY

General Literature
Beck, H. G. *Geschichte der orthodoxen Kirche im byzantinischen Reich.* Göttingen, 1980.
————. "Kirche und Klerus im staatlichen Leben von Byzanz." *Revue des études byzantines* 24 (1966): 1–24.
————. *Kirche und theologische Literatur im byzantinischen Reich.* Munich, 1959.
Hussey, J. *The Orthodox Church in the Byzantine Empire,* 2d ed. Oxford, 1990.
Michel, A. *Die Kaisermacht in der Ostkirche (843–1204).* Darmstadt, 1959.

Early Period

Guillou, A. "L'évêque dans la société méditerranéenne du VIe–VIIe siècles: Un modèle." *Bibliothèque de l'Ecole des Chartes* 131 (1973): 5–19; reprinted in idem, *Culture et société en Italie byzantine (VIe–VIIe s.)*. Study II. London, 1978.

Hohlweg, A. "Bischof und Stadtherr im frühen Byzanz." *Jahrbuch der Österreichischen Byzantinistik* 20 (1972): 51–62.

Jones, A. H. M. *The Later Roman Empire 284–602*, chapter 22, pp. 873–937, 1362–90. Oxford, 1964.

Liebeschuetz, J. H. W. G. *Barbarians and Bishops: Army, Church, and State in the Age of Arcadius and Chrysostom*. Oxford, 1990.

Noethlichs, K. L. "Materialen zum Bischofsbild aus den spätantiken Rechtsquellen." *Jahrbuch für Antike und Christentum* 26 (1973): 28–59.

Late Period

Macrides, R. "Saints and Sainthood in the Early Palaiologan Period." In S. Hackel, ed., *The Byzantine Saint*. University of Birmingham Fourteenth Spring Symposium of Byzantine Studies, 67–87. London, 1981.

Magdalino, P. "The Byzantine Holy Man in the Twelfth Century." In Hackel, ed., *The Byzantine Saint*, 51–66.

Talbot, A.-M. "The Patriarch Athanasius (1289–1293; 1303–1309) and the Church." *Dumbarton Oaks Papers* 27 (1973): 13–28.

Tiftixoglu, V. "Gruppenbildung innerhalb des konstantinopolitanischen Klerus während der Komnenenzeit." *Byzantinische Zeitschrift* 62 (1969): 25–72.

Art

Ruggieri, V. *Byzantine Religious Architecture (582–867): Its History and Structural Elements*. Orientalia Christiana Analecta 237. Rome, 1991.

Ševčenko, N. P. *The Life of Saint Nicholas in Byzantine Art*. Turin, 1983.

Walter, C. *Art and Ritual of the Byzantine Church*. London, 1982.

8

FUNCTIONARIES

André Guillou

HE BYZANTINE EMPIRE was unique in medieval Europe in that it
was the only government before the thirteenth century to exhibit a
centralized system of administration whose initiative reached the
most distant provinces, and because it was able for several centuries to
impose its will on different races speaking different languages, whose interests were sometimes divergent. It was only in Byzantium, and to a
lesser degree in Muslim countries, that one found government agents endowed with a part of state authority and answerable to that state.

In spite of what has been written on the subject, these agents were
few in number, which might appear paradoxical in a theocratic state in
which the emperor, God's chosen one, represented him on earth. As in
ancient oriental monarchies and in Hellenistic states, the emperor was in
fact regarded as ruling with other members of his administration, forming
a single governing body, receiving its orders from the sovereign, who had
chosen the members either directly or indirectly, and who were formally
required to perform those orders or be accused of a felony. John Ka-
taphloron, the *vestēs* and notary *tōn oikeiakōn, stratēgos* (governor) and
tax collector (*anagrapheus*) of the theme of Smolena with the new district
of Thessalonike and Serres in Macedonia, received "from the powerful
and divine emperor," says the official document he signed in 1079, an
order to examine the acts presented by his predecessors to reach the quota
of taxes due by a small religious establishment near Hierissos in Chal-
kidike.

One could not escape the imperial will. The text of acts written in
imperial offices was, in this respect, perfectly clear: "By virtue of the
power and force of the present *chrysoboullos logos* (a solemn imperial
document sealed with a gold bull) of my majesty," one reads in a
chrysobull of Andronikos III for the monastery of St. John Prodromos
on Mount Menecee in 1332, "all of this (the advantages granted to the

monastery) will be preserved in an unshakable and stable manner, without the possibility of an infraction or a violation occurring against them by any person at any moment; and anyone, a practicing governor, tax collector, or any other functionary who attempts to infringe upon them in any way will be convinced he tried the impossible, will be stripped of his duties and discharged." It has therefore been assumed that the empire was filled with more or less zealous functionaries serving the public interest (*tēn douleian tou koinou metacheirizomenoi*).

Returning to the concept passed down to historians from the medieval West, about the public and the private, we find another Byzantine peculiarity. In Byzantium there was no local administration in the current sense of the term, nor was there a monopolization of public power by the large property owners. The state was represented in the provinces by civilian or military governors and by prelates who were also answerable directly to it. All these representatives did in fact have a few government officials under them whom one might call "functionaries." But, for the most part, in carrying out their duties they delegated their authority to local notables, to professional guilds grouped into a consortium who were collectively responsible before state representatives for a certain public duty, like the later rural communes (*chōria*) responsible for levying taxes in their territories, following the orders of the state and in conformity with its regulations. Thus we see, for example, that the accounts of the large properties, both lay and ecclesiastical, were established and managed under the control of the state and in conformity with its regulations by private citizens who had been given a public responsibility.

The emperor represented a concentration of all political authority in the hands of one person. And as the sacred imperial palace was, until the twelfth century, his residence and thus the seat of government, we can understand why palace personnel throughout time held a preeminent place among the agents of political power. This is because every public office was tied directly to the palace. The emperor governed the state with agents closely connected to him through a more or less honorific palatine function, through a court title that gave them a rank in the hierarchy.

The importance of such priority at court was enormous: "Any renown in life, which is connected to the glorious value of titles, is revealed to spectators only by one's being called in one's order of priority at the splendid table and the coveted meal of our very wise emperors," wrote Philotheos, the author of a manual of ranks in Constantinople, in 899. The eminent place someone occupied in Byzantine society and the value of the titles he bore corresponded to an established order, which was natural in an empire that claimed to be heir to the Roman Empire and in which the emperor, "crowned by God," had among other missions that of maintaining the order and of guaranteeing the well-being of his subjects: order (in Greek, *taxis*) was part of the imperial cult. Emperor Constantine VII Porphyrogennetos explained it in this way in the preface of his *Book of Ceremonies:* "Indeed, just as one would label 'disordered' a badly formed body whose parts had been connected pell-mell and without unity, so, too, would be the imperial state if it were not conducted and governed with order," and he adds that not to respect order would be like amputating what is most important in imperial glory, and he who tolerated it was neglecting the people and destroying everything.

THE RECRUITMENT OF FUNCTIONARIES

Quintus Aurelius Symmachus, prefect of Rome, wrote to Emperor Valentinian II in 384: "In the future you will act in the better interest of your city if you confer offices upon those who have not sought them," and in 450 Emperor Marcian confirmed that point of view in a Novel that deals with the incompetence and dishonesty of functionaries: "since your majesty had put an end to the venal intrigues of functionaries and had acted against their will to govern loyally the private affairs of the crown and the state of appreciated and informed men—for your majesty knows that the state will be fortunate if it is led by men who have not sought to do so and who normally reject public offices."

The attraction and advantages of holding a government post were considerable. The writer Libanios, the most famous rhetorician of the fourth century, uses the following language to recommend his natural son Cimone, who could have been included on the list for the council of the city of Antioch, to Tatian, the praetorian prefect of the Orient: "He will be very happy with all that might be given to him, because it will give him the same guarantee, regardless of how long it lasts, even if it is only for a month."

In fact, for the great majority of functionaries, the emperor was in no position to evaluate the worth of candidates personally, and he depended upon the recommendations of those of his entourage in whom he had confidence: "The emperor is a man," wrote Ammianus Marcellinus, "and he does not know to whom he should confer the affairs of state," unlike God who knew everyone's merits and had no need to hear recommendations from anyone.

This non-gratis recommendation (*suffragium*) did not benefit candidates of modest origins. But the pressure was such that the imperial government capitulated by requiring only that the candidate promoted by way of recommendations pay 50 gold solidi and that anyone promoted through seniority alone pay between 5 and 10 gold solidi!

One can understand that such imperial tolerance gave free rein to corruption: high-level positions were sold to such a degree that, in the sixth century, Justinian, just as Theodosios had done in the preceding century, imposed the following oath upon provincial governors, their deputies, and other equivalently ranked functionaries: "I swear that I have given nothing and will give absolutely nothing to anyone for the office that has been conferred upon me . . . nor for the recommendation to the emperor, or to the prefects or other dignitaries or to those close to them." We must keep in mind that the sum paid by a candidate to obtain the post of provincial governor corresponded to approximately twice an annual salary, and more than one such official had to borrow money to obtain that sum, even if it meant subsequently retrieving his losses through the people under his jurisdiction.

Justinian's successors attempted in vain to put an end to that practice, and under Leo VI (886–912) the government succeeded in fixing a rate that took into account whether or not the newly promoted official received a salary, which might be seen as a public loan and for the candidate as a lifelong investment. Chancery duties were naturally added to that sum, payable for every appointment or promotion. An anecdote told by Constantine VII Porphyrogennetos illuminates in a cruel light how the Byzantine state thus conducted its affairs. An old priest named Ktenas, the incomparable cantor of the New Church in Constantinople, had control over a large fortune; he wanted to become *prōtospatharios,* a very high-ranking dignity, in order to be able to carry the *epikoutzoulon,* a gala cloak, and to sit in the Lausiakos, a hall in the palace close to the throne room, where the high functionaries gathered either to be received by the emperor or to accompany him to some ceremony; seats were reserved there for each class of functionary. The *prōtospatharios'* salary was 1 lb. of gold and the price of the dignity was 12–18 lbs. of gold. Ktenas offered to pay 40 lbs., but the emperor felt it was completely out of the question for a priest to become *prōtospatharios;* Ktenas then offered to add some jewels and other goods valued at 20 lbs. of gold. The emperor's favorite, the patrician Samonas, intervened. Leo VI gave in. Two years later Ktenas died.

The way functionaries were recruited did not vary. They were less expected to have technical training than more general knowledge, ranging from epistolary art to rhetoric, and especially knowledge of the law. Here is what was required at the beginning of the tenth century of those who wanted to enter the guild of the twenty-four imperial notaries, according to the *Book of the Prefect* of the city of Constantinople:

A notary cannot be appointed without deliberation and a vote by the *primikērios* (chief) and the other members of the guild of notaries. He must, in fact, have perfect knowledge of the laws, excellent handwriting, be neither a chatterbox nor insolent, nor have dissolute habits; his character must command respect, his judgment must be sound, he must combine training with intelligence, speak with ease, and possess a perfectly correct style, a quality without which mistakes that might alter the tenor or punctuation of a text would very easily embarrass him. If from this point of view a notary were ever inspired to circumvent the law and the written instructions issued by those in authority, anyone who had testified on his behalf (at the time of his candidacy) would be held responsible. The candidate must know by heart the forty titles of the manual (the *Prochiron*, or abridged law code of Basil I) and know the sixty books of the *Basilika* (also by Basil I); he must also demonstrate a general education without which he might commit errors while writing his acts and err against good style. He will be granted the time necessary to prove his physical and intellectual abilities fully. He will draft an act on the spot in front of the members of the guild in order to protect them from any unpleasant surprises on his part. If, in spite of this precaution, he is caught making any mistakes, he will be forced to leave his post.

This is how a nomination is carried out. Following the depositions of witnesses and the examination of the candidate, that candidate, wearing the cloak, appears before the very illustrious prefect of the city (of Constantinople), with the guild of notaries and their *primikērios,* who swears, while invoking God and the salvation of the emperors, that neither favoritism nor intrigue, nor any consideration of kinship or friendship have caused the candidate to be called to occupy a seat, but rather his virtue, his training, his intelligence, and his capabilities in all areas. Following the formality of the oath, the acting prefect of the city confirms the candidate's election to the prefectural tribunal; the candidate is henceforth a member of the guild of notaries and will be considered as one of their own. Upon leaving the tribunal he goes to the church closest to his home, and there, in the presence of all the notaries wearing their cloaks, he takes off his own, puts on a surplice, and is consecrated by the priest's prayer. All the notaries, wearing their cloaks, fall into line behind him, the *primikērios* himself holding the censer and directing its smoke toward the newly elected one, who has the Bible in his hands and carries it in front of him. The straight and narrow paths upon which he is expected to walk are symbolized by the incense smoke directed right in front of the Lord. The elected one takes possession of the post that has been conferred upon him amidst this pompous display of ceremonial garments; he remains in his robes when he returns home, to celebrate and rejoice with everyone in attendance.

Beginning in the sixth century, and undoubtedly well before then, students who wanted to become functionaries were always advised to learn the law. This concern on the part of the Byzantine authorities is expressed with particular clarity in a law by Constantine Monomachos: "The earlier legal provisions concerning notaries and lawyers, which have been forgotten, should be put back in use. Not only will they be instructed alongside the *nomophylax* (or guardian of the laws, a post created in 1045), but they will not be received in their guilds without the *nomophylax* having attested to their good judicial training and their ability to speak and write well. Anyone who does not adhere to that policy will be immediately discharged, so that he knows it is no longer the recent neglect, but the former exactitude of the laws that reigns in public affairs." Future administrators thus had to have earned the diploma issued by the *nomophylax*.

The examination taken to enter into public service was difficult and very complicated, therefore the higher officials, with few exceptions, were always well educated. Among them one finds all the great known authors, from the rhetorician Ausonius, the master of Emperor Gratian, who made him a consul in 379, to the humanist philosopher Theodore Metochites, the grand logothete (a sort of prime minister) of Andronikos II in the fourteenth century, including Patriarch Photios in the ninth century and Michael Psellos, an encyclopedist and statesman, two centuries later. All had received their training at the university, in the years when there was one in Constantinople, or with private tutors at their own expense.

In principle, access to the highest offices was open to all subjects of the empire; residents of the provinces of humble origins came to Constantinople as students, and could gain entrance into offices as simple employees and then reach the summits of the bureaucratic hierarchy. In the sixth century, John of Cappadocia, the all-powerful minister of Justinian, began his career in the offices of the head of the militia; in the eleventh century, the eunuch Nikephoritzes, Psellos, Xiphilinos, Leichoudes, and John Mauropous, all men of obscure origins, but talented and ambitious, also climbed all the rungs of the ladder of power. In the fourteenth century, the grand duke Alexios Apokaukos, beginning as a simple scribe in the offices of the *domestikos* of the themes (head of the provinces) in the Orient, succeeded in obtaining the office of his superior and successively became, in spite of his incompetence, *parakoimōmenos* (overseer of the imperial chamber), administrator of taxes, grand duke (head of the fleet), and prefect of the capital. All the same, and very early on, the powerful families of large landowners monopolized the high administrative offices of the empire, and after the twelfth century the highest positions were even occupied by relatives and allies of the reigning dynasty; very soon a true closed caste of functionaries was created, which welcomed foreign princes, and under the Palaiologoi, frequently monks and clerics who held civilian and even military jobs. The monk Theodotos became general logothete, a sort of minister of finances in the seventh century, and, at the beginning of the following century, that office was held by a deacon of

Hagia Sophia, who also received the command of a fleet. Such intervention by the clergy into the administration of the state was especially frequent in the fourteenth and fifteenth centuries.

THE FUNCTIONARY'S OATH

The act of assuming one's post was preceded by a more or less solemn ritual ceremony whose essential element was always the candidate's oath and his veneration of the emperor. Beginning in the fifth century, an oath of loyalty was demanded of all high officials of the court and of dignitaries of the empire. It was a religious act that strengthened imperial authority and served as a symbolic recognition by the functionaries of the divine nature of imperial power. Each new functionary was required to swear this oath before receiving his investiture, and all functionaries renewed that oath upon the election of each new emperor. In the time of the Palaiologoi in the fourteenth century, upon the death of an emperor, all the provincial governors resigned. They then gathered together and swore an oath of loyalty to the new emperor, who in due time once again conferred their functions upon them. The dignitaries' and functionaries' oath of loyalty was given in writing, and the document remained in the palace archives, listed in a register.

I swear by All-Powerful God, by his only son Jesus Christ our God, by the Holy Spirit, by Mary the saintly and glorious mother of God, forever a virgin, by the four Gospels which I am holding in my hands, by the holy archangels Michael and Gabriel, that I will maintain a pure conscience with regard to our very divine and pious masters, Justinian and his wife Theodora, and that I will render them loyal service in the exercise of the duties that have been given to me through their piety; I will willingly accept all pain and all fatigue resulting from the office they have conferred upon me in the interest of the empire and the state. I am in communion with the holy Catholic and apostolic Church of God; in no form and at no moment will I oppose it, nor will I permit anyone to do so, insofar as I am able to prevent it. I do also swear that I have truly given nothing to anyone nor will give anything for the position that has been conferred upon me or to obtain a patronage, that I have neither promised nor agreed to send anything at all from the provinces in order to obtain the support of the emperor, nor to the very glorious prefects, nor to other famous people who govern the administration, nor to their entourage, nor to anyone else, but that I have been granted my position virtually without salary and can thus appear pure in the eyes of the subjects of our very holy emperors, and am content with the sum that has been granted me by the state.

Such was the commitment made in the sixth century by the praetorian prefect of Illyricum, and it extended to the administrative personnel he had under his orders, of whom he promised diligence and disinterestedness in their fiscal duties, fairness and justice, before concluding: "And if I do not act exactly as I have said here, may I be subject here and in the beyond to the terrible judgment of our great master, God, and of our savior Jesus Christ, the fate of Judas, the leper of Gieze (the swindler in the Bible), the fear of Cain; and may I be subject to the punishment provided by the law of their piety." This oath in all its significance continued to be sworn until the end of the empire. A simple formulary of the fourteenth century stated:

> I swear by God and his holy Gospels, by the venerable and vivifying cross, by the very holy Mother of God Hodegetria, and by all the saints that I will be for our prince and emperor, the powerful and holy N. (the name of the emperor) a faithful servant throughout my entire life, loyal not only in words but through those actions that good servants carry out for their masters. And this, that I be so not only with regard to a master, but also to the majesty he has and will have, I am the friend of his friends and the enemy of his enemies; against them, against his majesty, I will never plot, I will undertake no action and will give my consent to no one, I will commit neither treachery nor acts of cruelty, I will reveal to the emperor any plans against him and will name those responsible. A true and faithful servant of the emperor, this I will be, if he reigns successfully according to the exact truth and in all honesty, just as truth really asks of the servant to be true and honest with regard to his master, and if, with God's permission he falls into misfortune or is banished, I will accompany him, will share his suffering, and will incur the same risks as he until death itself, and this throughout my entire life.

The patriarch of Constantinople and the prelates of the church were subject to this oath, in their capacity as state officials, at least beginning in the eighth century.

During the ritual ceremony marking his "appointment," the new functionary received ceremonial garments whose color and ornamentation varied according to the celebrations at hand. In the ninth century, the rector, a personal palatine position, was thus given a white robe with a cloak woven with gold that fell on his shoulders, and with sleeves embroidered with gold, a cope also embroidered with gold, and a purple veil strewn with roses woven of gold. In the fourteenth century, the *despotēs* (despot) wore a hat enhanced with pearls, with his name embroidered in gold on the lower rim. The *megas domestikos* (grand domestic) wore a scarlet and gold hat and a cloak embroidered with the image of the emperor standing between two angels within a frame of pearls. Fashion played a role here; in time this apparel became less flowing, ever more rich, strewn with pearls and gemstones, and the headgear, a brimmed hat, became the essential distinctive symbol of each dignity.

THE CONDITION OF FUNCTIONARIES AND THEIR AUTHORITY

Earlier I explained why the number of civil servants in the Byzantine Empire was lower than is commonly believed. In fact, it remains impossible to provide exact figures for most of the empire. We will therefore limit ourselves to examining the functionaries who governed in North Africa, which had been reconquered in the sixth century; this is made possible by existing documentation. We will then offer a sketch of the later evolution of civil administration and its functionaries.

An imperial rescript of April 534 named the patrician Archelaos praetorian prefect, the head of the new government of Africa in its capital of Carthage. He had already carried out the same duties in Constantinople and Illyricum, and thus found himself in Africa as general treasurer of the expeditionary force. To assist him in his multiple tasks and to insure the smooth functioning of the numerous departments under his supervision, Archelaos had a staff of deputies, attachés, and employees under him. He was assisted primarily by a certain number of advisers, young legal experts, who were training as interns for a career in business, and it frequently happened, in fact, that provincial governors were chosen from among them. In the administration of justice, the prefect was again assisted by his chancellors. Then came the true staff, which included a total of 396 people divided into two categories: employees distributed among ten offices (118 functionaries), and deputies grouped into nine guilds (278 functionaries). There were also five doctors and four teachers in the prefect's entourage. The entire staff was appointed by the prefect and were answerable only to him. Beneath the praetorian prefect, seven governors shared the civil administration of the provinces of the diocese; they were aided in their various duties by a staff of fifty functionaries.

The evolution and development of the administrative organization, and therefore of the status of functionaries of the Byzantine Empire, were the result of changes made from day to day. They did not follow any preconceived system but were a constant adaptation to the evolving life of the various regions that comprised the empire, showing a flexibility completely contrary to a doctrinal frame of mind.

In the fourth century, Constantine reformed the system initiated by Diocletian, who, a century earlier, had militarized the civil service. Several department heads responsible to the emperor led departments in which the staff, who were subordinate to the leaders, were grouped into a hierarchical system. With civil and military powers henceforth separated, the imperial administration contained a double hierarchy. With one exception, the praetorian prefect of the Orient, the former praetorian prefects became regional functionaries and lost their military connections. Their responsibilities were divided among new department heads. The *magister officiorum* ran the emperor's dwelling with several offices. He had authority over the imperial bodyguard; he was also responsible for the arsenals, the mail services, and the state police. In his offices, the palace quaestor (*quaestor sacri palatii*) prepared legal documents and sent them out; he represented imperial judicial power and the emperor's knowledge of the law. Cassiodorus wrote that "the skill of his speech should be such that no one can find fault with it," as that speech was considered to be the very thoughts of the emperor.

The administration of finances was distributed between two independent departments: that of the sacred largesses and that of the private estate. The first, managed by a count, oversaw the treasury that was maintained by levying taxes on luxury items, and was used to pay for gifts made by the emperor to the army, government officials, foreign ambassadors, and foreign princes. He controlled customs, the mining industry, government factories, and the administration of currency flow through the intervention of counts or procurators. The private estate was administered by a count whose subordinate staff was comprised of counts in the imperial regions of Cappadocia and Africa, and the count of the private largesses, who was responsible for the traditional gifts made specifically to churches. The officer in the "sacred chamber," a eunuch, was in charge of the imperial chambers; with his close representative, the *primikērios* of the sacred chamber, who also held the title of *parakoimōmenos* ("he who sleeps near his sovereign"), and his army of chamberlains, he had an important place in the palace and could have, in certain circumstances, a role in the coronation, for example, a very high-profile position. The five department heads made up the prince's consistory, a state council and supreme tribunal that included among others a certain number of established members, called the counts of the consistory, which was aided in its work by the important guild of notaries discussed above.

In the final years of the fourth century, the provincial administration was organized into four prefectures: the Orient, Illyricum, Italy, and Gaul. Within the territory of their administration, the prefects had full imperial authority: they legislated, made final judgments, and directed the imperial mail service, public works, deliveries in kind, and even education. They paid salaries and remunerations, recruited the army, and also oversaw the arsenals. In the reign of Constantine, the military duties of the prefects were passed on to the leaders of the militia, who were recruited from among career soldiers and who had dukes under their command who were responsible for the troops of their province.

The sixth century was not so much a period of profound change—as certain historians, misled by the amount of legislation left by Justinian, have believed—as it was a stage in the administrative reorganization conceived by a power that was always sensitive to the concrete situation of the empire. The central administration was being broken up: the imperial treasurer came out from under the control of the count of the sacred largesses; the count of the private estate was replaced by two of his subordinates, the logothete of the herds and the count of the stable; the departments of the imperial chamber gained importance, and the emperor conferred civil and military offices upon whomever he deemed worthy; the lawyer Tribonian was thus both *magister officiorum* and quaestor. The provincial administration still watched over local events: the diocese of Egypt was closed down; the augustalis of Alexandria became a simple governor, and the five independent provinces, which were under the direct control of the praetorian prefect of the Orient, were overseen in both the military and civil domains by a duke who was chosen most often from the palatine nobility, and whose troops simultaneously were responsible for civil defense, acted as police, and collected taxes. Concern over the protection of the territories reconquered in Italy and in Africa against Lombard and Berber invasions led the Byzantine powers to transform those two provinces definitively into military command posts called exarchates by granting the exarchs, from the end of the sixth century, all responsibility for financial and judicial matters, public works, defense of the territory—which turned them into de facto sovereigns, just like the dukes in their duchies. Only Sicily preserved its individual government placed under the authority of a patrician, which then became the highest-ranking title in the hierarchy.

The empire lost territory and wealth as a result of invasions by Avaro-Slavs, Bulgarians, and Arabs. These losses led to new administrative reforms between the seventh century and the end of the eleventh: the *sakellarios,* the senior financial officer and keeper of the emperor's privy purse, replaced the count of the sacred largesses and the count of the private estate; and the three former financial offices of the praetorian prefecture—that of the army, general finances, and individual finances—became autonomous under the management of their department heads, three logothetes, who were soon joined by a fourth, that of the public mail service. This latter functionary took over some of the duties of the *magister officiorum,* whose functions were then limited to the court; the others were distributed among the *domestikos* of the *scholae,* the head of an army regiment, the quaestor, who ran the various offices, and the officers in charge of requests and ceremonies. They were almost all former subordinates of high-ranking officials.

A measure of the administrative decentralization of central power was found in the new division of the Byzantine territory into "themes." The theme, at first perhaps an army corps of soldiers registered or enrolled in the military records, then in general a corps of troops, in the eighth century became an army corps billeted in a province, and finally just the province itself or the military and administrative district where an army regiment had been billeted. Former special units with historical names, such as Opsikion or the *boukellarioi,* gave their names to the territories on which they had been stationed. Other administrative themes, such as Armeniakon, Anatolikon, derived their names from those of the corps of troops that once occupied them. The evolution consecrated by this profound reform of provincial administration was seen by the theoreticians of imperial absolutism as a limitation of the emperor's powers, who was delegating part of his civil and military authority to the *stratēgoi* whom he placed at the head of each theme. "With the Byzantine Empire shrunken and mutilated in the East as in the West, the emperors who succeeded Herakleios (610–641), no longer knowing where or how to exercise their power, broke up their command into small pieces, and the large regiments of troops abandoned their ancestral Latin to adopt Greek," wrote Constantine Porphyrogennetos. This is certainly a military expression of the remodeling of the provincial administration necessitated by the needs of defense, but also by the economic and social evolution of the province, with a scholarly reference to the ideal Roman Empire.

Administrative reform brought about important changes in the government hierarchy. The palace henceforth triumphed over the entire administration, and the dignity that had always accompanied a specific function was no longer distinguished from the office connected to it. Beneficiaries of this were thus designated in official acts where their signatures were at the bottom of written documents: for example, Nikephoros, *proedros* and duke of Thessalonike, Botaneiates—the surname coming last; or Prokopios, patrician, imperial *prōtospatharios* and *stratēgos* of Sicily—his titles at the end; or John, *magistros,* proconsul, imperial *prōtospatharios* and logothete of the drome; Andronikos, *prōtoproedros, prōtovestiarios,* and *domestikos* of the *scholae* of the Orient, Ducas.

In the first half of the eleventh century, the former system of the themes, which had dominated provincial administration, was profoundly modified. The new system was characterized by the centralization of the military organization, begun with the creation of the high command of the army of the Orient, then of the high command of the army of the West, carried out by the *domestikoi* of the *scholae.* The provincial army of the themes, which was by and large unreliable, as one is led to believe by the complete absence of sources dealing with it, was gradually replaced by the professional army made up of citizens or foreigners in the service of the empire and maintained by the state. The professional army (the *tagmata*), placed under the command of dukes or *katepani,* officers who acquired great importance in the military hierarchy, was stationed in the various regions of the empire, whose names were taken on by the commanders, regions chosen especially for military reasons, independent of the confines of the administrative districts (themes). The *stratēgos,* formerly a governor of the vast territories of the first themes in the seventh and eighth centuries, became a subaltern officer of dukes and *katepani,* a fortress commander without precise administrative duties. The army's provincial commands no longer necessarily corresponded to the former themes, which continued to exist, governed by a judge-praetor, head of the civil administration, now independent of and separate from the military administration.

The success of the Turkish invasions in Asia Minor completely shook up the administration of that region. The reorganization of the reconquered territory, begun by Alexios I Komnenos (1081–1118), was carried out primarily during the reign of Manuel I Komnenos (1143–80). The theme, an administrative district, was once again placed under the control of a high-ranking military official, no longer the *stratēgos,* who disappeared entirely, but a duke who also took on certain civil tasks, assisted by a series of new functionaries. Only the theme of Peloponnese-Hellas, placed under the high command of an admiral (the grand duke), continued to be governed by a civilian governor (the praetor), until the Latin occupation of 1204, which unleashed a new evolution in the provincial administration of the empire. The three Byzantine states of the thirteenth century—the Empire of Nicaea, the Empire of Trebizond, and the despotate of Epiros—pursued their own experiments, and the administrative reforms of the Komnenoi found very different applications in each of these regions, ones adapted to the specific political and economic conditions of each state.

ECCLESIASTICAL FUNCTIONARIES

The church may be seen as having been a large department of the state, connected as closely as any other department to the chief executive, the emperor. We find proof of this in a letter written between 1394 and 1397 by the patriarch of Constantinople, Antony IV, to Basil I, grand prince of Moscow, who had just put a ban on citing the name of the Byzantine emperor in the Russian Orthodox liturgy:

Very noble great king of Moscow and of all Russia, in the Holy Spirit very dear son of our moderation (this was the patriarch's title) Basil, our moderation begs God Pantokrator to grant your nobility (title given to the prince) grace, peace, his compassion, health of soul and body, the object of your wishes, his benediction, all good and all salvation. . . . I have been told of certain words spoken by your nobility concerning my very powerful and holy *basileus autokratōr* that have saddened me; you prohibit, I am told, the metropolitan (of Moscow) from commemorating in the diptychs (in the service) the divine name of the *basileus,* which is impossible, and you say, "We have a church, but we have no emperor and do not believe we have one," which is not good at all: the holy *basileus* (the emperor of Constantinople) occupies an important place in the church, not that of other notables and princes, for throughout time the emperors have strengthened and fortified piety all over the earth, they have organized ecumenical councils, they have upheld the rules set by the holy and divine canons on the true dogmas and on the life of Christians by giving them many laws, they have led many battles against heresies, imperial decrees together with the synods have established priorities among prelates, the division of their eparchies, and the distribution of dioceses; this is why they have an important function in the church. Even if, with God's permission, the barbarian peoples have encircled the realms of the emperor, the emperor still presently receives the same investiture from the church, the same rank, the same prayers, through holy unction he is ordained *basileus* and *autokratōr* of the Romans, that is, of all Christians, and everywhere, by all the patriarchs, the metropolitans, and the bishops, the name of *basileus* is mentioned along with that of the Christians, a privilege granted to no notable, nor to any other leader; and his power is so great that even the Latins, who have no connection to our church, give him the same title and show him the same submission as before, when they were associated with us; Orthodox Christians should therefore show him even more respect. Indeed, it is not because the barbarian peoples have encircled the territory of the *basileus* that the Christians should scorn him; for, on the contrary, that should be a source of instruction and wisdom for them: if the great *basileus,* master and lord of the earth, he who holds such power, has come to such distress, what might be the suffering of the rulers of small territories or of notables of small populations: and when your nobility and your territory experience much misfortune, the assaults and occupation by the impious (the Mongols), it is not just that we should despise your nobility because of that—quite the contrary—our moderation and the holy emperor write to you according to the former custom, and we confer upon you in our letters, in our notifications of elections, through the voices of our legates, the title held by the great kings who have preceded you. It is not good at all, my son, that you say, "We have a church, not an emperor," for it is not possible for Christians to have a church and no emperor, for the empire (that is, the state) and the church form a very close community, and it is impossible to dissociate them. The *basileis* rejected by Christians are only those who are heretics and lead a furious struggle against the church, who introduce false dogmas, foreign to the teaching of the apostles and the fathers; my very powerful and very holy *autokratōr*, thanks be to God, is very orthodox and very loyal; he is a defender of the church, he fights for it, he protects it, and it is not possible for a prelate not to mention his name. Listen, then, to the head of the apostles, Peter, in the first apostolic letter: "Fear God, honor the emperor." He did not say the emperors, so that one does not include those who, here and there, are called emperors among the barbarian peoples, but the *basileus*, to signify that the universal *basileus* is unique.

The administration of the church therefore came directly under the authority of the emperor, and that of the patriarchate, whose hierarchy was included in that of the sacred palace, merged with that of the patriarchal church of Constantinople, Hagia Sophia, which, through the Augoustaion, communicated with the imperial palace.

The palace staff was very large; Justinian limited it to 525, but in the seventh century it reached nearly six hundred people and continued to increase. Those who held offices were either clerics, priests or deacons, except the apparitors and the vergers (called *manglabitai*). Like other bishops, the patriarch was originally elected by the clergy and the people; his election was then ratified by the civil authorities, and he was ordained by a bishop. Justinian maintained this rule but restricted the electoral body and exercised great influence over the choice. In the ninth century it became common to allow only metropolitans to elect the patriarch, but the emperor retained the legal right to intervene: the metropolitans presented a list of three names, among which the sovereign chose the one who suited him, or a fourth, if he preferred. Some emperors even chose the patriarch directly: Basil II named Alexios from the Studios monastery on his deathbed (1025) and had him enthroned immediately; John Kantakouzenos successively imposed three patriarchs on the metropolitans: John XIV Kalekas in 1334, Isidore in 1347, and Kallistos in 1350. The patriarch received his investiture in the palace following the same protocol as that of lay dignitaries. The formula in the fourteenth century was the following: "The Holy Trinity, through the power it has granted us, promotes you to archbishop of Constantinople, New Rome, and to ecumenical patriarch"; the patriarch, after receiving the cross from the emperor, then traveled through the city on horseback from the Blachernai Palace to Hagia Sophia, where he was received by the archbishop of Herakleia. The metropolitans maintained their electoral rights, however, until the end of the empire, and the emperors never succeeded in suppressing its judicial legitimacy.

Leader of the Orthodox Church and second-in-command of the state, the patriarch had a powerful deputy, the *synkellos,* chosen by the emperor and made a member of the court of *magistroi* in the tenth century, who had seniority over the metropolitans and who could be sent on important political missions. The function became a title; it was multiplied and disappeared; the archdeacon, first deputy of the patriarch for the liturgy, endured the same fate. Five departments ran the administration: the high steward, chosen by the emperor until Patriarch Michael I Keroularios intervened in 1057, oversaw the vast temporalities of the patriarchate; the high *sakellarios,* aided by the archon (superintendent) of the monasteries, maintained order and discipline in the monasteries; the high *skeuophylax* was the guardian of the liturgical vessels, vestments, and books of the patriarchal treasury; the high *chartophylax,* archivist and librarian of the patriarchate, saw the importance of his role increase dramatically: authenticating patriarchal documents and verifying the accuracy of the copies and translations made of the books in the library, he ultimately obtained a right of inspection over all the offices of the patriarchate, "because he is the mouth and the hand of the patriarch," wrote Alexios Komnenos. He and his offices were also responsible for the staff. Finally, there was the *sakelliou,* who, with one or several archons, had control over the parish churches and their personnel.

In addition, the *prōtekdikos* and the guild of *ekdikoi* (defenders), jurists and legal auxiliaries, intervened in the defense of the accused, cases involving the freeing of a slave, to judge the beneficiaries of the right of sanctuary, and to instruct the converted; then came the *prōtonotarios,* the secretary of the patriarch; the logothete, the official in charge of ceremonies who, in particular, read speeches during festivals; the *kanstresios,* who supervised offerings; the referendary, who transmitted communications from the patriarch to the emperor; the *hypomnematographos,* who wrote solemn acts and kept official records of the sessions of the synod; the *hieromnemon,* responsible for ordinations; the *hypomimnēsikōn,* adviser and private secretary to the patriarch; officials in charge of offices, judgments, and requests; the head of ceremonies; notaries; the archons of monasteries and churches; the *didaskaloi* of the Gospel, of the Apostles, and of the Psalter; the archant of the *antimēnsion,* who introduced the communicants; the archon of the lights, who took care of the neophytes; the rhetor, who acted as teacher and orator; the two gatekeepers; the *noumodotēs,* who distributed money to clerics and the poor; and the primicerius of the notaries. People frequently held several offices simultaneously. Officers received a written act of nomination or of promotion and agreed in writing to fulfill the duties of their office, under penalty of expulsion. We have no information on how they were paid.

In the provinces, ecclesiastical administration was in the hands of the metropolitans and the bishops, who were at the head of metropolitanates and suffragan bishoprics, the latter subordinate to the former, with the exception of the autocephalous archbishops, whose offices were answerable to the patriarch. Metropolitans and bishops were recruited first from among the dignitaries of the patriarchate and the metropolitanates, then from among abbots of the monasteries or simple monks. The bishops were under the metropolitans. Metropolitans and bishops oversaw the churches and their property, assisted in the beginning by deacons, then by various deputies, whom they appointed themselves and who were a microcosm of the patriarchal court: for example, the archdeacon, assistant to the metropolitan or the bishop, the *synkellos, ekdikos* (defender), referendaries, *apokrisiarioi, dioikētai, skeuophylax,* and notaries. In Constantinople, as in the provinces, the key principle of ecclesiastical hierarchy was never challenged, in the sense that the dignity of the person was always based on his title of ordination (priest, deacon); but from the outside, the functions performed by the different orders caused disturbances and developments that were continually related to the changes in society and in civil institutions: there was a close connection between the ecclesiastical and the civil hierarchies. The monastic world remained separate; it was never controlled by one or the other, even if, by rights, those institutions might have claimed to do so.

THE STATUS OF FUNCTIONARIES

The status of functionaries can be examined in six aspects: salaries, advancement, duties and responsibilities, punishments, controls, and retirement.

Salaries
In the fourth century, salaries were paid in kind: regulation rations, units of fodder, and quality food for the functionary's table. At the end of the century, salaries were still paid in kind. In 439 salaries, at least for the higher-level positions, were paid in gold, at rates fixed for each province by the praetorian prefect. Here is the list of the salaries of the highest-ranking officials under Justinian, who raised them significantly, in order to put an end to the extortion that had been taking place until that time in the provinces:

Praetorian prefect of Africa	7,200 gold solidi
Prefect of Egypt	2,880 gold solidi

Proconsul of Palestine (including his offices)	1,584 gold solidi
Duke of Tripolitania	1,582 gold solidi
Duke of Byzacena	1,582 gold solidi
Duke of Numidia	1,582 gold solidi
Duke of Mauretania	1,582 gold solidi
Duke of Sardinia	1,582 gold solidi
Proconsul of Cappadocia	1,440 gold solidi
Duke of Lybia	1,405 ¼ gold solidi
Moderator of Arabia	1,080 gold solidi
Praetor of Pisidia	800 gold solidi
Praetor of Lycaonia	800 gold solidi
Praetor of Thrace	800 gold solidi
Count of Isauria	800 gold solidi
Moderator of Hellespont	725 gold solidi
Praetor of Paphlagonia	725 gold solidi
Moderator of Phoenicia	720 gold solidi
Quaestor	720 gold solidi
Praetor of the plebs (with his assessor)	720 gold solidi
Count of Armenia III	700 gold solidi
Consulars of Africa	448 gold solidi

These were low salaries, but functionaries had many ways to become rich. In their capacities as judges they were able to reap many benefits, as did the governor of Sardinia in the sixth century who levied a regular tax on his pagan subjects, who were then allowed to practice their legally prohibited cult. Numerous times the emperors—in vain—forbade provincial officials and their families to acquire property in the territory of their jurisdiction or to marry rich local heiresses. It appears that many administrators were corrupt and indulged in much abuse of power at the expense of the local populations. This was, however, not true of everyone, as we learn in a letter from the bishop of Cyrrhus, Theodoret, dated around 434, to the former prefect Antiochos:

> One can certainly see in many ways the fairness of your judgment, but that which exhibits it most clearly is the way in which you choose the magistrates to whom you confer the government of peoples and towns: taking equal care of all subjects and choosing the most incorruptible of men, those who are above money and who hold the scales of justice in fairness, and who, in a word, are the best; you place them at the head of towns like fathers, doctors, or pilots. Nevertheless, if we have encountered many of these virtuous men who have received their power through choices made by you, the one who has appeared to us the most worthy of love and respect is the very magnificent Neon. We have known him better, in fact, since it is he who has been chosen to be at the helm of our land and because, during

the term of his appointment, through his wise government, he has seen to it that his ship is always blown by favorable winds. If this man, upon leaving his position today, has, for his part, set down the burden of his troubles and concerns, he has, on the other hand, deprived his subjects of his paternal solicitude; he hurries to rejoin your greatness, after having acquired glory instead of fortune, and with the brilliance of that admirable poverty so worthy of praise. Send him back to us invested with a new mandate as governor, for God protect us that a man who knows how to do good not be stripped of the occasion to do so.

The organization of dignities and positions in the ninth century had an effect on the way salaries were paid. More than ever, salaries resembled favors granted, not reflecting the importance of the services rendered, but rather that of the brilliance of the dignity. There is an important fact: all dignitaries, with assigned functions or not, had the right to a salary. For example, in 1082 Alexios Komnenos sent Emperor Henry IV, with whom he was seeking an alliance against the Normans in Italy, documents conferring dignities upon members of his court, but accompanied by the salaries associated with them.

In the tenth century the distribution of salaries had become a court ceremony that took place during the week preceding Palm Sunday. Liutprand, ambassador of Emperor Otto I, alongside Constantine VII in 950, described the ceremony he attended which lasted three days:

A large table 10 cubits long and 4 cubits wide was set; it was covered with sacks full of gold solidi, and signs set on each of them indicated the person who was to receive each sack. People began to file before the emperor with the greatest decorum; they were called in succession according to the dignity of their office. The first called was the rector of the palace upon whom was set, not in his hands, but on his shoulders, sacks of gold coins and four ceremonial cloaks (called *skaramangia*). Then came the *domestikos* of the *scholae* and the *drungarius* of the fleet, the first of whom was the head of the army and the other the head of the navy. As they both held an equal dignity, they received the same quantity of coins and *skaramangia*. But the large quantity of objects received was such that they could not carry it all on their shoulders; not without difficulty, and with the help of their retinue, they pulled their goods behind them. Then the twenty-four *magistroi* were admitted; each received 24 lbs. of gold and two *skaramangia*. Then came the order of patricians, each of whom received 12 lbs. of gold solidi and one skaramangion. I know neither the rank of those who came next, nor the amount of money they received. Responding to the call, one saw a huge group of *prōtospatharii, spatharokandidatii, koitōnitai, manglabitai,* and *prōtokaraboi,* each of whom, depending on his dignity, received from 7 to 1 lb. of gold.

The ceremony began on the fifth day of the week preceding Palm Sunday and lasted one to four hours each day; it was repeated again on the sixth and seventh days. As for those who earned a salary less than 1 lb. of gold, they received their pay not from the emperor but from the chamberlain. The distribution ceremony extended into the whole week before Easter. The practice endured, and in the eleventh century the *nomophylax,* or *didaskalos* of the laws, a professor of legal issues, each year received from the emperor 4 lbs. of gold and a purple cloak, and in addition was entitled to payment in kind. Of course, only the dignitaries who lived in Constantinople received their salaries in this way; most others received theirs locally, with their salaries taken from taxes collected in the provinces before these revenues were sent to the capital. The sums distributed directly by the emperor thus represented only a very small percentage of salaries.

Advancement

All government officials regularly advanced in their careers through seniority, but there were a great many exceptions to this. At the beginning of the fifth century, functionaries in the imperial chamber were divided into three categories (*forma prima, secunda, tertia*), which they successively passed through. But the supernumeraries were themselves divided into categories, and one could thus find a supernumerary of the first rank apply for a position as titulary of the same rank, thereby blocking any promotion from the second rank. A law of 422 sought to avoid this anomaly by establishing that vacant first-class positions would alternately be filled by second-class titularies and first-class supernumeraries, and the same would hold for vacant second-class positions; and anyone who attempted to jump a turn, obtaining a titulary position before it was his turn, was demoted to the lowest-ranking position of third-class supernumeraries.

In the offices of the imperial palace, seniority was the only means of advancement; one climbed a single rung of the professional ladder at a time until one reached the rank of *proximos* held by the employee who had been there the longest. At the beginning of the fifth century, after having been set at three, then at two years' duration, each "rung" was reduced to one year. But it was possible for a supernumerary to have to wait many years to enter among the titularies. At that time, titulary positions in the palace offices were bought and sold. With the *proximos* in each office leaving every year, he had the possibility of selling the vacated position at the bottom of the administrative ladder for the sum of 250 solidi (the going rate in 444) to the first of the supernumeraries; if the latter refused, it was offered to the next in line, and this continued until he found a taker. The seniority of supernumeraries was not fixed in a rigorous fashion, for it could be altered according to the will of the thirteen oldest employees in favor of those who worked most industriously. If a position became vacant through the death of the functionary, the heirs of the deceased could sell the vacated position to the oldest supernumerary for the sum of 250 gold solidi.

Responsible directly to the *magister officiorum,* the imperial couriers formed a large guild that in the fifth century included 1,248 functionaries. As in other departments, advancement was by seniority, except for agents of exceptional merit. For this reason the emperor reserved the right to grant two supplemental promotions. In the fourth century one of these functionaries, after having completed his career, was still young enough to seek a nomination as provincial governor. But in the fifth century, it seems that those who thought they would never reach the final level of their category were able to retire after twenty or twenty-five years of service.

We are relatively better informed about career conditions in one of the financial departments of the empire, that of gifts (largesses). Every agent admitted into this department was placed in one of the offices; he was promoted through seniority and retired after putting in his time as office chief, but one could not go from one office to another in the department. The rhythm of promotions was accelerated in time. Thus it was that the rank of office chief, which once lasted three years, was reduced to one year at the beginning of the fifth century. But promotion was not connected to the same length of service in all offices: technicians, such as those who worked with gold, silver, or stone, had to complete thirty, forty and even fifty years of service, whereas in the majority of administrative offices a dozen years were enough to climb all the rungs of the career ladder.

Duties and Responsibilities

In a sixth-century Novel, Emperor Tiberios gives a succinct description of the duties of government officials: "We order that governing belongs to those who enjoy a good reputation and who have a strong interest in justice; next, that functionaries assume public posts without having previously offered gifts or anything else. Governors must preserve their subjects from all prejudice; they must also devote themselves with great care to the collection of public taxes. That governors, their coadjutors, chancellors, or assistants, or any of their friends or relatives must receive nothing from their subjects; otherwise they will be forced to pay them back fourfold. They must be content with their emoluments, which are paid to them from the public treasury in accordance with the current laws." In general, being agents of the emperor, functionaries were expected to remain loyal to him, to perform his orders and those of his representatives in a rigorous manner, and to apply the current laws.

Beginning in the sixth century, functionaries had to remain in their posts for fifty days after the date their terms expired, in order to respond to citizens who might want to bring suits against them. If a trial against a functionary was not concluded within the fifty days, and it was a civil trial, the accused had to arrange for a proxy; if the case was penal, the functionary had to remain until the end of the proceedings.

Justinian demanded that, upon assuming their duties, all officials should receive a communication of the imperial ordinances listing those duties and should swear an oath on the Gospels to govern without misrepresentation or fraud. He forbade functionaries in Constantinople to buy goods or property or to build without imperial authorization, and forbade all functionaries to receive any donation as long as they were in office. These were very wise ancient laws that unfortunately were constantly violated and that Justinian's successors had to renew. Justin II (565–578) conceived of choosing governors upon presentation by the bishops and landowners of the region, and forced them to pay a deposit to guarantee that taxes would be collected. They had to promise to levy them gently but with accuracy, and to render justice when needed.

All these regulations were incorporated into the corpus of the *Basilika* at the beginning of the tenth century, whereas new texts relating to the responsibilities of government officials were enacted. By virtue of his providential mission, the emperor's government could only be beneficial to its subjects. They were thus encouraged to complain about any violations or violence of which they might be the victims from functionaries on all levels. Another law forbade officials to marry not only the children, but anyone with whom they had any sort of kinship in the province they were governing. The aim of this law was to prevent functionaries from forming family ties in the provinces for which they were responsible, which might have led to the development of favoritism and subjectivity with regard to specific areas of their administration.

The law also aimed at discouraging functionaries from being tempted to acquire property at low prices. They were thus always forbidden, in the capital as well as in the provinces, to buy either goods or buildings, to have structures built, and to accept bequests, trusts, or donations within the scope of their administration throughout the term of their office.

Leo VI (886–912) rescinded these restrictions in his Novel 84:

The decisions made on the subject of government officials by our predecessors, that functionaries of the imperial city have been forbidden to buy either goods or property, or to undertake construction without the authorization of the emperor; in addition, a contribution made to the functionary during the term of his office can be accepted only if the contributor confirms it through the authority of a written document after the functionary leaves office, or if it has been five years since the functionary has left office. These decisions, however strict they may appear, have rightly been made to prevent the reign of violence; but given that it is easy to prevent violence in other ways, they no longer seem necessary to us. This is why we wish them to be repealed, especially taking into account the fact that, since they did not provide for any sanctions, the daily transgression of them remained unpunished, and they even had no authority before our present law. Why, then, are they not necessary? Because the path for requests and petitions to the emperor is open to everyone, rich or poor; those who live in this city, anyone who suffers violence is permitted to call upon the emperor so as not to be completely overwhelmed by the menacing party; where, then, henceforth is the necessity, as if it were a matter of a land deprived of all help, to maintain such a requirement in a city where one can freely seek aid?

We therefore decree that, in accordance with the current state of things, functionaries may buy and build and will not be incriminated with regard to what they have received in voluntary gifts, with the understanding that those who are subject to violence will not be deprived, when the occasion arises, of the means to escape it through an appeal to the emperor. Regarding provincial functionaries we have decided the following: the *stratēgos* (governor of the theme) will be able neither to buy nor to build anything for his personal use as long as he holds office, nor may he freely accept gifts. As for other functionaries subordinate to him, when the issue has been referred to the *stratēgos,* he will decide whether to dismiss them or keep them in office.

Was this a shrinking of central power, progress made by the corps of functionaries? What was predicted occurred: all or almost all functionaries acquired real estate and created large domains using any means necessary, to the detriment the small landowners in particular.

Punishments

One notes the same weakening of central power in the reduction of penalties inflicted on offending functionaries. One of the strengths acquired by Byzantine bureaucracy was that it quite naturally engendered a reduction in responsibility for functionaries because of their professional offenses. With the legislative reform of Leo VI, penal sanctions, previously brought against functionaries guilty of either not executing at all or poorly executing official orders, had been set forth with much less severity than before. In accordance with the ancient law still in effect, the functionary found guilty of theft or of the sale of objects belonging to the state was eligible for capital punishment. Leo VI ruled that any functionary guilty of such infractions would simply lose his administrative post and would pay a fine representing twice or four times the value of the object stolen or sold, depending on the circumstances of the theft or the sale:

> Our power decides that the law (of Emperor Justinian) that decrees that the death penalty will be the sentence for a functionary found guilty of having stolen goods from the public treasury, indeed, not only for him, but also for any accomplices he may have, will no longer be included among the constitutions that have legal authority, acknowledging that it represents an inhuman punishment, one not in accordance with what a law should be; and this law will no longer be in force, and will be rejected as being contrary to the good of the state and useless: henceforth the punishment to be incurred by those officials brought to justice for theft from the public treasury will be the loss of their office and reimbursement at twice the value of what they have stolen, and their accomplices, if they are rich, will be subject to the same penalty, and if they are poor, will submit to the punishment of the lash, the shame of the tonsure of their hair, and deportation.

In another ordinance the same emperor ordered that "whoever invites an operator of that guilty practice (castration) here to perform his profession, if the sponsor is on the list of people in the emperor's employ, he will first be stricken from that list and will then be fined 10 lbs. of gold (3,600 solidi) to be paid to the tax office, and will be incarcerated for ten years." Castration had been prohibited since the Roman era, and in the sixth century Justinian, noting the high death rate associated with the operation, which only a few more than 3 percent of all patients survived, had imposed heavy penalties against the instigators and their accomplices which included castration, working in the mines for those who survived the operation, and the confiscation of their property; but the populations of the Caucasus at that same time practiced castration on a large scale. And we know that, from the fifth century on, the royal palace, then the central administration, employed a great many eunuchs; certain duties and certain court titles were reserved for them; moreover, they could exercise all public functions with very few exceptions. During ceremonies, eunuchs took precedence over everyone else. In the church, in the army, and in the civil hierarchy, they were able to obtain the highest offices. Among the eunuchs one found patriarchs, like Germanos I in the eighth century, Methodios I in the mid-ninth century, Stephen II in the tenth century, Eustratios Garidas in the eleventh century; metropolitans, clerics, and monks; and the eunuch Narses, *prōtospatharios* and chamberlain under Justin II (565–578), had the monastery of Katharoi built in Constantinople, reserving it for eunuchs; the most famous monasteries of the capital, such as the Studios, were open to them.

Many military leaders were also eunuchs, such as Staurakios in the reign of Irene (797–802); the *stratēgos* of Calabria, Eustathios, in the tenth century; the patrician Niketas, who was beaten by the Arabs, held prisoner, and bought back by Emperor Nikephoros II Phokas a half-century later; the patrician Nicholas, who delivered Aleppo and Antioch in 970; and almost all the officers in the armies of Constantine IX and Theodora in the middle of the eleventh century. Until the thirteenth century, eunuchs often played a very important role in the emperor's entourage, and the officer of the imperial chamber governed the state: Stephen of Persia was able to attack Anastasia, the mother of Emperor Justinian II, with impunity; Baanes was made responsible for managing the business of the empire when Basil I was at war; under Leo VI the chamberlain, a former slave and eunuch, Samonas, perhaps of Arab origin, succeeded in temporarily ousting the powerful Nicholas, former head of an imperial office, from the patriarchical throne; Basil, an illegitimate son of Romanos I Lekapenos and a Slavic slave, is an even more striking example since, following his victory over the Arabs, he received the triumph of the Hippodrome, which he enjoyed with great credit under Romanos II, became prime minister under John Tzimiskes, and one of the largest landowners in the empire; under Michael IV (1034–41), three of whose brothers were eunuchs, eunuchs managed the empire, and again under Michael VI, Michael VII, and later under Alexios III Angelos at the end of the twelfth century, when the *sakellarios* Constantine gave orders to the imperial bodyguard. The palace eunuchs, whose success was perhaps connected to the fact that they could have no claim to the imperial purple, lost all importance in the second half of the thirteenth century following the return of the Palaiologoi, under the influence of western prejudice which considered them to be physically inferior persons.

By reducing the impact of sanctions brought against guilty functionaries, legislation demonstrated the ascendancy of a group of state agents and the relaxation of the authority exercised over them by the central government. At the end of the eleventh century, after the Komnenoi family came to power, the administrative nobility, made up of large landowners, gained momentum and began increasingly to escape the control of central power.

Controls

Through a constitution dated 24 June 530, Justinian placed bishops at the head of the entire financial administration of cities, including procurements and public works, and ordered them to resist emphatically any state officials who might attempt to circumvent the law, even if they availed themselves of orders from the court or the prefecture. In addition, Justinianic legislation ordered the bishops to maintain control over all activity of the provincial governors, to keep close watch over them so they would carry out their duties, and to include in their reports to the emperor any offenses or misdeeds by dishonest governors. A law of 17 April 539 even provided that in trials in which one of the parties contested the fairness of the governor, the bishop or the metropolitan would judge the matter conjointly with him; and it went so far as to relegate governors to the jurisdiction of bishops in suits that were brought against them by those living in their district. Only four years earlier Justinian had relegated to the civil jurisdiction of bishops those governors completing their terms who were attempting to flee during the fifty-day period that followed the end of their mandate, during which they were supposed to remain available to respond to potential accusations from those in their jurisdiction.

But this control over the government of functionaries by the ecclesiastical administration could not suffice insofar as it was directly involved with the levying of taxes. Indeed, in 530 Justinian had reserved to the emperor the right to send representatives, called *discussores* or logothetes into the provinces, men who, by controlling the entire financial management of the cities, also oversaw construction projects. These were most often important men who had the full confidence of the emperor. The most famous example in Justinian's time was Alexander Psalidios, from the Greek *psalidion* (a pair of clippers or shears), because, said the historian Prokopios, he could clip the edge of gold coins so adeptly using that implement and without changing the coins' appearance. Undoubtedly promoted to the dignity of ex-consul, after having been office chief at the Prefecture of the Orient, probably in the office of military finances, in 540 he was sent to Italy as imperial commissioner wielding very extensive powers. Responsible for rebuilding a budgetary deficit in a region that, following a harsh war that lasted five years, was not yet completely at peace, he began by carrying out some very strict budget cuts. Thus the "poor" of Rome were deprived of certain distributions of wheat delivered until that time to St. Peter's at the expense of the state; salaries were no longer paid to the imperial guard, which was being maintained by the Ostrogothic royalty, even though its functions had become pure sinecures ever since military service had been closed to Romans; the salaries of silentiaries, senators, and probably all other civil servants of a court that had ceased to exist, were no longer paid; soldiers found themselves applying the methods Alexander had employed with so much success in the Orient (see below), which they did their best to emulate to compensate themselves using the Italian populations; moreover, Alexander did his utmost in the most pitiless way, going back to the time of Theodoric a century earlier to hunt down delinquent taxpayers and seize sums from functionaries that he accused them of having embezzled.

As he went along, Alexander stopped in Greece to reorganize the defense of the Pass of Thermopylae, which had just proven insufficient during the Bulgarian invasion in the same year. He replaced the peasant militia, which until then had been responsible for defending that site, with two thousand regular soldiers. He assigned municipal funds to maintain that force, funds that in Greek cities had previously been earmarked for games and public works. This measure led to the visible decline of the artistic heritage.

The ex-consul Leontios, a friend of Emperor Maurice's family and of his uncle Domitian, the bishop of Melitene, and certainly a former chief in the office of finances in Constantinople, undertook a similar inspection of local finances on the orders of the emperor. He landed in Sicily at the end of the summer of 598, settled in Syracuse, a sort of capital of Byzantine Sicily, and, working with the ecclesiastical administration (especially the bishop of Syracuse), as provided for in the laws, for two years summoned lay and ecclesiastical officials there, notables and important personages of Italy and Sicily, who had retired from their duties, to verify their accounts.

Retirement

An agent of the state spent many years without doing very much, badly paid, and very often in an unpleasant office atmosphere. In a letter Michael Psellos described what went on during his time at the chancellory of Constantinople, where he modestly began a career that carried him to the summits of power:

> I had the misfortune of being in the office of the *asēkrētis*. . . . The work there is so hard and so overwhelming, the pressure to write such that one cannot, so to speak, either scratch one's ear or raise one's head, or eat when one is hungry or drink when one is thirsty, or go wash up when one is so tempted to, with the sweat running down your forehead and onto your face; and the great compensation for this effort? Outbursts of anger, remarks over mistakes, and so on. Here there is no relief, every day the same thing. . . . Closed up in tight quarters without a hallway, everyone squeezed in together, as if piled on top of each other . . . everyone seeks to displace his neighbor. . . . One demonstrates the speed with which he writes, another claims to have superior knowledge and does his best to create doubt about that of his superiors; another promotes his physical strength and his talent in fighting; another the fluency of his speech; another his licentiousness or vulgarity; another his seniority . . . ; he who has nothing else attempts to derive some benefit from his extreme zeal for business or for discussions on language. Whence the great quarrels and the indescribable and interminable fights. This is why old Phasonlas and Achiras, who was

even older, could not be reconciled despite the efforts of many intermediaries. . . . Fits of anger by the one against the other, the divulging of secrets . . . the one declares that his colleague is an imbecile, the other becomes even angrier, increases his insults; they come to blows.

When an official had achieved the highest seniority, he became qualified to occupy a position that entailed more responsibility and to receive a higher salary. Finally, at the end of his career, generally in the last or next to last year, the functionary received compensation by selling his position or in the form of a departure bonus. These final payments took the place of a retirement pension. The historian Prokopios explains the situation of an agent in this way: "All agents of the state, civil or military employees, are first placed at the bottom of the ladder and throughout the years take the place of those who die or retire; they then obtain a higher post and reach the highest position. And those who reach that echelon, following an ancient tradition, receive an appropriate sum of money so that they may see to their needs in old age." If a functionary died one or two years before the end of his career, his widow and children could receive the final compensation for the service rendered by the father.

SOME NOTABLE GOVERNMENT CAREERS

John, the all-powerful minister of Justinian in the sixth century, was born in Cappadocian Caesarea and was of humble origins. He had so little instruction that he could not write correctly in Greek, and his knowledge of Latin was undoubtedly among the most deficient. The same was true of his Christian education. It was undoubtedly at the time when Justinian became master of the resident militia, responsible for the garrisons of the imperial residence and for other regiments of troops scattered throughout the empire, that the future emperor met John, who was at the time an accountant for one of the three masters of the militias. Justinian quickly noted the true abilities of his humble subaltern, who explained his ideas for reforming public finances to him in a persuasive fashion. Justinian's interest in John enabled him to enter into the employ of the prefecture, where he appears to have become the head of a financial office; and he was promoted to the then vacant position of *illustris* even before he was named prefect, which shows the extraordinary position he already held. Once he had reached a position of power, John indulged in the most vulgar of vices: he was a drunk, a glutton, and a rake, to such a degree and with such offhandedness that it became a scandal. Brutal, sometimes even sadistic in his manners, without scruple in pursuing his goals, he was not an honest functionary: he was able to accumulate so much wealth that before his final fall he was maintaining thousands of soldiers; the general

Belisarios wielded as much power in the same period, but for a civil servant it was unheard of. He did not flatter the emperor, and talked to him in a very frank manner, similar to that of Narses, whereas his position at the palace was much more vulnerable than that of the eunuch, administrator of the civil list, and favorite of Empress Theodora, whom John only scorned and who in her turn felt an unrelenting hatred for him, which ultimately led to his ruin. John seems not to have been a disinterested civil servant, but in his own way he was truly devoted to the state, if not to the emperor, and was sincere in his passion to cure the ills with which the empire was most profoundly stricken. It is noteworthy, moreover, that the historian Prokopios, who heartily detested him, exalted his energy, political foresight, and ability to overcome the greatest difficulties.

Photios, patriarch of Constantinople (858–867; 877–886) was a scholar and a statesman. An aristocrat by birth, his family was connected to the imperial family through marriage, since his father was Empress Theodora's brother-in-law. The family's orthodoxy was never in doubt, as his father, an uncle, and he himself had suffered, during the period of Iconoclasm, for their attachment to the cult of icons. His training and scholarship in theological matters as well as in profane subjects were legendary, and it was claimed that he had sold his soul to the devil to obtain them. Having been educated to pursue a lay career, it was believed he would go into the civil administration and diplomacy. In 858 he was at the head of the imperial chancery, but for a long time before that he had been a dominant figure in Byzantine political and social circles. He had been launched into the world with all the advantages—birth, intelligence, good manners, and also money—and he was able to derive the greatest benefit from it all. He was a close friend of Bardas, the emperor's uncle. Thus, when that statesman came to power in 856, Photios naturally became his counselor and confidant, and when Patriarch Ignatios was forced to resign, he advanced to the highest position in the Byzantine Church. Photios is credited with seeing more clearly than anyone the opportunity for the Byzantine Church to extend its influence and power in the Slavic world. He saw the new possibilities of that influence beyond the frontiers of the empire and prepared for its accomplishment by establishing the international power and credit of the patriarchate of Constantinople. The assassination of the Caesar Bardas, his protector, and of Emperor Michael III brought about Photios' downfall, and he was incarcerated in a monastery by the new emperor, Basil I. In 875, convinced that the change he had made in ecclesiastical policy had ameliorated neither the internal situation of the empire nor its relationship with Rome, Basil recalled Photios to Constantinople, entrusted his son's education to him, and put him back on the patriarchical throne upon the death of old Ignatios in 877. A change in sovereign overthrew him a second time. Leo VI in fact dismissed the patriarch and in his place put his own very young brother, Stephen. Photios died in exile in Armenia.

A writer and statesman, Michael Psellos was born and raised in Constantinople. He took his first classes in the monastery school of Ta Narsou. He studied orthography and poetry, then rhetoric either there or at another school. When he was about twenty-five he was still a "student" and took part in oratory competitions. He then taught for quite some time in a public school. He taught just about everything: spelling, subjects of the quadrivium, law, and especially rhetoric and philosophy. After a modest beginning, his qualities soon brought him to the forefront in Constantinople, and he specialized in teaching at a higher level and became a renowned professor. He received the title of "consul of the philosophers," and there was no branch of knowledge in his time in which he did not make a name for himself. The court and the emperors delighted in his talent. He became secretary of state, high chamberlain, prime minister, and soon the maker and undoer of emperors; he died out of favor in March 1078.

In the eleventh century there appeared the familial dynasties of high government officials; the notables of the fourteenth century believed that positions of responsibility rightfully fell to them. Here are a few examples: Michael Glabas Tarchaneiotes was born around 1240; he was successively named *primikērios* of the court (33rd grade), high *papias* (22nd grade), *pinkernes* (15th grade), high constable (12th grade), and high *primikērios* (11th grade). At the end of his reign, Michael VIII Palaiologos named him *prōtovestiarios,* but above all placed that dignity at the fourth rank of the court hierarchy. Made *prōtostratōr* in 1293, Tarchaneiotes refused the title of caesar on principle, but at the end of the century was named grand duke. His long career was completely contained within the highest ranks of the court hierarchy, but it took him forty years to reach the top. This is an example of the normal advancement of a faithful and successful servant of the empire. His father-in-law, Alexios Philanthropenos, experienced a slightly different fate. He was named *prōtostratōr* in 1261; he was covered in glory in several battles, but was named grand duke only after 1271. His promotion was thus rather slow. There were four possible careers for members of the important families: the civil administration, the court, the army, and the church. In principle there were very few high-ranking officers and dignitaries. This is explained very well by the exceptional role they played in affairs of state or in service at court. The grand duke commanded the fleet: there could not be several grand dukes, by virtue of a completely unitary concept of the commander in chief, an expression of imperial authority. Alexios Philanthropenos was named grand duke only upon the death of the titulary grand duke, Michael Laskaris.

Reflections of a Retired Functionary

Kekaumenos, the author of these reflections, was a general who took part in the Bulgarian campaign in 1041, was *stratēgos* of the theme of Hellas, and lived in Larissa. Kekaumenos recommends to his reader two ways to meet his needs: enter into the service of the state, into the army or administration, and expect pensions, dignities, and compensation from the emperor; if the reader is a simple individual or retired, he should cultivate the earth: "If you are not rich, do not undertake to build, rather, plant vines and work the land . . . if you are not in active service, there is no better source of revenue for you than that of the land." Raising vineyards was particularly advantageous. In general it was necessary to seek forms of rural farming that each year, either tenant-farmed or sharecropped, brought returns without too much difficulty: "Build mills; cultivate gardens; plant trees of all sorts, and reeds, which each year will yield returns without trouble; keep livestock, oxen, pigs, sheep, and anything that grows and multiplies by itself each year: this is what will provide you an abundant table and pleasure in everything."

An older man, sententious, moralizing, cautious, and wary, Kekaumenos expresses a thought whose New Testament origin is obvious, but that loses its banality because it is addressed to the emperor: "There are ignorant people who proclaim that a certain man is of a great and old family, and another of low and humble birth: I say that all men are the sons of Adam, whether they are emperors, notables, or peasants." This opinion might be that of all Byzantium. The rules Kekaumenos lived by led him to fear God and the emperor, to be just in the eyes of some and loyal in the eyes of others, and for everything else, "beware." He advanced in life prudently and, in his own words, with eyes lowered: "it is a profitable thing," he says, "to fear."

His piety was sincere and true, but religion did not provide him with food for thought. For Kekaumenos, humanity was divided into two: on the one hand, there were the good Christians, on the other, the heretics, Jews, and Muslims. For him, devotion consisted of attending services and saying prayers: those of matins, four o'clock, vespers, and compline; it was good in the middle of the night to add the recitation of a psalm, for at that hour one communed with God without being distracted. It was also good to read the Scriptures, without excessive curiosity. One had to venerate the holy images, but not wear phylacteries, except perhaps a cross, a holy image, or a relic; Kekaumenos was not superstitious and refused to believe in dreams or divines. It was excellent to visit monks, even if they appeared rather simpleminded: after all, the apostles were like them. On the other hand, one had to keep one's distance from those disturbing beings, the "fools of God."

With regard to the emperor, from whom everything emanated, "honors and good deeds," a single rule of behavior applied: be loyal to the one who ruled in Constantinople, for he was always right. But that supreme power was distrustful, and his entourage was dangerous. One thus had carefully to avoid joining in a conversation about the emperor or the empress, especially during a banquet. One had to look out for jealous people, gossips, slanderers, and, through modest and reserved behavior, lay oneself open to no suspicion. One even had to take care to intervene on behalf of a friend only rarely and with discretion. The same rules applied in relationships with notables and in general with all superiors: do not be a nuisance, keep one's distance, do not complain, ask for nothing, and above all maintain the greatest reserve with their spouses, even if they make advances. On the other hand, one had to beware of subordinates, who were often treacherous, quick to let themselves be corrupted or to slander. Finally, if one held an important position, one had to watch over everything, be aware of everything, have spies everywhere. The image given is one of a close network of backbiting, spying, and denunciations that extended into the court, the capital, and the high-level administration.

The warning that recurs most often in Kekaumenos' memoirs is "Trust no one." It is curious to see this general address another general and recommend to him, in accordance with the purest Byzantine tradition, to weaken enemies through ruse, strategies, and traps, and to fight only as a last resort, only if absolutely necessary, while then taking care to maintain the happy medium between daring and cowardice. His goal was to succeed through competency.

Kekaumenos must have been a brave general and a circumspect governor, a man with much common sense but little finesse. He had no imagination, but he had seen a lot. He was not uneducated and spoke of reading with a touching simplicity: "Read a lot; you will learn a lot; and if you do not understand, persevere; God will ultimately send you knowledge; and don't be shamed to inquire of those who know concerning that which you do not understand." Subject to the absolute authority of an all-powerful state and of the religion of that state, he did not for a moment dream of judging the established order on earth, an imperfect replica of the celestial order that was promised to him.

SELECTED BIBLIOGRAPHY

Primary Sources

Theodosiani libri XVI cum constitutionibus Sirmondianis, ed. Th. Mommsen and E. Meyer. 2 vols. Berlin, 1905.

Notitia dignitatum utriusque imperii, ed. O. Seeck. Berlin, 1876.

Corpus juris civilis, ed. Th. Mommsen, P. Krueger, R. Schoell and W. Kroll. 3 vols. Berlin, 1870–95.

von Lingenthal, Zachariae. *Jus graeco-romanum,* vol. 3: *Novellae constitutiones.* Leipzig, 1857.

Les novelles de Léon VI le Sage, ed. P. Noailles and A. Dain. Paris, 1944.

Basilicorum libri LX, ed. G. E. Heimbach. Leipzig, 1833–70.

Constantini Harmenopuli Hexabiblos, ed. G. E. Heimbach. Leipzig, 1851.

Le Livre du préfet, ed. J. Nicole. Geneva, 1893.

Oikonomides, N. *Les listes de préséance byzantines des IXe–Xe siècles.* Paris, 1972.

Pseudo-Kodinos. *Traité des offices,* introduction, text, and translation by J. Verpeaux. Paris, 1966.

Dölger, F. *Regesten der Kaiserurkunden des oströmischen Reiches.* 4 vols. Munich, 1924–65.

Ioannis Lydi De magistratibus, ed. R. Wuensch. 2d ed. Stuttgart, 1967.

Procopi Caesarensis Anecdota, ed. J. Haury. Leipzig, 1906.

Constantini Porphyrogeniti imperatoris de cerimoniis aulae byzantinae libri duo, critical edition by I. I. Reiskii. 2 vols. Bonn, 1829–30.

Die Werke Liudprands von Cremona, ed. J. Bekker. 3d ed. Leipzig, 1915.

General Literature

Ahrweiler, H. *Études sur les structures administratives et sociales de Byzance.* Variorum Reprints, London, 1971.

Angold, M. *The Byzantine Empire 1025–1204: A Political History.* London–New York, 1984.

Bréhier, L. *Le monde byzantin,* vol. 2: *Les institutions de l'empire byzantin.* Paris, 1949.

Guillou, A. *La civilisation byzantine.* Paris, 1989.

Jones, A. H. M. *The Later Roman Empire 284–602.* Oxford, 1964.

Maksimovič, L. *The Byzantine Provincial Administration under the Palaiologoi.* Amsterdam, 1988.

Raybaud, L. P. *Le gouvernement et l'administration centrale de l'empire byzantin sous les premiers Paléologues (1258–1354).* Paris, 1968.

Stein, E. *Histoire du bas-empire,* ed. J.-R. Palanque. 2 vols. Paris, 1949–59.

Svoronos, N. *Études sur l'organisation intérieure, la société et l'économie de l'empire byzantin.* Variorum Reprints, London, 1973.

9

EMPERORS

Michael McCormick

"THE SUN ACTS LIKE AN EMPEROR" (*ho hēlios basileuei*). With these words, medieval men and women of Byzantium used to describe the resplendent purple and gold hues of the Mediterranean sunset. In a few words the idiom tells us a number of important things. As the sun presided over the Byzantines' natural world, so the emperor seemed the pinnacle and supreme organizing principle of their society. Like the rays of the Mediterranean sun, his power and splendid presence pervaded Byzantium's reality and imagination. Our efforts to evoke the Byzantines cannot fail to consider the emperor without missing an essential, perhaps even defining, facet of the Byzantine life experience.

We shall begin with that aspect of the emperor that was most visible to the Byzantine "man in the street" and that still dominates our understanding of him today, the symbolism of his power. From there we shall attempt to penetrate the precincts of the sacred palace, to uncover the physical structures of power. Only then can we begin to assess the nature of that power and the men—and women—who exercised it. And we can conclude where we started, with the public manifestation of power, this time not in its static symbols but in the dynamic symbolic projections of power, in the great ceremonial celebrations of the emperor that sought to bridge the gap between ruler and ruled, to incarnate in elaborately scripted gestures the deeper verities and falsehoods of imperial rule.

But first I must caution the reader that this historian will have to draw chiefly on his own research and concentrate on the Byzantine imperial experience down to the watershed of 1204, the Latin sack of Constantinople. There is virtue to this necessity, for it will help us remember that, for all the real continuity in the imperial government's traditions and routines, the Byzantine ruling class stridently and incessantly asserted and thereby magnified and distorted that continuity.

POWER SYMBOLIZED

The imperial idea's visible incarnation was swathed in the shimmering hues of finest purple silk—use of which was jealously restricted to the emperor and his closest associates—threaded with gold wire to catch the sunlight. The symbolism of ultimate status served a practical purpose as well, since the combination of brilliant purple and glittering gold immediately directed all eyes to the key figure in a large cortege. Little wonder that echoes of ancient solar ideology have been detected in the erudite underpinnings of imperial ceremonial and that Michael Psellos, an eleventh-century courtier and intellectual, imagined a campaigning emperor's anticipated return to his capital as the "sunrise" his subjects awaited.

Purple was the emperor's color par excellence. His most solemn diplomatic documents were dyed in it; purple floor markings organized the movements of participants in the elaborate ballet of imperial audiences; purple ribbons were attached to property confiscated by the emperor's agents. Legitimate emperors were quite literally born to the purple: the chamber of the Great Palace in which medieval empresses gave birth was paved with porphyry, so that the newborn infant's first experience of this world was infused with his unique, divinely acknowledged status. Indeed, the connection of color and empire was perhaps powerful enough to survive the Ottoman conquest of 1453 and influence the Turkish name of the striped red mullet (*tekfur baligi,* where the first word is believed to come from the Greek *tou kyriou*).

The Christian emperors of Byzantium were the direct heirs of the masters of the Roman world. In fact, "Byzantium" and "Byzantine" are modern scholars' conventions, a convenient shorthand to designate the millenary survival of the Roman Empire in its mighty eastern heart of New Rome, modern Istanbul (from the Greek *eis tēn polin*). Constantinople lay athwart the route connecting the strategic frontiers of the Danube and Iran, and this fact was not lost on Constantine I when he transferred there the institutions of central government to escape the impoverished, besieged western provinces of Italy, Gaul, and Spain. In informal usage, the Christian emperors were always emperors of the Romans, and when an upstart western barbarian by the name of Charlemagne had himself acclaimed "emperor" by a pliable pope, the heirs of Augustus and Justinian in Constantinople dispelled any confusion by proclaiming on their coinage that they were "Emperors of the Romans." Their law was Roman law: indeed, the two great codifications of Roman law were both issued at Constantinople by the early Byzantine emperors Theodosios II and Justinian, and paleographers believe that the magnificent Florence codex of the *Digest* was prepared in imperial (Latin) workshops on the Bosporos in Justinian's own lifetime.

The ideology of the emperor's power came from Rome, but it was deepened, refashioned, and transformed by the powerful Christian and Hellenistic currents that swept through the world of a dying antiquity. The ruler's most important title, *basileus,* once borne by the successors of Alexander of Macedon, had crept from common parlance into official Roman titulature by the seventh century and, in so doing, shed its classical meaning of "king" to occupy the semantic zone of "emperor." The Latin word *rex* was transliterated into Greek to designate the lesser form of rulership that prevailed on the empire's fringes.

The divinely promoted emperor was still elected commander-in-chief, whether the army, the *synklētos* or senate of Constantinople, or citizens acted as God's agents by voicing the cadenced shouts, the acclamations that legally recognized his status. In the early centuries of the Byzantine era, this nonhereditary aspect of the republican ideology of old Rome remained vital. Pope Gregory the Great still considered the hereditary transmission of power a characteristic of barbarian peoples like the Franks or Persians. Emperors were legitimized by success, particularly of the military variety, and their successors had to be designated co-emperors during their own lifetime to insure a smooth transmission of power. Indeed, this constitutional requirement of success as a prerequisite for political—and even biological—survival struck foreign observers, for example, a medieval Arab who claimed the Byzantines deposed their emperor if ever he returned from war without victory. Whence the tremendous vitality of usurpations, which constantly challenged the rule of individual emperors yet never challenged the idea of emperor.

This providential man was chosen by God: his coins proclaimed the fact that he was "from God" (*ek theou*). His subjects called themselves *douloi,* which in the time of Thucydides had meant "slaves" but now perhaps connoted something closer to "servants." The *basileus* was God's own representative on earth who had inherited the trappings of the cult of his pagan Roman predecessors' divinity. His person was sacred, which yet did not protect him from the threat of assassination. Alone among laymen he enjoyed special privileges within the Orthodox Church. If his special relations with God, who lived at the heart of the Byzantine worldview, derived from divine election of him to rule, they were continuously manifested and reinforced through the emperor's piety and orthodoxy and in his special munificence to God. Where Roman emperors had built vast baths, markets, or triumphal columns, Byzantine emperors preferred to build churches. Propagandizing pictures showed the emperor giving gifts to the Virgin and her Child, as for instance in a celebrated mosaic of Hagia Sophia, and carefully calibrated acts of generosity concluded his ritual visits to the capital's shrines.

Every emperor was, moreover, indirectly sanctified by the official cult the Eastern Orthodox Church granted to Constantine I, the semi-mythical prototype of the perfect emperor—at least in his legendary incarnation of the Middle Ages—and by the regular commemorations of the ruler's imperial predecessors in the *synaxarion,* or festal calendar of the church of Constantinople. Each year the emperors' obits were marked by liturgical anniversaries, processions, and services, just as their victories, accessions, and the like demarcated public space and time, via the empire's monuments and holidays.

STRUCTURES OF POWER

The palace was the stage on which the symbolism of power played. Infused with the general sacrality that attached to the imperial figure, this building—or rather, complex of buildings—both fascinated and mystified the Byzantine imagination. Magical palaces chock full of gold might appear and disappear on the old parade grounds outside the city and supply a mythical Justinian with the money to raise the great dome of Hagia Sophia. The sacral status of the emperor's dwelling was such that one hagiographical story has a grandee accused of polluting the palace because he dared to enter it after he had made love to his wife on a Sunday. Even the palace walls themselves might "speak," supplying mute but eloquent testimony on impending events. When, for instance, the citizens of Constantinople awoke to discover that the emperor's sword and shield had been hung from the palace gate, they knew war was at hand and that the *basileus* would lead the army into battle. The presence or absence of a mosaic of the Virgin above the palace entrance declared the current emperor's theological views, and tampering with it might trigger riots in the streets.

By the early fifth century, the new capital of Constantinople had mushroomed into one of the great urban centers of the Roman Empire's more economically advanced eastern half. The main palace had been founded by Constantine I at the southeast end of the hilly peninsula on which New Rome was built, in the heart of the city's splendid monumental downtown. The palace's size and magnificence soon warranted the name of "Great" to distinguish it from the lesser imperial residences established elsewhere in the city and its suburbs. Its approach was marked by the Golden Milestone, which listed the distances to each of the Roman Empire's great cities from this, the heart of the empire. Visitors to Istanbul can see a recently discovered fragment of this monument at the beginning of Divan Yolu, which approximates ancient Constantinople's great Middle Avenue. The splendid porticoes leading from the Milestone to the Brazen House, the palace's monumental main entry, were reserved for perfume merchants, so that the approaches to the emperor's home would delight the nose as well as the Byzantine eye.

To the western or land side, the massive Hippodrome, scene of so many sporting and political dramas in the empire's early centuries, shielded the Great Palace complex from the fires and riots that wracked the burgeoning capital in late antiquity. Inside the Hippodrome, a fortified loge (the *kathisma*) allowed the emperor to view circus races and manifest himself to his city's population in complete safety; this imperial box was physically joined to the palace by a secure passage. Just north of the palace, a monumental square adorned with the great triumphal column of Justinian and the Senate House provided the backdrop for imperial processions to services in Hagia Sophia on great holy days. To the south and east, the palace spread down the slope toward the sea in a series of gardens, terraces, balconies, and residential and official buildings. The magnificently luxurious Boukoleon Palace that so impressed the Crusader archbishop William of Tyre rose above the beach and private landing at the foot of the southern slope.

The Great Palace's expansion probably peaked in the fifth and sixth centuries, but significant new building continued for another six hundred years. In the ninth and tenth centuries, improving imperial finances allowed extensive remodeling. The Komnenian dynasty, however, shifted their main residence to the newer Blachernai Palace on the city's northwest fringe, overlooking the Golden Horn and the plain beyond the walls, and the Great Palace slowly slipped from a ceremonial residence into semi-abandonment.

The court espoused Roman society's *villeggiatura* lifestyle and enjoyed seasonal vacations in the rural surroundings of the capital's Asiatic and European suburbs. The seaside palaces that dotted the shorelines of the Sea of Marmara and the Bosporos ranged from the magnificent structures erected by Justinian and Theodora across the bay from Chalcedon to Michael III's pleasure pavilion at St. Mamas, the modern Beşiktaş, an area the Ottoman sultans would also appreciate.

However many holiday villas the emperors might build, for most of the empire's history the physical structures of power were identified with the Great Palace. It is striking that, for all the archaeological and topographical attention lavished on its scarce remaining rubble, the abundant evidence on how the palace *functioned* as an institution has never been completely assembled and questioned.

The Great Palace constituted a kind of city within the city, and its structures reflected its many functions. Walls separated the palace from the city around it from an early date, if the perimeter wall identified at the late antique palace in Ravenna is any indication of Constantinopolitan practice. Certainly later emperors like Justinian II and Nikephoros II Phokas strengthened and extended the Great Palace fortifications. The autocracy's security was enhanced by crack military units quartered just inside the Great Palace's main entrance, barring the way to the imperial family. Dissenters and conspirators disappeared into the complex's own prisons. If all else failed, a private harbor allowed a threatened emperor to escape from the Great Palace. In better times, the harbor allowed swift and secure water transport to most points in the city aboard the emperor's scarlet-painted yacht. After nearly losing his throne in the Nika revolt, Justinian I constructed both granaries and bakeries inside the Great Palace to insure its self-sufficiency; cisterns guaranteed a secure water supply. Personnel lists suggest that the palace included stables and artisan's workshops. A private polo court allowed the emperors and their family to indulge in a favorite medieval sport. A number of chapels and churches constructed inside the complex ministered to the palace's religious needs; by the end of the ninth century, their permanent staff of a dozen priests and many deacons resided behind the palace walls.

The Great Palace's ancient structures were likely articulated in a series of rectangular peristyle porticoes, the garden courtyards of which might be adorned with statuary or fountains, while the porticoes themselves could feature magnificent mosaics like the one still visible in Istanbul's Mosaic Museum. In mild weather, high officials sometimes conducted government business in the open-air porticoes. This is where they congregated for the discussions that led to Anastasios I's election in 491, and Constantine V once held an audience on a terrace overlooking the sea. Around such porticoes we might expect to find the buildings that housed key ministries of the imperial government. "The Palace," in fact, was sometimes used as a kind of shorthand for "government establishment." And, from an early date, some elements of the bureaucracy, such as the master of the offices and the count of the sacred largesses—and presumably the gold mint—were headquartered in the palace. We know that, in this cash-based society, the emperor kept his vast reserves of coinage and precious metals safe inside the palace; Basil II had to construct special spiraled galleries underneath it to store his accumulation. The number of government offices actually located within its walls seems only to have increased with the centuries, as administrative services as diverse as the imperial chancery and judicial tribunals took their seats there. Triple doors led from the porticoes into the large halls that served as the stage for solemn acts of government such as the reading out of new laws, audiences granted to foreign ambassadors, or promotions of high-ranking officials. The emperor occupied a raised platform at one end. Curtains separated him from the rest of the hall, while floor inlays helped guide the movements of those admitted into his presence. How these halls were used will become clear when we examine the ritual projection of imperial power.

The emperor's residence constituted yet another structural unit within the palace. It was separated from the rest and secluded, its precincts presided over by the all-powerful corps of palace eunuchs. Privileged indeed were the ordinary mortals who were allowed into the emperor's private residence.

A large and heterogeneous crowd populated the physical structures of this city within a city. We have already noted the bureaucrats and imperial guards. The emperor of course lived there with his mother, wife, and children, and members of their extended families might well join them. Others, like the many relatives of Emperor Constantine VI's first wife, were given houses close to the palace.

The smooth functioning of the private and public spheres of the imperial entourage's life required careful organization. In the early Byzantine era, each ranking resident of the palace apparently constituted a kind of autonomous organizational cell, since he lived with his own personal domestic staff, including slaves, bodyguards, and a cellarer, the last of whom suggests separate arrangements for each unit's food storage and preparation within the palace milieu. Separate revenue arrangements financed each unit. Thus, in the late ninth century, the private yacht of the empress was paid for by the revenues flowing into and managed in her own "table" or provisions account.

The men and women who served the palace fulfilled all the functions one might expect in a large and fabulously wealthy household. A host of people contributed to the well-being of the palace establishment. Late Roman laws reveal lamplighters, doorkeepers, and interpreters; craftsmen and workers were attached to the imperial mint, and it is likely that palace artists helped churn out the artworks and dies required by the coinage and imperial propaganda, whether they were intended as gifts or special commissions. Medieval ceremonial prescriptions reveal artists and artisans attached to the palace. We hear of the emperor's tailors, gold-thread workers, and goldsmiths. *Atriklinai,* maître d's at state banquets, played a delicate role in establishing the precedence and seating each guest. Eunuchs managed the daily routine of the palace: the *papias,* assisted by his "number two man" (*deuteros*), first appears in the eighth century and oversaw the functioning of the palace's physical plant, buildings, lighting, and so on. Under him were the lower-ranking palace personnel (*diaiterioi*), who were organized into sections called "weeks" reflecting their work schedule. In the tenth century, an effort was made to restrict their recruitment to residents of the capital and its immediate environs.

The highest-ranking members of the palace's domestic personnel were the eunuch chamberlains who staffed the imperial apartments or *kouboukleion* (from Latin *cubiculum*). Genderless and—in theory at least—kinless, the eunuch cubicularies constituted the ultimate outsiders.

From their powerlessness sprang, paradoxically, great influence in the form of absolute confidence and authority within the emperor's household. Eunuchs served his table and prepared his bed and clothing. Every night they locked themselves and their emperor in his bedroom and lay down to sleep next to his bed and the door. They controlled the emperor's private schedule and cared for his insignia. Their cooperation was indispensable for anyone who wished to reach the emperor's ear: imperial support for his theological positions cost St. Cyril of Alexandria bribes for the chief eunuchs ranging from 50 to 200 lbs. of gold.

Early in the Byzantine millennium, Roman law prohibited the castration of citizens, and most imperial eunuchs stemmed from beyond the empire's northeastern frontiers. By the eighth century, the recruitment pattern seems to have changed: one of Empress Irene's leading eunuch ministers is reported to have schemed to obtain the purple for his own family—clearly implying that he was a Byzantine—while a little later a Paphlagonian peasant beseeched God to grant him a son so he could castrate him and provide for his own old age through his son's palace service. We even find an illegitimate member of the imperial family, Basil Lekapenos, occupying a central position within the imperial *kouboukleion* in the second half of the tenth century.

Eunuchs' statutory power so increased that by the tenth century, the head eunuch presided over the organizing of imperial ceremonies, a privilege wrested from the hands of the leading bearded ministers of state sometime after the sixth century. The eunuch *castrensis* or majordomo oversaw the palace's lesser-ranking staff in late antiquity, and we have already seen the importance of his medieval successor, the eunuch *papias*. Eunuchs helped raise the imperial children: the notorious Antiochos had tutored Emperor Theodosios II, and Pope Gregory I expressed concern about the example the eunuchs set for Emperor Maurice's children. When a marriage was planned between Charlemagne's daughter and Empress Irene's son, a eunuch official was dispatched to the West to instruct the Frankish girl on the customs and language of the Byzantine court. And a constant concern to enunciate the privileges and advantages that accrued to the eunuchs of the *kouboukleion* hints that, beneath the explicit authorship claimed by Emperor Constantine VII, the great tenth-century treatise *On Imperial Ceremonies* owed much to this social group. Such was their prestige that the medieval mind imagined angels in their image. Until their power was curtailed by the triumph of kinship networks as an organizing principle of public life under the Komnenoi, trusted eunuchs could even be found commanding imperial armies.

The court that passed its days and nights in this splendid setting was a melting pot of ethnicities. In the empire's early days, Gothic bodyguards, Persian eunuchs, and Italian and North African bureaucrats hovered around the imperial person; so too again in the twelfth century, when Turkish and Norman commanders watched over imperial security, Latin interpreters and their relatives from Bergamo worked for the palace, while a Hungarian or French empress and their ladies-in-waiting presided over the court's social life. It is scarcely surprising that down to the sixth century the court in Constantinople constituted a powerful enclave of Latin speakers in the Greek East; the full impact of this bilingualism can still be read in the technical jargon of the medieval Greek bureaucracy, which is studded with Latinisms ranging from *patrikios* (Latin *patricius,* "patrician") or *doux* (Lat. *dux,* "duke") to *sekreton* (Lat. *secretum,* "office"). In the twelfth century, the enthusiasm of Emperor Manuel I Komnenos and the Latins in his entourage for the fashions of the feudal West fostered the diffusion of a western lifestyle in the Byzantine upper class; jousts and tournaments replaced the ancient chariot races as the court's favorite entertainment in the Hippodrome.

THE EXERCISE OF POWER

Who were these emperors, what did they do, and why were they so important in the life of this great civilization? The recruitment of emperors and the patterns by which power was transmitted changed over the Byzantine millennium. Election by the senate and army declined, although successful usurpation, itself often not overly distinct from election, took up some of the slack. Family succession grew in importance across the last seven Byzantine dynasties. From 610 to 1204, thirty-two designated co-emperors succeeded to the purple; twenty-five of them were imperial offspring, and six more were co-opted into the imperial family. A single dynasty, the Palaiologoi, presided over the empire's last two centuries.

The institutional background of emperors reflects a changing political structure. Down to the early seventh century, the army supplied the largest share of emperors, followed closely thereafter by the imperial family; the civilian bureaucracy could boast only the exceptional election of Anastasios I. From Herakleios down to the Venetian conquest of Constantinople in 1204, the bureaucracy and palace milieux gained against the army. But thereafter the civil service played no role as a recruiting ground for the late Byzantine emperors. So, too, Byzantium's shifting geographical horizons can be read in the fact that, even excluding Constantinople, the empire's European provinces supplied all sovereigns whose background is known down to Tiberios II, except for Zeno. After Phokas, and until the final centuries when the empire's sharply reduced size severely limited the possibilities and their significance, most emperors born outside of the capital came from Asia Minor and so reflected Anatolia's enhanced political and social importance. The aristocracy supplied the bulk of emperors. Nonetheless, in an exceptional but persistent phenomenon, a few nonaristocrats clawed their way to the top through imperial service, whether they were peasants like Justin I and Basil I, or stemmed from a more urban milieu like Michael IV.

The emperors' position in Byzantine political ideology fairly approximated the role they played in the Byzantine state. The word "state" seems almost a historical anomaly in the medieval world. Yet, alone in medieval Christendom, Byzantium preserved a political system grounded on professional salaried institutions, which in turn structured and defined the Byzantine aristocracy down to the twelfth century. As the source of law, the emperor was not bound by it, and frequently acted accordingly. In fact, Byzantine legal thinking in some respects even expanded the extensive imperial prerogatives Roman law had recognized: the emperor was the sole source of the administrative promotions that made the political system tick, and he was felt to enjoy extraordinary confiscatory powers that perhaps limited the very notion of private property.

Though the emperor's authority might sometimes appear ambiguous or even be thwarted the farther one got from the imperial capital of Constantinople—*hē basileuousa polis,* "the ruling city"—the power at his disposal was real enough. Unlike any other European ruler before the thirteenth century, Byzantine emperors commanded a professional army and a highly organized bureaucracy expert at extracting wealth from the layers of the population least able to afford it, thanks to an elaborate tax system. When the creaky system was whipped into action, the empire's professional administrators were capable of performances that were astonishing by medieval standards. Even so hostile an observer as an anonymous Crusader was forced to register the bureaucracy's logistical feat in swiftly transporting boats across mountains and through forests in order to facilitate an assault on the Turkish-occupied town of Nicaea in 1097.

This sophisticated government was so structured that the tasks of governance were split up among a large number of independent bureaucracies. The series of autonomous lines of authority that resulted discouraged opposition to the top, since they converged in one place only, in the hands of the emperor himself. In other words, all power was centralized.

Wealth too. Every March and September, great trains of gold flowed into the palace in the form of the imperial land tax, which must have supplied the bulk of the empire's operating budget. Tolls levied at the empire's customs stations and markets, payments (which were really investments) for imperial titles and the pensions they entailed, confiscations, and fines all fed the palace cash reserves. Added to these regular sources of public income were the profits and production of the emperor's vast private estates, not to mention the proceeds from the state monopoly workshops that produced the luxury textiles for which Constantinople's markets were famous. Hence palace treasure piled up under thrifty emperors; the sums of gold Byzantine historians mention measure in tons. All of these sources of revenue combined to finance a monetary economy largely centered on the emperor and his expenditures for armies, officials, munificence, and pleasure, thus giving real economic weight to the powers granted him by law and by custom.

Naturally emperors' style of rule varied greatly over one thousand years of history. There were emperors who, like Herakleios or Manuel I, insisted on leading their troops to war in person and who actually played the role of chief general. Other emperors followed in the footsteps of Justinian and remained buried in the palace, working through the night to examine policy options and issue orders across a far-flung bureaucracy, or peppering their commanders with orders and trying to micromanage military expeditions from the capital. And there were scholar emperors like Theodosios II, who might leave the reins of power effectively in the hands of their most trusted advisors, or playboy emperors like Alexander, under whom the bureaucracy chugged along under its own steam.

What did an emperor's routine look like? The nature of this society and therefore of the surviving sources makes this question more difficult to answer than might appear at first glance. Despite his essential position in actually working the levers of power, the emperor tends chiefly to be visible as he revealed himself to his contemporaries in the carefully staged circumstances of imperial ceremonial, rather than actually running the government or leading his private life. An early Byzantine preacher even exploited this circumstance for its shock value by asking his audience to imagine the all-powerful emperor snoring away in his bed, in an unflattering comparison with the nocturnal prayers of contemporary monks. Combing through the sources, we can nonetheless piece together a mosaic of our own that would look something like this.

Like other Byzantines, emperors arose around dawn in order to take full advantage of the day's sunlight. The first serious order of business in the day would have been prayers in one of the palace's several churches; knowledge of this fact guided the assassins of Leo V. In the tenth century, the Great Palace opened for public business twice daily, for three or more hours before lunch and the same afterwards. After the completion of the morning office, the eunuch *papias,* who kept the keys to the palace's various gates, and his team of palace servants accompanied the commander of the imperial guards and his men through the palace, unlocking the various gates and doorways from the inside outward. It is typical that this critical security duty was divided between the rival social groups of eunuchs and soldiers. We know that important affairs of state, such as great processions or the distribution of gold to the empire's dignitaries, began immediately in the day's first hour, about 6 A.M. and might last until late morning. When more routine affairs needed his attention, the emperor might ascend the throne in the apse of the Chrysotriklinos (golden banquet hall), where he would await his chief minister, who would join him behind the curtain that separated the imperial apse from the rest of the room. The chief minister or logothete, or any other official the emperor needed to consult, might come and go several times before lunch. When the emperor was ready for lunch, the *papias* would parade through the palace shaking his keys, signaling the closing of the palace. The whole procedure was repeated when the palace opened again after lunch.

During his normal working day, the emperor consulted with his chief ministers on pressing affairs. He might take a personal interest in judicial proceedings. He granted audiences to officials departing or returning from the field. The handful of governmental memorandums that Constantine VII had recopied into the treatises on rulership that he prepared for his son suggest that the imperial bureaucracy generated a significant flow of documents that worked their way back to the Great Palace, documents ranging from intelligence reports of recent events beyond the Black Sea to detailed logistical reports on the costs and administrative measures required to outfit a fleet for operations against Arab-occupied Crete. Some emperors intervened personally in the composition of laws. A sixth-century church historian has left a vivid picture of Justin II presiding over a series of discussions with leading dissident prelates, as various imperial officials attempted to goad and cajole them into furnishing language for a religious edict that would foster theological compromise. After long wrangling, the emperor was satisfied with the proposed text and ordered that twenty copies be brought to him and the others for signature before sunset. One specialist has even detected what may be Justinian I's personal stylistic ticks in the impatient staccato phrases that are strewn through some of his Latin laws. In any case, and in any period when the emperor actually appended his autograph subscription to the various privileges, administrative orders, and new laws prepared by his chancery, he must have been quite busy practicing his purple penmanship in obsolete Latin so long as he signed documents with the word *legimus,* certainly as late as the eighth century. By the tenth century, this element of the imperial signature had devolved to the master of the inkstand (*ho epi tou kanikleiou*), and emperors signed their names and titles: "John [I] in Christ God faithful emperor of the Romans." No less important than the administrative business of state was the palace's ceremonial business, as we shall see. On these occasions, the morning or indeed the entire day might be devoted to the onerous but indispensable duties of imperial ritual.

Imperial leisure might take many forms. In striking contrast to the patterns that obtained in the Latin West, aristocratic background and the premium Byzantine civilization placed on literacy combined with the routine role of written documents in civil and military administration to foster literary pretensions among emperors, a phenomenon that extended to the women of the imperial family. Justinian composed learned theological treatises. Whatever the role of his ghostwriters, Constantine VII, a scholar emperor like Theodosios II half a millennium earlier, clearly aimed at a literary legacy by composing or commissioning treatises on different aspects of imperial governance—precious sources on foreign policy, the provinces, the central administration, and the ceremonial articulations of the court and state aristocracy—not to mention his vast encyclopedic project of extracts from ancient authors. His father, Leo VI, had composed hymns and speeches for various state occasions. Manuel II wrote a polemical treatise on Christianity against Islam. John VII Kantakouzenos paraphrased the *Nicomachean Ethics* and devoted himself to his autobiography in forced retirement.

Nor were the men of the imperial family alone in wielding the pen: the highly educated Eudokia turned her talents to versifying the Bible, while lower-class origins and nearsightedness did not prevent Theodora from receiving Monophysite theological treatises transcribed in large letters so she could read them. The remarkable Anna, Alexios I Komnenos' purple-born daughter, glorified her father's reign in the *Alexiad,* whose rich tapestry of classical allusion adorns a historical work that ranks this talented woman as one of the Middle Ages' great historians. Such cultural ambitions in the imperial family help explain how the imperial court played a significant role in Byzantium's remarkable cultural florescence.

Emperors like Michael III, who descended into the arena to taste the thrills and dangers of chariot racing, were exceptions. More dignified and aristocratic exercise took them out of doors for hunting trips. A lovely enclosed park, the Philopation, lay just beyond the Blachernai Palace and provided a convenient and agreeable setting for falconry and hunting the animals with which it was stocked. More elaborate expeditions accompanied the emperors' quest for big game, especially wild boars, in Asia Minor and Thrace. The palace polo grounds allowed them to hone their equestrian skills in imperial privacy. Indoor amusements like dice or Alexios I Komnenos' daily morning game of chess with his relatives provided less strenuous diversion.

Though many purple-clad monarchs were justly celebrated for their piety—even, as we have just seen, the notorious former courtesan Theodora, whose premarital sexual license her determined detractor Prokopios detailed—not a few rulers, male and female alike, indulged their fancies with the men and women of their entourage. Constantine VI's dalliance and then second marriage with one of his mother's ladies-in-waiting plunged the eighth-century elite into a political crisis. Michael III was accused of drunken orgies during which he and his boon companions parodied the mysteries of church and state and taunted the religious devotion of his mother the empress, even as he married his favorite mistress to his peasant protégé and future murderer Basil the Macedonian, in order to facilitate his own nocturnal escapades. Constantine IX Monomachos created a new court dignity that allowed his mistresses to appear in the limelight along with his wife.

Some empresses were no less enterprising than their male counterparts: Romanos II had been bewitched by a tavern keeper's daughter who took the name of Theophano when she climbed out of bed and into the throne. When her husband died, she preserved her status by marrying the empire's greatest general and the standard-bearer of a great military clan, Nikephoros II Phokas. Yet this monkish warrior emperor was happier on the frontier with his troops than at home with his beautiful young wife, who soon yielded to the attractions of his handsome lieutenant, John Tzimiskes. Together they plotted her husband's murder, and John ascended the throne. But the opposition of an outraged church blocked Theophano's success and led to her expulsion from the palace. Two generations later, Theophano's fifty-year-old spinster granddaughter Zoe was obliged to marry a prominent civil servant in his sixties in order to maintain her family's hold on power. She soon discovered the charms of a younger man who, not coincidentally, was related to an influential eunuch. When her husband succumbed in his bath, Empress Zoe married her young lover the same night. After her lover's death and a disastrous interlude when his nephew occupied the throne, the sixty-four-year-old empress married once again.

Family ties played an important role in the imperial entourage. To be sure, the emperor's family had often figured prominently in public life since the time of Augustus. But the phenomenon gained new strength in the Byzantine period. The trend toward governance through kinship networks reached a first peak under Maurice, at the end of the sixth century, when the emperor's brother was master of the offices (foreign affairs) and *curopalatus* (palace security), his brother-in-law commanded the crack palace regiments and led the army on a number of campaigns, and yet another relative, the bishop of Melitene, remained Maurice's closest adviser and warranted an imperial funeral. Across the society a broad trend toward cross-generational lineages may have misfired more than once before it started its final ascent under the long-lived Macedonian dynasty. An important consequence was a gradual blurring of the boundaries between the state as a public entity and a vision of the state that came closer to a family patrimony, a view unmistakably conveyed by aspects of Komnenian policy. From the late eleventh century, the degree of kinship to the emperor actually came to supplant the old distinctions of the state aristocracy as a basis for precedence within the state.

The importance of kinship networks underscores the historical significance of empresses. *Augoustai,* as their official title ran, were legally dependent on the emperors. The *Digest* clearly states that their power and position derived from the emperor, and later Byzantine law echoed it. Nonetheless, circumstance combined with the progressive development of lineage as a primary factor of social organization to grant some empresses remarkable power and authority. A systematic analysis of empresses' social backgrounds across the Byzantine millennium would probably illuminate changing patterns of the imperial political and social structure (for example, both Honorius and Arkadios were married to generals' daughters), while empresses like the wives of Justinian or Theophilos show how marriages to the throne generated power for the imperial woman's family. Newcomers to the throne might seek to consolidate their new power by marrying an established empress; thus Marcian married the fifty-one-year-old consecrated virgin Pulcheria in 450, and Nikephoros III Botaneiates married Empress Maria in 1078.

Selecting an empress was no small matter. We have already seen that a few empresses came from nonaristocratic milieux. From 788 to 881, Byzantine sources mention bride shows in which various eligible young ladies were paraded before the emperor and his mother. Although some doubt has been cast on the accounts of this unusual selection process, it appears to have been emulated by Charlemagne's son in the West. Perhaps such a procedure represented one stratagem for liberating the emperor's choice from the tremendous pressures that prominent aristocrats at court might have worked to insure the success of women from their family.

Diplomacy began bringing emperors foreign wives in the eighth century when Constantine V's marriage with a Khazar princess was followed by failed negotiations for daughters of Frankish kings. Foreign brides were coached in the Greek language and court customs before arriving in their new home. Typically they changed their names when they assumed their new Byzantine identity, often receiving names of ideal qualities like Irene ("peace"). The geopolitical level at which the Byzantine emperors were able to conclude such alliances peaked under the Komnenoi, when brides came from the rulers of the German Empire and Capetian France. The significance of imperial marriages was not diminished by a political structure that was increasingly reshaped along the lines dictated by kinship networks and a patrimonial state. One marvelous pamphlet that survives in the Vatican Library (Vat. gr. 1851) documents with vernacular poetry and pictures the ceremonies and celebrations that heralded the arrival in Constantinople of Agnes, daughter of Louis VII of France. Indeed, such alliances became so usual that Palaiologan masters of ceremony concocted a standard ritual to mark the arrival of the emperor's foreign bride in Byzantium, but the late empire's diminished status meant that foreign empresses now came from lesser echelons of regional potentates.

It would be a mistake to assume that all imperial wives automatically became empresses, at least in the early period. Over the three centuries from Constantine's accession to that of Justinian and Theodora, only about a third of emperors' known wives were granted the title of empress. The exalted status of these early Byzantine empresses can be seen in various privileges: they issued coinage, authenticated documents with lead seals, wore imperial insignia, and possessed their own revenues and the appropriate staffs to manage them. And they held the official title of *Augousta*. Some empresses, like Theodora, wife of Justinian, or Leontia, wife of Phokas, became empresses immediately on their husbands' accession. Others did so in connection with their marriage to the emperor, while still others became empresses only later in the marriage or not at all. The reasons are not always clear, but there is some indication that down to the eighth century at least, the status of empress might be granted in connection with the birth of an heir.

The public life of empresses was largely separate from that of their husbands. In this they reflected a general tendency of Byzantium's upper classes toward sexual segregation. Empresses were particularly important to the female court aristocracy inasmuch as they provided the pivot for the public lives of the grand ladies of Byzantium. Thus Michael II's associates are supposed to have claimed that "it is not proper for an emperor to live without a wife or for our wives to be deprived of a mistress and empress." One rare occasion when senatorial women might occupy ceremonial center stage in the capital's streets was when they welcomed the emperor's future bride, for instance, when Irene arrived in Constantinople from Athens. The empresses presided over their own autonomous ceremonial and social sphere formed by the wives of the ranking members of the state hierarchy of dignities, who held ranks corresponding to those of their husbands. Thus, during the eucharistic liturgy at Hagia Sophia, the empress, surrounded by her own and the emperor's eunuch cubicularies and sword bearers, granted solemn audience to the wives of the imperial dignitaries, and each rank was admitted to receive the kiss of peace from her. So, too, when Princess Olga of Kiev was presented to the empress, the seven *vela* (raisings of the curtain that marked the ceremonial entrées) differentiated the women of the court according to precise precedence. The emperor appeared for Olga's private audience with the empress and imperial children in the imperial chamber, and two state banquets were held, apparently simultaneously, one for women and one for men.

Paradoxically this kind of gender-based segregation did not preclude the energetic involvement of empresses, like other Byzantine women, in a host of various activities. Thus the sight of a particularly magnificent merchant ship prompted a ninth-century emperor to discover to his horror that his wife was running a shipping business out of the palace. The enraged Theophilos is reported to have asked his retinue sarcastically, "Didn't you know that God made me an emperor, but the empress my wife has made me a bosun?" He torched the vessel. Whether this ever actually happened in this way may perhaps be questioned, but the story itself suggests that an empress running a business unknown to her husband was a plausible situation for the ninth century. And why not? After all, empresses disposed of vast private estates, which they had to administer like any other Byzantine aristocrat.

The political influence of empresses can be read in different ways. For instance, from 425 to A.D. 600, during the early stages of the great crisis that ended the ancient world and brought forth the Middle Ages, empresses averaged more than twenty years of reign, substantially more than their male counterparts. In concrete terms, Empress Verina and her daughter Ariadne maintained themselves in the Great Palace, while the crown passed in and out of the hands of males from four biological families, including their own. The celebrated Theodora seems to have played a vigorous role behind the scenes in Justinian's governance. Prokopios claims that the imperial couple consciously manipulated their divergent religious opinions: Justinian held orthodox views about the nature of Christ and made them the law of the land; but his wife, like a large segment of the empire's eastern provinces, was an ardent heretic and protectress of the Monophysite doctrine. Prokopios may in fact be borne out in the way that Justinian innovated by introducing his wife's name into the religious oath of allegiance required of all state officials. In any event, Theodora's niece Sophia, who married Justinian's nephew Justin II, played an even more active role. She also took the public status of the empress a step further when her portrait appeared next to the emperor's on the bronze coinage, precisely the coins that circulated most intensively in the economic transactions of daily life. No less significantly, Sophia and her immediate successors joined their husbands in the public oaths on the emperors' health and victory that citizens were required to swear when paying their taxes or establishing contracts.

Only under exceptional circumstances did empresses run the empire directly, for instance, during an emperor's minority or, like Justin II's Sophia, when their husbands' health failed and they took up the slack. Formal regencies were established on a number of occasions, and the empresses could then personally control the levers of power. So the imperious Irene even assumed sole rule, perhaps contemplated marriage to Charlemagne, and certainly commanded that her own son be blinded when he threatened her power. The sister empresses Zoe and Theodora, the Macedonian dynasty's last surviving members, also ruled briefly in their own names. Co-ruling regents were officially acknowledged in the symbols of sovereignty: on coins, in acclamations, and dating formulas of documents. Although in such circumstances the empress customarily yielded formal precedence to the young emperor, here the fourteenth-century empress Ann of Savoy was an exception. Although she did not formally receive the imperial dignity, Alexios Komnenos' mother Anna Dalassene took full control of the empire's administration while her son fought desperately to fend off the assault Robert Guiscard had launched from Italy. From her time on, acts issued by empresses survive and document their very considerable wealth. Clearly the seclusion of the imperial palace and the privileges of supreme power fostered the position and influence of the *augoustai*.

Screened from the population by a crowd of genderless men and rough barbarian soldiers, the rulers' lifestyle constituted a kind of living archaism. The imperial couple's most distinctive robe, the *lōros,* a kind of elaborate silk scarf that wrapped them in a glorious swath of purple and gold brocade, was the ultimate avatar of the classical Roman consuls' *toga trabeata;* its own origins are connected with those of the priestly stole and the archepiscopal pallium of the Roman Catholic Church. It bore no relation to the average Byzantine's everyday wear, of course. Centuries after normal Byzantines had adopted the modern style of eating seated on stools or chairs at table, state banquets presided over by the emperor in the palace's magnificent dining halls continued to use the ancient Roman style of eating while reclining together on large couches or *akkoubita.* Centuries after Latin had ceased to be a living language in Constantinople, the lettering of imperial coins and the address clauses of imperial privileges continued to use the old Roman alphabet, even if their legends were now usually in Greek.

How could a secluded, sacralized, archaized emperor play such a dominant role in Byzantine self-understanding? This was partly due, as we have seen, to the structure of the imperial government, which wove together, in one pair of hands alone, all the strings that needed to be pulled. Part of the answer lies also in the nature of the Byzantine aristocracy. Social status in Byzantium was determined by one's position in an elaborate and changing hierarchy of precedence with respect to the emperor: each person's precise rank in society was determined by the combined rank of his dignity—the honorific titles and pensions granted by the emperor to an individual for his own lifetime and nonhereditary—and the government offices currently held or held in the past at the emperor's pleasure. Even after the Komnenian revolution at the close of the eleventh century, when kinship links supplanted the old title system, degree of kin relationship to the emperor became the deciding factor. In other words, imperial connections supplied the ladder of social preferment; one's status was largely in the hands of the emperor himself. Notwithstanding the conventional—and erroneous—image of Byzantium as an eternally unchanging society, "monuments of unaging intellect" in the words of the Irish poet, the connection between government service and aristocratic status opened the door to a kind of social mobility that might catapult to the supreme office individuals of no social standing whatsoever: Basil I, former wrestler, stable hand, and bodyguard, or Michael IV. And there is no reason to think that such vertiginous social ascensions were confined to the supreme office alone.

POWER PROJECTED

A further factor that helped make the emperor into the linchpin of the elite's self-image was the way in which each individual's status was communicated to his peers and the world at large. In a society that lacked the technological means of mass communication, symbolic gestures bridged the gap between ruler and ruled and conveyed to each their respective parts in the Byzantine world order. Ceremony lay at the heart of the Byzantine attitude to the political order; indeed, the same word (*taxis*) designates both "order" and "ceremony" in Byzantine Greek. The public projection of the imperial idea was the very essence of imperial ceremony, whose carefully scripted rituals broke the emperor's seclusion and punctuated Byzantine civic life. These elaborate ceremonies, which seemed to incarnate in unchanging fashion the eternal gestures and truths of imperial rule, were in fact anything but immutable; recent research has uncovered how imperial ceremonial managers cleverly fashioned each performance of an ancient ritual by combining new and old elements in order to transmit messages about power and society that were finely calibrated to a changing situation. Thus the classical Roman triumph had been thoroughly Christianized, and each performance was tailored to the precise political and spiritual configuration of the moment. In the tenth century, for instance, the victorious John I Tzimiskes, who reached the throne over the body of his relative and benefactor, resurrected the ancient Roman triumphal chariot. This he did so he could place on it a victory-giving icon of the Virgin, humbly dismount, and walk behind the icon through the capital's Golden Gate, thereby sending a powerful signal of both his victory and religious devotion to a popular cult.

A tenth-century emperor expressly recognized the political function of such ceremonies in projecting imperial prestige and enhancing his power. From the vast repertory of imperial symbolic gestures, two ceremonies in particular played a crucial role in Byzantine public life from beginning to end and accurately convey its tenor: solemn audiences and processions.

We might return for a moment to the magnificent halls that faced the porticoes of the Great Palace. Everything within such a hall was organized to impress foreign or domestic delegations. The Byzantines were ingenious makers of mechanical devices that profoundly impressed and mystified in a pretechnological culture. In fact, they have left traces as far away as in an Anglo-Norman epic about Charlemagne. A good example was the medieval "Throne of Solomon" from which the emperor was adored by the stunned, confused suppliants and ambassadors who were admitted into his presence when the curtain concealing the seated ruler opened. Tenth-century descriptions show that the sights and sounds that accompanied the emperor's self-manifestation to foreign diplomats were geared to produce a disorienting psychological impact: as the foreign diplomat prostrated himself before the throne, the hall echoed with acclamations cued by bursts on the imperial organs. Mechanical beasts reared up on their stands around the imperial throne and roared, even as the emperor's throne ascended toward the ceiling. The din and distance engulfing the participants obviated any discussion; the intention seems to have been to soften up the imperial government's interlocutors before actual discussions began.

Perhaps the most striking self-manifestation of the emperor and his elite came in the great public processions. These had grown out of the dynamics of public life in the late Roman world's teeming capitals; all kinds of significant events in the life of the community from the baptism of a child to marriage, to displays of corporate identity, to the liturgical life of the church (the stational liturgy of the church of Rome is but another fossil of this public life in late antique cities) assumed public shape in the form of processions. Medieval Constantinople preserved and developed the stately parade of social groups as an essential element of civic life: students, newly licensed notaries, or state functionaries all staged them with the cooperation of their peers and the applause of their audiences; so, too, the clergy of "the Great Church," Hagia Sophia, who celebrated different liturgical feasts at different points in the city's sacred topography.

Of these diverse processions, those of the imperial court were the keystone. Elaborate parades marked the emperor's movement even within the palace's more public precincts, and especially when he left the sacred palace for the capital's leading shrines or on great occasions of state, like a triumphal return from battle or to welcome an heir's fiancée. So processions dominated even the court's imagination: a nightmare placed a very judgmental St. Peter and menacing apparitions of eunuch cubicularies at the conclusion of an imperial procession to Hagia Sophia and forewarned

Bardas Caesar, regent of Michael III, of his impending doom. And even beyond the court: around the year 1000, Symeon "the New" Theologian, played on analogies deriving from such imperial ceremonies in homiletic exhortations to his monks. Similar metaphors abound in the late antique preaching of patriarchs such as John Chrysostom or Proklos of Constantinople.

What did such a procession look like? The details vary from one end to another of the Byzantine millennium, and the changes can be most revealing of the ways in which the civilization itself developed. In the tenth century, a typical parade looked something like this. If the procession was to take the emperor out of the sacred, secure precincts of the palace, the first step was to clean the road, repair, grade, and sprinkle it with rosewater-scented sawdust. The route was decorated with flowered wreaths, sweet-smelling plants, and various expensive hangings—textiles or silverware—which were at least in part solicited from the capital's wealthy merchants and which glorified the emperor's passing and advertised their wares. The whole procedure was aptly named the "coronation of the city," given the semantic identity of "crown" and "wreath" in Greek.

The most powerful officials at court oversaw the selection of the precise locations of the various staged encounters at which acclamations would be chanted to the emperor; the texts themselves were composed or updated and singers and choruses arranged. Bleachers were erected for spectators. A fountain near where performers would stand might be filled with pistachios, almonds, and wine.

After an elaborate series of preparatory ceremonies within the palace, during which the emperor and any junior co-emperors donned their heavy processional garb, and the various constituent elements of the cortege greeted the rulers and took their places in the procession, the emperor made the sign of the cross, the parade got under way and appeared in public. First to emerge were the standard-bearers, carrying the ancient *vexilla* of Roman power, standards and long "dragon" banners, and of course the great golden cross reputedly made by Constantine I. The various elements of the hierarchy of state dignities who had received the command to appear on the eve walked in front of the imperial group. They were arranged in ascending order of precedence and wore ceremonial robes that were carefully regulated so as not to detract from the splendor of the emperor's raiment. At the tail end of the cortege, the elite corps of imperial bodyguards and eunuch cubicularies surrounded the emperor. The procession passed through the assembled ranks of city merchants and guilds and municipal authorities of the capital, as well as any foreign ambassadors who happened to be in the imperial city.

Along the route to the Great Church, the procession halted, and the government choruses who still bore the name of the ancient circus factions sang complex acclamations to the world ruler. Once inside, the emperor was greeted by the patriarch and stepped behind a curtain where, in deference to the celestial ruler, the chief eunuchs removed his crown. After entering the sanctuary, kissing the altar cloth, and censing the great golden crucifix within, the emperor retired to a nearby chamber, emerging only to escort the eucharistic gifts to the altar and again for communion. After this the ruler breakfasted in the chamber with his grandees, while the service concluded. As he left, the emperor distributed purses of gold to the clergy, the chanters, and a group of mendicants and finally made a large customary donation of 10 lbs. of gold to the church. The procession back to the palace followed the same model as on the way in; it often concluded with a sumptuous banquet in which the empire's highest dignitaries were summoned to the ancient dining couches according to their rank.

Scripted though they were, parades like this nonetheless functioned as a point of contact between ruler and ruled. For the onlookers of the capital—and the numerous foreign and Byzantine visitors it attracted—the pageant of imperial pomp and circumstance played out in simple symbolic gestures the key themes of imperial propaganda: the emperor's power, wealth, and sacral presence and the solidarity with the emperor of the ruling elite who processed with him, whether he was ostentatiously acting out his public piety by going to Hagia Sophia on a great feast day or trumpeting his triumph as he returned from campaign brandishing booty and captives. Subjects might seize the occasion to toss petitions in the emperor's path. For those who marched with him, their insignia and their concomitant position in the parade relative to the emperor himself were on display for all to see. Their public prominence was carefully calibrated by their dignity, their precedence in the procession, and the consecration of years of toil, intrigue, or service. For the emperor, it was an opportunity to confirm all these things and broadcast the political message of the moment: who was up, who was down, war or peace, joy or mourning.

Yet even when he remained within the palace, the emperor was constantly forced onto his subject's minds. His ubiquitous face stood watch in every place where public authority was exercised, and the official portraits were accorded the same honors as his person: small wonder the iconography of imperial power was the most developed artistic repertoire of Byzantine figurative art, after religious themes. The emperor was united to his subjects by the exercise of his powers, particularly his justice—a ninth-century ruler like Theophilos was legendary for his prompt dispensation of justice on his weekly processions through the capital's marketplace—and by his much-touted virtue of *philanthrōpia,* which in this era meant "mildness" or "clemency" as much as "philanthropy." In this age of religion, Byzantine emperors were expected to contribute to the upkeep and glorification of the empire's churches, monasteries, and hospitals and to fulfill his obligations as eternal victor par excellence, notably by maintaining and improving the defensive works of his cities, whence a remarkable and millenary series of inscriptions proclaiming the emperors' restorations of the great walls of Constantinople and other cities. His subjects prayed aloud for him—nineteenth-century printed texts of the Eastern Orthodox liturgy still contain prayers for the emperor's victory over the barbarians—on Sundays and special feasts in a unique public synthesis of religiosity and political allegiance. They accepted payment in his coins and thereby recognized him, for accepting a usurper's coin was treason. They swore oaths of allegiance or proclaimed their loyalty by acclaiming him and by paying their taxes, itself an act of allegiance.

So the emperor was a kind of social focal point and model for the Byzantine elite; late Roman poets and Byzantine thinkers enunciated this point clearly, and we can easily detect the repercussions of the emperor's lifestyle throughout the hierarchy of Byzantine officialdom and high society, and indeed beyond its frontiers. A caustic Greek proverb, "Bitches mimic their mistress" (hai kunes tēn despoinan mimoumenai), suggests that the culture was aware of its own imitative dispositions. Just like the emperor, eighth- or ninth-century grandees might well have helpers called prōtostratōr or prōtovestitōr in their entourage, while a seventh-century patriarch of Alexandria consciously imitated imperial custom by ordering his tomb immediately upon his promotion, as an ostentatious sign of humility. The christomimetic emperors themselves realized this standard-setting aspect of their conduct: at least the exhortations attributed to Basil I reveal an awareness of how subjects followed the emperor's every example. And anyone who has ever considered the ceremonial of the kings and popes of the medieval West in conjunction with that of the Byzantine emperor cannot fail to be struck by the connections.

Sum, sun, and apex of the Byzantine political and mental world, the emperor was, in some sense, indistinguishable from Byzantium's very existence. Loyalty to the basileus lay at the heart of Byzantine political ideology and even of Byzantine patriotism. His capital bore the name of its founder and great, sainted model-emperor Constantine I. Even when, in the later Middle Ages, the factual coterminousness of imperial power with areas of Greek language and culture coalesced with resentment of the Latin sack of Constantinople and popular resentment against the papacy's demands to precipitate a new Hellenic variant on the old cosmopolitan patriotism of the traditional empire, emperor and Byzantium seemed indissoluble. And so it is not surprising that the last day of the last emperor, Constantine XI, who died defending the great land walls of Constantinople on 29 May 1453, was also the last day in more than a thousand years of Byzantium's history.

SELECTED BIBLIOGRAPHY

Ahrweiler, H. *L'idéologie politique de l'empire byzantin.* Paris, 1975.

Beck, H. G. "Senat und Volk von Konstantinopel." *Sitzungsberichte der bayerischen Akademie der Wissenschaften 6.* Munich, 1966.

———. "*Nomos, Kanon* und Staatsraison in Byzanz." *Sitzungsberichte der Österreichischen Akademie der Wissenschaften,* Philos.-hist. Kl. 384, 1–60. Vienna, 1981.

Cameron, Alan. *Circus Factions: Blues and Greens at Rome and Byzantium.* Oxford, 1976.

Cameron, Averil. "The Construction of Court Ritual: The Byzantine *Book of Ceremonies.*" In *Rituals of Royalty: Power and Ceremonial in Traditional Societies,* 106–36. Cambridge, 1987.

Dagron, G. *Naissance d'une capitale: Constantinople et ses institutions de 330 à 451.* Paris, 1974.

Dölger, F. *Byzanz und die europäische Staatenwelt.* Ettal, 1953.

Grabar, A. *L'empereur dans l'art byzantin: Recherches sur l'art officiel de l'empire d'Orient.* Paris, 1936.

Hendy, M. F. *Studies in the Byzantine Monetary Economy, c. 300–1450.* Cambridge, 1985.

Hunger, H. *Prooimion: Elemente der byzantinischen Kaiseridee in den Arengen der Urkunden.* Vienna, 1964.

———, ed. *Das byzantinische Herrscherbild.* Darmstadt, 1975.

Kantorowicz, E. H. "*Oriens Augusti — Lever du roi.*" *Dumbarton Oaks Papers* 17 (1963): 119–77.

Kazhdan, A. P. "Das System der Bilder und Metaphern in den Werken Symeons des "Neuen" Theologen." In *Unser ganzes Leben Christus unserm Gott überantworten,* 221–39. Göttingen, 1982.

———. "Certain Traits of Imperial Propaganda in the Byzantine Empire from the Eighth to the Fifteenth Centuries." In *Prédication et propagande au moyen âge,* 13–28. Paris, 1983.

———. "Do We Need a New History of Byzantine Law?" *Jahrbuch der Österreichischen Byzantinistik* 39 (1989): 1–28.

Kazhdan, A. P. and M. McCormick. "The Social World of the Byzantine Court." In *Byzantine Court Culture from 829 to 1204,* Dumbarton Oaks Symposium, April 1994 (in press, Dumbarton Oaks).

Maslev, S. "Die Staatsrechtliche Stellung der byzantinischen Kaiserinnen." *Byzantinoslavica* 27 (1966): 308–43.

McCormick, M. "Analyzing Imperial Ceremonies." *Jahrbuch der Österreichischen Byzantinistik* 35 (1985): 1–20.

———. *Eternal Victory: Triumphal Rulership in Late Antiquity, Byzantium, and the Early Medieval West,* 2d ed. Cambridge-Paris, 1990.

McCormick, M. "Emperor and Court." In the *Cambridge Ancient History*, vol. 14 (in press, Cambridge University Press).

Pertusi, A. "Insegne del potere sovrano o delegato a Bisanzio e nei paesi di influenza bizantina." In *Simboli e simbologia nell'alto medioveo, 3–9 aprile 1975*, 2. Settimane di studio del Centro Italiano di Studi nell'Alto Medioevo 23, 481–563. Spoleto, 1976.

Rösch, O. "*Onoma basileos*": *Studien zum offiziellen Gebrauch der Kaisertitel in spätantiker und frühbyzantinischer Zeit*. Vienna, 1978.

Treitinger, O. *Die oströmischen Kaiser- und Reichsidee nach ihrer Gestaltung im höfischen Zeremoniell*. Jena, 1938.

See also numerous articles in the *Oxford Dictionary of Byzantium*, ed. A. P. Kazhdan et al. (Oxford, 1991), e.g., "Emperor," "Empress," "Political Structure," "Basileus."

10

SAINTS

Cyril Mango

I WOULD INVITE THE READER to visit any Byzantine church that has retained its decoration in reasonably good condition and to gaze at the paintings or mosaics on its walls. At the summit of the dome he or she will see a bust of Christ the Universal Ruler (Pantokrator) holding the book of Gospels and looking down with a fairly stern expression. Just below him, between the windows of the dome, may be a group of prophets holding scrolls upon which the texts of their respective prophecies are inscribed and pointing up to Christ, whose Incarnation they had foreseen. They are the only representatives of the Old Testament. In the apse will be an image of the Virgin Mary, the Queen of Heaven, holding the Christ child in her lap. High up in the vaults the key episodes of the New Testament will be unfolded in schematic form: the Annunciation, the Nativity, the Baptism, and so forth, down to the Resurrection and the Ascension. All the remaining space in the arches and the vertical surface of the walls will be devoted to saints, who represent the New Dispensation, that is, the Church Universal. The saints are not engaged in any action; they are either in bust or full figure, facing the beholder frontally and dressed in the costume appropriate to their calling: martyrs, holy warriors, bishops, physicians, deacons, monks. To facilitate recognition, each saint is clearly inscribed with his name. If you are familiar with Byzantine iconography, you may be able to recognize the more famous saints by their facial characteristics, their hairstyle, the shape and color of their beard (if indeed they are bearded), but for the majority of them, the inscription is the only means of identification.

The mural decoration of a Byzantine church may not be a *speculum mundi*, but it is a *speculum salvationis*, conveying in abridged form the main stages of God's grand design (*oikonomia*). The role of the Old Testament is merely to announce the Incarnation, which is the nodal point of the providential scheme, while the history of the faithful after the coming of Christ is embodied in the saints, who sustain the edifice of the Church and bridge the gap between the ordinary believer and the timeless presences higher up.

It is true that the majority of saints represented in a Byzantine church are not what we, from our historicist perspective, would call Byzantine saints. Such a distinction held no meaning for the Byzantine mind. The story of humanity after Christ was one: it was the realm of grace (*charis*) as opposed to the realm of the law (*nomos*) and was exemplified by human beings who had pleased God and who formed, next to the angelic host, God's court or retinue. Chronology was of no consequence: the apostles lived in timeless communion with the victims of the persecutions of the second to fourth centuries, the desert fathers, the bishops of the patristic age, and the heroes of the struggle against Iconoclasm in the eighth and ninth centuries. The most popular saints, the ones most frequently portrayed, tended to be shadowy figures from a distant past: St. George, St. Theodore, St. Demetrios, St. Nicholas, Sts. Cosmas and Damian. Nothing definite was known about them except that many of them had been tortured and put to death by some "tyrant" in the days when Christians were persecuted. Every Byzantine knew, however, that St. Demetrios was the patron of Thessalonike, St. Nicholas of Myra, St. Theodore of Euchaita in the Pontos, whereas Sts. Cosmas and Damian had their principal power base in a suburb of Constantinople. In that sense the saints were the successors of local gods and heroes.

From Martyr to Confessor and Holy Monk

The beginning of the Byzantine period (if we define it as starting in the reign of Constantine) was immediately preceded by the Great Persecution (303–312). In some places more than in others, in fits and starts, depending on the zeal or slackness of the government bureaucracy, the persecution left behind it a trail of many thousands of victims whose memory needed to be kept alive before it was forgotten. Eusebios of Caesarea, in the last part of his *Ecclesiastical History,* recorded all the cases known to him, especially in his native Palestine, setting down in detail the tortures that were inflicted on each victim and the exact date of death. He parades before our eyes a long string of heroes—priests and state officials, young and old, virgins and married women—all uniformly brave and unswerving. Soon memorial shrines (*martyria*) would be built to them and their names inscribed in commemorative calendars. The church did not forget its martyrs, but the martyrs themselves were denied all personality. They became names in a list: Anthimos, bishop of Nikomedeia, beheaded, 3 September.

After the Edict of Toleration, opportunities for martyrdom greatly diminished, if they did not disappear altogether. The brief pagan interlude under Emperor Julian (361–363) is said to have produced a number of martyrs, some of them certainly fictitious. Others are said to have suffered under the Arian Valens (364–378). Finally, the iconoclastic crisis in the eighth and ninth centuries led to the death of a few especially determined defenders of the cause of icons. With these exceptions, it was only outside the empire that Christians could still die for their faith, in Zoroastrian Persia followed by the Muslim caliphate and in pagan Bulgaria.

Broadly speaking, however, the era of the martyrs had ceased with Constantine, and their mantle was assumed by two other categories of Christian heroes, the confessor and the holy monk. The confessor is usually defined as the person who suffers persecution and hardship, but not violent death, in upholding his faith or, more specifically, the correct doctrine. That occurred more often than not when the imperial government was of a heretical persuasion, the heresies in question being Arianism, Monothelitism (in the seventh century), and Iconoclasm. The archetypal confessors were Athanasios of Alexandria (d. 373), who suffered five successive periods of exile for upholding the Catholic doctrine against an Arian government, and John Chrysostom (d. 407), who was unjustly deposed and died in exile for having stood up, not against heresy, but against malevolence and intrigue in high places.

A semantic *glissement* contributed to the blurring of boundaries between categories of sanctity. Witness (*martyria*) and confession or profession (*homologia*) were cognate terms. "Fight the good fight of faith," wrote St. Paul (1 Tim. 6:12–13), "lay hold of eternal life, whereunto thou hast been called, and hast professed a good profession (*homologian*) before many witnesses. I give thee charge in the sight of God . . . and of Christ Jesus, who before Pontius Pilate witnessed (*martyrēsantos*) a good confession (*homologian*)." It was the duty of all Christians to bear witness to Christ. The meaning of *witness* could be narrowed to those who paid the ultimate price, but also widened to include other forms of endurance and renunciation, seeing that martyrdom was a special gift or grace conferred by God. The transition from the martyr, who was the "athlete of Christ" to the monk, who was likewise the "athlete of Christ," was largely prepared in the third century by Origen, who himself vainly sought martyrdom and had to content himself with lifelong renunciation. Furthermore, martyrdom was momentary, whereas the monk's "witnessing" was constant and continued to the moment of his death.

If we were to count all the saints who distinguished themselves in the Byzantine world down to the fifteenth century, we would surely find—making allowance for overlap between categories—that the number of confessors was quite small compared to that of holy monks. This is not the place to delve into the highly complex problem of the origin of monas-

ticism, which antedates the Byzantine period, but it is proper to emphasize the rapid and extraordinary success that this somewhat anarchic institution enjoyed. From Egypt, its presumed home, it spread like wildfire
to Syria and Mesopotamia, Palestine, and eastern Asia Minor, reaching
Constantinople by the end of the fourth century. The typical Byzantine
saint was and remained the monk, a person who, strictly speaking, stood
outside the structures of the official church in spite of repeated efforts to
bring monasticism under episcopal authority. He found his ultimate
model in St. John the Baptist and was, moreover, the ideal Christian inasmuch as he followed to the letter Christ's injunction, "If thou wilt be
perfect, go and sell that thou hast, and thou shalt have treasure in heaven"
(Matt. 19:21).

The monk's contest—for he, too, metaphorically speaking, was a soldier—was not with an iniquitous state, as had been the case with the
martyrs, but with the invisible powers of darkness, the demons who assail
human beings in various ways so as to block their salvation. The battlefield had shifted, but the adversary remained the same, seeing that paganism with all its institutions and deceptions, its sacrifices and oracles,
was a demonic invention. It was the Devil who had engineered the persecution of the church and who, after suffering a setback with the defeat of
paganism, diverted his energies to the multiplication of heresies. Seen
from that angle, martyrs, confessors, and monks all strove in the same
cause, which was the fight against the Devil and his demons, a fight that
would only be resolved by the Second Coming; and in that great battle the
monks, by virtue of their training (askēsis), were the true professionals.

The modern reader, who does not believe in demons, but does believe
in sociology, economic factors, and the like, is in a poor position to understand the world of early Christianity. He or she will either relegate
demons to the realm of fantasy or interpret them metaphorically as per-
sonifications of sins and passions. It is important, therefore, to state that
in the fourth and following centuries demons were perceived as perfectly
real beings. There were myriads of them filling the air above the earth,
lurking in the countryside, in caves, mountains, and marshes, and especially numerous among the vestiges of paganism, in statues and old
tombs. Demons took possession of human beings and farm animals,
causing various diseases, such as epilepsy and madness, and, once installed in a body, were unwilling to be ejected. They could also be im-
planted in persons by magicians, who used their incantations and curse
tablets (defixiones) to that end. The holy monk, who had acquired power
over the demons, was therefore best equipped to heal the sick.

It would require a separate chapter to plot the progress of demonology in the Mediterranean world. Suffice it to say that a belief in the existence of numberless maleficent powers was not part of classical paganism.

It had penetrated from the outside, largely, it seems, from Mesopotamia and Egypt, capturing the dispersed world of Judaism before the beginning of the Christian era. The New Testament acknowledges the existence of demons that cause derangement in humans and animals, but also refers to the Devil, who holds in his power all the kingdoms of the earth and sows the weeds that choke up the good wheat. The relation of the Devil to the inferior demons is not made explicit in the New Testament. The fact, however, that the Gospel does not contain a coherent theory of demonology cannot be construed to mean that demonology is marginal to its message. Christ (if he is correctly delineated) and his disciples believed in demons, as did the Jews of the diaspora. The Christian message was, in the first instance, addressed to an audience that held similar views, and its potency was demonstrated by successful acts of exorcism. The task of constructing a "science" of demonology on the basis of the obscure evidence provided by the Bible, coupled with the "experience" of the public, was accomplished by Christian theologians, largely in the second and third centuries.

As we enter the fourth century, we see that demonology, which had earlier been regarded with disdain by Greek and Roman intellectuals, had won almost universal acceptance and become a very potent instrument in the hands of the church. Christians held a magic more efficacious than that of Jewish or Egyptian sorcerers. They were able to expel demons in the name of Christ with additional help from angels and archangels.

We are now in a better position to enter the world of the holy monk. If his primary role is to conduct the fight against demons, he must make himself a specialist in that kind of warfare. He knows that mastery over the forces of darkness is not granted without adequate training. Demons are basically weak, but they are persistent and resourceful. They act upon the imagination by inflaming passions—concupiscence in the first instance, gluttony, avarice, envy, and anger. They cause delusions. They frighten human beings by appearing to them in the guise of wild beasts, repulsive insects, reptiles, giants, or soldiers. On the other hand, they may impersonate saints, angels, or even Jesus Christ. By abstaining from food and drink, by hardship and constant prayer, the true monk gradually purifies his intellect until he has acquired the gift of "the discernment (*diakrisis*) of spirits." He can now see the demons under their various disguises and even smell them, for demons emit an evil stench. By being able to recognize them and to tell the difference between the more and the less dangerous kind, he is in a position to undo their work and drive them away.

The archetypal monastic saint is St. Antony, who is also the subject of the earliest known biography of a Christian saint, probably composed in the 360s. It does not concern us here whether the Life was or was not

written by Athanasios, patriarch of Alexandria, to whom it is tradition-
ally attributed, but it is worth noting that it proved an instant best-seller,
was immediately translated into Latin (twice) and other languages, and
exercised a lasting influence on all subsequent hagiography. If we had possessed information about Antony from a variety of sources, we would
have been in a better position to judge if his Life was reliable in factual
terms and in presenting a convincing portrait of the man. Such, however,
is not the case. We know Antony only through his Life: the man and the
document are for us one and the same.

The modern reader who picks up the Life of Antony will be struck
by the omission of certain kinds of information that we normally expect
of a biography. First, no dates are given. Admittedly, a number of clues
are scattered up and down the text, and it is possible by combining them
to work out an approximate chronology. That, however, is left to the historian to do for himself. Second, the geographical setting is extremely
vague. Antony is born and bred in a village in Egypt, but we are not told
where that village was. He withdraws to an unspecified desert and, once
again, to a remoter wilderness, which appears to be at the foot of a mountain and where he is thirteen days' journey from Nitria. Third, and most
important, there is no characterization of the hero either physically or
morally. Beyond the facts that he was illiterate, spoke only Egyptian, was
neither too tall nor too broad, always wore a happy expression, and remained in robust good health to the age of 105, there is nothing in the
text to convey a mental picture of the man. Beyond being a saint, Antony
has no personality.

We are left, therefore, with his reported actions. He remains at home
until the age of eighteen or twenty, when his parents die, whereupon he
gives away his inheritance, making some provision for his sister. He then
embarks on his *askēsis*, which falls into three stages both in terms of physical remoteness and of perfection: first, at a short distance from his village, where he supports himself as a laborer; second, in the desert, where
he remains confined for twenty years, finally emerging in public as a
healer and propagator of the monastic ideal; third, in the "inner desert."
He visits a city only twice, the first time during the Great Persecution,
when he follows the arrested Christians to Alexandria and ministers to
the confessors in prison and in quarries. He wishes to become a martyr
himself, but for reasons that are not explained, does not succeed in so
doing. His second visit to Alexandria, on the invitation of unnamed bishops, is to denounce the Arian heresy. Except for these two interludes on
a wider stage, Antony's career may be described by our standards as un-
eventful. It is, however, dominated by an unceasing inner struggle against
the devil, which is what the biography is really about. The temptations
are described as a "dust storm of imaginings" and form a progression,

starting with a longing for family, possessions, and the comforts of home life, going on to sexual desire, and culminating in hallucinations accompanied by physical violence. The long sermon that Antony is made to deliver is largely devoted to the nature and behavior of demons, presented in accordance with an elaborate and coherent system. Demons are envisaged as inhabiting the air, which is by nature turbulent in contrast to the serenity of the heavens. Having their station in the air, demons are able to intercept the upward progress of human souls, claiming those that are subject to them and letting pass only those that are pure. Here already we meet the curious concept of the aerial customs houses (*telōnia*), which was to play an important part in Byzantine speculation about death and the afterlife.

In addition to its emphasis on demonology, Antony's Life has been deliberately slanted to serve the interests of a particular ecclesiastical party, namely, that of Patriarch Athanasios. Antony is represented as the declared enemy of heretics (Meletians, Arians, and Manichaeans) and the upholder of the order of the church. He shows due respect for bishops and priests. We may well wonder if a man who, under Constantine, was apparently ignorant of the fact that the reigning emperor was Christian, and who, by his withdrawal from society, had placed himself outside the ministry and sacraments of the church, was really in a position to hold strong views about the very subtle theological doctrines that divided the Catholics from the Arians. We may also wonder whether monasticism in the form in which Antony practiced it was not a threat to the established church, whose organization it entirely bypassed. Whoever wrote the Life appears to have been anxious to harness to the Catholic cause a charismatic figure and a movement that he saw as wielding great influence.

We have stopped to examine the Life of Antony for a number of reasons. It offers us the earliest and one of the clearest statements of monastic ideology and of its intimate link with the world of the demonic. It provides the model for all subsequent hagiography. Furthermore, it teaches us that the study of the saint is really the study of hagiography. More of that later.

WHO WAS A SAINT?

We have said that the majority of Byzantine saints were monks, but that does not answer the question how one became a saint. The Eastern Orthodox Church, until the very end of the Middle Ages, did not have a regular process of canonization. In theory, sanctity was conferred by God, not by a committee of men, and was normally manifested by posthumous miracles. In practice, of course, it was a different matter. If we may look at the process in reverse, the final stage of recognition was inclusion in the liturgical calendar (*synaxarion*), of which the fullest and most authoritative redaction was that of Constantinople. It is a bulky compilation listing, at a rough guess, some two thousand saints and indicating the church or churches of the capital in which each saint's commemorative service (*synaxis*) was celebrated, many entries being accompanied by a brief biographical sketch. The *synaxarion*, as we have it, is a product of the tenth or eleventh century. Once it had been compiled and disseminated, it had the effect of limiting the number of later entrants. The company of saints became a *numerus clausus*. Indeed, very few new members were added from the twelfth to the fifteenth century.

If we look more closely at the saints commemorated in the *synaxarion*, we find them to be a pretty mixed bag. They include, for example, Emperor Justinian I (527–565), who, far from being a saint, was regarded by his contemporary, the historian Prokopios, as a demon incarnate. There is also an entry for the emperor "Justinian the Younger of pious memory." Can that really be Justinian II (685–695; 705–711), a monster of iniquity and cruelty? Patriarch Photios (858–867; 877–886), a great scholar but hardly a saint, is there along with his lifelong enemy, the austere patriarch Ignatios (847–858; 867–877). There are, of course, many other bishops and patriarchs of dubious credentials (forty-nine of Constantinople alone), many founders of monasteries, even saints who have been split into two or three separate persons. How did all of them get into the *synaxarion*? Presumably by a lengthy process of compilation from earlier calendars, both urban and monastic, from literary sources (like the *Ecclesiastical History* of Eusebios), and from the diptychs of individual churches. It goes without saying that a great many mistakes occurred in the course of transmission.

That still does not answer our initial question, but only pushes it back to an earlier stage. Granted that the *synaxarion* of Constantinople was compiled from earlier calendars, how did the latter come to include certain saints and not others? The answer is not always the same, but in some cases is quite clear. Let us take a concrete case. The monastery of St. Glykereia, situated on a little island about halfway between Constantinople and Nikomedeia, was refounded in the first half of the twelfth century and became for a time a prestigious establishment. Its renovator was an Armenian nobleman called Gregory Taronites, possibly the general of that name who rebelled against Emperor Alexios I (1081–1118) and was punished by imprisonment. Gregory became a monk and founded his own monastery. The only miracle he is said to have performed was expelling from his island the multitude of field mice that had infested it, but he is also described as being endowed with the gift of second sight. After his demise he was naturally entered in the monastery's own calendar, which was later copied and copied again in manuscripts that traveled beyond the confines of the monastery. In this manner a figure of strictly local interest entered the wider circle of recognized saints.

The lesson to be drawn from our short digression is that in our quest for the Byzantine saint we cannot take the list of some two thousand members contained in the *synaxarion* or any similar list and reduce them to a common denominator. Emperor Justinian bore as little resemblance to St. Antony of the desert as the latter did to Patriarch Photios. We shall, therefore, confine ourselves to what, rightly or wrongly, we may regard as typical representatives of Byzantine sanctity. Most of them will belong to the class of "holy men and women," but we shall add a few other examples to round off the picture.

The Living Dead

Since early Christian times the tomb of the saint had been the locus of his cult. The tomb was also the ultimate test of sanctity, for there was a fundamental distinction between the bones of an ordinary mortal and those of the saint. The case is expressed very clearly in the Miracles of St. Thekla, who had a great shrine at Seleukeia in Isauria (southeastern Asia Minor). In about the year 400, the bishop of Seleukeia, acting under some pressure, authorized the burial, in the south aisle of Thekla's shrine, of a prominent and respected person. No sooner had the grave diggers started to lift up the paving slabs than the saint stopped them in their tracks. She then appeared in a nocturnal vision to the bishop and reproached him for dishonoring her church by implanting in it "the stench of cemeteries and tombs." Tombs and churches, she explained, had nothing in common, except in the case of the dead who were not dead, but were living in the Lord and were consequently worthy of sharing the habitation of martyrs. One could not have asked for a clearer definition. There were the dead dead and the living dead, who were the saints. A supernatural sign of approval was sometimes manifested at the time of burial. Thus, when St. John the Almsgiver (to whom we shall return) was being interred in a sarcophagus that contained the bodies of two predeceased holy bishops, these two bodies made a space between themselves as if they had awakened to welcome St. John in their midst. In this way they indicated to the assembled congregation the glory that had been granted to the saint. The opposite phenomenon was also common: the body of a sinner was often cast out by his neighbors in burial.

The seal of divine approval was thus conferred on the saint at the time of his interment, and he remained alive in his tomb, which regularly emitted a sweet smell. The tomb became a source of healing. Even the oil of the lamp that burnt in front of it had miraculous powers to cure disease and drive away demons. The tombs of some exceptional saints had the further distinction of exuding oil (St. Demetrios, St. Nicholas) or blood (St. Euphemia). Who was a saint was not, therefore, a question that occurred to the Byzantine mind. God himself provided the answer at the point of death. On a few occasions he might even remove the body to an undisclosed location, as happened to St. Symeon, the holy fool of Emesa (Homs in Syria), who was active in the sixth century. Symeon died a pauper as he lay under a heap of twigs in his humble hut. When his absence had been noticed, some people discovered his corpse and, without washing it, without candles or incense, took it unceremoniously to the common cemetery for strangers and buried it. Symeon's protector and confidant, a certain deacon John, was alerted; he had the grave opened so as to give the body an honorable burial, but found it missing, for the Lord had moved it and thereby glorified it. That, in the hagiographer's words, was "the seal and confirmation" of the saint's immaculate way of life. To put it another way, there was neither tomb nor relics.

HAGIOGRAPHY

Some Byzantine saints are known to us from their writings, their public actions, and references to them by contemporaries, which make it possible to gain some understanding of their personality and express a judgment that may not be entirely favorable. Cyril of Alexandria may remind us more of a gangster than a saint, and even the great John Chrysostom has evoked among historians fairly mixed feelings. In most cases, however, hagiography provides the only (or the principal) record. That being so, we must familiarize ourselves with the mechanisms of Byzantine hagiography, which was neither a naive nor a candid medium.

No two cases are exactly alike, so let us take a hypothetical one. St. X, let us assume, was the founder of a monastery in the sixth century. He had come from another province, embraced the monastic life in a certain community, then became a solitary. After many years of ascetic struggle and several changes of location, he had come to his final abode, gathered a number of disciples, and organized an independent establishment. A monastery, it must be understood, was not simply a spiritual brotherhood; it needed buildings, no matter how simple, a chapel, a mausoleum, fields to till. In other words, it needed an endowment. By his supernatural gifts and powers of healing, St. X extracts benefactions from rich people. His fame spreads. As he is already at an advanced age or even dead, one of his disciples decides to compose his biography. He recollects such stories as he may have heard from the saint and questions his brethren concerning their memories. The chances are that the saint's distant origin and early career have been quite forgotten. They can be glossed over or, better, invented according to a recognized schema. The rest is likely to consist of disconnected episodes, whose chronological sequence has become obscured. With whatever materials come to hand, a biography is composed. If it is not in sufficiently good Greek, a man of letters may be commissioned to correct it. The purpose of the Life is to advertise the monastery through the person of its saintly founder and to provide a lection, that is, a text that will be read out on his anniversary, public recitation being more widespread than private reading. Consequently, the founder needs to be presented as a typical saint, an embodiment of all the monastic virtues, not as an individual with all the peculiarities and foibles that distinguish one human being from another.

The biography is now launched on what is often a long and tortuous course. Its fate in the first instance is tied up with the monastery for whose benefit it was composed. If the monastery declines and disappears, the text may disappear with it. Let us assume, however, that the text survives by being copied into a menologion, a collection of Lives arranged in the order of the calendar. Thus salvaged, it may even be translated into another language, for example, Syriac, and from Syriac into Arabic and from Arabic into Georgian. In the most favored cases we happen to possess the original Life. Such, for example, are those of Hypatios by Kallinikos (fifth century), the several excellent biographies composed by Cyril of Skythopolis (sixth century), the Life of St. Theodore of Sykeon (seventh century), of St. Ioannikios by Peter (ninth century), and many others. Very often, however, only a translation, a paraphrase, or a résumé has come down to us.

We now reach the tenth century, which witnessed a massive effort to collect and reedit in uniform style the Lives of the important saints, an enterprise that is principally associated with the activity of an imperial official named Symeon Metaphrastes (the Paraphraser). Our biography, if judged of sufficient interest, may then have been retold by Symeon's team of ghostwriters, a process that involved not only a stylistic facelift but also the elimination of all unnecessary or unsuitable detail. When that had been done, the "improved" text was assured of survival, given the fact that Symeon's edition was issued in hundreds of copies, but the original text, now no longer necessary, may well have been lost. That was not the end of the process: the biography would then have been abbreviated in several forms for inclusion in various liturgical calendars. The saint's memorial day would have inspired rhetorical laudations and hymns in verse.

Why have we set down all these details? Because, to repeat, the Byzantine saint in most cases is not an entity separate from his hagiographic dossier. He is entirely contained in that dossier and is himself a liturgical construct. His personality has been almost completely obliterated. What remains is a partial account of certain actions (which may be true or false) and some particulars about his cult. To sift out the factual content of his actions is the task of historical criticism. The historian cannot simply accept what he reads in the text if he wishes to establish what the saint actually did, but he can use the entire text for other purposes. He will often find in it a sprinkling of authentic and vivid information bearing on daily life, which is why Byzantine hagiography has been quarried by social and economic historians. He is also entitled to treat the text as the expression of a certain *mentalité*, of the ideals that the Byzantines set before themselves and the limits of their intellectual world. Now for some concrete examples, which I have chosen not only to introduce certain types of saint, but also to show the workings of the hagiographic process.

St. Matrona, Founder of a Nunnery

The first thing to be said about Matrona—for one can never be too careful in such matters—is that she did exist. She is mentioned in a chronicle source as being in circa 499 one of the leaders of monastic establishments at Constantinople who opposed the religious policy of the reigning emperor Anastasios. In the prolonged dispute between Catholics and Monophysites, Anastasios, like his predecessor Zeno (474–491), adopted a policy of conciliation toward the "heretical" party and sought to enforce the "edict of union" (Henotikon) that Zeno had issued to that effect. The patriarch of Constantinople, Makedonios (496–511), was supposed to make sure that the recalcitrant monks and nuns, who rejected the Henotikon as a dangerous fudge, followed the imperial line, but faced with their obstinate opposition, decided to leave them alone and not persecute them. Among the recalcitrants who refused communion with the official church is mentioned our Matrona. She is described as "being still alive" (which means that she must have died soon thereafter) and as having performed "many wonders" while pressure to conform was being applied to her by a certain Chrysaorios, deacon of the cathedral. In other words, Matrona gained some notoriety in the good fight for the Catholic doctrine, and one might have expected that her principled stand in the face of coercion would have been one of the elements of her posthumous fame.

Matrona's hagiographic dossier is very simple. It consists of a Life, its paraphrase done in the *officina* of Symeon Metaphrastes, and a résumé of the same. The Life, therefore, is all we have to read. It was written not before 550 by an anonymous author who does not claim personal knowledge of the saint, but states that he had drawn his information from Matrona's lifelong companion named Eulogia. The Life tells the story of a woman who was pursued by her tyrannical husband from one country to another until she found peace in a nunnery she established with a number of female companions. Is it, broadly speaking, a true story or a fiction?

A native of Perge in Pamphylia (in southern Asia Minor), Matrona turns up at Constantinople, aged twenty-five, with her husband Dometianos and a small daughter, Theodote. We are not told why they have come to the capital, but we may suspect that Dometianos had some official business there. Being of a pious disposition and evidently repelled by her husband, Matrona makes contact with a group of devout women who served in one capacity or another in the church of the Holy Apostles. With their help she moves out of her family home, entrusts her daughter to the care of a widow, and decides to abscond. Suspected by Dometianos of practicing prostitution, she disguises herself as a eunuch and enters a men's monastery directed by one Bassianos, a Syrian, who may be described as a monastic entrepreneur. Soon she is detected because her ears are pierced and is escorted out of the monastery. She finds that her daughter had died in the meantime. Dometianos is on her heels, so the companions of Bassianos take counsel and ship her out secretly to a nunnery at Emesa (in Syria) with which they have contact. Matrona does well there and rises to the position of abbess. She performs a vicarious miracle (the only one credited to her) by curing a blind man with the holy oil that exuded from the recently discovered head of St. John the Baptist (found in 452). Her fame spreads. Apprised of it, the persistent Dometianos hurries off to Emesa to claim his wife, but she slips off to Jerusalem. From there, still pursued by Dometianos, she flees to Mount Sinai and thence to the outskirts of Berytus (Beirut), where she takes up residence in an abandoned pagan temple haunted by demons. She becomes something of a local celebrity. Rich ladies of Beirut, mounted on chariots or carried in litters, go out to visit her and she converts daughters of pagans. She is anxious, however, to return to Constantinople and see again Bassianos and her former fellow monks who had been so kind to her. Dometianos having by now dropped out of the picture, she takes ship to the capital in the company of some highly placed ladies. She makes contact with Bassianos, who is delighted to see her again, and takes up hired lodgings together with eight other women she had brought from Beirut. Soon she attracts the attention of Empress Verina, wife of Leo I, and of the Augusta Euphemia, wife of Anthemios, former emperor of Rome, but asks no favors of them. The wife of the immensely rich patrician Sporakios presses her to take possession of one of her many estates, and she chooses one, just within the walls of Constantinople, in a quiet neighborhood, next to several monasteries, including that of Bassianos. It is small but has a rose garden. The deeds are drawn up, and Matrona with her imported companions comes into full ownership of the estate.

All that remains now is to build a monastery and that requires money.

Fortunately, there are many rich women at Constantinople, and a bene-factress soon turns up. She is called Athanasia and is only eighteen years old. Married to a dissolute husband whom she heartily dislikes, she has a small child who dies soon thereafter. After various adventures, Athanasia packs off her husband, recuperates her considerable patrimony, and joins Matrona's community. Resources are now available to wall the property, build a three-storey chapel, endow the establishment, and even distribute some money to other monasteries as well as to anchorites in Jerusalem, Emesa, Beirut, and the entire East. Athanasia dies fifteen years later, but Matrona lives on to the age of nearly a hundred. The Devil, whom she had offended at Beirut, torments her in her dreams, but shortly before her death she is accorded a vision of the Virgin Mary in Paradise, that being the divine "seal" signifying approval of her saintly career. No post-humous miracles are recorded.

Such in outline is the Life of Matrona. How far can we trust it? Its learned editor, Hippolyte Delehaye, one of the greatest connoisseurs of Greek hagiography, was somewhat skeptical of it. Indeed, some reasons for doubt are not lacking. Particularly surprising is the omission of Ma-trona's main claim to fame, the resistance she offered to the religious pol-icy of Emperor Anastasios. The deacon Chrysaorios, who exerted pres-sure on her, never appears in the story. There is only an oblique statement toward the end of the Life to the effect that most of her exploits have been obscured by the storm that had overtaken the holy church and that she kept the Orthodox faith to the end. But if the author obtained his information, as claimed, from the saint's lifelong companion and was, therefore, writing soon after Matrona's demise, how is it that her exploits had been obscured? Was the author's reticence due to the fact that em-peror Anastasios was still on the throne? Yet there are clear signs that the Life as we have it could not have been written before 550.

Whatever the answers may be, the Life of Matrona does evoke a pre-cise setting, all the more interesting because it is one of a female society. Matrona evidently came from a rich family and moved with ease among women of wealth and influence. The only virtuous men who are intro-duced into the story are monks, whereas husbands are evil and children do well to die young, thereby releasing their mothers from worldly obliga-tions. Matrona finds contentment in the company of her fellow nuns, whom she dresses not in woolen girdles and veils, as was customary among women, but in wide leather belts and men's white cloaks. A psy-chologist may make something out of that. Matrona works practically no miracles, nor does she undertake any harsh form of asceticism. The de-monic element plays a very modest part in her Life. One is left wondering whether her claim to sanctity was due to the persecution she endured at the hands of her husband or to the fact that she founded a nunnery and instituted in it a particular form of discipline.

A CHARITABLE BISHOP

St. John the Almsgiver served as patriarch of Alexandria during a particularly critical period of history. A Cypriot by birth and himself the son of a governor of Cyprus, he was neither a monk nor a clergyman but a rich married man and the father of children. In 609 the Byzantine Empire was not only under attack from Persia but also rent by a civil war between the detested emperor Phocas and the leaders of an insurrection that had started at Carthage, namely Herakleios (who was to become emperor the following year) and his cousin Niketas. The rebels managed to win Egypt and Cyprus, and John, whose wife and children had apparently died, was ordained patriarch of Alexandria.

To serve as imperially appointed bishop of Alexandria was a risky business at the best of times because the greater part of Egyptians tended to the Monophysite persuasion and Alexandrians were notoriously addicted to rioting. When John assumed the post, things were even worse because of the Persian invasion of Syria and Palestine, the flood of refugees flowing into Egypt, food shortages, and the need to ransom prisoners and help the Christians in the Holy Land. It seems that John performed his duties with vigor and tact. In the tenth year of his ministry, as the Persians were advancing on Alexandria, he fled to his native Cyprus. He built and endowed a church in honor of St. Stephen in the city of Amathos and died shortly thereafter (some time after 620). That much seems reasonably certain.

There is no reason to doubt that John was a compassionate man in addition to being a skillful administrator. He may even have deserved the honors of sanctification. However that may have been, two of his friends named John Moschos (author of the immensely popular *Pratum spirituale*) and Sophronios (later to become patriarch of Jerusalem) delivered in his honor a funerary laudation in which some of his notable achievements were narrated. These included his struggle against the Monophysites, his charity to refugees, the building of hostels and maternity wards, measures against sodomy, help sent to captured Jerusalem, and a few other incidents of the same kind, all perfectly credible. The laudation, originally written in high literary style, has not come down to us *in toto,* but we have a résumé of it. A little later, in 641 to be precise, the then archbishop of Cyprus decided that a supplementary biography of John was needed and commissioned it from one of his suffragans, Leontios of Neapolis, who had already given proof of his talent as a hagiographer. That was probably done for the benefit of the city of Amathos, where John lay buried and where his tomb was beginning to prove miraculous; perhaps also in the interests of anti-Monophysite propaganda. As far as we can tell, Leontios had not known John, but was nevertheless able to compile a whole string of lively anecdotes, which he falsely pretended to have either witnessed himself or heard from an Alexandrian informant. The anecdotes are well told in colloquial Greek, and many of them are certainly of Alexandrian provenance, but it is difficult to tell if they actually had anything to do with John the Almsgiver; some certainly did not. The next step was to combine the résumé of the funerary laudation and the supplementary Life (paraphrased into more elegant Greek) into a single text, which was again paraphrased in the tenth century and then boiled down to less than a page for insertion into the *synaxarion* of Constantinople under John's feast day of 12 November. Here we read that John was canonically ordained to the patriarchal see of Alexandria. He served many years, performed innumerable miracles, distributed alms to the poor, converted to the true faith many infidels, and finally migrated unto the Lord in extreme old age. The lineaments of a real person have been completely obliterated. John has become an icon to be hung on the wall alongside the icons of other holy bishops. What, finally, do we know about John? Perhaps only what survives in the résumé of the laudation by Moschos and Sophronios. As to the anecdotes told in the supplementary Life by Leontios, they cast much incidental light on life in Alexandria but prove impervious to historical verification.

AN INVENTED SAINT

Byzantine hagiography is full of fictions. There are Lives of saints who in all probability never existed. There are Lives of historical personages, indeed very famous ones, that completely distort their known actions and turn them into a fable: the numerous Lives of Emperor Constantine, those of St. Epiphanios of Salamis and St. John Chrysostom fall into this category. There are also Lives of saints of whom nothing whatever happened to be known. Here is an example of the third group.

St. Sampson the *xenodochos* (administrator of a hostel) was the reputed founder of the biggest and most famous hospital of Constantinople, a multistorey building that was situated between the churches of St. Sophia and St. Irene and formed part of the welfare system administered by the cathedral. There is an icon of Sampson, carved in marble, in the Istanbul Archaeological Museum. It shows a man with a medium-length beard holding a Gospel book (hence a priest) and looking, as usual, straight ahead. We would dearly like to know something about Sampson.

Until recently all the available documentation was a Life, augmented by posthumous miracles, in the edition of Symeon Metaphrastes and a derivative notice in the *synaxarion*. The late Father F. Halkin, an indefatigable editor of Greek hagiographical works, was able to discover an earlier text, not so much a Life as a laudation, which Symeon Metaphrastes must have had before him. What do we learn from the new text? First, that its anonymous author was writing a long time after Sampson's lifetime. The saint's deeds, he says, had been almost obscured by the passage of time—almost, but not entirely. Indeed, Sampson hailed from Rome and was the scion of a rich and aristocratic family, descended, no less, from Emperor Constantine. He was educated in holy Scripture and later, it seems, in medicine. When his parents had died, he gave all his wealth to the poor, manumitted his slaves, and came to Constantinople, where he attracted the notice of Patriarch Menas (536–552) and was ordained priest at the age of thirty. He lived in a small house, which is still to be seen, and there tended the sick. Emperor Justinian happened to fall gravely ill with a disease of the genital organs and saw in a dream that he was surrounded by a throng of prominent physicians. An angel pointed out to him a man of humble mien and said, "No one but he can cure you." After a search, Sampson was found and, of course, healed the emperor. He refused all reward, only insisting that at his house, which was next to St. Sophia then under construction (532–537), a hospital be built, and so it was done. At that time the general Belisarios returned from Africa bringing with him the immense treasure of the Vandal king Gelimer (534), one-third of which was allotted to the hospital. And so, after tending the sick for many years and attaining extreme old age, Sampson died and was buried on 27 June in the big church of St. Mokios in the crypt underneath the altar table. His tomb proved miraculous and emitted a holy oil. As for the hospital, it remained as a wonder to future generations, even if it had suffered from fires in the course of civil disorders.

All that can be said in favor of the above account is that the chronological indications it furnishes are more or less contemporary with one another: the author had done a little historical research. In fact, however, the hospital is known to have burned during the so-called Nika revolt in January 532, and in recording this event the historian Prokopios states that it had been built "in earlier times" by a certain pious man called Sampson. In other words, Sampson, of whom nothing was apparently known, had lived well before the time of Justinian. The Life or laudation, probably composed for public delivery on the saint's feast day, is a complete fabrication woven round two physical features: the little house, perhaps contained in the hospital complex, in which Sampson was believed to have started his medical career, and the miraculous tomb in the basilica of St. Mokios, which was a cemeterial church in the western section of the city. The existence of a cult created the need for a biography, and so

Sampson the *xenodochos,* like so many other saints whose identity had been forgotten, was launched on his hagiographical career.

Escalating the Mortifications

Monasticism, the breeding ground of Byzantine sanctity, did not at first seek publicity; indeed, it desired—or so we are led to believe—the very opposite. By its very success, however, it was bound to attract widespread curiosity. Before the end of the fourth century, "reporters" risked being pursued by brigands and devoured by crocodiles to penetrate to the very depths of Egypt so as to bring back a firsthand account of the accomplishments of the new breed of "philosophers." And so a new genre of literature was born that may be termed "sketches of monastic life." It proved enormously popular. The *Historia monachorum in Aegypto* was quickly followed by the *Lausiac History* (ca. 420), so called because it was dedicated to the imperial chamberlain Lausos, one of the most influential men in the empire. To claim the same measure of celebrity for Syria as had been enjoyed by Egypt, Theodoret of Cyrrhus composed his *Historia religiosa,* while in the sixth century the Monophysite John of Amida (often called John of Ephesos after the name of his see) wrote *The Lives of the Eastern Saints* in which he exalted the exploits of his coreligionists. In the seventh century John Moschos, who had traveled all over the Near East collecting monastic stories, championed in his *Pratum spirituale* the Catholic, that is, anti-Monophysite wing. Regional and interconfessional rivalries are not far from the surface in these collections, which were endlessly anthologized in the following centuries.

The public, eternally simpleminded, wanted to know above all the precise technique whereby those holy men attained their legendary powers. There was, indeed, no uniformity in this respect: different monks put into practice different kinds of discipline. All of them underwent some kind of deprivation, but there were many degrees of deprivation. Food, drink, and sleep, clothing and bedding were obvious areas of interest. The Egyptian monks, as has often been remarked by others, avoided, on the whole, any excessively harsh or unnatural form of mortification. The great Apollô, leader of a community of five hundred, disapproved of those who wore irons on their body or grew their hair long. "These men," he would rightly say, "are exhibitionists and are seeking human praise, whereas they ought to subdue their body by means of fasting and do good works in secret. But instead of doing that, they are making themselves conspicuous." Apollô himself abstained from all cooked food, including bread, confining himself six days a week to such plants as grew naturally in the desert. He performed a hundred genuflections every day and another hundred every night. He slept in a cave. He wore a short-sleeved tunic and a turban on his head. All these details are carefully set down because they constituted the saint's particular regimen (*ergasia*), which invited imitation or simply curiosity.

The future, however, lay with the exhibitionists. The analogy with martyrdom may have been one motivation: for, just as the martyrs had endured the most horrible tortures (lovingly detailed in their Passions), so the monks, too, being the successors of the martyrs, should subject themselves to the most severe punishment. A more cynical reading of the evidence suggests, however, that a quest for notoriety was, as Apollô had seen, an important factor. Conventional monasticism was no longer news; it needed to be made more eye-catching to excite the interest of the public. It was especially in Syria and Mesopotamia that the "excesses" of asceticism reached their most extreme expression and from there were carried to other parts of the empire. The monasticism of Constantinople was largely created by Syrians.

When we turn to the *Historia religiosa* of Theodoret, we find an increased severity of mortifications: monks inhabit huts or caves too small for the human body, they wear iron collars and chains, some of them never lie down, others remain entirely in the open, exposing themselves to the extremes of heat and cold. One monk spends ten years in a narrow cylindrical cage, which he has fashioned out of two wheels joined by planks and suspended in the air from a kind of tripod. Theodoret's prize exhibit is, however, St. Symeon Stylites (d. 459), the originator of one of the most bizarre and certainly the most spectacular form of asceticism. What induced Symeon to spend thirty-seven years standing on top of a column? Was it, as was said at the time, to serve by his physical position as intermediary between God and his angels in heaven and men on earth? Or was it to expose himself all the more to the attacks of demons, whose habitat was the air? Whatever explanation we find the most plausible (and many have been advanced), the fact remains that Symeon, like his imitators Daniel on the Bosporos and Symeon the Younger near Antioch, chose with particular care the location of his column. It was clearly visible from a main route of communication in an area that was then much more populous than it is now. All three stylites attracted great crowds of pilgrims and came to enjoy immense influence not only over ordinary people but also over dignitaries and emperors.

Writing at the end of the sixth century, the church historian Evagrios, himself a Syrian, describes with evident admiration the advances of monastic discipline. In addition to the monks who starved themselves in communities, he singles out the "grazers" (*boskoi*), men and women who went out into burning deserts, discarded their clothes, and fed off the ground. Over the years they came to resemble wild beasts and ran away from all human contact. Evagrios is especially enthusiastic about the small band of monks of whom St. Symeon of Emesa was the most famous representative. These were the holy fools who simulated madness and lived in cities, completely insensible to all human needs and passions. So deadened was their nature that they were able to converse with women and frequent baths and taverns without any moral danger—a gift they had acquired at the price of prolonged and scrupulous training. By casting themselves in the role of the most despised members of society, namely, the insane, they exposed themselves to complete humiliation and so overcame the sin of pride.

Of the monastic refinements pioneered in Syria and Mesopotamia, only that of the "grazers" was not destined for great success, perhaps because of the colder climate of the more northerly parts of the empire. Stylites and holy fools became, however, part of the common repertoire and produced many notable representatives in later periods. After the sixth century, no new or more bizarre form of mortification appears to have been introduced. Monasticism flowed on, with minor adjustments, in its two preestablished main channels, the communal (cenobitic) and the solitary (anachoretic). While the discipline recommended by St. Basil of Caesarea was generally respected, no monastic "orders" with specialized aims were introduced. In this regard Byzantium differs sharply from the West.

The Saint in Society

The pagan emperor Julian (361–363), who had been raised as a Christian and knew his opponents intimately, ridiculed Christian monks for their hatred of mankind: whereas human beings are naturally sociable, monks departed from the city and, being possessed by demons—note how the argument has been turned around—loaded themselves with chains and iron collars. Indeed, to the ancient mind, society was an urban phenomenon: by forsaking cities the monks manifested their misanthropy. Julian has here identified and exaggerated a fundamental antinomy in the model of sanctity offered by monasticism. How was withdrawal from the world to be reconciled with the ideal of philanthropy? Were the example and healing action of the saint to be addressed only to such rustics as happened to come in contact with him? Two courses were open: either the city dweller was to travel to the desert (which could only be done in a few cases), or the monk was to come to the city. In the city, however, the monk was like a fish out of water. The city was full of bustle and vain pursuits, of taverns, theaters, and brothels; it was not conducive to a life of quiet contemplation. Furthermore, it contained another source of spiritual authority, namely, the episcopal church, whose attitude toward monks was often ambivalent. Even so, we do find in the fourth and following centuries a growing movement of monks toward urban centers, where they establish themselves, at first not so much within the city perimeter as in the suburbs. By so doing they maintain a measure of separation, yet place themselves within easy reach of the urban people. Seeing that this migration was voluntary, we can only conclude that monks set a value on proximity to city dwellers. Did they wish to extend their ministry or, more cynically, gain better access to sources of influence and power?

Except for the "grazers," who entirely withdrew from human society, all Byzantine saints, even anchorites of the desert, exercised some social action. They healed the sick, exorcized demons, protected farm animals, admonished sinners, converted pagans, fought heresy, intervened on behalf of the wronged. The nature of his action depended not only on the saint's background, personality, and ambition, but also on his geographical location and the structure of the society in which he found himself. To illustrate the complexity of the situation I have chosen the example of a fifth-century "suburban" saint, Hypatios, who established himself close to Constantinople, on a rather grand estate that had once been owned by the praetorian prefect Rufinus (d. 395), hence on the border between rural Bithynia and the world of the capital. The variety of his social contacts reflects his intermediary position between country and city.

Although he never completed his education, Hypatios came from a respectable and lettered provincial family. He abandoned his station in society by running away from home and joining a monastic community in Thrace, where he pretended to have been a slave, but resumed contact with his family when his father, now widowed, discovered him in his hiding place. A more austere monk would have refused all commerce with relatives, but Hypatios accompanied his father to Constantinople, helped him with some business (perhaps a lawsuit) while lodging in the mansion of a rich citizen, and then decided not to return to the Thracian countryside. Joined by two companions, he crossed the Bosporos, allegedly in search of some remote mountain or cave, but discovered within a couple of miles of Chalcedon an abandoned and haunted monastery on the estate of Rufinus and established himself there for the rest of his life. Rufinianae, as it was called, was surely a very splendid complex and contained a palace in which members of the imperial family and other distinguished visitors would lodge from time to time—hardly a place where one would have sought anonymity and withdrawal from the world.

If we read carefully the biography of Hypatios, we discover several strands running through it: a paternal attitude toward neighboring peasants and other ordinary people, a criticism of the established church, and a cultivation of the rich and powerful. Hypatios is the beneficiary of donations from several important dignitaries, even the emperor himself, thanks to which the monastery is built up and provided with resources.

He repays his debt by performing various services: he exorcises the brother of a military count and refuses to be paid in gold for his trouble; heals the horses of the public post; helps a secretary who served in the prefecture to find some state papers he had lost; even consents to go out of his monastery in order to exorcise an imperial lady in waiting. While being the client of the powerful, Hypatios is also able, by virtue of his moral authority, to stand up to them in a manner that no ordinary person could afford. When, for example, he accepts as monks the runaway slaves of the consul Monaxios, he is able to refuse flatly their master's legitimate request for their surrender. He is warned of the danger he is incurring, yet manages to put the consul in his place by asserting God's superior claims.

What Hypatios is in relation to the powerful, the peasants, the poor, and the oppressed are in relation to him. In other words, he acts as an intermediary patron, channeling downward the benefactions he receives from above—a redistributor of wealth, usurping the role that was normally reserved to the church. Foreseeing famine, he buys with borrowed money large stocks of corn and then hands out free bread to the starving peasantry. He tends the sick with his own hands, cures farmers' animals and listens to complaints from the oppressed. The emperor's architect Elpidios, immensely rich, seeks his help to be delivered of a demon. Hypatios begins the treatment, but happens to hear from contractors and poor workmen that Elpidios had been cheating them. So he says to Elpidios, "It has been revealed to me that you are going to die. Go home and make amends to those you have defrauded if you wish to save your soul." Elpidios is about to do so, but is assured by his physicians that he is going to live and so dies in sin.

Hypatios also acts on the religious stage, making converts in a countryside that is still to a considerable extent pagan and combating widespread magical practices. He is driven to do so because the regular clergy is lazy and given to drunkenness. Even the bishop of Chalcedon, in whose jurisdiction the monastery of Hypatios lay, approves the restoration of the Olympic festival in his city's theater and needs to be told by a delegation of monks that the festival in question was an expression of unadulterated paganism and ought to be prohibited.

The model provided by Hypatios is more typical of the later Byzantine saint than that of the harsh ascetic from the East. Not being some exotic foreigner, he is not obliged, so to speak, to stand on his head to attract attention. His mortifications are moderate, and he is portrayed as a gentle person, although the precise nature of his spiritual authority remains elusive. His teaching, as reported, is conventional: love of God and one's neighbor, the importance of temperance (meaning the abstention not from all food but from varied food other than vegetables, legumes, and grains), avoidance of pride and *akēdia,* continuous prayer. It is possible, according to Hypatios, but difficult to live virtuously in the world. Marriage, in particular, leads to injustice because it creates a need for money and that leads to quarrels and perjury. The heart becomes hardened through daily cares, and one even stops going to church. Yet Hypatios does not advocate any social reform and singles out among the advantages enjoyed by monks the fact that they are honored by Christian kings and dignitaries. For that alone God can hardly be thanked enough.

In the centuries after Hypatios, the character of Byzantine society underwent many changes. The cultured provincial elites, to which Hypatios appears to have belonged, faded away. With the decline of cities in the seventh and eighth centuries, the former balance between town and country was completely altered. A new aristocracy of appointed or hereditary warlords sprouted up in Asia Minor. The loss of the eastern provinces (Syria, Palestine, Egypt) to the Arabs removed from the Byzantine scene the exponents of oriental asceticism who had been so conspicuous before. If the saint is defined by his involvement in society, it would follow that, in the different society of the Middle Ages, the saint would have acquired a different role. Yet that is not the impression we gain when we read the hagiography of the ninth, tenth, and eleventh centuries, not to go any later. True, the background landscape of the texts has changed: the scene of the saint's action is usually more restricted, there is greater insecurity and a lower level of "material culture." Even so, the ideals of sanctity appear to remain the same and so, *mutatis mutandis,* is the saint's role in society vis-à-vis both a changed aristocracy and the lower classes. Is it an optical illusion created by the texts which, by a strange quirk, tend to be written in more and more elegant Greek, while the general level of life has declined?

One last example may help us focus the issue. St. Luke or Hosios Loukas, as he is usually called, is probably the most famous saint of medieval Greece and founded an impressive monastery in Boeotia that is still standing. Its principal church is by medieval standards a big and sumptuous structure, decorated with costly marbles and mosaics, among which one can see a portrait of Loukas himself with intense eyes and pointed beard, his arms raised in prayer. In a crypt under the church, Loukas was laid to rest, and special arrangements were contrived to cater to an influx of pilgrims.

The fortunes of Loukas and his ancestors were overshadowed by the foreign invasions that swept over Greece in the ninth and tenth centuries. Himself descended from refugee farmers, Loukas had to flee twice in the face of barbarian attack from his chosen habitat. Even so, he did not travel very far: Athens, Thebes, and the two coasts of the gulf of Corinth marked the limits of his movements. Loukas never learned to read and write, but respected education and used to consult a scholar who was established at Corinth; he also respected the established church. He appears to have been something of a gardener and endears himself to the modern reader by his kindness to animals, a trait also recorded of earlier Palestinian saints. His "social" activity consists of acts of charity, which he began to practice as a boy, and giving hospitality to strangers. He helps two impoverished brothers to find buried treasure, causes a murderer to repent, enables a sea captain to catch fish, performs menial tasks for a stylite for a period of ten years, feeds refugees on an offshore island, saves a passing ship. Not so much a miracle worker as a clairvoyant, Loukas naturally comes to the attention of the authorities and is consulted in cases of need: he is invited to Corinth to help recover a sum of money that had been stolen from an imperial ambassador and advises the governor of Greece, one Pothos, to pay a visit to Constantinople at a juncture that appeared to threaten the official's career. Another governor, Krenites, invites him to dinner and, after an initial misunderstanding, becomes greatly attached to him. Krenites contributes money for the erection of a church at the saint's monastic retreat, the first stage of an ambitious building program that was to follow Loukas' death in 953.

Compared to Lives of saints who had flourished five centuries earlier, that of Loukas strikes us by the narrowness of its horizons and the relative triviality of its content. The rigors of the saint's ascetic initiation, the occasional demonic temptations, the insensibility (apatheia) he achieves, the afflictions that are visited on him are all true to type, as is also his relation to the world of officialdom and the aristocracy established in the provincial capital of Thebes. It is thanks to the financial support of the governor that the monastery is eventually built and becomes a place of pilgrimage—the posthumous miracles at the saint's tomb are more spectacular than any he is said to have accomplished in his lifetime. Once the cult is in place, the biography is commissioned in "high" literary Greek (for it is not the peasants that need to be impressed but members of the gentry), and the rustic clairvoyant is elevated to the status of a saint.

Here we may be approaching one of the reasons for the apparent uniformity through the centuries of Byzantine saints. Most of them were not only monks, but founders of monasteries because it was in the context of an organized community that their memory was most likely to be preserved and recorded in writing. Another type of saint, say a holy fool, had no institutional framework. He was by definition a "hidden servant of God" who concealed his sanctity and had neither following nor cult. There were certainly a great many holy fools down to the end of the Byzantine period, yet, not surprisingly, only two biographies of them are preserved, that of Symeon of Emesa, already mentioned, and that of Andrew of Constantinople, who is probably a fictitious figure and whose verbose "Life" was intended as a moral tract. In the twelfth century, St. Leontios, who ended as titular patriarch of Jerusalem, started his ascetic career as a holy fool at Constantinople, repeating the same exploits that Symeon had practiced in the sixth. Had he remained a fool to the end of his days, we would never have heard of him, but he went on to become abbot of the great monastery of St. John the Evangelist on the island of Patmos, and that is why his Life was written down and preserved in a manuscript that is still on Patmos.

The founder or abbot of a monastery, however much his biography may conceal his actual circumstances, was an administrator and fund-raiser who stood in a position of dependence toward wealthy patrons: that was as true of Hypatios in the sixth century as of Loukas in the tenth. The patron's generosity was the precondition of the establishment and expansion of the institution: hence the tension that may be observed in Byzantine hagiography. On the one hand, the genre demanded that the saint be portrayed as a man of God who sought nothing but quietude and rejected all worldly ambition; on the other hand, his association with the high and mighty needed some acknowledgment. Of course, the saint could not be represented as a sponger: donations were conferred on him freely and were not solicited. Even the lowly Loukas asserts his independence vis-à-vis the governor Krenites by upbraiding him for unseemly behavior, and only after Krenites had apologized does he consent to accept his familiarity and his money.

Undoubtedly, too, the model of the saint was self-perpetuating. It is not only we who read Byzantine saints' Lives (for purposes other than those intended); the Byzantines also read them, indeed, some of them read little else. They took careful note of the saints' exploits and discipline and were inspired to emulation. Far from being an obstacle, the antiquity of the models was a guarantee of recognized sanctity. Most of the monks depicted on the walls of Byzantine churches belong to early times: Antony, Euthymios, Onouphrios, Theodosios the Cenobiarch, Amun of Nitria. Only rarely does a medieval monk like John Klimakos or Loukas join their company. That may well explain the remarkable similarities we observe across a gulf of centuries. The Cypriot St. Neophytos (twelfth/thirteenth century), who did not receive the honors of a Life, clearly modeled himself on the great St. Sabas (sixth century).

The prestige of a distant past and the constraints of hagiography are among the reasons why the Byzantine saint, insofar as we can perceive him, remained faithful to early types. The nature of the Byzantine monastery, which tended more and more to become a small agricultural enterprise independent of ecclesiastical control, though often exploited by a private patron, was another factor. That is not to say that a more minute analysis may not reveal in different periods and in different regions greater departures from the norm than we have allowed here. To do so, however, one would have to write a whole book of a kind that has not been written yet.

Selected Bibliography

Antonius magnus eremita, ed. B. Steidle. Studia Anselmiana 38. Rome, 1956.

Brown, P. "The Rise and Function of the Holy Man in Late Antiquity." *Journal of Roman Studies* 61 (1971): 80–101.

The Byzantine Saint, ed. S. Hackel. University of Birmingham Fourteenth Spring Symposium of Byzantine Studies. London, 1981.

Canivet, P. *Le monachisme syrien selon Théodoret de Cyr.* Paris, 1977.

Dagron, G. "Les moines et la ville: Le monachisme à Constantinople jusqu'au concile de Chalcédoine (451)." *Travaux et Mémoires* 4 (1970): 229–76.

Delehaye, H. *Les légendes hagiographiques,* 4th ed. Subsidia Hagiographica 18a. Brussels, 1955.

———. *Les passions des martyrs et les genres littéraires.* Brussels, 1921.

———. *Les saints stylites.* Subsidia Hagiographica 14. Brussels, 1923.

———. *Sanctus: Essai sur le culte des saints dans l'antiquité.* Subsidia Hagiographica 17. Brussels, 1927.

Festugière, A. J. *Les moines d'Orient,* 4 vols. in 7 parts. Paris, 1961–65.

Patlagean, E. "Ancienne hagiographie byzantine et histoire sociale." *Annales: Economies, sociétés, civilisations* 23 (1968): 106–26.

Ševčenko, I. "Hagiography of the Iconoclast Period." In idem, *Ideology, Letters and Culture in the Byzantine World,* Study V. London, 1982.

———. "L'agiografia bizantina dal IV al IX secolo." In *La civiltà bizantina dal IV al IX secolo,* 93–173. Bari, 1977.

Of the texts analyzed in this chapter, the Life of St. Matrona is edited by H. Delehaye, *Acta Sanctorum, Novembris,* III (Brussels, 1910), 790–813; that of St. John the Almsgiver (by Leontios) by A. J. Festugière, *Vie de Syméon le Fou et Vie de Jean de Chypre* (Paris, 1974); that of Sampson by F. Halkin, *Rivista di studi bizantini e neoellenici,* n.s. 14–16 (1977–79): 5–17; that of Hypatios by G. J. M. Bartelink, *Callinicos: Vie d'Hypatios,* Sources chrétiennes 177 (Paris, 1971); that of Hosios Loukas by D. Z. Sophianos, *Hosios Loukas* (Athens, 1989); and that of Leontios by D. Tsougarakis, *The Life of Leontios Patriarch of Jerusalem* (Leiden, 1993).

INDEX